MCAT

CRITICAL ANALYSIS and REASONING SKILLS: STRATEGY AND PRACTICE

Printed in the United States of America

First Printing, 2016

ISBN 978-1-944935-03-0

Next Step Pre-Med, LLC
4256 N Ravenswood Ave
Suite 303
Chicago, IL 60613

www.nextstepmcat.com

ABOUT THE AUTHORS

Bryan Schnedeker is Next Step Test Prep's Vice President for MCAT Tutoring and Content. He manages all of our MCAT and LSAT instructors nationally and counsels hundreds of students when they begin our tutoring process. He has over a decade of MCAT and LSAT teaching and tutoring experience (starting at one of the big prep course companies before joining our team). He has attended medical school and law school himself and has scored a 44 on the old MCAT, a 525 on the new MCAT, and a 180 on the LSAT. Bryan has worked with thousands of MCAT students over the years and specializes in helping students looking to achieve elite scores.

Anthony Lafond is Next Step's MCAT Content Director and an Elite MCAT Tutor. He has been teaching and tutoring MCAT students for nearly 12 years. He earned his MD and PhD degrees from UMDNJ - New Jersey Medical School with a focus on rehabilitative medicine. Dr. Lafond believes that both rehabilitative medicine and MCAT education hinge on the same core principle: crafting an approach that puts the unique needs of the individual foremost.

To find out about MCAT tutoring directly with Clara, Anthony, or Bryan visit our website:

http://nextsteptestprep.com/mcat

Updates may be found here: http://nextsteptestprep.com/mcat-materials-change-log/

If you have any feedback for us about this book, please contact us at mcat@nextsteptestprep.com

Version: 2016-07-01

FREE ONLINE MCAT DIAGNOSTIC and

FULL-LENGTH EXAM

Want to see how you would do on the MCAT and understand where you need to focus your prep?

TAKE OUR FREE MCAT DIAGNOSTIC EXAM

Timed simulations of all 4 sections of the MCAT

Comprehensive reporting on your performance

Continue your practice with a free Full Length Exam

These two exams are provided free of charge to students who purchased our book

To access your free exam, visit:

http://nextsteptestprep.com/mcat-diagnostic/

TABLE OF CONTENTS

INTRODUCTION

Hello and welcome to Next Step's Strategy and Practice book for the new Critical Analysis and Reasoning Skills Section of the MCAT. Since that name is quite the mouthful, we're just going to keep it simple for this book and call it "the CARS section".

The book you're holding contains all of the information and practice that you need to start mastering this challenging part of the MCAT. We'd like to start by giving you a brief overview of the CARS Section here in the Introduction.

The CARS section will consist of 53 questions which you'll have 90 minutes to answer. Those 53 questions will be presented as a series of questions associated with a reading passage (much like the old Verbal Reasoning section of the prior MCAT). The section will include approximately 9 passages with four to seven questions with each passage. We've followed that estimate for the practice sections in this book.

Each section will have roughly 50% of the questions drawn from Humanities topics and 50% from Social Sciences topics. You will not be required to have any prior knowledge of any of the topics discussed. Within those broad categories, the AAMC estimates that the questions will break down as 30% comprehension based, 30% inference based, and 40% extrapolation based (applying the passage reasoning to new situations or incorporating new information into the passage).

The disciplines discussed in a CARS passage can be drawn from any of the following areas:

Humanities: architecture, art, dance, ethics, literature, music, philosophy, pop culture, religion, theater

Social Sciences: anthropology, archaeology, cultural studies, economics, education, geography, history, linguistics, political science, population health, psychology, sociology

As with the science sections, the key to mastering this new section involves taking a step-by-step approach, starting with untimed practice to master your technique, then short timed work on a few passages, and finally full timed sections.

Everyone here at Next Step would like to wish you the best of luck with your studies!

Thank you,

Bryan Schnedeker
Co-founder and National MCAT Director
Next Step Pre-Med, LLC

APPROACH I: THE HIGHLIGHTING TECHNIQUE

This balanced technique is by far the most popular, most common, and most successful.

Passage: 4.5 minutes

Highlighter: Key terms, contrast, opinion, cause-and-effect

Scratch paper: don't use

Questions: 5.5 minutes

With this approach, you will be using the highlighter as your main tool for synthesizing what you're reading. You must ***absolutely NOT highlight as you go along***. Instead, stop every 3-4 sentences, ask yourself, "okay what did I just read?" and then select a few words that capture the important ideas you just read. If you just highlight as you read along, you end up with the "paint roller effect" where everything gets highlighted.

Then, when you get to the end of the passage, take a moment to ask yourself what the Main Idea was of what you'd just read. Focus on the author's overall opinion and tone. You needn't write it down, but some students find it helpful to do so.

When solving questions, you should be aiming to answer 2-3 of them without looking anything up, and then 2-3 of them may require you to go back and look up facts from the passage. Since you'll have something like 5 minutes to answer the questions, you should have plenty of time to do a bit of "look it up" work.

On the next page you'll find two practice passages. Get a highlighter pen and work through them – don't worry about time for now. Focus on making good choices about what to highlight. Then answer the questions.

After that, you'll see our explanations. There, we have **bold** text as a way to indicate what's worth highlighting. Compare your choices to our suggestions to see if you missed anything important, or highlighted something that was a minor detail.

Compare your highlighting choices to what came up in the questions – did your highlighting help focus your attention on the things that came up in the questions? If so, great job! If not, you can help your review by going back through the passage with another color of highlighter pen and "fixing" the highlighting so that it's perfect. Then come back and review the passage a week later to remind yourself about what good highlighting looks like.

Highlighting Practice Passage I

Epiphenomenalism is a theory of mind that posits that mental events are caused by underlying physical events, but that those mental events cannot then cause physical changes. That is, it is not the subjective sensation of nervousness that causes perspiration, but rather the perspiration is caused by a physiological reaction. This reaction also produces a sensation of nervousness, but that "feeling" is just a side-effect. Thomas Henry Huxley likened the mind to the whistle on a steam locomotive; while the whistle may announce that the train is coming, it has no effect on the actual operation of the train itself.

The development of epiphenomenalism as a school of thought is rooted in the attempt to solve the basic problem of Cartesian dualism. In the 19th century, philosophers wrestled with the problem of interaction between two seemingly incompatible substances: the mental and the physical. The huge successes of the Enlightenment and the scientific tradition that grew out of it demonstrated humanity's increasing mastery over the realm of the physical, but the mental remained largely opaque, governed by theories and attitudes that could at best be called "folk psychology". In light of this disparity, thinkers in the early 19th century wondered how it was that mind and body could interact.

Descartes posited that there was a special organ – the pineal gland – in the center of the brain that provided a two-way link between the substances of mind and body. This organ explained the truth of our basic perception that the body can affect the mind (e.g. putting wine into the body can cloud the mind), and that the mind can affect the body (e.g. our desire to get some fresh air can send the body out for a walk).

The epiphenomenalists countered that although the mind may be a substance different from the body, it has no causative power on the body. This view flourished as it was consonant with the scientific behaviorism that was coming into vogue at the turn of the 20th century. Such scientific behaviorists, notably Ivan Pavlov, John Watson, and Burrhus Skinner, found great success in their efforts to investigate the relationship between environmental stimuli and behavior exhibited by animals (including humans), while making no reference whatsoever to the mental state of the subject. While such behaviorists would not have made the absurd proposal that the subject has no mental state at all, they simply treated the mental state as causally irrelevant. If an animal's "feelings" cannot have any effect on its behavior, then we may safely ignore them in constructing our experiments and our theories about how animals behave, they held.

Epiphenomenalism faced a number of challenges throughout the past century, but since the cognitive revolution in the 1960's, it has received a number of surprising new avenues of support. In the more modern understanding, mental states are simply physical states in the brain–a thought is simply a pattern of electrical impulses traveling along neurons, a memory a growth of new connections between neurons, a feeling an increased level of certain neurotransmitters in certain anatomical regions. The epiphenomenon is the purely subjective, qualitative aspect of an experience. Such aspects are usually referred to as the "raw feel" of an experience, or the "what-it-is-like", or most often, "qualia". Thus if a dog and a robot that can perfectly mimic the behavior of a dog are both fed a piece of bacon, they will exhibit exactly the same behavior, but only the real dog will be experiencing the qualia of the food. The saltiness of the salt, the richness of the smell, the pleasure of eating will only be present in the epiphenomenal world that is the dog's brain. Both will bark happily, wag their tails, and scarf the food down in a single bite, but only the dog has a mind that will be experiencing the qualia of the food.

A large body of neurophysiological data seem to support epiphenomenalism. Such data includes a number of kinds of electrical potentials which occur in the brain and which cause behavior, and yet happen before the subject is mentally aware of the event. Research shows that it takes at least half a second for a stimulus to become part of conscious experience, and yet subjects are capable of reacting to that stimulus in less than half that time. Thus it is not our consciousness that controls our behavior, but rather our brain reacts and the "mental feeling" of what's happening comes after the fact.

[Adapted from: *Train Whistle in the Head* by Kristen O'Connell-Choate, Tucson Upstairs University Press, 2007]

1. Consider the case of the dog and dog-like robot discussed in the fifth paragraph. Descartes would assert that:
   A) the existence of a robot dog that can perfectly mimic the real dog refutes his theory of dualism.
   B) both the real dog and the robot dog have minds that are linked to their bodies through the pineal gland.
   C) the real dog has a rudimentary mind that is fundamentally different from its body, whereas the robot has only a body.
   D) the robot dog's qualia have some additional, unknowable property that separates the robot dog from the real one.

2. According to the passage, the raw feel of an experience arises from a brain state that is also the cause of any behavior we exhibit in response to that experience but that the feel itself is causally irrelevant. That view would most be weakened if it were discovered that which of the following were true?
   A) The electrical potentials that happen in response to a stimulus before the subject is aware of the experience happen most strikingly in the case of olfactory stimuli.
   B) When a subject is unconscious they are still capable of reacting to a number of different stimuli.
   C) Anger management classes have been shown to stimulate a portion of the prefrontal cortex that is associated with "cooling down" and "thinking things through before you act" and that those regions exhibit activity before subsequent behavioral actions designed to reduce physiological arousal.
   D) Meditation techniques that teach a person to avoid harmful repetitive thought patterns have been shown to be effective in the treatment of a number of mental illnesses that had previously only been considered treatable through powerful drugs or surgery.

3. Why does the author discuss the belief of Descartes that the brain has a special gland to mediate interactions between the body and the soul?
   A) To show that Descartes's error about the function of the pineal gland serves as a fatal blow to the soundness of his philosophical theory
   B) To refute Descartes's theory of mind/body dualism
   C) To acknowledge that even Descartes knew that true dualism was impossible and that the mind must, at least in part, be a physical thing
   D) To demonstrate that Descartes was aware that physical things that affect the body could alter the mind even though the mind is a fundamentally different substance from the body

4. The common experience of a violent shocked reaction (shouting, flinching, etc.) when seeing someone in the same room when you thought you were alone, even when that person is someone very familiar serves as evidence:
   A) for both epiphenomenalism and materialism.
   B) for neither dualism nor epiphenomenalism.
   C) for dualism but not epiphenomenalism.
   D) against the notion that mind/body interactions are mediated by the pineal gland.

5. Which of the following is most analogous to the function of the mind in epiphenomenalism?
   A) The gasoline used to run a motor that drives a boat forward.
   B) The beauty of a flower that inspires a poet to write a poem.
   C) The tension an audience feels while watching a suspenseful movie.
   D) The sunlight glinting off waves on the surface of a calm lake.

6. In an experiment subjects are made to look at a series of shocking and disturbing images flashed on the screen for a very short period of time. What does the passage suggest may happen in the brains of these subjects?
   A) Their pineal glands will suffer stress in response to the disturbing images.
   B) Some physiological responses may occur before the subject is mentally aware of what they're looking at.
   C) The parts of their brains responsible for registering disgust will be stimulated only after the subjects have a subjective feeling of disgust.
   D) At least some of the subjects will stop looking at the screen after they realize the images are all disturbing.

Highlighting Practice Passage I Explanation

Epiphenomenalism is a theory of mind that posits that **mental** events are **caused by underlying physical** events, but that **those mental events cannot then cause physical changes**. That is, it is not the subjective sensation of nervousness that causes perspiration, but rather the perspiration is caused by a physiological reaction. This reaction also produces a sensation of nervousness, but that "**feeling**" is just a **side-effect**. **Thomas Henry Huxley** likened the **mind** to the **whistle on a steam locomotive**; while the whistle may announce that the train is coming, it has **no effect on the actual operation** of the train itself.

Here we've highlighted two technical words – epiphenomenalism and Huxley's name. That's so we can find them again later. We've also highlighted some terms that reveal opinion – the opinion of epiphenomenalism. Remember that opinions can be a school of thought.

The development of epiphenomenalism as a school of thought is rooted in the attempt to **solve** the basic problem of **Cartesian dualism**. In the 19th century, philosophers wrestled with the problem of **interaction** between two **seemingly incompatible** substances: the mental and the physical. The huge successes of the **Enlightenment** and the scientific tradition that grew out of it demonstrated humanity's increasing mastery over the realm of the physical, but the mental remained largely opaque, governed by theories and attitudes that could at best be called "**folk psychology**". In light of this disparity, thinkers in the early 19th century wondered **how it was that mind and body could interact**.

Key terms: Cartesian dualism, Enlightenment, folk psychology

We're given another opinion here – the opinion of philosophers. Highlighting "interaction" "seemingly incompatible" lets us know what they were thinking, "how it was that mind and body could interact".

Descartes posited that there was a special organ – **the pineal gland** – in the center of the brain that provided a **two-way link** between the substances of mind and body. This organ explained the truth of our basic perception that the **body can affect the mind** (e.g. putting wine into the body can cloud the mind), and that the mind can affect the body (e.g. our desire to get some fresh air can send the body out for a walk).

Key terms: Descartes, pineal gland

Opinion: Descartes (and thus Cartesian Dualism) asserts that mind can affect physical and physical can affect body.

The epiphenomenalists countered that although the **mind may be a substance different from the body**, it has **no causative power** on the body. This view flourished as it was consonant with the **scientific behaviorism** that was coming into vogue at the turn of the 20th century. Such scientific behaviorists, notably **Ivan Pavlov**, **John Watson**, and **Burrhus Skinner**, found great success in their efforts to investigate the **relationship between environmental stimuli** and **behavior** exhibited by animals (including humans), while making **no reference whatsoever to the mental state** of the subject. While such behaviorists would not have made the absurd proposal that the subject has no mental state at all, they simply treated the **mental state as causally irrelevant**. If an animal's "feelings" cannot have any effect on its behavior, then we may safely **ignore** them in constructing our experiments and our theories about how animals behave, they held.

Key terms: behaviorism, Pavlov, Watson, Skinner

Opinion: Behaviorism supports epiphenomenalism by showing you can analyze and predict behavior with no reference to mental states (not that they don't exist, but they don't matter)

Epiphenomenalism faced a number of **challenges** throughout the past century, but since the **cognitive revolution in the 1960's**, it has received a number of **surprising new avenues of support**. In the more modern understanding, **mental** states are simply **physical states in the brain**—a thought is simply a pattern of electrical impulses traveling along neurons, a memory a growth of new connections between neurons, a feeling an increased level of certain neurotransmitters in certain anatomical regions. The **epiphenomenon** is the **purely subjective, qualitative aspect** of an experience. Such aspects are usually referred to as the "**raw feel**" of an experience, or the "what-it-is-like", or most often, "**qualia**". Thus if a dog and a robot that can perfectly mimic the behavior of a dog are both fed a piece of bacon, they will exhibit exactly the same behavior, but **only the real dog** will be experiencing the **qualia** of the food. The saltiness of the salt, the richness of the smell, the pleasure of eating will only be present in the epiphenomenal world that is the dog's brain. Both will bark happily, wag their tails, and scarf the food down in a single bite, but only the dog has a mind that will be experiencing the qualia of the food.

Key terms: cognitive revolution, raw feel, qualia

Opinion: After the cognitive revolution we've come to see mental states as just physical states in the brain.

Contrast: A robot dog that exactly mimics a real dog could reproduce all of the behaviors but wouldn't experience the qualia the way the dog does.

A large body of **neurophysiological data** seem to **support epiphenomenalism**. Such data includes a number of kinds of **electrical potentials** which occur in the brain and which cause behavior, and yet **happen before the subject is mentally aware** of the event. Research shows that it takes at least half a second for a stimulus to become part of conscious experience, and yet subjects are **capable of reacting to that stimulus in less than half that time**. Thus it is not our consciousness that controls our behavior, but rather our brain reacts and the "**mental feeling**" of what's happening **comes after** the fact.

[Adapted from: *Train Whistle in the Head* by Kristen O'Connell-Choate, Tucson Upstairs University Press, 2007]

Key terms: neurophysiological data, mental feeling

Cause-and-effect: New data show that the brain is capable of reacting to things faster than the person is capable of becoming consciously aware. Thus the conscious awareness is not the thing causing the physical reaction.

Main Idea: Epiphenomenalism contrasts with dualism by saying that physical can affect mental but that mental has no control over physical. Support for epiphenomenalism has come from behaviorism, the cognitive revolution, and neurophysiology.

Remember, on Test Day you don't necessarily have to stop and write out the Main Idea. What you do need to do is stop, take a moment to gather your thoughts – look over all of your highlighting, essentially re-skimming the passage just looking to your highlights. In doing so, formulate the Main Idea in your mind.

1. Consider the case of the dog and dog-like robot discussed in the fifth paragraph. Descartes would assert that:
    A) the existence of a robot dog that can perfectly mimic the real dog refutes his theory of dualism.
    B) both the real dog and the robot dog have minds that are linked to their bodies through the pineal gland.
    C) **the real dog has a rudimentary mind that is fundamentally different from its body, whereas the robot has only a body.**
    D) the robot dog's qualia have some additional, unknowable property that separates the robot dog from the real one.

Descartes thinks that mind and body are two fundamentally different things, but that they can have a causal relationship with each other through the pineal gland. Descartes would certainly not think that a robot dog had a mind or qualia of any kind. Thus choice C is correct.

2. According to the passage, the raw feel of an experience arises from a brain state that is also the cause of any behavior we exhibit in response to that experience but that the feel itself is causally irrelevant. That view would most be *weakened* if it were discovered that which of the following were true?

    A) The electrical potentials that happen in response to a stimulus before the subject is aware of the experience happen most strikingly in the case of olfactory stimuli.

    B) When a subject is unconscious they are still capable of reacting to a number of different stimuli.

    C) **Anger management classes have been shown to stimulate a portion of the prefrontal cortex that is associated with "cooling down" and "thinking things through before you act" and that those regions exhibit activity before subsequent behavioral actions designed to reduce physiological arousal.**

    D) Meditation techniques that teach a person to avoid harmful repetitive thought patterns have been shown to be effective in the treatment of a number of mental illnesses that had previously only been considered treatable through powerful drugs or surgery.

To refute epiphenomenalism we need a case where someone can mentally think something through (have a conscious experience of thinking something over) and that is able to then cause physical responses. In the case of choice C, the person is able to think things through before activating the physiological response that lets them calm down. Thus C is the correct answer because it suggests that the conscious experience of thinking things through comes before and leads to the actual physiological calming down.

3. Why does the author discuss the belief of Descartes that the brain has a special gland to mediate interactions between the body and the soul?

    A) To show that Descartes's error about the function of the pineal gland serves as a fatal blow to the soundness of his philosophical theory.

    B) To refute Descartes's theory of mind/body dualism.

    C) To acknowledge that even Descartes knew that true dualism was impossible and that the mind must, at least in part, be a physical thing.

    D) **To demonstrate that Descartes was aware that physical things that affect the body could alter the mind even though the mind is a fundamentally different substance from the body.**

Descartes believed that mind and body could interact with each other somehow – that mind could cause physical changes and that physical changes (like drinking alcohol) could affect the mind. If mind and body are two very different things, we're left wondering how they could interact. So the author tells us Descartes's answer: the brain had a special organ (the pineal gland) to achieve that end. Thus choice D is correct.

4. The common experience of a violent shocked reaction (shouting, flinching, etc.) when seeing someone in the same room when you thought you were alone, even when that person is someone very familiar serves as evidence:

    A) for both epiphenomenalism and materialism.

    B) **for neither dualism nor epiphenomenalism.**

    C) for dualism but not epiphenomenalism.

    D) against the notion that mind/body interactions are mediated by the pineal gland.

The argument about dualism and epiphenomenalism rests on causality: can the mind cause physical changes or not? Dualism says yes, epiphenomenalism says no. Shouting in surprise does not, in itself, address the question. Thus choice B is correct. For the situation in the question to be relevant we would have to be told something about the causal links – did the person shout before experiencing surprise, or have the feeling of surprise and then shout in response.

5. Which of the following is most analogous to the function of the mind in epiphenomenalism?
   A) The gasoline used to run a motor that drives a boat forward.
   B) The beauty of a flower that inspires a poet to write a poem.
   C) The tension an audience feels while watching a suspenseful movie.
   D) **The sunlight glinting off waves on the surface of a calm lake.**

The example in the passage says that the mind is like the whistle on a train: related to the arrival of the train, but not with any causal power over the train itself. So we need something where the epiphenomenon has no ability to cause the underlying phenomenon. Choice D is the best fit – the glint of sunlight is caused by the small ripples in the water's surface, but the glinting doesn't cause (and can't cause) the underlying waves.

6. In an experiment subjects are made to look at a series of shocking and disturbing images flashed on the screen for a very short period of time. What does the passage suggest may happen in the brains of these subjects?
   A) Their pineal glands will suffer stress in response to the disturbing images.
   B) **Some physiological responses may occur before the subject is mentally aware of what they're looking at.**
   C) The parts of their brains responsible for registering disgust will be stimulated only after the subjects have a subjective feeling of disgust.
   D) At least some of the subjects will stop looking at the screen after they realize the images are all disturbing.

The final paragraph tells us that some neurophysiology studies have shown that people's brains are capable of reacting faster than the person actually becomes aware of something. That matches choice B.

Highlighting Practice Passage II

The needs that are usually taken as the starting point for motivation theory are the so-called physiological drives. Two recent lines of research make it necessary to revise our customary notions about these needs, first, the development of the concept of homeostasis, and second, the finding that appetites (preferential choices among foods) are a fairly efficient indication of actual needs or lacks in the body.

Thus it seems impossible as well as useless to make any list of fundamental physiological needs for they can come to almost any number one might wish, depending on the degree of specificity of description. We cannot identify all physiological needs as homeostatic. That sexual desire, sleepiness, sheer activity and maternal behavior in animals, are homeostatic, has not yet been demonstrated. Furthermore, this list would not include the various sensory pleasures (tastes, smells, tickling, stroking) which are probably physiological and which may become the goals of motivated behavior.

In a previous paper it has been pointed out that these physiological drives or needs are to be considered unusual rather than typical because they are isolable, and because they are localizable somatically. That is to say, they are relatively independent of each other, of other motivations and of the organism as a whole, and secondly, in many cases, it is possible to demonstrate a localized, underlying somatic base for the drive. This is true less generally than has been thought (exceptions are fatigue, sleepiness, maternal responses) but it is still true in the classic instances of hunger, sex, and thirst.

It should be pointed out again that any of the physiological needs and the consummatory behavior involved with them serve as channels for all sorts of other needs as well. That is to say, the person who thinks he is hungry may actually be seeking more for comfort, or dependence, than for vitamins or proteins. Conversely, it is possible to satisfy the hunger need in part by other activities such as drinking water or smoking cigarettes. In other words, relatively isolable as these physiological needs are, they are not completely so.

Undoubtedly these physiological needs are the most pre-potent of all needs. What this means specifically is, that in the human being who is missing everything in life in an extreme fashion, it is most likely that the major motivation would be the physiological needs rather than any others. A person who is lacking food, safety, love, and esteem would most probably hunger for food more strongly than for anything else.

[Adapted from "A Theory of Human Motivation", *Psychological Review*, by A.H. Maslow, 1943.]

1. The author would probably agree with which of the following statements about physiological drives?
    A) A few of the fundamental physiological needs still need to be identified.
    B) Homeostasis is the result of satisfying a physiological need.
    C) The physiological drives do not form a discrete, clearly-defined category.
    D) The strongest physiological drives refer to those needs which are socially-oriented.

2. What is the author's purpose in writing, in the final paragraph, that food would take precedence over the other needs listed?
    A) To support his argument that urgency and priority are a better definition of physiological needs than homeostasis.
    B) To argue that hunger is a fundamental physiological drive, while love and safety aren't.
    C) To show an example of the non-isolable nature of even the fundamental physiological needs.
    D) To prove that fundamental physiological needs cannot be met by alternate activities.

3. An energy-dense drink like soda often meets energy needs far before it provides the person consuming it with a sense of fullness. The author would probably consider this
    A) an example of the overlapping nature of some physiological needs.
    B) evidence of the non-physiological nature of hunger.
    C) evidence that social training can overcome or confuse physiological drives.
    D) an indication that hunger is non-homeostatic.

4. What is the author's purpose in writing, in the second paragraph, that not all physiological needs have been confirmed to be homeostatic?
    A) To support the inclusion of sensory pleasures to the list of recognized physiological needs.
    B) To introduce the unconfirmed needs, sexual desire, sleepiness, maternal instinct, etc.
    C) To provide further evidence against homeostasis as a dominant organizing principle.
    D) To provide evidence that the present definition of physiological needs is problematic.

5. Biologist Ernst Mayr argued that complex biological phenomena generally could not always be broken down to sets of simple, isolated relationships, but would remain intertwined and mathematically inexact. The author would likely
    A) agree that biological reductionism is a dead end.
    B) admit that perfect isolability is impossible.
    C) acknowledge the difficulty in reductionism, but not its irrelevance.
    D) dismiss the idea that a simple, rule-based understanding can never be achieved.

Highlighting Practice Passage II Explanation

The needs that are usually taken as the starting point for **motivation theory** are the so-called **physiological drives**. Two recent lines of research make it necessary to revise our customary notions about these needs, first, the development of the concept of **homeostasis**, and second, the finding that **appetites** (preferential choices among foods) are a fairly efficient **indication of actual needs** or lacks in the body.

Key terms: motivation theory, physiological drives, homeostasis

Cause-and-effect: knowledge of homeostasis and the relation between appetites and bodily needs both affect prior understanding of drives

Thus it seems **impossible** as well as useless to make any **list of fundamental physiological needs** for they can come to almost any number one might wish, depending on the degree of specificity of description. **We cannot identify all physiological needs as homeostatic**. That sexual desire, sleepiness, sheer activity and maternal behavior in animals, **are homeostatic, has not yet been demonstrated**. Furthermore, this list would not include the **various sensory pleasures** (tastes, smells, tickling, stroking) which are probably physiological and which may become the goals of motivated behavior.

Contrast: some physiological needs are homeostatic, some may not be, some definitely aren't

Cause-and-effect: the way in which needs are defined determines which can be thus classified

Opinion: an unobjective, uncertain classification has no use

In a previous paper it has been pointed out that these physiological drives or needs are to be considered **unusual rather than typical** because they are **isolable**, and because they are **localizable somatically**. That is to say, they are relatively independent of each other, of other motivations and of the organism as a whole, and secondly, in many cases, it is possible to demonstrate a **localized, underlying somatic base** for the drive. This is true less generally than has been thought (exceptions are fatigue, sleepiness, maternal responses) but it is still true in the **classic instances of hunger, sex, and thirst**.

Key terms: isolable, localizable

Contrast: previously isolability and localizability were considered defining characteristics, now considered exceptional

Cause-and-effect: a clear location and physiological cause define classic, well-understood drives

It should be pointed out again that any of the physiological needs and the **consummatory behavior** involved with them serve as **channels for all sorts of other needs** as well. That is to say, the person who **thinks he is hungry** may actually be seeking more for comfort, or dependence, than for vitamins or proteins. Conversely, it is possible to **satisfy the hunger** need in part **by other activities** such as drinking water or smoking cigarettes. In other words, **relatively isolable** as these physiological needs are, they are not completely so.

Key terms: consummatory behavior

Contrast: traditional consummatory behavior, a need arises from a biological imperative, leading to behavior that satisfies the underlying cause (dehydration causes thirst causes rehydration through drinking), but other causes and consummations can be the cause or result of this need

Cause-and-effect: other needs (than need of food)may cause hunger, other responses (than eating) may satisfy hunger

Undoubtedly these physiological needs are the most **pre-potent** of all needs. What this means specifically is, that in the human being who is missing everything in life in an extreme fashion, it is most likely that the **major motivation** would be the **physiological needs** rather than any others. A person who is lacking food, safety, love, and esteem would most probably hunger for food more strongly than for anything else.

[Adapted from "A Theory of Human Motivation", *Psychological Review*, by A.H. Maslow, 1943.]

Key terms: pre-potent

Contrast: hunger is pre-potent and takes precedence, love and safety are secondary

Cause-and-effect: of several needs, physiological needs (being pre-potent) are strongest, take precedence in consummatory behavior

Main Idea: Homeostasis doesn't fully explain even physiological needs as motivators and what may seem like fundamental physiological needs can't fully be isolated, since they may be expressions of emotional needs, or may be satisfied by other behaviors.

1. The author would probably agree with which of the following statements about physiological drives?
    A) A few of the fundamental physiological needs still need to be identified.
    B) Homeostasis is the result of satisfying a physiological need.
    C) **The physiological drives do not form a discrete, clearly-defined category.**
    D) The strongest physiological drives refer to those needs which are socially-oriented.

The passage describes the current difficulties in clearly categorizing physiological drives, citing their imperfect isolability as a major issue.

A: This is not supported by the passage.
B: This contradicts the passage, which cites several needs that are not homeostatic in nature.
D: This contradicts the passage, which states that hunger would override drives involving other people, such as love or esteem.

2. What is the author's purpose in writing, in the final paragraph, that food would take precedence over the other needs listed?
    A) **To support his argument that urgency and priority are a better definition of physiological needs than homeostasis.**
    B) To argue that hunger is a fundamental physiological drive, while love and safety aren't.
    C) To show an example of the non-isolable nature of even the fundamental physiological needs.
    D) To prove that fundamental physiological needs cannot be met by alternate activities.

Throughout the passage, the author has been arguing about the difficulty in recognizing and categorizing different drives/needs. He shows the problem with homeostasis as a defining factor. In the last paragraph, he returns to some of the currently acknowledged needs, but alights on their pre-potency, demonstrating the urgency to satisfy these needs, and the way they take priority over other needs. The implication is that this definition works where others have failed.

B: This may be true, but the author seems to have assumed from the start that hunger, one of the classic drives, is physiological. The question at hand was, why is this so?
C: This paragraph had nothing to do with isolability.
D: This is contradicted elsewhere in the passage and irrelevant to the section being discussed.

3. An energy-dense drink like soda often meets energy needs far before it provides the person consuming it with a sense of fullness. The author would probably consider this
    A) **an example of the overlapping nature of some physiological needs.**
    B) evidence of the non-physiological nature of hunger.
    C) evidence that social training can overcome or confuse physiological drives.
    D) an indication that hunger is non-homeostatic.

The statement in this question stem suggests that, despite hunger being a drive leading to the ingestion of food, the need can be met, at least from a caloric perspective, without curtailing the hunger itself. This is similar to another example given in the passage, where something with no calories can satisfy hunger, given enough of it, and likewise suggests that needs are not perfectly isolable. A is a match.

B: The physiological nature of hunger is not at question in this passage.
C: Nothing like this is discussed in the passage.
D: That the hunger drive can be fooled does not necessarily mean it is not homeostatic, and, again, were this evidence, it's not an argument the passage author had made about hunger.

4. What is the author's purpose in writing, in the second paragraph, that not all physiological needs have been confirmed to be homeostatic?
    A) To support the inclusion of sensory pleasures to the list of recognized physiological needs.
    B) To introduce the unconfirmed needs, sexual desire, sleepiness, maternal instinct, etc.
    C) To provide further evidence against homeostasis as a dominant organizing principle.
    D) **To provide evidence that the present definition of physiological needs is problematic.**

The entire passage is devoted to sussing out the difficulties in identifying the physiological needs, given several contradictory definitions, none of which work for each need traditionally listed. That paragraph is devoted to the issues with the homeostatic definition, but is still in service to that larger goal. D is thus a match.

A: This answer choice switches evidence and conclusion. The sensory pleasures were cited as another problem with the homeostatic definition; the author took it as a given that they were physiological in nature.
B: These were clearly only included as examples to support the claim that many needs are not homeostatic, not the main purpose of the paragraph.
C: The author does not attack homeostasis itself, which explains many bodily processes, merely the definition of physiological needs as homeostatically-motivated.

5. Biologist Ernst Mayr argued that complex biological phenomena generally could not always be broken down to sets of simple, isolated relationships, but would remain intertwined and mathematically inexact. The author would likely
    A) agree that biological reductionism is a dead end.
    B) admit that perfect isolability is impossible.
    C) **acknowledge the difficulty in reductionism, but not its irrelevance.**
    D) dismiss the idea that a simple, rule-based understanding can never be achieved.

The passage suggests that the non-isolability of many physiological needs is, in fact, a problem, making it more difficult to understand the drives they feed. At the end, the passage author suggests a new definition, based on a simple hierarchy, to classify physiological and non-physiological needs. C is the best match for this.

A: This is not supported by the passage.
B: Though not all needs are isolable, it seems to be assumed that some biological processes are.
D: Too extreme. Reductionism may be desirable, but the passage acknowledges the difficulty.

1. The passage asserts that the uniqueness of the poet stems from his:
  I. habit of separating himself physically from the drudgery and commonality of day-to-day experience.
 II. acute sense of the immediate as an entity removed from the confounding filter of human interpretation.
III. ability to reshape verbal imagery according to a specific design.
     A) I only
     B) III only
     C) I and III only
     D) II and III only

2. Throughout the passage, the author advances his primary argument by comparing and contrasting:
     A) the poet and his poetry.
     B) false vision and real experience.
     C) poets and other artists and thinkers.
     D) the subtlety and palpability of poetry.

3. If this passage were included with other pieces of writing on poetry containing central themes consistent with that of this passage, writings with which of the following themes would be most appropriate to include?
     A) Modern native poets
     B) Universal techniques of poetic analysis
     C) That which typifies the poetical
     D) A critical belief that the parallels between poetry and other fine arts threaten the uniqueness of its literary province

4. The sentence "It is rather in what we call psychical vision that the poet is wont to excel, that is, in his ability to perceive the meaning of visual phenomena," in the first paragraph is most probably included by the author in order to:
     A) define the distinct provenance of the poet by offering a descriptive insight into his interpretive process.
     B) highlight the poet's great difficulty in transcending the limitations of immediate vision in their writing.
     C) emphasize the poet's exclusive role as a seer.
     D) underscore the uniqueness of the poet's capacity for interpreting the meaning of that which he sees.

5. The author seems to suggest that a reader's appreciation of a poet's work stems from:
     A) the need to separate out the elements of poetry born from the poet's multiple roles as seer, marker and singer.
     B) the difficulty of navigating the literal meaning of a poet's work.
     C) the need to transcend the barrier of dissimilar experience between reader and poet.
     D) the reader finding insight in the mind of a poet.

6. Based upon the passage text, the author most probably finds the role of the critic in relation to the poet to be one of:
     A) imposing strict limitations on the work poets may produce.
     B) interpreting the common elements of poets' work.
     C) liaison, bridging the gap between reader and poet.
     D) judge, putting forth a positive or negative assessment of the absolute merit of poetic works.

7. In the final sentence of the second paragraph, the author makes reference to "The intellect of Newton," in order to:
     A) provide an example illustrating a preceding assertion qualifying an element of the poetic temper.
     B) emphasize his claim that the scientific mind operates differently than that of the poet.
     C) support his assertion that a vivid sense of relation, shared by the philosopher, is necessary and sufficient to define the poetic mind.
     D) strengthen his description of the role of the poet as a thinker according to his "intellectual capacity".

Note-taking Practice Passage I Explanation

The mere physical vision of the poet may or may not be any keener than the vision of other men. There is an infinite variety in the bodily endowments of habitual verse-makers: there have been near-sighted poets like **Tennyson**, far-sighted poets like **Wordsworth**, and, in the well-known case of Robert **Browning**, a poet conveniently far-sighted in one eye and near-sighted in the other! No doubt the life-long practice of observing and recording natural phenomena sharpens the sense of poets, as it does the senses of Indians, naturalists, sailors and all outdoors men. The quick eye for costume and character possessed by a **Chaucer** or a **Shakespeare** is remarkable, but equally so is the observation of a **Dickens** or a **Balzac**. It is rather in what we call psychical vision that the poet is wont to excel, that is, in his ability to perceive the meaning of visual phenomena. Here he ceases to be a mere reporter of retinal images, and takes upon himself the higher and harder function of an interpreter of the visible world. He has no immunity from the universal human experiences: he loves and he is angry and he sees men born and die. He becomes according to the measure of his intellectual capacity a thinker. He strives to see into the human heart, to comprehend the working of the human mind. He reads the divine justice in the tragic fall of Kings. He penetrates beneath the external forms of Nature and perceives her as a "living presence." Yet the faculty of vision, which the poet possesses in so eminent a degree, is shared by many who are not poets. **Darwin's** outward eye was as keen as Wordsworth's; St. Paul's sense of the reality of the invisible world is more wonderful than Shakespeare's. The poet is indeed first of all a seer, but he must be something more than a seer before he is wholly poet.

Scratch Notes:

Auth thinks poets are different from other men in their psychical vision, true poet = seer but more than that.

Another mark of the poetic mind is its vivid sense of relations. The part suggests the whole. In the single instance there is a hint of the general law. The self-same Power that brings the fresh rhodora to the woods brings the poet there also. In the field-mouse, the daisy, the water-fowl, he beholds types and symbols. His own experience stands for all men's. The conscience-stricken **Macbeth** is a poet when he cries, "Life is a walking shadow," and **King Lear** makes the same pathetic generalization when he exclaims, "What, have his daughters brought him to this pass?" Through the shifting phenomena of the present the poet feels the sweep of the universe; his mimic play and "the great globe itself" are alike an "insubstantial pageant," though it may happen, as Tennyson said of Wordsworth, that even in the transient he gives the sense of the abiding, "whose dwelling is the light of setting suns." But this perception of relations, characteristic as it is of the poetic temper, is also an attribute of the philosopher. The intellect of a Newton, too, leaps from the specific instance to the general law.

Scratch Notes:

Poet must be seer + able think in univ. + general. Facility for the univ. also in philos + sci

The real difference between "the poet" and other men is … in his capacity for making and employing verbal images of a certain kind, and combining these images into rhythmical and metrical designs. In each of his functions—as "seer," as "maker," and as "singer"—he shows himself a true creator. Criticism no longer attempts to act as his "law-giver," to assert what he may or may not do. The poet is free, like every creative artist, to make a beautiful object in any way he can. And nevertheless criticism—watching countless poets lovingly for many a century, observing their various endowments, their manifest endeavors, their victories and defeats, observing likewise the nature of language, that strange medium (so much stranger than any clay or bronze!) through which poets are compelled to express their conceptions—criticism believes that poetry, like each of the sister arts, has its natural province, its own field of the beautiful. … In **W. H. Hudson's Green Mansions** the reader will remember how a few sticks and stones, laid upon a hilltop, were used as markers to indicate the outlines of a continent. Criticism, likewise, needs its poor sticks and stones of commonplace, if it is to point out any roadway. Our own road leads first into the difficult territory of the poet's imaginings, and then into the more familiar world of the poet's words.

[Adapted from *A Study of Poetry*, Chapter II. Bliss Perry, 1920.]

Scratch Notes:

What sep. poet from other = verbal images in metrical designs, criticism believe poetry beautiful and crit. has own tools to look at poet's imaginings and words.

Main Idea: A poet must have a keen insight into the world, possess an ability to see the universal underlying the particular, and have a unique ability to craft verbal images in a rhythmical pattern. Critics of poetry recognize its beauty and use their own "sticks and stones" to appreciate it.

1. The passage asserts that the uniqueness of the poet stems from his:
  I. habit of separating himself physically from the drudgery and commonality of day-to-day experience.
 II. acute sense of the immediate as an entity removed from the confounding filter of human interpretation.
III. **ability to reshape verbal imagery according to a specific design.**
     A) I only
     B) **III only**
     C) I and III only
     D) II and III only

I: False. The passage explicitly states in the first paragraph that the poet "has no immunity from the universal human experience."

II: False. The second paragraph in particular describes the poet's work as having a vivid sense of the relations [between things], of finding a hint of the general in specific instances and, in the second paragraph, as having a "sense of the abiding" and of the "sweep of the universe." Taken together, the author suggests that the poet does not have a strictly isolated sense of the immediate, but that he interprets and relates events by way of his human experience. But, in any case, this statement is incorrect because, from the end of the second paragraph, "this perception of relations, characteristic as it is of the poetic temper, is an also an attribute of the philosopher" and is not, as the question asks, something that is unique to the poet.

III: True. The passage explains in the last paragraph that "the real difference between "the poet" and other men is … in his capacity for making and employing verbal imagery … combining these images into rhythmical and metrical designs."

2. Throughout the passage, the author advances his primary argument by comparing and contrasting:
     A) the poet and his poetry.
     B) false vision and real experience.
     C) **poets and other artists and thinkers.**
     D) the subtlety and palpability of poetry.

The main thrust of the passage is describing the common habits of poets and how they are similar or dissimilar to those of other thinkers and artists in support of the passage's main goal of defining what makes a poet unique.

A: The author never directly compares or contrasts poets with their individual works.

B: While the passage does explore the nature of a poet's vision, the author explains the process in terms of expanding and interpreting experiences and relationships. He doesn't suggest that any "vision" is less real than "experience."

D: While the subtlety and palpability of poetry may be referred to obliquely as elements of different poets' works in the first and second paragraphs, it's not a continued or central theme of the poet. That main theme is, instead, explaining, as the first sentence of the third paragraph says, "the real difference between 'the poet' and other men."

3. If this passage were included with other pieces of writing on poetry containing central themes consistent with that of this passage, writings with which of the following themes would be most appropriate to include?
    A) Modern native poets
    B) Universal techniques of poetic analysis
    C) **That which typifies the poetical**
    D) A critical belief that the parallels between poetry and other fine arts threaten the uniqueness of its literary province

The passage seeks out and explains those things that are both common and unique to the poet in the process of writing; such an exposition would fit well in a more general discussion of what defines poetry.

A: The passage includes examples of poets from different time periods and places, not just modern or native poets. The passage's central theme is what universally makes poets unique from other artists, and doesn't focus on sub-groups of poets.
B: While the passage does touch on poetic analysis when discussing the place of criticism, it's less central to the passage than the main theme of what uniquely defines poets.
D: This choice implies that drawing parallels between poetry and other art threatens poetry's place as a separate art form. The third paragraph specifically claims agreement among critics that poetry does occupy its own space in the realm of fine arts, contradicting the choice and meaning that any effort to draw parallels between poetry and other art forms would pose no threat to poetry's place.

4. The sentence "It is rather in what we call psychical vision that the poet is wont to excel, that is, in his ability to perceive the meaning of visual phenomena," in the first paragraph is most probably included by the author in order to:
    A) **define the distinct provenance of the poet by offering a descriptive insight into his interpretive process.**
    B) highlight the poet's great difficulty in transcending the limitations of immediate vision in their writing.
    C) emphasize the poet's exclusive role as a seer
    D) underscore the uniqueness of the poet's capacity for interpreting the meaning of that which he sees.

The sentence gives context to the first paragraph's concluding claim that the poet acts importantly as a seer, by explaining and emphasizing the poet's ability to see psychically (through interpretation in the mind's eye) visual phenomena.

B: This is precisely the opposite of what the sentence claims; according to the sentence, and in keeping with the passage, the poet is adept at transcending the limitations of physical vision and interpreting the implications of both the seen and unseen. Be careful to correctly interpret the use of the word "wont" in the sentence, by keeping in mind the logical progression of the passage.
C: While the final sentence of the first paragraph does state that the poet must first act as a seer, it continues on to say that "… he must be something more than a seer before he is wholly poet." Acting as a seer then, being a "mere reporter of retinal images" as the first paragraph describes it, is a common function performed by many, not by poets exclusively.
D: This is directly contradicted by the passage's claim that the poet's "faculty of vision … is shared by many who are not poets."

5. The author seems to suggest that a reader's appreciation of a poet's work stems from:
    A) the need to separate out the elements of poetry born from the poet's multiple roles as seer, marker and singer.
    B) the difficulty of navigating the literal meaning of a poet's work.
    C) the need to transcend the barrier of dissimilar experience between reader and poet.
    D) **the reader finding insight in the mind of a poet.**

In the final paragraph, the passage is fairly explicit about the role of the reader: to understand the imaginings of the poet. The last sentence of the last paragraph concludes that the "[reader's] road leads first into the difficult territory of the poet's imaginings" and only then into the easier and "more familiar world of the poet's words."

A: While the last paragraph does describe the multiple roles played by the poet, it's not suggested that tension exists in satisfying those roles, or that evidence of multiple roles is apparent in poets' work.

B: The last sentence of the passage states that understanding the poet's words is easier than placing those words in context of the "poet's imaginings."

C: While this may or may not be true in real life, the passage doesn't make reference to it. This choice is out of scope.

6. Based upon the passage text, the author most probably finds the role of the critic in relation to the poet to be one of:
    A) imposing strict limitations on the work poets may produce.
    B) **interpreting the common elements of poets' work.**
    C) liaison, bridging the gap between reader and poet.
    D) judge, putting forth a positive or negative assessment of the absolute merit of poetic works.

Answering this question correctly requires an understanding of the critic's role as described in the passage. In keeping with the larger goal being described in this passage—finding those things uniquely common to poets in accomplishing their work—the last paragraph describes how critics can act in this capacity to outline the creative paths followed by poets.

A: The final paragraph suggests that while critics in the past may have acted, or attempted to act, in this manner, they no longer do.

C: The author describes the critic and reader as facing similar challenges, but as having different tasks, as the reader must follow "…[his] own road."

D: This may be a tempting response but such a role for a literary critic isn't what's being specifically described in the passage. Instead, the passage conceives of the critic as one who seeks to understand the nature and dimensions of poetry.

7. In the final sentence of the second paragraph, the author makes reference to "The intellect of Newton," in order to:
    A) **provide an example illustrating a preceding assertion qualifying an element of the poetic temper.**
    B) emphasize his claim that the scientific mind operates differently than that of the poet.
    C) support his assertion that a vivid sense of relation, shared by the philosopher, is necessary and sufficient to define the poetic mind.
    D) strengthen his description of the role of the poet as a thinker according to his "intellectual capacity".

This question asks about the author's intent. Pay close attention to the preceding sentences describing poets' minds moving from specific instances to the general. This is the same as the description of Newton's intellect in the reference sentence. The passage refers to Newton (as an example of another thinker who generalizes from specific examples in the course of a creative process) in order to support the passage's claim that generalization is a quality common to, but not unique to, poets. If Newton, a scientist, generalized from the specific, then, while generalization is held to be an important characteristic of the poet as highlighted by the examples of generalizing poets in the second paragraph, it can't be unique to the poet. The inclusion of Newton then serves to make the point that generalization is not exclusive to the poetic mind.

B: No such claim is made. In fact, this sentence draws a parallel between the functioning of the poetic and scientific mind; both the poet and scientist, as represented by Newton, infer the general from specific instances.

C: The vivid sense of relation referred to in the opening sentence of the second paragraph is "characteristic" of a poet, but not alone sufficient to define the poetic mind, as others share the characteristic.

D: In spite of the common use of the word "intellect" in both lines, the reference to Newton's intellect isn't included in order to draw a comparison to the role of the poet as a thinker, but rather to act as a specific example of Newton as a generalizing thinker.

Note-taking Practice Passage II

Bright young scientists must learn through trial-and-error to separate failure to achieve the expected results from failure of the experiment altogether, and when it comes to the latter, technical failures (such as mis-calibrations of instrumentation or other careless oversights) from personal failure. For scientists who are just starting to conduct real research – that is, research in which one does not know what to expect as an outcome, rather than the carefully controlled "experiments" students conduct in the lab solely as a way to learn good lab techniques – a series of setbacks or the failure of a major project can quickly lead to a lack of faith in the experimental process itself. Such failure can create a sense of anxiety over the future of the project, especially in an environment in which the need for funding creates a pressing need to generate positive results quickly. This mental and financial pressure robs the young scientist of the fundamental right of all experimenters: the right to make mistakes. The greatest scientific discoveries have come not after a carefully and elegantly controlled series of pre-planned steps, but rather through the lumpy, uneven process of trial-and-error in which serendipity plays a significant role. But to that scientist who learns the wrong lesson from failure too strongly and too early in her career, the basic enterprise of science ceases to be a learning from failure and instead simply becomes failure.

The scientist's main recourse is to simply recast all lab work as a learning process in which it is the process of experimenting itself that is a success, such that there are no failures. The real sense of oneself as a scientist comes from an ability to understand "failures" as a chance to learn either something about the mechanics of lab work, or something about the system being investigated. The exploration itself becomes the central process of developing the young scientist. If the scientist makes a technical mistake in the operation of a piece of lab equipment, it is an opportunity to develop the toolset that will allow future investigations to proceed more smoothly, whereas if the results are simply wildly different than expected, it gives the scientist an opportunity to investigate something new and interesting about the world. In either case, the central mental faculty being prodded is the scientist's primary tool: curiosity.

An openness and curiosity about the world itself is, of course, the primary motivator for most of those who embark on the scientific journey to begin with. And failure is not always a frustrating setback that many first believe. It was, after all, the failure of Alexander Fleming to properly care for his petri dishes that led to the discovery of penicillin, or Wilson Greatbach's inadvertent use of a resistor a thousand times too strong that led to the development of the pacemaker. These sparks of genius and the exhilaration they bring are scattered liberally throughout the entire history of science. Ironically, one of the great curses that can befall a fledgling scientist is to experience not a great stroke of failure at the start of his career, but rather one of these great strokes of luck. If the talented young researcher has such a lucky moment, and comes to believe that such breakthroughs are the normal course of affairs, he may come to think after a subsequent few years of failure that he critically lacks some skill at research and may be driven into a more reliable profession, such as science teaching or science journalism.

Anyone who has devoted their life's work to the laboratory must ultimately have a moment in their career when their curiosity about the research itself, rather than the accolades it may bring, creates a sense of joy. This joy for working in the lab, in which the enterprise ceases to be work and becomes neither a vocation nor an avocation and instead becomes simply a way of life, is the foundational basis for that critical transformation: from a mere technician to a true scientist. Whatever technical mishaps may happen, whatever moments of serendipity may arrive, and whatever the results may show or fail to show, it is the curiosity and joy of discovery that define the scientist.

[Adapted from *Failure Across Professions* Audrey O'Connell, Sussex County Historical Press, 1993]

1. In paragraph three, the author mentions a "failure" of Alexander Fleming and an "inadvertent" action by Wilson Greatbach. In context, these words suggest that at least part of scientific discovery:

    A) requires making technical mistakes.

    B) can only happen to fledgling scientists who have a great stroke of luck.

    C) involves doing things that might typically be considered mistakes.

    D) is motivated by a desire for accolades.

2. The author implies that scientists who persist in their careers as research scientists do so because they:

    A) seek the accolades that come from making a major breakthrough.

    B) are compelled by a sense of curiosity about the world.

    C) would not be happy in a reliable profession such as teaching or journalism.

    D) experience pressure to obtain funding by demonstrating positive results.

3. All of the following are stated in the passage EXCEPT:

    A) Making discoveries in the lab creates a sense of curiosity about the world.

    B) Failure to produce positive results quickly can discourage new scientists.

    C) Recasting both technical failures and unexpected results as successes can encourage scientists.

    D) Failure is not always a setback.

4. In another work, the author of the passage states that approximately half of promising young Ph.D. candidates who appear as second or third authors on research papers early in their studies eventually either fail to complete their degree or do so without publishing any other original research. This is most likely due to:

    A) new researchers failing to cultivate a sense of curiosity that lets failure be reinterpreted as success.

    B) a stroke of serendipity occurring early in the career of young scientists.

    C) a failure to distinguish between mere technical failures and a failure to achieve the expected results.

    D) a desire to become either a science journalist or a science teacher.

5. One science journalist remarked, "no one likes the blind fumbling about that leads to the lucky discovery; everyone likes having made the lucky discovery". The passage suggests that fledgling scientists who prefer "having made the lucky discovery" might be expected:

    A) to make more lucky discoveries.

    B) to give up research science.

    C) to increase their technical facility in the lab.

    D) to develop a stronger curiosity about the world.

6. The passage most strongly supports which of the following in regards to scientists?

    A) They frequently experience failure through the process of trial-and-error.

    B) Some of the greatest scientists had sloppy lab technique that led to technical failure.

    C) Whether or not one achieves great success as a scientist depends solely on luck.

    D) Their work transforms who they are by transforming their way of life.

7. Which of the following, if true, would most *weaken* the assertions made by the author?

    A) Scientists should treat the lab as something of a playground in which their imagination can be given free rein.

    B) A scientist prone to technical errors is displaying a personal failure through carelessness and should seek another line of work.

    C) Scientists must cultivate a deep sense of patience since the lucky discovery may come along only after many years.

    D) A scientist is fundamentally an explorer and is at her best when she is off the map: there can be no mistakes because there are no lines to cross.

Note-taking Practice Passage II Explanation

Bright young scientists must learn through trial-and-error to separate failure to achieve the expected results from failure of the experiment altogether, and when it comes to the latter, technical failures (such as mis-calibrations of instrumentation or other careless oversights) from personal failure. For scientists who are just starting to conduct real research – that is, research in which one does not know what to expect as an outcome, rather than the carefully controlled "experiments" students conduct in the lab solely as a way to learn good lab techniques – a series of setbacks or the failure of a major project can quickly lead to a lack of faith in the experimental process itself. Such failure can create a sense of anxiety over the future of the project, especially in an environment in which the need for funding creates a pressing need to generate positive results quickly. This mental and financial pressure robs the young scientist of the fundamental right of all experimenters: the right to make mistakes. The greatest scientific discoveries have come not after a carefully and elegantly controlled series of pre-planned steps, but rather through the lumpy, uneven process of trial-and-error in which serendipity plays a significant role. But to that scientist who learns the wrong lesson from failure too strongly and too early in her career, the basic enterprise of science ceases to be a learning from failure and instead simply becomes failure.

Scratch Notes: Failing can cause scientists to feel pressured and to give up. Real discov. from tri-al-and-error + luck.

The scientist's main recourse is to simply recast all lab work as a learning process in which it is the process of experimenting itself that is a success, such that there are no failures. The real sense of oneself as a scientist comes from an ability to understand "failures" as a chance to learn either something about the mechanics of lab work, or something about the system being investigated. The exploration itself becomes the central process of developing the young scientist. If the scientist makes a technical mistake in the operation of a piece of lab equipment, it is an opportunity to develop the toolset that will allow future investigations to proceed more smoothly, whereas if the results are simply wildly different than expected, it gives the scientist an opportunity to investigate something new and interesting about the world. In either case, the central mental faculty being prodded is the scientist's primary tool: curiosity.

Scratch Notes: Auth thinks new sci. need dev. curiosity + see fail as chance to learn.

An openness and curiosity about the world itself is, of course, the primary motivator for most of those who embark on the scientific journey to begin with. And failure is not always a frustrating setback that many first believe. It was, after all, the failure of Alexander **Fleming** to properly care for his petri dishes that led to the discovery of penicillin, or Wilson **Greatbach**'s inadvertent use of a resistor a thousand times too strong that led to the development of the pacemaker. These sparks of genius and the exhilaration they bring are scattered liberally throughout the entire history of science. Ironically, one of the great curses that can befall a fledgling scientist is to experience not a great stroke of failure at the start of his career, but rather one of these great strokes of luck. If the talented young researcher has such a lucky moment, and comes to believe that such breakthroughs are the normal course of affairs, he may come to think after a subsequent few years of failure that he critically lacks some skill at research and may be driven into a more reliable profession, such as science teaching or science journalism.

Scratch Notes: Great luck at start of career can be bad. Journalism + teaching more reliable jobs. Curiosity in the first place drives ppl to sci.

Anyone who has devoted their life's work to the laboratory must ultimately have a moment in their career when their curiosity about the research itself, rather than the accolades it may bring, creates a sense of joy. This joy for working in the lab, in which the enterprise ceases to be work and becomes neither a vocation nor an avocation and instead becomes simply a way of life, is the foundational basis for that critical transformation: from a mere technician to a true scientist. Whatever technical mishaps may happen, whatever moments of serendipity may arrive, and whatever the results may show or fail to show, it is the curiosity and joy of discovery that define the scientist.

[Adapted from *Failure Across Professions* Audrey O'Connell, Sussex County Historical Press, 1993]

1. Based on the information in the passage, the presence of barking behavior in the absence of other dogs or humans supports the idea that:

    A) dogs' highly flexible vocal cords permit them to bark for a variety of purposes.

    B) some barking behavior indicates the emotional state of the dog without communicative intent.

    C) the arousal model fails to account for a common observation made by dog owners.

    D) Hare's work is fundamentally flawed.

2. The passage suggests that recordings of dogs barking, to be useful in studying dog communication, must be:

    A) made when attempting to take food away from a dog.

    B) of particularly high quality so as to be recognizable by other dogs.

    C) intelligible to a human audience.

    D) recorded in response to a specific situation being studied.

3. Animal researchers have recorded a set of vocalizations made by hyenas in conjunction with several different hyena behaviors commonly exhibited in the wild. If the researchers wanted to speculate on the function of those vocalizations, Hare would suggest that they:

    A) play those recordings to human listeners and ask the humans to distinguish between the vocalizations.

    B) use a spectrograph to analyze the pitch, loudness, or timbre of the vocalizations.

    C) compare the vocalization behavior of hyenas with their nearest domesticated relative.

    D) play those recordings to other hyenas and observe their reactions.

4. Based on the passage, which of the following pieces of background knowledge would be most helpful in evaluating Hare's contentions?

    A) Knowledge of how vocalization developed as a communication tool in people

    B) An understanding of the different sorts of jobs for which dogs have been bred

    C) A familiarity with the normal set of behaviors and vocalizations exhibited by wolves

    D) A familiarity with the skeletal anatomy of a typical dog

5. Which of the following would most strengthen Coppinger's theory about the function of barking?

    A) There are perceptible differences between the barks of dogs who are being threatened by larger animals and those being threatened by smaller animals.

    B) When fed a slight sedative, the barking activity of dogs tended to increase in response to strangers.

    C) Wolves show an increased amount of barking when kept in captivity.

    D) When given food that contained small doses of stimulant drugs but provided with no environmental cues, dogs increased the duration and frequency of their barking.

Skimming Practice Passage I Explanation

In his recent book, ***The Genius of Dogs: How Dogs are Smarter than You Think,*** **Brian Hare** argues that the **communicative abilities of dogs extend** well past the blunt signifiers of tail and ear position and bared teeth that humans have long known. If you ask the typical lay person, he would suggest that dog vocalizations consist of little more than barking, growling, and whining. And while Hare's work **doesn't expand on this basic repertoire**, he convincingly argues that **dogs are communicating far more** than we were previously aware, through some combination of pitch, loudness and timbre.

Key terms: book title, Brian Hare

Opinion: Hare thinks dogs communicate a lot with their vocalizations

Even many dog owners think that a **dog's bark contains very little information**. That is, the dog isn't "thinking" anything in particular, nor trying to communicate anything in particular. They bark just because "that's what dogs do". Research by **Raymond Coppinger** seems to support what he calls an "**arousal model**". That is, dogs simply **bark when they're excited** about something, and the barking is not a behavior over which the dog is exerting any conscious control and with **no attempt at communication by the dog**. In support of his hypothesis, Coppinger presents data gathered from several different breeds of working dogs whose job is to protect **free-range livestock**. In many instances, the dogs barked nearly continuously for six to eight hours, even when no other dogs or humans were within earshot. The bark simply communicates the fact that **the barking dog is excited**, with no attempt to communicate that message to any particular audience. Hare provides an anecdote that seems to align with the arousal model: he talks about a guard dog he had while working in Africa who would bark at every passerby throughout the night, even when they were people the dog had known and lived with for years.

Key terms: Coppinger, arousal model, livestock

Opinion: Coppinger thinks barking just means dog is excited with no communication behind it

More recent research, however, suggests that **barking and growling may communicate more** than had been previously thought. Dogs' **vocal cords** are highly flexible, permitting dogs to alter their vocalizations to produce a wide variety of different sounds. Scientists recorded the barking and growling done by dogs under a variety of situations. One involved a recording of a "**food growl" and a "stranger growl**". The first was recorded when researchers attempted to take food away from an aggressive dog, and the second when they simply approached aggressive dogs. They then placed food on the opposite side of the room from another dog and let it approach the food. They played back recordings of both the "stranger" and "food" growls as the dogs approached the food. **Only in response to the "food" growl did the dogs hesitate** before continuing.

Key terms: vocal cords, food growl, stranger growl

Cause-and-effect: recording of food growl made other dogs hesitate before approaching food, stranger growl didn't

In a similar experiment, researchers recorded the barks of dogs in two different situations. In the first, the dogs were simply left alone. In the second, a stranger would approach the dog, eliciting barking. When those barks were played later for other dogs, these other **dogs ignored all of the "alone" barking**, but perked up immediately when the "stranger" bark was played. Even more surprising, **humans were able to distinguish** between the barks, and correctly identify which was which, even if the human test subjects were not themselves dog owners.

Cause-and-effect: "alone" barking got no response from other dogs, but stranger barking did, humans were able to distinguish

Hare also notes that barking behavior itself seems to be an **unintended consequence of domestication**. While wolves and dogs share many behavioral characteristics (and, in fact, dogs were reclassified in 1993 as a **subspecies of wolf**), **wolves rarely bark**. Barking makes up only a small percent – by Hare's estimates as low as 3% – of wolf vocalizations. In addition, the experimental foxes in Russia that have been "force domesticated" over the span of just a handful of generations have shown the same split: the **wild-type foxes don't bark, whereas the domesticated ones do**. The artificial selection process that selects against aggression and fear in canids seems to have unearthed a propensity for barking.

[Adapted from "Sparky Speaks?" by Elliot Hirsen, 2011]

Cause-and-effect: domestication creates barking behavior

Contrast: wolves and wild foxes don't bark, dogs and domesticated foxes do

Main Idea: Dog vocalizations communicate more than we previously thought, and although dogs sometimes bark in response to general excitement, they are capable of barking to communicate a variety of different situations.

1. Based on the information in the passage, the presence of barking behavior in the absence of other dogs or humans supports the idea that:
    A) dogs' highly flexible vocal cords permit them to bark for a variety of purposes.
    B) **some barking behavior indicates the emotional state of the dog without communicative intent.**
    C) the arousal model fails to account for a common observation made by dog owners.
    D) Hare's work is fundamentally flawed.

The question makes specific reference to an example of dog barking from Coppinger's studies. As Coppinger stated, dogs bark in response to general arousal (emotional state) without communicating anything in particular, as choice B says.

2. The passage suggests that recordings of dogs barking, to be useful in studying dog communication, must be:
    A) made when attempting to take food away from a dog.
    B) of particularly high quality so as to be recognizable by other dogs.
    C) intelligible to a human audience.
    D) **recorded in response to a specific situation being studied.**

In analyzing the various types of barking, the researchers played the recordings of the barking back for other dogs to hear and for other humans. So both choice B and C seem tempting, but we can eliminate them both. After all, if C were correct, then B would also have to be correct. You can't have two right answers! Instead, we have to think not about who the recordings were played for, but when and why they were recorded – in response to different situations. Choice D nails it.

3. Animal researchers have recorded a set of vocalizations made by hyenas in conjunction with several different hyena behaviors commonly exhibited in the wild. If the researchers wanted to speculate on the function of those vocalizations, Hare would suggest that they:
    A) play those recordings to human listeners and ask the humans to distinguish between the vocalizations.
    B) use a spectrograph to analyze the pitch, loudness, or timbre of the vocalizations.
    C) compare the vocalization behavior of hyenas with their nearest domesticated relative.
    D) **play those recordings to other hyenas and observe their reactions.**

We must apply the technique used in the passage to a new situation. In the passage, the study was done by recording a dog's barks and then playing those barks back to listeners – first other dogs, then people who interact with dogs. A similar protocol would be choice D, to play hyena vocalizations back for other hyenas.

Skimming Practice Passage II

As one looks forward to the America of fifty years hence, the main source of anxiety appears to be in a probable excess of prosperity, and in the want of a good grievance. We seem nearly at the end of those great public wrongs which require a special moral earthquake to end them. There seems nothing left which need be absolutely fought for; no great influence to keep us from a commonplace and perhaps debasing success. There will, no doubt, be still need of the statesman to adjust the details of government, and of the clergyman to keep an eye on private morals, including his own. There will also be social and religious changes, perhaps great ones; but there are no omens of any very fierce upheaval. And seeing the educational value to this generation of the reforms for which it has contended, one must feel an impulse of pity for our successors, who seem likely to have no convictions that they can honestly be mobbed for.

Can we spare these great tonics? It is the experience of history that all religious bodies are purified by persecution, and materialized by peace. No amount of accumulated virtue has thus far saved the merely devout communities from deteriorating, when let alone, into comfort and good dinners. This is most noticeable in detached organizations—Moravians, Shakers, Quakers, Roman Catholics—they all go the same way at last; when persecution and missionary toil are over, they enter on a tiresome millennium of meat and pudding. To guard against this spiritual obesity, this carnal Eden, what has the next age in reserve for us? Suppose however many million perfectly healthy and virtuous Americans, what is to keep them from being as uninteresting as so many Australians?

I know of nothing but that aim which is the climax and flower of all civilization, without which purity itself grows dull and devotion tedious,—the pursuit of Science and Art. Give to all this nation peace, freedom, prosperity, and even virtue, still there must be some absorbing interest, some career. That career can be sought only in two directions,—more and yet more material prosperity on the one side. Science and Art on the other. Every man's aim must either be riches, or something better than riches. To advocate the alternative career, the striving of the whole nature after something utterly apart from this world's wealth,—it is for this end that a stray voice is needed. It will not take long; the clamor of the market will re-absorb us to-morrow.

[Adapted from "Literature as an Art", *The Atlantic Monthly*, December, 1867.]

1. The author's primary purpose in this passage is:
    A) to provide a call to arms for individuals to follow passionate, challenging lives.
    B) to draw attention to the dramatic irony of a society starved for evil.
    C) to acknowledge the death of art as the bittersweet but necessary price of peace and justice.
    D) to argue for Science and Art as the inevitable flower and final purpose of a mature civilization.

2. Which of the following, if true, would most *weaken* the author's main argument?
    A) Moravians, Quakers, and Roman Catholics are found to have most increased their prosperity in peacetime.
    B) During the last US-involved war, sculpture increased while live theater decreased.
    C) Hemingway's greatest novel, *A Farewell to Arms*, was based on his experiences in the Great War.
    D) A national survey shows that individuals insulated from social upheaval are rated as the most passionate.

3. Which of the following assumptions does the author make in the first paragraph?
    A) Challenging but laudable tasks benefit those who undertake them.
    B) Later generations are as likely to have strong moral convictions as the current one.
    C) A strong moral imperative can be gained from experience.
    D) Moral conviction is less desirable than an easy life.

4. According to the passage, which of the following exemplifies the decline of a people or organization after its battles are won and trials endured?
    A) The safe, boring lives of millions of Australians.
    B) The debasing success of America's latest moral earthquake.
    C) The Shaker's post-missionary-phase millennium of prosperity.
    D) The increase of peacetime science.

5. Which of the following does the author assume to be true, based on the second paragraph?
    A) Australia has never experienced war or serious social upheaval.
    B) Hard-earned virtue is preferable to meaningless ease.
    C) The Quakers have become materialistic and complacent.
    D) Pudding is contradictory to revolution.

6. In context, when the passage describes a "spiritual obesity, this carnal Eden", the author means
    A) that without some bitterness in life, the sweet can never be as sweet.
    B) that an excess of prosperity can lead to spiritual ill-health.
    C) that paradise on Earth is a part of humanity's future, rather than its past.
    D) that austerity, not prosperity, is necessary for moral uprightness.

7. Suppose a survey of Spanish poetry from the 13th to 21st century revealed that the frequency of highly-acclaimed and widely reprinted work (relative to the amount published during the period) spiked during revolutionary periods. The author would likely explain this as
    A) the result of unjust circumstances fostering a passion for truth and moral right.
    B) a result of the lack of lucrative employment making the arts more desirable.
    C) an anomaly, explainable by the heterogeneity of a nation in crisis.
    D) a result of a greater demand for beautiful things in difficult times.

Skimming Practice Passage II Explanation

As one looks forward to the **America of fifty years hence**, the main source of anxiety appears to be in a probable **excess of prosperity**, and in the **want of a good grievance**. We seem nearly at the end of those great **public wrongs** which require a special **moral earthquake** to end them. There seems nothing left which need be absolutely fought for; no great influence to keep us from a commonplace and perhaps **debasing success**. There will, no doubt, be still need of the statesman to adjust the details of government, and of the clergyman to keep an eye on private morals, including his own. There will also be social and religious changes, perhaps great ones; but there are no omens of any very fierce upheaval. And seeing the **educational value** to this generation of the **reforms** for which it has contended, one must feel an impulse of pity for our successors, who seem likely to have no **convictions** that they can honestly be mobbed for.

Key terms: America, public wrongs, moral earthquake , reforms, convictions

Contrast: contradictory terms: excess of good, want of bad, debasing success

Cause-and-effect: peace and prosperity give future generations no chance for education/conviction

Opinion: individual greatness requires difficult times

Can we spare these great tonics? It is the experience of history that all religious bodies are **purified by persecution**, and **materialized by peace**. No amount of accumulated virtue has thus far saved the merely devout communities from **deteriorating**, when let alone, into comfort and good dinners. This is most noticeable in detached organizations—**Moravians, Shakers, Quakers, Roman Catholics**—they all go the same way at last; when persecution and missionary toil are over, they enter on a **tiresome** millennium of meat and pudding. To guard against this **spiritual obesity**, this **carnal Eden**, what has the next age in reserve for us? Suppose however many million perfectly healthy and virtuous **Americans**, what is to keep them from being as uninteresting as so many **Australians**?

Key terms: purified, Moravians, Shakers, Quakers, Roman Catholics, Eden, Australians

Contrast: persecution purifies but peace leads to materialism; virtuous and persecuted Americans, boring (stable, wealthy?) Australians

Cause-and-effect: when no trials are left, groups and individuals become complacent and weak; spoils of victory destroy virtuous qualities

Opinion: turbulence and difficulty creates the best individuals; wealthy and peaceful are to be pitied for weakness

I know of nothing but that aim which is the climax and **flower of all civilization**, without which purity itself grows dull and devotion tedious,—the pursuit of **Science and Art**. Give to all this nation peace, freedom, prosperity, and even virtue, still there must be some absorbing interest, some career. That career can be sought only in two directions,—more and yet more **material prosperity** on the one side. Science and Art on the other. Every man's aim must either be riches, or something better than riches. To advocate the alternative career, the striving of the whole nature after something utterly apart from this world's wealth,—it is for this end that **a stray voice is needed**. It will not take long; the clamor of the market will re-absorb us to-morrow.

Key terms: civilization, Science, Art

Contrast: riches vs. something better

Cause-and-effect: lack of great war or social cause implies need for worthwhile individual pursuits

Opinion: art and science are the greatest pursuits; material prosperity is tempting but art is better

Main Idea: A society with no injustice, no pain, no evil, is at risk of losing its greatness, so one must advocate the pursuit of greatness through art and science.

1. The author's primary purpose in this passage is
    A) **to provide a call to arms for individuals to follow passionate, challenging lives.**
    B) to draw attention to the dramatic irony of a society starved for evil.
    C) to acknowledge the death of art as the bittersweet but necessary price of peace and justice.
    D) to argue for Science and Art as the inevitable flower and final purpose of a mature civilization.

At first glance, A , B, and C all seem relatively close matches for the main idea of the passage. D is almost exactly lifted from the passage, and is found in the concluding paragraph, but it doesn't fully encapsulate the main idea. However, it does show why A is the best match. The passage author not only elucidates the problem of a society with no more physical or moral battles to fight, he advocates a solution, for which A is a reasonably good match. He does not discuss the problem merely to make a point of its irony (B), nor to reluctantly accept it as an inevitability (C).

2. Which of the following, if true, would most *weaken* the author's main argument?
    A) Moravians, Quakers, and Roman Catholics are found to have most increased their prosperity in peacetime.
    B) During the last US-involved war, sculpture increased while live theater decreased.
    C) Hemingway's greatest novel, *A Farewell to Arms*, was based on his experiences in the Great War.
    D) **A national survey shows that individuals insulated from social upheaval are rated as the most passionate.**

The main argument is that great societal challenges such as war or social injustices that need changing provide a sort of moral education for the citizens who experience and face these great tasks, and, as a corollary, that the lack of such crises denies individuals the opportunity to learn virtue and conviction. Either evidence of a society with great challenges but little moral conviction, or a society without such challenges whose citizens nevertheless have great moral conviction, would weaken the argument. D is a pretty good match for the latter and, if true, would weaken the main argument. Both A and B are neutral, neither strengthening nor weakening the main argument, while C actually strengthens it.

3. Which of the following assumptions does the author make in the first paragraph?
    A) Challenging but laudable tasks benefit those who undertake them.
    B) Later generations are as likely to have strong moral convictions as the current one.
    C) **A strong moral imperative can be gained from experience.**
    D) Moral conviction is less desirable than an easy life.

A is not an assumption but an explicit statement. B is contrary to what the passage suggests in the first paragraph. But the first paragraph notes the educational value of the fight for reforms, stating that those who come later, in the peaceful era, will lack conviction. The implication is that the lack of such experiences will be responsible for the lack of conviction, which assumes that moral conviction can be learned, matching the statement in C. D is the exact opposite of another assumption the author makes, given the comment about pitying those who come later.

4. According to the passage, which of the following exemplifies the decline of a people or organization after its battles are won and trials endured?
    A) The safe, boring lives of millions of Australians.
    B) The debasing success of America's latest moral earthquake.
    C) **The Shaker's post-missionary-phase millennium of prosperity.**
    D) The increase of peacetime science.

Since the question stem specifically asks about the decline of a people, the answer choice must reflect the time of stability after all the battles are won. There was no mention in the passage itself of what previous trials and tribulations the Australians have or have not faced, so A can be eliminated. America's recent social upheaval is mentioned, but the expected decline is hypothetical and lies still in the future, so B is not a good match either. C is a perfect match, and is found in the passage. D is offered in the passage as a cure for such a decline, not a sign of it.

5. Which of the following does the author assume to be true, based on the second paragraph?
   A) Australia has never experienced war or serious social upheaval.
   B) **Hard-earned virtue is preferable to meaningless ease.**
   C) The Quakers have become materialistic and complacent.
   D) Pudding is contradictory to revolution.

Since the answer choices come from different parts of the paragraph, it's necessary to examine them one at a time. A is very tempting, as the author compares citizens of a turbulent America to those of Australia, suggesting that the latter country has been stable and free of war (and its citizens consequently boring). However, this does not necessarily mean that the country has never faced war or upheaval, only that it has not in the most recent generation at the time the passage was written. B, however, is assumed, given the tone of the passage. In this paragraph, the author describes a life of peace and material ease as tiresome, deteriorated, and boring. The author is operating under the assumption that such a life is undesirable. C is a consequence of that same assumption, and is outright stated, not assumed. D might be tempting, but on closer examination it is not integral to the argument. Although pudding is used as an example or indicator of sloth and complacency, it's not the main point. The author is not arguing against eating pudding, but against a life where everything is easy and passion has no place. It's not necessary to assume that a revolutionary cannot have the occasional pudding.

6. In context, when the passage describes a "spiritual obesity, this carnal Eden", the author means
   A) that without some bitterness in life, the sweet can never be as sweet.
   B) **that an excess of prosperity can lead to spiritual ill-health.**
   C) that paradise on Earth is a part of humanity's future, rather than its past.
   D) that austerity, not prosperity, is necessary for moral uprightness.

The author's colorful phrasing, a "spiritual obesity", uses the metaphor of overindulgence causing ill health to describe the surprising results of achieving prosperity and peace. The purpose of the passage is to warn against this danger, and the purpose of the quoted phrase is to sum up the problem, which is well-stated in B. Answer choice A sounds reasonable based on the phrasing itself, but does not match any of the arguments in the passage. C, too, is nowhere in the passage. D is tempting, as it nearly hits the passage author's main idea, but the problem is not the lack of "lack", but the lack of an actual injustice or challenge. The focus on prosperity versus austerity misses the mark somewhat.

7. Suppose a survey of Spanish poetry from the 13th to 21st century revealed that the frequency of highly-acclaimed and widely reprinted work (relative to the amount published during the period) spiked during revolutionary periods. The author would likely explain this as
   A) **the result of unjust circumstances fostering a passion for truth and moral right.**
   B) a result of the lack of lucrative employment making the arts more desirable.
   C) an anomaly, explainable by the heterogeneity of a nation in crisis.
   D) a result of a greater demand for beautiful things in difficult times.

The author's main argument describes social turbulence and injustice as moral teachers, and the lack of them as leading to a bland, convictionless populace. It follows that individuals of passion and moral strength are disproportionately created—taught—during turbulent times. It's assumed that this creates better and more meaningful art. A is a good match for this. B is nowhere in the passage. C contradicts the main idea, which predicts this outcome rather than calling it an anomaly. D too is not in the passage.

CHAPTER 2.
General Prep Strategies

HOW TO PREP FOR THE CARS SECTION

In the previous chapter we looked at narrow, focused strategies: how to tackle an individual passage. Now, let's spend just a few minutes talking about how to prep for the CARS section in general.

Step 1: Form a study group

The single most valuable way to prep for the MCAT is free, but it does take work. We've all had that experience in college: the professor says "you'll be doing this project in a group," and you feel an inward moan. You just know you'll spend the next three weeks dealing with lazy slackers. And in the end, you'll have to do all the work yourself anyway.

It's no surprise that many MCAT students prefer to "go it alone" given those types of experiences in college. However, the MCAT is a *very* different animal than college tests or projects. Having a good MCAT study group or study buddy is essential to your success on the CARS section. In my decade of working with MCAT students, the two biggest factors I've seen that lead to MCAT success are a good study buddy and a good attitude.

So if working with a study group is Step 1, how do you go about getting the most out of it?

First, don't be afraid to "break up" if things aren't going well.

You're not married to your study partner. If things aren't working well for you, address the issue immediately and directly (but politely!). Simply tell the other person, "I think our learning styles aren't really meshing that well and I'd really prefer to study on my own. Good luck with your prep!" Your MCAT prep timeline will end up being pretty tight, and you don't have time to waste with a partner that isn't clicking well with you.

Second, give each other homework.

The whole point of a study buddy (or workout buddy, etc.) is to create accountability to someone other than yourself. At the end of every review session with your study partner, discuss what homework you're going to be doing over the next several days.   Some assignments should be set for both of you, "Okay so we'll both take the AAMC Practice MCAT Test before we meet on Friday" but then other assignments should be divided between you: "It'll be my job to review the first five reading passages and your job to review passages six through ten." At the subsequent session, teach each other what you've reviewed. Any educator will tell you that the best way to learn something is to teach it to someone else. One of the main reasons to have a study buddy is to have someone who you can teach material to. Which brings us to…

Third, teach each other the material.

One of the goals in finding a study partner should be to find someone who has different strengths and weaknesses than you. So if you're really good at the social science and history passages, you should find someone who's got a knack for the art, dance, and music ones. The goal is not to have your partner teach you, but rather for you to teach him. It's that act of teaching that will turn your strengths into total mastery.

And finally, stay positive!

Sure, there's academic benefits of having a partner who can help you understand the material. But having a good study buddy also helps tremendously with the emotional support needed to get through such a huge challenge. Celebrate each others' successes and commiserate over difficulties. Rely on your study partner to provide a sympathetic ear, and offer her one in return.   In the end, success on the CARS section depends on attitude and motivation. And they're best found with a good study partner or study group.

Step 2: Set a study schedule

You need to be doing reading practice at least 6 days a week, but it doesn't need to be timed practice every day. Typically, you should be doing a full 90 minute timed section twice a week. The other days you should be doing a smaller chunk of verbal work – typically two to four passages. A typical weekly schedule might look like this:

Mon: Full MCAT Practice test (which obviously includes a CARS section)
Tue: Review day, no new reading passages
Wed: 2 untimed practice passages
Thu: 4 untimed practice passages
Fri: Full 90 min timed CARS section
Sat: 2 untimed practice passages
Sun: 4 untimed practice passages

The key here is consistency. You simply cannot boost your CARS score in a short time through some sort of "trick". There's no magic tricks on the MCAT – only hard work and lots of practice. Typically you'll need at least 8 – 10 weeks of practice to make a dent in your CARS score. Many find they need longer.

Step 3: Set aside time for outside reading

To give the reading muscles in your brain a good workout, you need to set aside about 30 minutes a day to do heavy MCAT-level reading. The best choice here is to go straight to hardest stuff the MCAT has to offer: philosophy.

You can buy an old, used copy of ***Reason & Responsibility*** on Amazon for less than ten bucks. It's a college-level philosophy textbook used around the country for people who are starting out as philosophy majors. The nice thing is that it has articles covering everything from the ancient Greeks up to modern day.

Read for 30 minutes each morning. At the end of each column of text, stop and try to summarize the author's overall main idea or main opinion and write it in the margin at the bottom of the page. After 30 minutes, stop reading that article. If you didn't finish the article, that's okay, just move on.

The next day, skip ahead to the next chapter in the book. If you just keep reading from the same section of the book, you're going to go a little nuts reading about the same topic over and over. Instead, rotate through the chapters so you're getting something a little different every day – Monday is the ontological proof of God's existence, Tuesday is morality, Wednesday the possibilities that computers have a mind, and so on.

Alternatively, if there's a particular part of the CARS section that you absolutely hate – art or history or public health – you can set time aside to read from a journal on that topic. A regular magazine isn't enough. Even the famous suggestion, "Oh just read The Economist every day" just isn't hard enough. You need to go to ***professional journals*** written by and for those working in that field.

Step 4: Keep track of your progress: Lessons Learned Journal

This was mentioned earlier in the book but it bears repeating – you have to be empirical about your approach to reading passages. You can't reject something out of hand just because you don't like it. You have to try lots of different approaches and keep track of how things are going.

We've given you a small worksheet in Appendix A at the back of the book. But don't be limited to that single page. The best choice is to just start a new Word document where you keep track of everything.

When I'm working with my own students, I call it their "Lessons Learned Journal". At the end of each chunk of work – whether that's a whole test, a timed section, or just some passages – you should stop and record your performance, your timing, what approach you took, and how confident you were.

Then, underneath that, take some notes about what you did wrong *and what you did right*. It's not enough to dwell on mistakes. You should also celebrate things you did correctly and write down reminders to yourself to do them right again.

Step 5: Review the alternative techniques and approaches discussed in Appendix C

The three main reading strategies discussed in the previous chapter are perfect for most students. But maybe you're not "most students" and you need to try other things. Read through Appendix C to get some more advice.

Panic Mode Practice Passage I

Recent research in the field of memory has led to an explosion of our knowledge ███████████████ ██ ███████investigators have focused on one particular aspect of memory failure, that of false memories.

The manner by which false memories are created is somewhat surprising to those who harbor the outdated view of memory as a sort of video recording that sits in our head and plays back correctly every time we recall an event. In fact, memories are fluid, ever-changing things. ████████████████████████████ ██ ██ ██ ██ ████████████████████████████████████ incorrect detail will work its way into the story and become fixed as a part of your "real" memory of the event.

False memories are not just limited to distortions or mis-rememberings of individual details of an event either. People can easily be made to remember entire events that never happened to them. The "Lost in the Mall" effect, first developed by Elizabeth Loftus, ████████████████████████████████████ ██ ██ ██ ██ ██ "lost in the mall" event was the real one, and that a real event was false. Since the original experiment in the early 1990's, the phenomenon has been studied across age groups and cultures, and been shown to exist in nearly every population studied.

Loftus's studies primarily demonstrate that belief in false memories hinges primarily on plausibility. In order for the subjects to be made to recall the false "lost in the mall" event, ████████████████████████████ ██ ██

Despite the ethical controversies surrounding these studies, their results have led to a significant new development in the psychology community: a new diagnosis of "false memory syndrome" (FMS). ████████████████████████ ██ ██ ███████ any attempt to correct the false memory leads the FMS sufferer to react with aggression and rejection.

The strongest objectors to the new diagnosis are those who work with recovered memory therapy and assert that the memories they help patients remember are not implanted memories that can trigger FMS, but rather are real memories of long-forgotten childhood trauma.

[Adapted from "Remember to Remember" by K.J.O.C. Choate, 2012.]

1. Which of the following would most *challenge* the author's argument about how false memories can be implanted?
    A) In a later study, Loftus found that women were more likely to report remembering a false memory than men, and there were no significant differences between different racial groups.
    B) When presented with childhood scenarios that are all false, subjects most commonly report being able to recall the event that includes the fewest details that are closely linked to the subject's childhood.
    C) True memories are more easily recalled when the memory has been encoded with a rich amount of detail linking the memory to other memories.
    D) Damage to the parts of the brain associated with forming new memories tends to reduce the frequency with which people will report being able to recall false memories.

2. According to the author's explanation of memory, which of the following is the most plausible?
    A) Certain individuals with autism have flawless recall of visual material.
    B) A singer incorrectly sings a particular word during one performance and that word becomes fixed in the singer's mind as a correct part of the song.
    C) An adult remembers his fifth birthday and is able to recall the birthday cake in vivid detail but is unable to remember any of his friends who were at the party.
    D) Those with false memory syndrome become so obsessed with their memory that they recall it exactly the same every single time.

3. The author asserts that every time we remember an event, we are actually remembering the last time we remembered that event. This most likely happens because:
    A) the brain's process of encoding memories always incorporates the mental process going on during the encoding, including the recalled experience and other contemporaneous inputs.
    B) the brain's memory mechanisms can only focus on encoding those parts of a memory with strong emotional content, leading us to re-experience the emotions that accompany a memory.
    C) we are especially vulnerable to developing false memories as a result.
    D) it is psychologically more reassuring to reinforce the positive aspects of a memory.

4. As used in the passage, the word *syndrome* is best described as:
    A) a false memory implanted by researchers studying memory.
    B) a process of reshaping memories every time they are recalled.
    C) a psychological disease with biological roots.
    D) a collection of distressing psychological symptoms.

5. As described by the author, false memory syndrome would most accurately describe which of the following situations:
  I. A subject in a psychology study who strongly insists that the false memory of being lost in a mall is the real memory and that another real memory never happened.
 II. A person represses their memory of a childhood trauma and by working with a therapist who does recovered memory therapy is able to recall the event and begin addressing it.
III. A psychiatric outpatient who recalls the death of a pet she never actually had and who experiences significant feelings of distress on a nearly daily basis from her recollection of the event.
    A) I only
    B) III only
    C) II and III only
    D) I and III only

Panic Mode Practice Passage I Explanation

Recent research in the field of memory has led to an explosion of our knowledge ██████████████████ ██ ████ investigators have focused on one particular aspect of memory failure, that of false memories.

We know more about memory now and false memories are being studied.

The manner by which false memories are created is somewhat surprising to those who harbor the outdated view of memory as a sort of video recording that sits in our head and plays back correctly every time we recall an event. In fact, memories are fluid, ever-changing things. ████████████████████████████████████ ██ ██ ██ ██ incorrect detail will work its way into the story and become fixed as a part of your "real" memory of the event.

Memory is fluid, not like a tape recorder in your head and apparently false details can get worked into your memory and fixed as part of the real memory.

False memories are not just limited to distortions or mis-rememberings of individual details of an event either. People can easily be made to remember entire events that never happened to them. The "Lost in the Mall" effect, first developed by Elizabeth Loftus, ███ ██ ██ ██ ██ ████████████████████████████████████ "lost in the mall" event was the real one, and that a real event was false. Since the original experiment in the early 1990's, the phenomenon has been studied across age groups and cultures, and been shown to exist in nearly every population studied.

Memory can make mistakes not just in details but you can remember whole events that never happened and people will really stick to it. This false event has been shown to be true across cultures.

Loftus's studies primarily demonstrate that belief in false memories hinges primarily on plausibility. In order for the subjects to be made to recall the false "lost in the mall" event, █████████████████████████████ ██ ███████████████████████████████

Memory depends on the false memories being plausible.

Despite the ethical controversies surrounding these studies, their results have led to a significant new development in the psychology community: a new diagnosis of "false memory syndrome" (FMS). ███████████████████ ██ ██ ████ any attempt to correct the false memory leads the FMS sufferer to react with aggression and rejection.

The "lost in the mall" studies led to a new disease being created – false memory syndrome and people who have this disease get really upset if you try to correct the false memory.

The strongest objectors to the new diagnosis are those who work with recovered memory therapy and assert that the memories they help patients remember are not implanted memories that can trigger FMS, but rather are real memories of long-forgotten childhood trauma.

[Adapted from "Remember to Remember" by K.J.O.C. Choate, 2012.]

Some people object to the new diagnosis because they work with helping people recover memories.

1. Which of the following would most *challenge* the author's argument about how false memories can be implanted?
   A) In a later study, Loftus found that women were more likely to report remembering a false memory than men, and there were no significant differences between different racial groups.
   B) **When presented with childhood scenarios that are all false, subjects most commonly report being able to recall the event that includes the fewest details that are closely linked to the subject's childhood.**
   C) True memories are more easily recalled when the memory has been encoded with a rich amount of detail linking the memory to other memories.
   D) Damage to the parts of the brain associated with forming new memories tends to reduce the frequency with which people will report being able to recall false memories.

Best guess: B (or maybe D)

We read that plausibility was a big part of the lost in the mall study of false memories of events. B says that people recall the thing with the fewest plausible details. That goes against what we read.

A: We didn't skim through and see anything about gender or racial differences so this is probably irrelevant.
C: Our skim gave us lots about false memories but nothing about how easy it is to remember true memories, so best not guess this.
D: Possible. Our skim didn't reveal anything about parts of the brain but at least this choice is on topic.

2. According to the author's explanation of memory, which of the following is the most plausible?
   A) Certain individual with autism have flawless recall of visual material.
   B) **A singer incorrectly sings a particular word during one performance and that word becomes fixed in the singer's mind as a correct part of the song.**
   C) An adult remembers his fifth birthday and is able to recall the birthday cake in vivid detail but is unable to remember any of his friends who were at the party.
   D) Those with false memory syndrome become so obsessed with their memory that they recall it exactly the same every single time.

Best guess: B (or maybe C)

We're told that memory isn't just a tape recorder in your head that plays back every time. We see that false details or events can be recalled as if they're the real thing. Choice B gives a good example of that false detail working its way into the memory.

A: We didn't see anything about flawless recall.
C: Possible. Our skim didn't address different kinds of things being recalled differently so this is a possible guess.
D: "exactly" is probably too strong, given that the passage is about how fluid memory is.

3. The author asserts that every time we remember an event, we are actually remembering the last time we remembered that event. This most likely happens because:

- A) **the brain's process of encoding memories always incorporates the mental process going on during the encoding, including the recalled experience and other contemporaneous inputs.**
- B) the brain's memory mechanisms can only focus on encoding those parts of a memory with strong emotional content, leading us to re-experience the emotions that accompany a memory.
- C) we are especially vulnerable to developing false memories as a result.
- D) it is psychologically more reassuring to reinforce the positive aspects of a memory.

Best guess: A

The question says that every time we recall an event we're actually recalling the last time we remembered it. The question doesn't contain any language about positive or negative memories, so we can avoid C and D. B is a good possibility, but again the question doesn't concern itself with emotional memories, it says all memories. Only choice A seems to address mechanisms that apply to memory in general.

4. As used in the passage, the word *syndrome* is best described as:

- A) a false memory implanted by researchers studying memory.
- B) a process of reshaping memories every time they are recalled.
- C) a psychological disease with biological roots.
- D) **a collection of distressing psychological symptoms.**

Best guess: D

As a rule, don't use outside knowledge. But when you're in quick-quick-skim-and-guess panic mode, use whatever you can. The word "syndrome" just refers to a collection of symptoms when used in outside contexts, so just guess D here.

5. As described by the author, false memory syndrome would most accurately describe which of the following situations:

- I. **A subject in a psychology study who strongly insists that the false memory of being lost in a mall is the real memory and that another real memory never happened.**
- II. A person represses their memory of a childhood trauma and by working with a therapist who does recovered memory therapy is able to recall the event and begin addressing it.
- III. **A psychiatric outpatient who recalls the death of a pet she never actually had and who experiences significant feelings of distress on a nearly daily basis from her recollection of the event.**
    - A) I only
    - B) III only
    - C) II and III only
    - D) **I and III only**

Best guess: D

We're told false memories are memories of things that didn't actually happen and it looks like I and III describe that, so our best guess is D.

Recent research in the field of memory has led to an explosion of our knowledge about how the brain encodes, stores, and retrieves memories and the anatomical structures associated with each of these processes. Along the way, a number of investigators have focused on one particular aspect of memory failure, that of false memories.

The manner by which false memories are created is somewhat surprising to those who harbor the outdated view of memory as a sort of video recording that sits in our head and plays back correctly every time we recall an event. In fact, memories are fluid, ever-changing things. We encode the information that makes up a memory and then when we recall that information, we are not simply passively "reading" the information back into our consciousness. We are, in fact, re-creating the memory fresh every time we remember it. Thus, in a very real sense, every time you remember an event, you're not remembering the event, you're remembering the last time that you remembered that event. If you find yourself telling a story about something that happened to you in childhood, and you happen to mis-remember one detail of that event due to some environmental cue during the story, that incorrect detail will work its way into the story and become fixed as a part of your "real" memory of the event.

False memories are not just limited to distortions or mis-rememberings of individual details of an event either. People can easily be made to remember entire events that never happened to them. The "Lost in the Mall" effect, first developed by Elizabeth Loftus, demonstrates that it is possible to implant false memories in people. In the technique, the subject is presented with four scenarios describing childhood events. These scenarios are provided by family members of the subject. Unbeknownst to the subject, one of the memories is false. The subject is asked to recall the event, and to write out details of their memory. If they are unable to remember the event, the subject is to honestly report an inability to recall the event. In a startlingly high 25% of cases, the subjects reported that they could, in fact, remember the false event of having been lost in the mall as a toddler. Even more surprising, at the conclusion of the study, the subjects were informed that one of the events was false and over 20% of the subjects asserted that the "lost in the mall" event was the real one, and that a real event was false. Since the original experiment in the early 1990's, the phenomenon has been studied across age groups and cultures, and been shown to exist in nearly every population studied.

Loftus's studies primarily demonstrate that belief in false memories hinges primarily on plausibility. In order for the subjects to be made to recall the false "lost in the mall" event, the researchers had to get corroborating details from family members, such as the name of a shopping mall that would have been visited by the subject frequently, as well as the names of other people who would have been involved in such an event.

Despite the ethical controversies surrounding these studies, their results have led to a significant new development in the psychology community: a new diagnosis of "false memory syndrome" (FMS). While researchers generally recognize that everyone has some number of inaccurate memories, those who suffer from FMS are strongly preoccupied with their false memories. In the worst cases, the person's entire personality and lifestyle are oriented around the false memory, and the person experiences great distress as a result. Further, the false memory is completely resistant to change: any attempt to correct the false memory leads the FMS sufferer to react with aggression and rejection.

The strongest objectors to the new diagnosis are those who work with recovered memory therapy and assert that the memories they help patients remember are not implanted memories that can trigger FMS, but rather are real memories of long-forgotten childhood trauma.

Answer key: 1-B, 2-B, 3-A, 4-D, 5-B

We ended up getting one wrong here – because we skimmed we didn't have a good sense of the definition of false memory syndrome so we got question 5 wrong. But when time is tight, getting just 2 or 3 right is plenty good enough.

Panic Mode Practice Passage II

The French have long been brought up with an emotional attachment to the image of the small wine grower, ████████ ███ ███████████████████████████████████ "oenogenic myth" and represents the particularly French exaltation of the man who is the fusion of the aesthete and rustic farmer.

Like any myth, this idea cannot be adequately described in a single sentence, but the broad outlines of the most common recurring examples of it can be seen to form a distinct pattern. At the center of the myth lies the independent man who is at once a viticulturist, a vintner, and an oenophile. ███ ██ ██ ████████████████████ Because he combined the virtues of all three areas, he avoided the provincialism of other agricul-turalists, the overly narrow technical vision of other craftsmen, and the detached self-indulgence of the wealthy sybarite.

The origin of this myth is not one rooted in the popular consciousness, but rather in the rarefied world of early 18th century French poetry. The myth began more as a literary trope than anything else. ████████████████████ ██ ██ ██ ██ █████████████████████████████████████ of the new Third Republic. This image was strengthened even further in contrast to the utilitarian technocrats of the Vichy regime under Nazi control, and served as a cultural touchstone of continu-ity through the Fourth Republic into the contemporary Fifth Republic.

Like all myths, the oenogenic myth contains the seeds of truth buried within falsehood. ██████████████████████ ██ produced on inde-pendent estates in which a single grower would develop his own cultivars, process them into wine, and select the finest bottles for sale in Paris.

By the 1880's, however, the basic nature of wine production had changed. Professional taste-makers in the finest French salons and bistros had taken it upon themselves to serve as the nation's palate. They were now the ones dic-tating what fine wine should taste like. ██ ██ ████████████████████████ the small wine grower was now relegated solely to viticulture.

This fracturing of the wine growing landscape carried with it startling advances in both the quality and quantity of production, the availability of different sorts of wines throughout the year, ████████████████████████████████ ██ ██ unified and interdependent France, in which fraternity between the rural grower, technocratic wine maker, and refined urban wine lover produced a product respected the world over: the French wine.

[Adapted from "Whining and Wine" by K. Roo, 2001.]

1. The author's main argument is that the oenogenic myth is:
    A) a myth with no factual basis in the realities of French viticulture or wine-making.
    B) a sentimental attachment to a particular representation of the independent wine-maker and his role in French society.
    C) an accurate reflection of the production of French wine, both in the past and today.
    D) an overly optimistic view of early wine-makers that downplays several key negative attributes of these wine producers.

2. According to the passage, the oenogenic myth has its foundations in:
    A) French literature.
    B) rural estates of the bourgeoisie.
    C) small vineyards in the southwest of France.
    D) the burgeoning Parisian middle-class.

3. Based on assertions made in the passage, the oenogenic myth assumes that the independent wine grower:
    I. possesses a combination of varied skills.
   II. is more sophisticated than other agriculturalists.
  III. is of a relatively lower class.
    A) I only
    B) I and II only
    C) I and III only
    D) I, II, and III

4. The author states that the oenogenic myth became a widely held belief because:
    A) the upheavals in French society following the Revolution required the stabilizing influence of a unifying national symbol.
    B) the French Revolution took as one of its symbols the independent wine grower who combined working class and middle-class values.
    C) most of the wine produced in France in the eighteenth century was made on small independent estates.
    D) the idealized image of the independent wine-grower corresponded to the realities of life for most French people at the end of the 1800's.

5. The passage suggests that the oenogenic myth implied that independent wine makers were:
    A) part of an interdependent revolutionary France.
    B) fond of tinkering with cross-breeding grape cultivars.
    C) strengthened in response to technocratic Nazis.
    D) less specialized than they are today.

6. The author implies which of the following about the truth of the oenogenic myth?
    A) It was entirely false.
    B) It was mostly false when first promulgated, but was close to the truth by the turn of the twentieth century.
    C) It was true only insofar as it depicted the wine grower who fiercely supported the French Revolution.
    D) Its typical images corresponded to the realities of many wine-growers in the early 1700's.

4. The author states that the oenogenic myth became a widely held belief because:
    A) the upheavals in French society following the Revolution required the stabilizing influence of a unifying national symbol.
    B) the French Revolution took as one of its symbols the independent wine grower who combined working class and middle-class values.
    C) most of the wine produced in France in the eighteenth century was made on small independent estates.
    D) the idealized image of the independent wine-grower corresponded to the realities of life for most French people at the end of the 1800's.

Quick, blind guess. Our skim of the beginning and end of each paragraph didn't say anything about the belief becoming widespread, so just guess here.

5. The passage suggests that the oenogenic myth implied that independent wine makers were:
    A) part of an interdependent revolutionary France.
    B) fond of tinkering with cross-breeding grape cultivars.
    C) strengthened in response to technocratic Nazis.
    D) ***less specialized than they are today.***

Best guess: D

We're told at the end of the passage that now there's this fractured landscape where everyone is specialized. So it's a good guess that the independent wine growers of the past were less specialized.

6. The author implies which of the following about the truth of the oenogenic myth?
    A) It was entirely false.
    B) It was mostly false when first promulgated, but was close to the truth by the turn of the twentieth century.
    C) It was true only insofar as it depicted the wine grower who fiercely supported the French Revolution.
    D) ***Its typical images corresponded to the realities of many wine-growers in the early 1700's.***

Best guess: D (or maybe C)

Our skim revealed that things changed in the late 1800's, so we might guess that the myth fit reality back in the 1700's.

A: "Entirely" is probably too strong
B: At the end of the passage we see in modern times France is interdependent, not based on small independent wine growers who do everything themselves.
C: Possible. Our quick skim didn't reveal anything about the French revolution.

The French have long been brought up with an emotional attachment to the image of the small wine grower, and to a set of ideas about the people and the lifestyle created around the small vineyards that dot the south west of the country. This collection of ideas has been called the "oenogenic myth" and represents the particularly French exaltation of the man who is the fusion of the aesthete and rustic farmer.

Like any myth, this idea cannot be adequately described in a single sentence, but the broad outlines of the most common recurring examples of it can be seen to form a distinct pattern. At the center of the myth lies the independent man who is at once a viticulturist, a vintner, and an oenophile. That is, the central conception of the oenogenic myth is an idealized man who represents the best of what is French: he is tied to his land through the viticulture, he is a skilled craftsman who can take the grapes through a complex series of steps to produce the final product, and he has the discerning palate of the true wine-lover. Because he combined the virtues of all three areas, he avoided the provincialism of other agriculturalists, the overly narrow technical vision of other craftsmen, and the detached self-indulgence of the wealthy sybarite.

The origin of this myth is not one rooted in the popular consciousness, but rather in the rarefied world of early 18th century French poetry. The myth began more as a literary trope than anything else. The newly well-to-do of a burgeoning French bourgeoisie who themselves owned small vineyards and who enjoyed tinkering with cross-breeding grape cultivars on their rural estates enjoyed reading about an idealized (yet more rustic, lower-class) version of themselves. So powerful was this myth that by the end of the 18th century it has become clearly defined and widely accepted. The change from literary myth of the elite to a tenet of the masses can be seen as tied to the French Revolution, in which the working and middle classes threw off the yoke of royalty, and in which the man who was both educated and worker became a symbol of the new Third Republic. This image was strengthened even further in contrast to the utilitarian technocrats of the Vichy regime under Nazi control, and served as a cultural touchstone of continuity through the Fourth Republic into the contemporary Fifth Republic.

Like all myths, the oenogenic myth contains the seeds of truth buried within falsehood. At the start of the 18th century when the myth first began to grow, a sizable portion of the wine output in France was indeed produced on independent estates in which a single grower would develop his own cultivars, process them into wine, and select the finest bottles for sale in Paris.

By the 1880's, however, the basic nature of wine production had changed. Professional taste-makers in the finest French salons and bistros had taken it upon themselves to serve as the nation's palate. They were now the ones dictating what fine wine should taste like. Similarly, the burgeoning science of chemistry had put some methodological meat on the bones of wine creation and with it came a cadre of professional wine makers who knew little of agriculture, but a great deal about how to turn the grapes into the final product. Having had two thirds of the rug yanked out from under him, the small wine grower was now relegated solely to viticulture.

This fracturing of the wine growing landscape carried with it startling advances in both the quality and quantity of production, the availability of different sorts of wines throughout the year, and an endless treadmill of new fads replacing old. The myth of the lone wine grower wrestling with the very earth to produce a bottle of fine vintage has only very recently been contested by an even stronger image: that of a unified and interdependent France, in which fraternity between the rural grower, technocratic wine maker, and refined urban wine lover produced a product respected the world over: the French wine.

Answer Key: 1-B, 2-A, 3-B, 4-B, 5-D, 6-D

So we see that with just a quick skim of the first and last sentences, we were still able to make very good guesses on five of the six questions. Even if you only got 2 or 3 right, count that as a "win". When you're at the end of the section and running out of time, we want to take what we can get.

CHAPTER 4.
Half-Section Practice

SECTION 1: HIGHLIGHTING TECHNIQUE

You can use any technique you'd like on the following half-section but I very strongly recommend you use this as a chance to start getting timed practice with the highlighting technique. When working your way through this section, there's only one absolute requirement: **you must time yourself strictly**. Don't set a timer counting down, but rather a stopwatch counting up. You do yourself no favors by casually working through the passages with no awareness of time.

If you would like to get the best practice for the highlighting technique, do the following before you start:

1. Get a stopwatch to count up (or a stopwatch app on your phone).
2. Get a yellow highlighter.
3. Go some place where you won't be interrupted and that is relatively quiet.
4. Get some foam earplugs to block out the noise.

When you start the section start the stopwatch counting up.

Every time you finish reading a passage, hit the "lap" button on the stopwatch. Every time you finish a set of questions, hit the "lap" button again. At the end of the section you'll have 10 data points showing you how long you took to read each passage and how long for the questions.

With the highlighting technique you should spend 4 - 5 minutes on the passage and 5 - 6 minutes on the questions.

Then, when reviewing the explanations afterwards, look to the **bold** text as a guide for what we suggest you highlight. Additional notes between the paragraphs can help guide your understanding of the passage.

Passage I

Two thirds of the United States lies west of the Mississippi River. This vast domain has already exercised a tremendous influence over our political destiny. The Territories were the immediate occasion of our civil war. During an entire generation they furnished the arena for the prelusive strife of that war. The Missouri Compromise was to us of the East a flag of truce. But neither nature nor the men who populated the Western Territories recognized this flag. The vexed question of party platforms and sectional debate, the right and the reason of slavery, solved itself in the West with a freedom and rough rapidity natural to the soil and its population. Climatic limitations and prohibitions went hand in hand with the inflow of an emigration mainly from the Northern States,—an emigration fostered by political emotions and fevered by political injustice. While the South was menacing and the North deprecating war, far removed from this tumult of words the conflict was going on, and was being decided. And it was because slavery was doomed in the great West, and therefore in the nation, that rebellion ensued.

It is worthy of note that the same generation which witnessed the growth of the Calhoun school of politics in the South, and of the Free Soil and (afterward) the Republican party in the North, and which followed with intense interest the stages of the Territorial struggle, witnessed also the employment of steam and electricity as agents of human progress. These agents, these organs of velocity, abbreviating time and space, said, Let the West be East; and before the locomotive the West fled from Buffalo to Chicago, across the prairies, the Rocky Mountains, the desert steppes beyond, and down the Pacific slope, until it stared the Orient into a self-contradiction.

It was on the part of our government a sublime recognition of the power of steam, that, while it was struggling for existence, it gave its sanction to the Pacific Railroad enterprise. Curiously enough, it is through Kansas and Nebraska—the Epidaurus of our Peloponnesian war—that the two great rival Pacific Railroad routes are to run.

America becomes at once interoceanic and mediterranean, commanding the two oceans, and mediating between Europe and Asia. By the Pacific Railroad, Hong Kong via New York is only forty days distant from London. The tea and silks of China and the products of the Spice Islands must pass through America to Europe. In this connection, also, there is a profound significance in our alliance, every year growing stronger, with Russia, whose extreme southern boundary joins Japan, our latest and warmest Asiatic ally.

But the development of American commercial power as against the world is secondary to the internal development of our own resources, and to the indissoluble bond of national union afforded by this inland route from the Atlantic to the Pacific, and by its future connections with every portion of our territory. In thirty years, California will have a population equal to that of New York to-day, and yet not be half full, and the city of St. Louis will number a million of souls. New York City and San Francisco, as the two great *entrepôts* of trade; Chicago and St. Louis as its two vital centres; and New Orleans at the mouth of our great national canal, the Mississippi,—will become nations rather than cities, out-stripping all the great cities of ancient and modern history.

[Adapted from "Our Pacific Railroads", *The Atlantic Monthly*, December, 1867.]

1. Which of the following titles most accurately describes the passage?
    A) A History of the US Pacific Railroad System.
    B) Post-Civil War Economics.
    C) The United States as the New Mediterranean.
    D) US Pacific and the Making of a Nation.

2. What is the significance of the comparison of Kansas and Nebraska to Epidaurus in paragraph three?
    A) The author is underscoring the unifying nature of the railroads by noting its passage through politically fractious territory.
    B) The author is supporting his description of these regions as critical hubs in both war- and peacetime.
    C) The author is making a point about the impossibility of discarding past political enmity.
    D) Epidaurus was a neutral territory, and the author is arguing that, as expected, similar neutral territories as Kansas and Nebraska are central to post-war diplomacy.

3. Why does the passage compare the post-railroad United States to the Mediterranean region?
    A) Because the Mediterranean region has historically included many warring nations comparable to the North and South during the US Civil War.
    B) Because the Mediterranean also has a comprehensive and effective transportation system.
    C) Because the Mediterranean region includes significant water transport, similar to the United States' Mississippi River and other "canals".
    D) Because the United States Pacific and Atlantic ports serve as connections to Asian and Europe, respectively, just as the Mediterranean bridges those continents.

4. Based on the passage, which of the following might have prevented the US Civil War from occurring?
    A) If the building of a railroad from the Northern states to the Western territories occurred earlier.
    B) If the Western territories were not settled by white Americans but remained sovereign Indian Territory.
    C) If California's population had increased more quickly.
    D) If the overland route from Europe to Asia became unusable.

5. Which of the following cities is not listed as a critical node of a newly-connected America?
    A) Buffalo.
    B) St. Louis.
    C) San Francisco.
    D) New Orleans.

6. In the context of the passage, the statement that " before the locomotive the West fled from Buffalo to Chicago" means
    A) citizens of Buffalo escaped the region as rail travel facilitated invasion from the East.
    B) the greater ease and speed of travel caused a mental shift, making the Western territories seem more isolated than before.
    C) greater accessibility caused formerly sparsely-populated territories to fill up, moving the bounds of "civilization" further away.
    D) unification of the South resulted in a redrawing of political boundaries according to the Missouri Compromise.

7. Based on the passage, which of the following situations, if true, would be the most unexpected?
    A) Although not directly connected by rail, more isolated communities experience a tourism boom for urbanites looking to "get away from it all".
    B) Within a few years, the rail connection of St. Louis to New York facilitates a post-war skirmish between former Union and Confederacy forces.
    C) The United States status as a trade center between Asian and Europe is partially supplanted by the building of the Panama Canal, providing easy ship passage through Central America.
    D) Cities near or on the Pacific Railway route increase in population at a higher than average rate.

Passage III

In the two supposed cases which have been considered, it has been judged wrong to believe on insufficient evidence, or to nourish belief by suppressing doubts and avoiding investigation. The reason of this judgment is not far to seek: it is that in both these cases the belief held by one man was of great importance to other men. But forasmuch as no belief held by one man, however seemingly trivial the belief, and however obscure the believer, is ever actually insignificant or without its effect on the fate of mankind, we have no choice but to extend our judgment to all cases of belief whatever. Belief, that sacred faculty which prompts the decisions of our will, and knits into harmonious working all the compacted energies of our being, is ours not for ourselves, but for humanity. It is rightly used on truths which have been established by long experience and waiting toil, and which have stood in the fierce light of free and fearless questioning. Then it helps to bind men together, and to strengthen and direct their common action. It is desecrated when given to unproved and unquestioned statements, for the solace and private pleasure of the believer. Whoso would deserve well of his fellows in this matter will guard the purity of his belief with a very fanaticism of jealous care, lest at any time it should rest on an unworthy object, and catch a stain which can never be wiped away.

It is true that this duty is a hard one, and the doubt which comes out of it is often a very bitter thing. It leaves us bare and powerless where we thought that we were safe and strong. To know all about anything is to know how to deal with it under all circumstances. We feel much happier and more secure when we think we know precisely what to do, no matter what happens, than when we have lost our way and do not know where to turn. And if we have supposed ourselves to know all about anything, and to be capable of doing what is fit in regard to it, we naturally do not like to find that we are really ignorant and powerless, that we have to begin again at the beginning, and try to learn what the thing is and how it is to be dealt with—if indeed anything can be learnt about it. It is the sense of power attached to a sense of knowledge that makes men desirous of believing, and afraid of doubting.

This sense of power is the highest and best of pleasures when the belief on which it is founded is a true belief, and has been fairly earned by investigation. For then we may justly feel that it is common property, and holds good for others as well as for ourselves. Then we may be glad, not that I have learned secrets by which I am safer and stronger, but that *we men* have got mastery over more of the world; and we shall be strong, not for ourselves, but in the name of Man and his strength. But if the belief has been accepted on insufficient evidence, the pleasure is a stolen one. Not only does it deceive ourselves by giving us a sense of power which we do not really possess, but it is sinful, because it is stolen in defiance of our duty to mankind. That duty is to guard ourselves from such beliefs as from a pestilence, which may shortly master our own body and then spread to the rest of the town. What would be thought of one who, for the sake of a sweet fruit, should deliberately run the risk of bringing a plague upon his family and his neighbors?

[Adapted from W.K. Clifford *The Ethics of Belief* 1879.]

15. According to the passage, what defines duty to mankind?
    A) Balancing pleasure and power to strengthen the body politic.
    B) Mastery of one's own body in order to avoid larger societal ills.
    C) To avoid beliefs that do not have evidence to support them.
    D) Binding men together as a means of directing group actions.

16. Based on the passage, how would the author react to a person insisting on adhering to an unproven, seemingly inconsequential, belief?
    A) Argue for the benefit to humanity of respecting free judgment as regards credence.
    B) Allow that certain beliefs offer well-deserved solace to the believer.
    C) Assert that such actions still might have an effect and thus must be vanquished.
    D) Remind him of his duty to prevent fanaticism by testing every belief.

17. The author uses the metaphors of "stains" and "plagues" in order to:
    A) Allude to the far-reaching effects of seemingly individual choices.
    B) Draw a parallel between the physical and mental results of belief.
    C) Warn of the physical effects of untested beliefs on the larger population.
    D) Argue for greater culpability for those who believe without a tested basis.

18. According to the author, people avoid doubt because they:
    A) seek personal pleasure.
    B) mistake duty for power.
    C) depend on a long history of testing and proving ideas.
    D) feel powerless without the knowledge of what to do.

19. Suppose that the owner of a shipping van chooses to believe that it is road-worthy without taking it to the mechanic to assure that this is the case. This action is best explained by which of the author's claims?
    A) "Then we may be glad, not that I have learned secrets by which I am safer and stronger, but that we men have got mastery over more of the world; and we shall be strong, not for ourselves, but in the name of Man and his strength."
    B) "Not only does it deceive ourselves by giving us a sense of power which we do not really possess, but it is sinful, because it is stolen in defiance of our duty to mankind."
    C) "Belief, that sacred faculty which prompts the decisions of our will, and knits into harmonious working all the compacted energies of our being, is ours not for ourselves, but for humanity."
    D) "To know all about anything is to know how to deal with it under all circumstances."

20. Based on the passage, which of the following reasons for personal belief is unworthy?
  I. it supplies personal enjoyment to the holder of the belief.
 II. it has withstood rigorous questioning, but not been proven.
III. it prevents the harmonious functioning of mental capacities.
    A) I and II only.
    B) I and III only.
    C) II and III only.
    D) I, II and III.

21. Based on the passage, with which of the following statements would the author be most likely to agree?
    A) Belief can be a tremendous asset to the advancement of humanity provided it is based on tested data.
    B) It is best to avoid mastery by submitting every belief to rigorous investigation and skepticism.
    C) Humans tend to act based on self-satisfaction rather than the advancement of humankind.
    D) Desire for power can be dangerous in terms of how it affects the larger community.

Passage IV

There are two fundamental types of control. The first of these is external, in which a person attempts to exert agency upon the world by controlling other people and, by extension, events outside the self. Such personality types are quite common, and can readily be seen in everything from the schoolyard bully to the sociopathic corporate CEO to the screaming drill sergeant.

The second type of control, however, is the one that ultimately brings greater self-empowerment and often, ironically, greater influence over external events. In this second type – internal control – a person does not seek to directly change the behavior of other people. Instead, the individual seeks total mastery over personal reactions, both cognitive and emotional, to the environment. Such an individual can then, through force of positive example, end up controlling other people.

In the majority culture of the United States, the first type of control is presented as the dominant narrative. Many of America's greatest cultural successes have come in the form of a person or a group of people actively working to change the world around them. America's dominant cultural paradigm is that of the scientist and the technological innovator working together to first discover, and then to exploit the laws of the natural world in a way that creates greater and greater control by humanity over nature. Historians may draw a straight line from the investigations of Benjamin Franklin to the great 19th century inventors of Fulton, Whitney, and Morse to the technical mastery of Edison and the industrial genius of Ford. The culmination of this worldview was the 1960's space race in which the American mindset of domination over nature put a man on the moon – still one of the most startling technological achievements in human history.

Those who wish to argue for the value of internal control face an uphill battle. When it is suggested that dominating the external world is ultimately a self-defeating process, most who listen will scoff. After all, can we not see the great riches of the businessman who dominates his competition? Are not the problems created by technological domination solved through technological means? The fundamental problems of external control seem mere by-products when they are not missed entirely.

The profound problem created by external control is that, by its very nature, it must create more losers than winners. If a business enterprise consists of a dozen competing sales representatives and only one of them can win the bonus for highest number of sales, then the "game" is rigged to create eleven losers. So it is too with technological domination over nature. If humanity's successful external control of nature makes us the winner, then every other species on Earth must be the loser (or in the case of domesticated species, relegated to a bland, bleached-out second place existence). The structure of external control social systems would seem to suggest to most participants that it is not in their best interests. For any one person, the odds of being a loser in an external control system is higher than being the lone winner. And yet rarely are people willing to shift their worldview when faced with this stark fact. Even after failing to successfully exert external control over and over, they simply blame their failure on bad luck or some other extenuating circumstance.

Ultimately, it is through examination of the greatest successes of external control that we may see the seeds for a successful argument for turning our vision inward. Time after time, when those who have gained great success through controlling others are interviewed near the end of their lives, they admit to the hollowness of their success. With little searching, we can uncover any number of autobiographies in which great and "powerful" people express regret over their lifestyle and come to realize in the end that their basic attitude toward the world, although generating short-term success, failed to create the true happiness and success that can only be attained by those whose control is turned inward.

[Adapted from "Innies and Outies: A Dialectic on Society and Control" by P. Bear, 2011.]

22. The assertion that historians draw a straight line from Ben Franklin to the space race is:
    A) true, on the basis of intervening successive technological achievements by other American inventors.
    B) supported by citations in the passage.
    C) possible but not supported by direct citations in the passage.
    D) false based on the author's conclusion that internal control is ultimately more successful.

23. The author's conclusion about external control and American society would be most *weakened* if which of the following were found to be true?
    A) A majority of working Americans describe their working lives as "collaborative" and their relations with their neighbors as "cooperative".
    B) In behavioral studies of group dynamics, most Americans will adopt a "dominating" stance and will continue to believe that that is the best strategy even after failing to achieve objectives.
    C) American sports that focus on competition with a sole winner, such as golf or tennis, are vastly more popular than cooperative sports such as hiking or mountain climbing.
    D) Only 5% of American adults categorize themselves as "technically adept" and answer "yes" when asked, "Do you eagerly look forward to new inventions and technology?"

24. The author implies that if the writer of a self-help book advocates internal control as the best way to approach life, many American readers would:
    A) go to great lengths to shift how they attempt to exercise control in their lives.
    B) read the book carefully and then offer a dispassionate, carefully reasoned argument to prove the writer wrong.
    C) refuse to shift their worldview and simply conclude that the writer was wrong.
    D) be curious enough to explore the idea further.

25. One can infer that if an American corporation structured itself along external-control lines in which a small number of "winning" employees were disproportionately rewarded, the company's workforce would:
    A) believe that such a structure is in their best interests.
    B) believe that such a structure is not in their best interests.
    C) feel so discontent that many would quit or retire early.
    D) take such a structure for granted.

26. The author believes that technology is relevant to the distinction between internal and external control as expressed in American culture because:
  I. technology permits improved human welfare and happiness.
  II. it facilitates a winner versus loser dichotomy that reflects the two types of control.
 III. opposing technologic domination garners a dismissive reaction.
    A) II only
    B) III only
    C) I and II only
    D) II and III only

27. A study demonstrating that most parents in the U.S. attempt to shape their children's behavior by telling the children what to do would:
    A) support the author's point that Americans tend to favor external control.
    B) support the author's main idea only if most parents also attempt to shape their children's behavior by setting a good example for them.
    C) directly contradict one of the author's supporting points, but not the main point.
    D) weaken the assertion that people failing at external control blame bad luck rather than the external control mindset.

Passage V

European investigators have endeavored to discover the influence of climate, season, weather, age, sex, marriage, profession, religion, upon suicide. These statistical tables are valuable. We require, however: (1) A separate table for those undoubtedly insane, putting in a class by themselves those sane enough to lie influenced by rational motives. (2) Under religion, those who really believe in some creed should be distinguished from those nominally attached to it. (3) There should be a table of statistics of the divorced. (4) There should be an earnest attempt made to get beneath the statistics to the hidden influences -- the 'moral causes.'

The commission and report by the Prussian government on suicides among school children indicates the need of similar inquiries into the causes and conditions leading to adult suicides. This might lead to insights that would guide preventive measures. These investigations should take into account the following: Physiological. The influence of epileptic, neurotic, dissipated parents. Influence of nerve exhausting vices, of mental overwork, of monotonous employment, of sedentary occupations. Psychical: The influence of monotony, of excitement, of excessive pursuit of wealth or pleasure, of disappointments, worries, of gambling. Literature: The influence of morbid sentimentalism in poetry and prose representing death as extinction, ignoring or denying the moral element in life conduct and destiny. The influence of dramatic representations of suicide, sometimes as in the case of Romeo and Juliet as the tragic ending of passionate love. The influence of realistic accounts of suicide in the newspapers, sometimes, it is claimed, initiating imitative epidemics. Social. The influence of solitariness, loneliness, brooding. The presence or absence of social or family ties. The sex instinct and the effect of the perversion or thwarting of this.

Then it might be in order to try to find out to what extent and in what ways educational, social, moral, or religious influences cooperate with the hygienic in keeping men and women in physical and mental health and normal, sane, and suitable activity. Even from the present data we may get some fairly obvious suggestions. Many suicides are undoubtedly insane, others are in the incipient stages, obsessed with various 'phobias' and probably all are in some degree morbid. Might not much be accomplished if we could succeed in convincing people of the hopefulness of cure and the need of expert advice and assistance in checking the earlier stages of threatened insanity? At present there is widespread despair.

Suicide accompanies civilization and education as an unerring index of maladjustment in society and defects in education. True education acts as a deterrent in teaching self-control, and in giving objective interests, literary, artistic, scientific, philosophical, philanthropic, moral, religious. The perverting influence of the realistic newspaper accounts of suicide should be checked by legislation.

[Adapted from "The Significance of Suicide", *Philosophical Review*, by James Gibson Hume, 1910.]

28. What was the author's goal in writing this passage?
    A) To make the argument that government needs to put a stop to newspaper accounts of suicide.
    B) To discredit existing studies of suicide which fail to take into account many major factors.
    C) To clearly delineate the division between the truly insane and rational depressives.
    D) To suggest and detail prospective future studies of the factors influencing suicide.

29. Which of the following factors in suicide did the author NOT discuss in detail?
    A) Divorce.
    B) Physiological conditions.
    C) Representations of suicide in art and media.
    D) Social ties.

30. Which of the following, if true, would weaken the author's argument of suicide acting as a social "index", as discussed in the last paragraph?
    A) A large-scale study in Norway finds a correlation between hours of daylight and suicide rates.
    B) A longitudinal study of one US city reveals increases in suicide rates coincide with the onset of economic recessions.
    C) A French study reveals that survivors of failed suicide attempts are two percent less likely to make an additional attempt for each week of treatment received.
    D) A Canadian study reveals that the nation's highest rates of suicide all occur in populations over 1000 people with the lowest levels of crime and unemployment.

31. In order to decrease suicide rates, the author would probably agree that governments should
    A) focus on treatment of those who have previously attempted suicide.
    B) devote funds to community wellness initiatives.
    C) sponsor a crisis response unit.
    D) increase prescription rates amongst community doctors.

32. In paragraph two, when the author writes about physiological, psychical and social influences, what must the author assume to be true?
    A) Suicide is entirely a response to external stimuli.
    B) A tendency towards suicide is inborn, and can be minimized to a limited extent by treatment.
    C) External factors can have a major effect on the likelihood of an individual committing suicide.
    D) A better understanding of the influencing factors of suicide can suggest preventive measures.

Half Section 1: Answer Key and Explanations

Passage 1
1. D
2. A
3. D
4. B
5. A
6. C
7. B

Passage 2
8. C
9. C
10. C
11. C
12. D
13. D
14. D

Passage 3
15. C
16. C
17. A
18. D
19. B
20. A
21. A

Passage 4
22. B
23. A
24. C
25. D
26. D
27. A

Passage 5
28. D
29. A
30. D
31. B
32. C

Passage I Explanation

Two thirds of the **United States** lie west of the **Mississippi River**. This vast domain has already exercised a tremendous influence over our political destiny. **The Territories** were the immediate occasion of our **civil war**. During an entire generation they furnished the arena for the prelusive strife of that war. The **Missouri Compromise** was to us of the **East** a flag of truce. But neither nature nor the men who populated the **Western Territories** recognized this flag. The vexed question of party platforms and sectional debate, the right and the reason of **slavery**, solved itself in the **West** with a freedom and rough rapidity natural to the soil and its population. Climatic limitations and prohibitions went hand in hand with the inflow of an emigration mainly from the **Northern States**,—an emigration fostered by **political emotions** and fevered by **political injustice**. While the **South** was menacing and the North **deprecating war**, far removed from this tumult of words the conflict was going on, and was being decided. And it was **because slavery was doomed** in the great West, and therefore in the nation, that rebellion ensued.

Key terms: United States, Mississippi River, The Territories, civil war, Missouri Compromise, East, Western Territories, slavery, West, Northern States, South

Contrast: East vs. West attitudes toward truce and politics; North vs. South attitudes toward war

Cause-and-effect: slavery ended in West, rebellion ensued

Opinion: people of Western territories decisive, rough, and practical

It is worthy of note that the same generation which witnessed the growth of the **Calhoun** school of politics in the South, and of the **Free Soil** and (afterward) the **Republican** party in the North, and which followed with intense interest the stages of the Territorial struggle, witnessed also the employment of **steam and electricity** as agents of human progress. These agents, these organs of velocity, abbreviating time and space, said, Let the West be East; and before the locomotive the **West fled from Buffalo to Chicago**, across the prairies, the Rocky Mountains, the desert steppes beyond, and down the Pacific slope, until it stared the Orient into a self-contradiction.

Key terms: Calhoun, Free Soil, Republican, steam, electricity

Contrast: South vs. North politics

Cause-and-effect: political ideas and technology grew up together; rail travel redefined "the West" as further away until all became one

It was on the part of our government a **sublime recognition** of the power of steam, that, while it was struggling for existence, it gave its sanction to the **Pacific Railroad** enterprise. Curiously enough, it is through Kansas and Nebraska—the **Epidaurus** of our **Peloponnesian** war—that the two great rival Pacific Railroad routes are to run.

Key terms: Pacific Railroad

Contrast: US civil war vs. Peloponnesian war

Cause-and-effect: government recognizing importance of steam, supported at critical juncture

Opinion: government had foresight to recognize importance of steam power

America becomes at once **interoceanic** and **mediterranean**, commanding the two oceans, and mediating between **Europe** and **Asia**. By the Pacific Railroad, Hong Kong via New York is only forty days distant from London. The tea and silks of **China** and the products of the Spice Islands must pass through America to Europe. In this connection, also, there is a profound significance in our alliance, every year growing stronger, with **Russia**, whose extreme southern boundary joins **Japan**, our latest and warmest Asiatic ally.

Key terms: interoceanic, mediterranean, Europe, Asia, China, Russia, Japan

Contrast: America vs. Mediterranean

Cause-and-effect: unification of US via railroad leads to hub status between Europe and Asia

But the development of American commercial **power as against the world is secondary to the internal development** of our own resources, and to the **indissoluble bond** of national union afforded by this inland route from the **Atlantic** to the **Pacific**, and by its future connections with every portion of our territory. In thirty years, California will have a population equal to that of New York to-day, and yet not be half full, and the city of St. Louis will number a million of souls. **New York City** and **San Francisco**, as the two great *entrepôts* of trade; **Chicago** and **St. Louis** as its two vital centres; and **New Orleans** at the mouth of our great national canal, the **Mississippi**,—will become **nations rather than cities**, out-stripping all the great cities of ancient and modern history.

Key terms: indissoluble bond, Atlantic, Pacific, New York City, San Francisco, Chicago, St. Louis, New Orleans, Mississippi

Contrast: development of unified US resources more significant than international economic position; nation-like future growth of US cities vs. comparatively small cities of the past in world history; cities as key international ports vs. key internal hubs

Cause-and-effect: connection of cities and nation will lead to incredible growth, outstripping all others in present and past

Opinion: America's global economic position is less important to its internal growth and development as a unified nation

Main Idea: The railroads will knit the states and territories of the United States into a true nation, transforming it politically, culturally, economically into something never seen before.

1. Which of the following titles most accurately describes the passage?
    A) A History of the US Pacific Railroad System.
    B) Post-Civil War Economics.
    C) The United States as the New Mediterranean.
    D) **US Pacific and the Making of a Nation.**

A is tempting, as the passage does give a good overview of the history around the development of the US Pacific railroads. But the passage doesn't merely recite the history, but argues for the important transformative effects of said railways to make a permanent, "indissoluble" bond throughout the nation. A doesn't capture this. B is out of scope, being neither specific enough (not touching on the centrality of the railroads to the passage), nor covering the scope of topics, which are not entirely economical. C focuses too much on one aspect, the new international role of the US, to the exclusion of the internal changes which are the bigger focus in the passage. D is the best match.

2. What is the significance of the comparison of Kansas and Nebraska to Epidaurus in paragraph three?
    A) **The author is underscoring the unifying nature of the railroads by noting its passage through politically fractious territory.**
    B) The author is supporting his description of these regions as critical hubs in both war- and peacetime.
    C) The author is making a point about the impossibility of discarding past political enmity.
    D) Epidaurus was a neutral territory, and the author is arguing that, as expected, similar neutral territories as Kansas and Nebraska are central to post-war diplomacy.

It is not necessary to bring any prior knowledge of ancient Mediterranean history to this question, merely to glean carefully the meaning in context of what's written in the passage. Prior to the referenced section, the author has described the US civil war, with a nation split into two warring nations (in paragraph one), and the different directions of the two regions' politics coinciding with the nascent steam/electricity revolution (in paragraph two). Following the referenced section, the remainder of the passage discusses the unifying and transformational effects of the railroads. Reading the actual section (which is not directly quoted in the question stem), what is so "curious" about a railroad passing through these particular states, and how do they compare to the state of Epidaurus, which was somehow involved in the Peloponnesian War? Without resorting to Wikipedia (unavailable when taking the MCAT), it's reasonable to infer that the author is making the historical reference to emphasize the contrast between regions that were at war with a future defined by political unity. B is not supported by the passage. C is contrary to the author's main argument, which describes unqualified, "indissoluble" unity. D is contrary to what's written in the passage, where the circumstance of a railroad through these states is described as "curious", while the answer choice says it is "as expected".

3. Why does the passage compare the post-railroad United States to the Mediterranean region?
   A) Because the Mediterranean region has historically included many warring nations comparable to the North and South during the US Civil War.
   B) Because the Mediterranean also has a comprehensive and effective transportation system.
   C) Because the Mediterranean region includes significant water transport, similar to the United States' Mississippi River and other "canals".
   D) **Because the United States Pacific and Atlantic ports serve as connections to Asian and Europe, respectively, just as the Mediterranean bridges those continents.**

Reading in context, the rest of the sentence containing this comparison in paragraph four specifically discusses the connection of Asia and Europe, which matches answer choice D. The other answer choices sound plausible but are not supported by the passage.

4. Based on the passage, which of the following might have prevented the US Civil War from occurring?
   A) If the building of a railroad from the Northern states to the Western territories occurred earlier.
   B) **If the Western territories were not settled by white Americans but remained sovereign Indian Territory.**
   C) If California's population had increased more quickly.
   D) If the overland route from Europe to Asia became unusable.

The passage cites the Western territories as a major cause of the war, as these territories were primarily filled by settlers from Northern states. Although railroads through the whole country are seen as unifying, a railroad connecting these regions would only speed the ideological separation of the Territorial populations from citizens of the South. On the other hand, if the region remained closed to white settlers as sovereign Indian Territory (which actually did happen on paper, but not in actuality), perhaps the war would not have occurred, given the information in the passage. B is thus a match. C is nowhere in the part of the passage discussing the war, and D would also be irrelevant in the absence of national railroad construction.

5. Which of the following cities is not listed as a critical node of a newly-connected America?
   A) **Buffalo.**
   B) St. Louis.
   C) San Francisco.
   D) New Orleans.

Each of these cities is cited as an important port or hub (New Orleans as the gateway to the Mississippi "canal") except Buffalo, which is only mentioned in the context of the shifting borders of the Western Territories.

6. In the context of the passage, the statement that " before the locomotive the West fled from Buffalo to Chicago" means
   A) citizens of Buffalo escaped the region as rail travel facilitated invasion from the East.
   B) the greater ease and speed of travel caused a mental shift, making the Western territories seem more isolated than before.
   C) **greater accessibility caused formerly sparsely-populated territories to fill up, moving the bounds of "civilization" further away.**
   D) unification of the South resulted in a redrawing of political boundaries according to the Missouri Compromise.

A is not supported by the passage. B is easy to pick by mistake as it sounds almost right, but reading it carefully, it states the opposite of what happened, as the West became less isolated, not more. C on the other hand is a good match, as the definition of the Western Territories is assumedly their isolated, inaccessible, and therefore sparsely-populated nature, which rail travel ameliorates or eliminates as it connects additional population areas. D involves several bits paraphrased from the passage, but is not actually supported by it.

7. Based on the passage, which of the following situations, if true, would be the most unexpected?
   A) Although not directly connected by rail, more isolated communities experience a tourism boom for urbanites looking to "get away from it all".
   B) **Within a few years, the rail connection of St. Louis to New York facilitates a post-war skirmish between former Union and Confederacy forces.**
   C) The United States status as a trade center between Asian and Europe is partially supplanted by the building of the Panama Canal, providing easy ship passage through Central America.
   D) Cities near or on the Pacific Railway route increase in population at a higher than average rate.

A is unrelated to any prediction made by the passage. B, however, contradicts the passage, which expects stronger bonds, not political fractiousness, as a result of railway unification, and would be quite surprising based on the passage. C neither supports nor contradicts the prediction of the railway system as making the United States increasingly central. It's reasonable that competition will take away from the United States' trade position, regardless of whether or not the railway system will add to it. D is predicted by the passage.

Passage II Explanation

To **summarize Jewish literature** is a **herculean effort**. To do justice to the literature of Judaism even in outline, it is clearly necessary to include the **Bible**, the **Apocrypha**, the writings of **Alexandrian** and the **writings of the time of the fall of Jerusalem**. Only by such an inclusion can the genius of the Hebrew people be traced from its early manifestations, through its inspired prime in the **Pre-Modern** and into its brilliant after-glow in the centuries of the **Modern Period**. Most works that have attempted this task have covered no more than **seventeen centuries of literary history**, beginning with the Pre-Modern. Even then, the **obstacles** incumbent on such an enterprise are **numerous and substantial**. One consideration has been in **determining the method** of such books

Key Terms: Jewish literature, pre-modern period, Bible, Apocrypha, Alexandrian, fall of Jerusalem

Opinions: summarizing Jewish literature is a herculean effort; including the Bible, the Apocrypha, the writings of Alexandrian and the writings of the time of the fall of Jerusalem is necessary to do justice to Jewish literature

Contrast: most works have limited the time-period summarized to no more than seventeen centuries, but obstacles still remain

Cause-and-effect: only by including certain works that preceded the Pre-Modern period can the genius of the Hebrew people be traced from that time through the Pre-Modern and into the Modern period

In presenting an **outline of Jewish literature three plans** are possible. One can divide the subject according to **Periods**. Such organization includes three Periods. **Starting with the Rabbinic Age** and closing with the activity of the earlier Gaonim, or Persian Rabbis, the **First Period** would carry us to the eighth or the **ninth century**. A well-marked **Second Period** is that of the **Arabic-Spanish writers**, a period which would extend from the ninth to the **fifteenth century**. From the sixteenth to the **end of the eighteenth century** forms a **Third** Period with distinct characteristics. Finally, the career of **Mendelssohn marks** the definite beginning of the **Modern Period**. Such a **grouping** of the facts presents **many advantages**, but it somewhat **obscures** the **varying conditions** prevalent at one and the same time in different countries where the Jews were settled. Hence **some writers** have preferred to arrange the material **under** different **Cantons**. After examining such a distribution, it is quite possible to draw a **map of the world's civilization** by merely **marking** the successive **places** in which **Jewish literature** has fixed its various head-quarters. **But**, on the other hand, such a method of classification has the **disadvantage** that it leads to much **overlapping**.

Key Terms: Periods, Rabbinic Age, Gaonim, Persian Rabbis, Arabic-Spanish writers, Mendelssohn, Modern period, Cantons

Contrast: grouping of facts by Periods provides advantages, but obscures conditions that existed contemporaneously in different countries where Jews were settled; possible to map world civilization via marking the location of Jewish literature's headquarters, but this method leads to overlapping

Cause-and-effect: because of obscuring concomitant conditions in various countries, some authors prefer arrangement by different Cantons

For long intervals together, it is **impossible to separate Italy from Spain,** France from Germany, Persia from Egypt, Constantinople from Amsterdam. This has induced other writers to propose a **third method** and to trace **Influences**, to indicate that, whereas **Rabbinism** may be termed the **native product of the Jewish genius**, the scientific, poetical, and philosophical **tendencies** of **Jewish writers** in the **Middle Age**s were due to the interaction of **external and** internal forces. Further, in this arrangement, the **Ghetto period** would have a place assigned to it as such, where it would not elsewhere, for it would again mark the almost complete sway of **purely Jewish forces** in Jewish **literature**. For by adopting this classification, we should have a **wave of Jewish impulse**, swollen by the accretion of foreign waters, once more breaking on a Jewish strand, with its contents in something like the **same condition** in which they left the **original spring**. All these **three methods are true**, and should impel an author to refuse to follow any one of them to the exclusion of the other two.

Key Terms: Influences, Rabbinism, Ghetto period

Opinions: an author should refuse to follow any of the three organizational methods to the exclusion of the remaining two

Contrast: Rabbinism is the native product of the Jewish genius, but the scientific, poetical, and philosophical tendencies of Jewish writers in the Middle Ages were due to the interaction of external and internal forces

Cause-and-effect: it is impossible to delineate between the literature of many locations at given times, which has induced some authors to propose sorting by Influences; Ghetto period is due purely to the influence of Jewish intellectual forces in Jewish literature

One thing of which **I am confident**, regardless of form, is that no presentation of the facts, can obscure the truth that such books deal with a great and an **inspiring literature**. In this and through them all may be detected the unifying principle that **literature** in its truest sense **includes life itself**; that **intellect** is the handmaid to **conscience**; and that the **best books** are those which **best teach men how to live**. This underlying unity gave more **harmony** to **Jewish literature** than is possessed by many literatures more distinctively national. Maxims teach, and the maxim, "**Righteousness delivers from death**," applies to **books as well as to men**. A literature whose consistent **theme** is **Righteousness is immortal**. On the very day on which Jerusalem fell, this theory of the **interconnection between literature and life** became the **fixed principle** of Jewish thought and writing, and it **ceased** to hold undisputed sway only in the **age of Mendelssohn**.

Key Terms: Righteousness delivers from death; Righteousness is immortal

Opinions: no presentation of facts can obscure the truth that such books deal with great and inspiring literature; the best books are those that teach men how to live; literature in its truest sense includes life; intellect is the handmaid to conscience

Contrast: Jewish literature possesses more harmony than many more distinctively national literatures

Cause-and-effect: the underlying unity of Jewish literature gives it harmony; "Righteousness delivers from death" applies to books as well as man; when Jerusalem fell, the theory of the interconnection between literature and life became a fixed principle of Jewish thought until the age of Mendelssohn.

Main Idea: Summarizing Jewish literature of the Pre-Modern period is typically done by categorizing works according to Period, Cantons or Influences. No organization, however, can obscure the value of the literature summarized. This value stems from the principle, embodied in Pre-Modern Jewish literature as well as all great literature, that writing has a moral component that connects literature and life.

8. The author is most likely to agree with which of the following evaluations regarding a book?
    A) Great books deal with inspiring literature.
    B) A great book challenges a reader's intellect.
    C) **Literature without an element of morality fails to meet the standard of the best works.**
    D) Summarizing the content of a great book detracts from the greatness of the literature which it contains.

One part of the main point of the passage is that the best books contain writing that instructs men how to live, and that these moral elements serve as a connection between literature and life. The author would be likely to endorse the view that books that do not contain a moral element would not meet the standard of the great works. The author doesn't specifically claim that all great work deals with inspiring literature, only that summaries of Jewish Pre-Modern literature deal with literature that inspires, contradicting choice A. The author clearly states that the organization, and ultimately the act of summarizing via organizing, the great works of Jewish Literature, does not obscure the underlying greatness of the literature (choice D), and that it is the connection between life and literature, not intellect, described as the hand-maid of conscience in the passage, to which the best books appeal, eliminating choice B.

9. As used in the passage, *Cantons* most nearly means:
    A) classification
    B) commonality
    C) **location**
    D) characteristic

The author mentions that organization by Periods obscures the conditions experienced by Jewish authors that were present simultaneously in different locations. The author states that organization by Cantons is a potential alternative that eliminates this problem, and discusses how mapping the locations where Jewish literature was principally produced reflects the sites of human civilization. Both facts imply that organization by Cantons is organization according to the location in which a work was written (C).

10. Based on passage information, a work of Jewish literature that principally explores themes that transcend the limitations of human experience, could have been written during all of the following times, EXCEPT:
    A) a time preceding the years included in the Periods of classification described in the passage.
    B) during the nineteenth century.
    C) **between the sixteenth and eighteenth century.**
    D) during the Modern period.

According to the passage, "On the very day on which Jerusalem fell, this theory of the interconnection between literature and life became the fixed principle of Jewish thought and writing, and it ceased to hold undisputed sway only in the age of Mendelssohn." A book that principally explores themes beyond the connection between literature and life is then not likely to have been written between the fall of Jerusalem and the time of Mendelssohn—the beginning of the Modern period. This is consistent with choice C, and eliminates choice D as well as choice B, since both choices D and C indicate dates during the Modern period. Choice A includes dates before and after the fall of Jerusalem, thus the work of literature described could have been written during this timeframe. This eliminates choice A.

11. If a scholarly work on the history of Hebrew literature is organized using the Periods described in the passage, then which of the following is necessarily true given passage information?
    A) Rabbinism and the works of the Persian rabbis would be included in different Periods.
    B) The Ghetto period would have a place assigned to it.
    C) **Literature written at the time of the Fall of Jerusalem would fall outside the years of the periods described.**
    D) The work of Mendelssohn marks the height of the Pre-Modern period.

The fall of Jerusalem preceded the establishment of the Pre-Modern period. It is the Pre-Modern period that is divided into the Periods defined in the passage; the fall of Jerusalem then falls outside the years of the periods described, choice C. The passage states that the Ghetto period is assigned a place only when work is organized by Influences, and that Rabbinism and the works of the Persian rabbis would both be assigned to the First Period, eliminating choices A and B. The passage also states that Mendelssohn's work marks the beginning of the Modern Period, eliminating choice D.

12. Which of the following, if true, would most challenge an assertion made in the passage?
    A) Via proper methods of categorization, it is possible to separate conditions in Italy from in Spain, and in Persia from in Egypt.
    B) Some books summarizing Jewish literature cover twenty centuries or more of works.
    C) The writings of the Gaonim are best included with those of Second Period authors.
    D) **Literary maxims cannot, by their nature, apply to men.**

The author asserts that maxims teach and that the best books fulfill a teaching role, particularly with respect to how one should live. The passage also asserts that Jewish literature is unified by, among other things, a moral thread and consistently contains maxims to that effect. If the assertion in choice D is true, then the maxims of righteousness central to Jewish literature could not act to instruct men in how to best live. If this is the case, then Jewish literature would fail to be among the best books, as they are described as being in the passage. Choice A is possible via application of sorting by Influences, and, accordingly, is incorrect.

13. According to the information presented in the passage, which method of organization of Pre-Modern Jewish literary works is appropriate for demonstrating works' consistent inclusion of truths of life at the time of their writing?
    I. Cantons
    II. Periods
    III. Influences
        A) I only
        B) III only
        C) I and II only
        D) **I, II and III**

The passage states that "no presentation of the facts, can obscure the truth that such books deal with a great and an inspiring literature ..." and that "... in this and through them all may be detected the unifying principle that literature in its truest sense includes life itself." Any organizational method, then, is appropriate for demonstrating this, making choice D correct.

14. Which of the following statements may be most reasonably inferred from the passage?
    A) Following the method of classification best suited to considering selected works of the Pre-modern period provides a better summary of those works than using a combination of less well-suited means of categorization.
    B) Distinctively national literatures lack harmony.
    C) Pre-modern Hebrew literature influenced by outside forces retains little of its native Jewish literary character.
    D) **Writers of Jewish literature occupied all major centers of civilization during the Pre-Modern period.**

According to the passage, "... it is quite possible to draw a map of the world's civilization by merely marking the successive places in which Jewish literature has fixed its various head-quarters." For this to be true, then the writers of Jewish literature cited in the passage must have been located at least in those locations most likely to define civilization. This supports the inference in choice D. The passage also states that no single organization scheme should be "... follow[ed] ... to the exclusion of the other two." This contradicts choice A. While the passage does state that Jewish Pre-Modern literature contains greater harmony than many more distinctively national literatures, it does not make the claim that national literatures are entirely without harmony, contradicting choice B. The passage also indicates that while Jewish literature of the period is a product of both internal and external forces, after "... the accretion of foreign waters", Jewish works still returned in "... much the same condition in which they left the original spring." That is, they retained much purely Jewish literary character even under foreign literary and intellectual influence. This eliminates choice C.

Passage III Explanation

In the two supposed cases which have been considered, it has been judged **wrong to believe** on insufficient evidence, or to nourish belief by suppressing doubts and **avoiding investigation**. The reason of this judgment is not far to seek: it is that in both these cases the belief held by one man was of great importance to other men. But forasmuch as no belief held by one man, however seemingly trivial the belief, and however obscure the believer, is ever actually insignificant or without its effect on the fate of mankind, we have no choice but to extend our judgment to all cases of belief whatever. **Belief**, that sacred faculty which prompts the decisions of our will, and knits into harmonious working all the compacted energies of our being, is ours not for ourselves, but for **humanity**. It is rightly used on **truths** which have been established by long experience and waiting toil, and which have stood in the fierce light of **free and fearless questioning**. Then it helps to bind men together, and to strengthen and direct their common action. It is desecrated when given to unproved and unquestioned statements, for the solace and private pleasure of the believer. Whoso would deserve well of his fellows in this matter will guard the purity of his belief with a very fanaticism of jealous care, lest at any time it should rest on an unworthy object, and catch a stain which can never be wiped away.

Key terms: belief; humanity

Contrast: belief vs doubt; individual belief vs "humanity" (established truths) belief

Cause-and-Effect: when a belief has been proven through testing and questioning, it can bind together humanity, but when it is held singularly, it can be dangerous and taint the believer

It is true that this duty is a hard one, and the **doubt which comes out of it is often a very bitter thing**. It leaves us bare and powerless where we thought that we were safe and strong. To know all about anything is to know how to deal with it under all circumstances. We **feel much happier** and more secure when **we think we know precisely what to do**, no matter what happens, than when we have lost our way and do not know where to turn. And if we have supposed ourselves to know all about anything, and to be capable of doing what is fit in regard to it, we naturally **do not like to find that we are really ignorant and powerless**, that we have to begin again at the beginning, and try to learn what the thing is and how it is to be dealt with—if indeed anything can be learnt about it. It is the **sense of power attached to a sense of knowledge** that makes men desirous of believing, and afraid of doubting.

Key terms: doubt, power

Contrast: belief vs doubt

Cause-and-Effect: when people have doubt they feel like they have lost the power of knowledge; thus they would rather believe in things than have doubt

This **sense of power** is the **highest and best** of pleasures when the belief on which it is **founded is a true belief**, and has been fairly earned by investigation. For then we may justly feel that it is common property, and holds **good for others as well as for ourselves**. Then **we may be glad**, not that I have learned secrets by which I am safer and stronger, but that *we men* have **got mastery over more of the world**; and we shall be strong, not for ourselves, but in the name of Man and his strength. But if the belief has been accepted on insufficient evidence, the pleasure is a stolen one. Not only does it deceive ourselves by giving us a sense of power which we do not really possess, but it is **sinful**, because it is stolen in defiance of our duty to mankind. That **duty is to guard ourselves from such beliefs** as from a pestilence, which may shortly master our own body and then spread to the rest of the town. What would be thought of one who, for the sake of a sweet fruit, should deliberately run the risk of bringing a plague upon his family and his neighbors?

[Adapted from W.K. Clifford *The Ethics of Belief* 1879.]

Contrast: "I" safer and stronger vs "Man" having increased mastery over world

Cause-and-Effect: believing things with insufficient evidence leads to pestilence

Main Idea: The passage examines morally acceptable and unacceptable reasons for belief. Morally acceptable belief must be tested and proven and can help to strengthen mankind, while unacceptable belief has no foundation but makes things more personally pleasurable.

15. According to the passage, what defines duty to mankind?
    A) Balancing pleasure and power to strengthen the body politic.
    B) Mastery of one's own body in order to avoid larger societal ills.
    C) **To avoid beliefs that do not have evidence to support them.**
    D) Binding men together as a means of directing group actions.

According to the third paragraph, "if the belief has been accepted on insufficient evidence" our "duty is to guard ourselves from such beliefs as from a pestilence," supporting choice C.

A, B: neither the body politic nor mastering one's body are topics of the passage, eliminating choices A and B.
D: While proper beliefs can "knit" mankind "into harmonious action" that is not the duty discussed in paragraph 3.

16. Based on the passage, how would the author react to a person insisting on adhering to an unproven, seemingly inconsequential, belief?
    A) Argue for the benefit to humanity of respecting free judgment as regards credence.
    B) Allow that certain beliefs offer well-deserved solace to the believer.
    C) **Assert that such actions still might have an effect and thus must be vanquished.**
    D) Remind him of his duty to prevent fanaticism by testing every belief.

In paragraph 2, the author states that "no belief held by one man, however seemingly trivial the belief, and however obscure the believer, is ever actually insignificant or without its effect on the fate of mankind," supporting choice C.

A, B: the author opposes holding on to untested beliefs, so neither choice A nor B, which support the right to hold untested beliefs, can be supported.
D: the passage states that one should "guard the purity of his belief with a very fanaticism of jealous care," but not that one ought to prevent fanaticism, as in choice D.

17. The author uses the metaphors of "stains" and "plagues" in order to:
    A) **Allude to the far-reaching effects of seemingly individual choices.**
    B) Draw a parallel between the physical and mental results of belief.
    C) Warn of the physical effects of untested beliefs on the larger population.
    D) Argue for greater culpability for those who believe without a tested basis.

Stains and plagues, as they are used in the passage, are examples of negative effects that spread through the community from false beliefs, supporting choice A.

B, C, D: the passage does not focus on the physical effects of belief nor culpability, eliminating choices B, C, and D.

18. According to the author, people avoid doubt because they:
    A) seek personal pleasure.
    B) mistake duty for power.
    C) depend on a long history of testing and proving ideas.
    D) **feel powerless without the knowledge of what to do.**

The second paragraph states that "it is the sense of power attached to a sense of knowledge that makes men desirous of believing, and afraid of doubting." Thus people avoid doubt because they prefer to have a sense of power, as in choice D.

A: while the passage does argue that some belief is held for personal pleasure, it does not suggest people avoid doubt for that reason, as in choice A.

B: power, according to the passage, comes from a sense of belief, but it is not connected to duty.

C: testing and proving ideas is the kind of belief the author supports, so should not be replaced by doubt, as in choice D.

19. Suppose that the owner of a shipping van chooses to believe that it is road-worthy without taking it to the mechanic to assure that this is the case. This action is best explained by which of the author's claims?
    A) "Then we may be glad, not that I have learned secrets by which I am safer and stronger, but that we men have got mastery over more of the world; and we shall be strong, not for ourselves, but in the name of Man and his strength."
    B) **"Not only does it deceive ourselves by giving us a sense of power which we do not really possess, but it is sinful, because it is stolen in defiance of our duty to mankind."**
    C) "Belief, that sacred faculty which prompts the decisions of our will, and knits into harmonious working all the compacted energies of our being, is ours not for ourselves, but for humanity."
    D) "To know all about anything is to know how to deal with it under all circumstances."

The owner is choosing to have a belief without testing it, primarily for his convenience. This goes against the duty defined in the last paragraph: guarding oneself against beliefs based on unsubstantiated beliefs, as in choice B.

A, C: these statements address beliefs that humanity shares, not untested beliefs.

D: In this situation the owner chooses not to know, eliminating choice D.

20. Based on the passage, which of the following reasons for personal belief is unworthy?
  I. **it supplies personal enjoyment to the holder of the belief.**
  II. **it has withstood rigorous questioning, but not been proven.**
  III. it prevents the harmonious functioning of mental capacities.
    A) **I and II only.**
    B) I and III only.
    C) II and III only.
    D) I, II and III.

According to the passage, personal belief is "desecrated when given to unproved and unquestioned statements." Choice II has something that has not been proven, so it is a credited answer. The passage also states that personal belief is not good if it is "for the solace and private pleasure of the believer," as in choice I.

21. Based on the passage, with which of the following statements would the author be most likely to agree?
    A) **Belief can be a tremendous asset to the advancement of humanity provided it is based on tested data.**
    B) It is best to avoid mastery by submitting every belief to rigorous investigation and skepticism.
    C) Humans tend to act based on self-satisfaction rather than the advancement of humankind.
    D) Desire for power can be dangerous in terms of how it affects the larger community.

The passage suggests that belief can be positive in allowing "men" to get "mastery over more of the world" and increase "man and his strength," as long as the ideas are "earned by investigation." Thus choice A is the credited answer.

B: the passage does not discuss how to avoid mastery, as in choice A.

C: while the passage suggests that people will hold on to beliefs for "private pleasure," it does not make a general claim about their overall motivations as in choice C.

D: desire for power is why people eschew doubt, according to the passage, but not necessarily itself a danger to the community, as in choice D.

Passage IV Explanation

There are two fundamental types of **control**. The first of these is **external,** in which a person attempts to **exert agency upon the world** by controlling other people and, by extension, **events outside** the self. Such **personality types are quite common**, and can readily be seen in everything from the schoolyard bully to the sociopathic corporate CEO to the screaming drill sergeant.

Key terms: control, external

Opinion: external control tries to directly control events outside the self and is quite common

The **second type** of control, however, is the one that ultimately **brings greater self-empowerment** and often, ironically, **greater influence** over external events. In this second type – **internal control** – a person does **not seek to directly change** the behavior of other people. Instead, the individual seeks total **mastery over personal reactions**, both cognitive and emotional, to the environment. Such an individual can then, through **force of positive example**, end up controlling other people.

Contrast: external control vs. internal control

Opinion: author thinks internal control leads to great self-empowerment, greater influence

Cause-and-effect: internal control lets you set a good example which ultimately leads to greater influence

In the **majority culture of the United States**, the **first type** of control is presented as the **dominant** narrative. Many of **America's greatest cultural successes** have come in the form of a person or a group of people actively working to change the world around them. America's dominant cultural paradigm is that of the **scientist** and the **technological** innovator working together to first discover, and then to exploit the laws of the natural world in a way that creates greater and greater **control by humanity over nature**. Historians may draw a straight line from the investigations of Benjamin **Franklin** to the great 19th century inventors of **Fulton, Whitney, and Morse** to the technical mastery of **Edison** and the industrial genius of **Ford**. The culmination of this worldview was the 1960's **space race** in which the American mindset of domination over nature put a man on the moon – still one of the most startling technological achievements in human history.

Key terms: United States, Franklin, Fulton, Whitney, Morse, Edison, Ford, space race

Opinion: author sees US as favoring an external control model, primarily through its favoring science and technological advancement

Those who wish to argue for the value of **internal control** face an **uphill battle**. When it is suggested that dominating the external world is ultimately a self-defeating process, **most who listen will scoff**. After all, can we not see the great riches of the businessman who dominates his competition? Are not the **problems** created by **technological domination solved through technological means**? The **fundamental problems of external control** seem mere by-products when they are not **missed entirely**.

Opinion: author thinks most will just scoff or ignore calls for internal control, since people either miss the problems of external control entirely, or think that the problems it creates are solved by more of the same

The profound **problem** created by external control is that, by its very nature, it **must create more losers than winners**. If a business enterprise consists of a dozen competing sales representatives and only one of them can win the bonus for highest number of sales, then the "game" is rigged to create eleven losers. So it is too with technological domination over nature. If **humanity's successful external control of nature** makes us the winner, then **every other species on Earth must be the loser** (or in the case of domesticated species, relegated to a bland, bleached-out second place existence). The structure of external control social systems would seem to suggest to **most participants** that it is **not in their best interests**. For any one person, the odds of being a loser in an external control system is higher than being the lone winner. And yet **rarely are people willing to shift their world-view** when faced with this stark fact. Even after failing to successfully exert external control over and over, they simply **blame their failure on bad luck** or some other extenuating circumstance.

Cause-and-effect: external control systems are rigged to create more losers than winners

Opinion: author thinks that people can't change their views, and even after losing repeatedly will just blame bad luck rather than change their outlook

Ultimately, it is through examination of the **greatest successes of external control** that we may see the seeds for a **successful argument for turning our vision inward**. Time after time, when those who have gained great success through controlling others are interviewed near the end of their lives, **they admit to the hollowness of their success**. With little searching, we can uncover any number of autobiographies in which great and "powerful" people **express regret over their lifestyle** and come to realize in the end that their basic attitude toward the world, although generating short-term success, **failed to create the true happiness** and success that can only be attained by those whose control is turned inward.

[Adapted from "Innies and Outies: A Dialectic on Society and Control" by P. Bear, 2011.]

Opinion: author thinks that by looking at the deathbed regrets of those few "winners" who were created by external control systems we see the basic problem – that it leads to hollowness and dissatisfaction

Main Idea: Despite the overwhelming preference of Americans for an external-control view of the world, it is ultimately internal control that creates more happiness, more success, and ironically more control over the external world.

22. The assertion that historians draw a straight line from Ben Franklin to the space race is:
    A) true, on the basis of intervening successive technological achievements by other American inventors.
    B) **supported by citations in the passage.**
    C) possible but not supported by direct citations in the passage.
    D) false based on the author's conclusion that internal control is ultimately more successful.

The author cites several examples of inventors and technological innovators when moving from Franklin to the space race – Fulton, Morse, etc. Thus choice B is correct.

23. The author's conclusion about external control and American society would be most *weakened* if which of the following were found to be true?
    A) **A majority of working Americans describe their working lives as "collaborative" and their relations with their neighbors as "cooperative".**
    B) In behavioral studies of group dynamics, most Americans will adopt a "dominating" stance and will continue to believe that that is the best strategy even after failing to achieve objectives.
    C) American sports that focus on competition with a sole winner, such as golf or tennis, are vastly more popular than cooperative sports such as hiking or mountain climbing.
    D) Only 5% of American adults categorize themselves as "technically adept" and answer "yes" when asked, "Do you eagerly look forward to new inventions and technology?"

To weaken the author's view we need to see that Americans aren't interested in a world view in which they dominate the external environment and control it. Thus choice A is correct.

B: This would support the author's view that Americans take an external, dominating stance to dealing with the world.

C: The popularity of sports that involve a sole winner and many losers (as opposed to noncompetitive sports like hiking) would support the author's view.

D: Technology was merely an analogy for the types of control, and the lack of tech savvy among lay people doesn't directly address the question.

24. The author implies that if the writer of a self-help book advocates internal control as the best way to approach life, many American readers would:

    A) go to great lengths to shift how they attempt to exercise control in their lives.

    B) read the book carefully and then offer a dispassionate, carefully reasoned argument to prove the writer wrong.

    C) **refuse to shift their worldview and simply conclude that the writer was wrong.**

    D) be curious enough to explore the idea further.

The author tells us that Americans would scoff at such a book, or miss the problems of external control entirely. They just don't want to change their world view. Thus choice C is correct.

25. One can infer that if an American corporation structured itself along external-control lines in which a small number of "winning" employees were disproportionately rewarded, the company's workforce would:

    A) believe that such a structure is in their best interests.

    B) believe that such a structure is not in their best interests.

    C) feel so discontent that many would quit or retire early.

    D) **take such a structure for granted.**

We're told that Americans just assume that an external control system that creates few winners and many losers is simply accepted by most, and that even when they end up as the loser they can't see the problem – they just blame bad luck. Thus they would take such a system for granted and choice D is correct.

26. The author believes that technology is relevant to the distinction between internal and external control as expressed in American culture because:

  I. technology permits improved human welfare and happiness.

  II. **it facilitates a winner versus loser dichotomy that reflects the two types of control.**

 III. **opposing technologic domination garners a dismissive reaction.**

    A) II only

    B) III only

    C) I and II only

    D) **II and III only**

The author discusses technology as an example of the American cultural preference for external control. We're told that Americans will dismiss the idea that there's anything wrong with external control (the problems created by technological domination are solved by more technology). II and III both fit the author's main idea and reflect his arguments about external control. Thus choice D is correct.

27. A study demonstrating that most parents in the U.S. attempt to shape their children's behavior by telling the children what to do would:

   A) **support the author's point that Americans tend to favor external control.**
   B) support the author's main idea only if most parents also attempt to shape their children's behavior by setting a good example for them.
   C) directly contradict one of the author's supporting points, but not the main point.
   D) weaken the assertion that people failing at external control blame bad luck rather than the external control mindset.

Directly giving a child an order telling him what to do would be the perfect archetype of external control. Thus choice A is correct.

Passage V Explanation

European investigators have endeavored to discover the **influence of** climate, season, weather, age, sex, marriage, profession, religion, upon suicide. These statistical tables are valuable. We require, however: (1) A separate table for those undoubtedly **insane**, putting in a class by themselves those sane enough to lie influenced by **rational motives**. (2) Under religion, **those who really believe** in some creed should be distinguished from those nominally attached to it. (3) There should be a table of statistics of the divorced. (4) There should be an earnest attempt made to get beneath the statistics to the hidden influences -- the **'moral causes.'**

Key terms: moral causes

Contrast: existing tables are valuable, but future tables should include more information; some suicides are insane, others are rational, have clear causes; some religious believe deeply, others only nominally

Cause-and-effect: climate, season, marriage, etc., all influence likelihood of suicide

Opinion: there are underlying causes beneath the statistical relationships

The commission and report by the Prussian government on suicides among school children indicates the need of similar inquiries into the causes and conditions leading to adult suicides. This might lead to **insights** that would guide **preventive measures**. These investigations should take into account the following: **Physiological**. The influence of epileptic, neurotic, dissipated parents. Influence of nerve exhausting vices, of mental overwork, of monotonous employment, of sedentary occupations. **Psychical**: The influence of monotony, of excitement, of excessive pursuit of wealth or pleasure, of disappointments, worries, of gambling. **Literature**: The influence of morbid sentimentalism in poetry and prose representing death as extinction, ignoring or denying the moral element in life conduct and destiny. The influence of dramatic representations of suicide, sometimes as in the case of Romeo and Juliet as the tragic ending of passionate love. The influence of realistic accounts of suicide in the newspapers, sometimes, it is claimed, initiating imitative epidemics. **Social**: The influence of solitariness, loneliness, brooding. The presence or absence of social or family ties. The sex instinct and the effect of the perversion or thwarting of this.

Key terms: physiological, psychical, literature, social

Contrast: physiological versus psychical versus media versus social causes of suicide

Cause-and-effect: better understanding suicide can aid prevention; various classes of difficulty will increase the chance of suicide

Then it might be in order to try to find out to what extent and in what ways **educational, social, moral, or religious influences** cooperate with the **hygienic** in keeping men and women in physical and mental health and normal, sane, and suitable activity. Even from the present data we may get some fairly obvious suggestions. Many suicides are undoubtedly insane, others are in the incipient stages, obsessed with various '**phobias**' and probably all are in some degree morbid. Might not much be accomplished if we could succeed in convincing people of the **hopefulness of cure** and the need of expert advice and assistance in checking the earlier stages of threatened insanity? **At present there is widespread despair**.

Key terms: educational, social, moral, religious, hygienic

Cause-and-effect: various influences can lead to good physical and mental health; engendering hopefulness can prevent suicide

Opinion: there is widespread despair

Suicide accompanies civilization and education as an unerring index of maladjustment in society and defects in education. **True education acts as a deterrent** in teaching **self-control**, and in giving **objective**

SECTION 2: NOTE-TAKING TECHNIQUE

You can use any technique you'd like on the following half-section, but I very strongly recommend you take this as an opportunity to start doing timed practice with the note-taking technique. When working your way through this section, there's only one absolute requirement: **you must time yourself strictly**. Don't set a timer counting down; rather use a stopwatch counting up. You do yourself no favors by casually going through with no awareness of time. The first step to improving your timing is to see exactly where your time is going.

If you would like to get the best practice for the note-taking technique, do the following before you start:

1. Get a stopwatch to count up (or a stopwatch app on your phone).
2. Get separate scratch paper to take notes and two pencils.
3. Go some place where you won't be interrupted and that is relatively quiet.
4. Get some foam earplugs to block out the noise.

When you start the section start the stopwatch counting up.

Every time you finish reading a passage, hit the "lap" button on the stopwatch. Every time you finish a set of questions, hit the "lap" button again. At the end of the section you'll have 10 data points showing you how long you took to read each passage and how long for the questions.

With the note-taking technique you should spend 6.5 - 7 minutes on the passage and 3 - 3.5 minutes on the questions.

Then, when reviewing the explanations afterwards, look to the notes underneath each paragraph for a guide about what sorts of things you should notice and jot down.

Please note: our notes are not a literal transcription of what you should be writing on your scratch paper. Your own notes are going to be quick, abbreviated, and will only make sense to you. Rather, we've given you these notes to show you the sorts of ideas that are important and worth jotting down in some way.

Passage II

There are many who acknowledge that the political structures of the day have an influence on the development of literature but vehemently oppose the notion that a subtle biological evolution of the brain has anything to do with the matter. Yet consider the difference between the forms of literature created by pre-literate societies in ancient times and those made during and after the Industrial Revolution: each exhibits a stark contrast with the other, and the production, consumption, and goals of such literature have a subtle interplay not just with the political ecology in which they were created, but on the kind of brain intended to receive the literary message.

Pre-literate societies had to transmit their literature orally, whereas industrialized societies did so in writing. The primary mental tool by which oral literature is both transmitted and consumed is memory, which requires development of the hippocampus and amygdala. Reading literature, however, triggers a series of mechanical controls for the eyes, and in the brain's visual processing centers in the occipital lobe, bypassing much of the memory activation centers.

It may seem absurd that the biological evolution of the brain influences the sorts of literature produced, and yet when neuroimaging studies are done on the brains of present-day peoples whose cultures most nearly approximate ancient ways of living, they reveal strong differences in both structural and functional development from contemporary brains.

Surviving for millennia as hunter-gatherers required the development of a brain with an astounding spatial memory. Early humans roved over vast territories in their search for food, and they had to be able to store this data and recall it effortlessly in order to survive. This lifestyle both selected for and subsequently promoted the neural architecture for memory. It is unsurprising, then, that the literature developed under such circumstances would depend heavily on memory. This memory-based literature persisted long after agriculture and civilization became the predominant mode of living; the ancient Greeks were well known to equate memory with intelligence itself. By contrast, once man developed systems for externalizing memory (first the written word, then later recorded sound and images), the primary mental virtue became speed of processing that information. Thus the literature that developed from medieval times onward tended towards exceptionally lengthy tomes that the reader would move through relatively quickly.

These differences are not merely technological or cultural. The neuroimaging studies done on "ancient peoples" were extended to comparing the brains of infants less than a week old. Those children born in industrial and post-industrial societies already showed stronger initial development of visual processing and prefrontal cortical regions whereas infants in pre-agricultural tribal societies (most notably the Etoro people of Papua New Guinea and the Pano tribe in the Amazon rainforest) had more well developed hippocampal and amygdalar architectures.

It is speculated that these difference also relate to the functions that literature develops in each situation: in pre-literate societies, the oral transmission of a culture's stories also functions to develop a mindfulness about the environment in which the listeners find themselves. These stories seek to inculcate traditional values. Modern literature, on the other hand, tends to serve mostly as a distraction from the environment. The entertainment value of the work crowds out other possible meanings.

The central fact that both forms of literature have in common, however, is the assumption that the creator of the literature – either the author of the novel in one case, or the reciter of the story in the other – shares the same basic framework of neural architecture as the listener.

[Adapted from "Novels and Neurons" by C. Robin, 2011.]

8. In the fifth paragraph, the "differences" the author mentions refer to:
   A) the differences in the speed with which literature is consumed in different societies.
   B) the fact that literature serves very different social functions in pre-literate and industrialized societies.
   C) the differences in neuroanatomy that are correlated with different forms of literature.
   D) minor differences in neural architecture between the creator and consumer of literature.

9. The author suggests that the consumption of literature in contemporary society:
   A) increases development in most areas of the brain.
   B) decreases environmental awareness while not conveying deeper meanings.
   C) is motivated by a desire to develop visual processing ability.
   D) encourages a slower, more careful evaluation of the meanings of printed words.

10. The author asserts that children born in modern societies have more advanced prefrontal cortical regions (which are associated with careful, reasoned judgments that take time to make) but also consume literature in a way that rewards speed of information processing. Are these two assertions reconcilable?
   A) Yes; the author makes no assertions that would prevent a particular type of literature from contributing to the development of areas of the brain with disparate functions.
   B) Yes; faster information processing requires more careful judgment about what parts of that information are important.
   C) No; the close relationship between increased processing speed and written forms of literature is incompatible with slowed brain activity.
   D) No; careful, reasoned judgments are the antithesis of the kind of brain activity described by the author.

11. When the author asserts in paragraph four that a certain lifestyle selected for the neural architecture of memory, the author means that:
   A) a lifestyle that required an exceptionally strong memory promoted the survival of the offspring of parents with well-developed hippocampal and amygdalar architectures.
   B) those individuals with well-developed memories selected a lifestyle that rewarded them for having a strong memory.
   C) ancient Greek civilizations rewarded those with strong memories.
   D) hunter-gatherers developed their memory throughout their lives.

12. Which of the following, if true, would most clearly *disprove* the author's thesis?
   A) Comprehension and appreciation of literature is enhanced when the creator and consumer of the literature have similar physiological and sociological backgrounds.
   B) The type of literature we consume can influence how our brains develop.
   C) When children from pre-literate societies are brought to schools and taught to read, they are able to develop a proficiency at reading that is roughly similar to children from literate societies.
   D) Widespread genetic testing of human remains demonstrates that no evolution has taken place in *homo sapiens* over the past 50,000 years.

Passage III

It will be well to consider, what is the value of philosophy and why it ought to be studied. It is the more necessary to consider this question, in view of the fact that many men, under the influence of science or of practical affairs, are inclined to doubt whether philosophy is anything better than innocent but useless trifling, hair-splitting distinctions, and controversies on matters concerning which knowledge is impossible.

This view of philosophy appears to result partly from a wrong conception of the kind of goods which philosophy strives to achieve. Physical science, through the medium of inventions, is useful to innumerable people who are wholly ignorant of it; thus the study of physical science is to be recommended, not only, or primarily, because of the effect on the student, but rather because of the effect on mankind in general. Thus utility does not belong to philosophy. If the study of philosophy has any value at all for others than students of philosophy, it must be only indirectly, through its effects upon the lives of those who study it. It is in these effects, therefore, if anywhere, that the value of philosophy must be primarily sought.

But further, if we are not to fail in our endeavour to determine the value of philosophy, we must first free our minds from the prejudices of what are wrongly called 'practical' men. The 'practical' man, as this word is often used, is one who realizes that men must have food for the body, but is oblivious of the necessity of providing food for the mind. It is exclusively among the goods of the mind that the value of philosophy is to be found; and only those who are not indifferent to these goods can be persuaded that the study of philosophy is not a waste of time.

Philosophy, like all other studies, aims primarily at knowledge. The knowledge it aims at is the kind of knowledge which gives unity and system to the body of the sciences, and the kind which results from a critical examination of the grounds of our convictions, prejudices, and beliefs. But it cannot be maintained that philosophy has had any very great measure of success in its attempts to provide definite answers to its questions. There are many questions—and among them those that are of the profoundest interest to our spiritual life—which, so far as we can see, must remain insoluble to the human intellect unless its powers become of quite a different order from what they are now. Has the universe any unity of plan or purpose, or is it a fortuitous concourse of atoms? Is consciousness a permanent part of the universe, giving hope of indefinite growth in wisdom, or is it a transitory accident on a small planet on which life must ultimately become impossible? Are good and evil of importance to the universe or only to man? However slight may be the hope of discovering an answer, it is part of the business of philosophy to continue the consideration of such questions, to make us aware of their importance, to examine all the approaches to them, and to keep alive that speculative interest in the universe which is apt to be killed by confining ourselves to definitely ascertainable knowledge.

The value of philosophy is, in fact, to be sought largely in its very uncertainty. The man who has no tincture of philosophy goes through life imprisoned in the prejudices derived from common sense, from the habitual beliefs of his age or his nation, and from convictions which have grown up in his mind without the co-operation or consent of his deliberate reason. To such a man the world tends to become definite, finite, obvious; common objects rouse no questions, and unfamiliar possibilities are contemptuously rejected. As soon as we begin to philosophize, on the contrary, we find that even the most everyday things lead to problems to which only very incomplete answers can be given. Philosophy, though unable to tell us with certainty what is the true answer to the doubts which it raises, is able to suggest many possibilities which enlarge our thoughts and free them from the tyranny of custom. Thus, while diminishing our feeling of certainty as to what things are, it greatly increases our knowledge as to what they may be; and it keeps alive our sense of wonder by showing familiar things in an unfamiliar aspect.

[Adapted from *The Problems of Philosophy*, by Bertrand Russell, 1912.]

13. The author cites which of the following as a difference between the study of physical science and the study of philosophy?

    A) Physical science directly benefits those who study it, but the study of philosophy benefits mankind in general.

    B) Physical science can benefit those who are ignorant of it, whereas philosophy benefits primarily those who study it.

    C) Physical science aims primarily at knowledge, while philosophy does not.

    D) Unlike philosophy, physical science avoids controversies on matters concerning knowledge.

14. Which of the following does the author NOT describe as a benefit of the study of philosophy?

    A) Studying philosophy encourages interest in our world.

    B) The study of philosophy helps us see the value of questioning our world.

    C) By studying philosophy, we are more likely to provide definitive answers to the most profound questions.

    D) Philosophy enlarges our world by freeing us from our customary ways of thinking.

15. According to the author, what fault might "practical men" find with the study of philosophy?

    A) Philosophy is nonessential; it does not contribute to the survival to humankind.

    B) Philosophy benefits the individual, but not humankind in general.

    C) Philosophy raises questions, but neglects to provide answers.

    D) Philosophy challenges widely held beliefs that are essential to man's survival.

16. Which of the following might convince a "practical" man of the value of philosophy?

    A) Definitive answers to questions regarding spiritual life

    B) A theory that philosophers are actually likely to answer the questions they raise

    C) Evidence that students of philosophy are likely to contribute useful goods that benefit society in general

    D) A revelation that the study of physical science is useful to fewer people than previously thought

17. What is the primary goal of the passage?

    A) To assert that the study of philosophy benefits not just those who study it, but society as a whole.

    B) To explore what value lies in studying philosophy.

    C) To argue that studying philosophy is equally important as studying physical science

    D) To describe the essential questions that philosophy attempts to answer

18. The author believes that an individual who excludes the study of philosophy from his/her life risks which of the following consequences?

    A) An overvaluation of the usefulness of physical science

    B) A preoccupation with hair-splitting distinctions

    C) An inability to reach definite answers to profound questions

    D) Imprisonment in one's own convictions and beliefs

19. How does the author address the criticism that philosophy raises questions, but fails to answer them?

    A) By postulating that few disciplines actually answer the questions they raise

    B) By suggesting that raising questions, not providing answers, is philosophy's chief value

    C) By emphasizing the value of philosophy to the survival of humankind

    D) By criticizing the idea that seeking answers has value to philosophers

Passage IV

The barriers to entry into the medical field and the training of physicians creates a twofold process by which those who end up spending their lives as doctors are those who most strongly filter their experiences through the basic defense mechanism of intellectualization. They are expected to approach diseases through a rational analysis of signs, symptoms, diagnoses and prognoses, rather than the raw immediacy of sensation, intuition, feelings and family. To even apply to medical school with a realistic hope of matriculating, students must complete coursework that both demands a strong native ability to solve intellectual problems and tends to develop that intellectual capacity at the expense of other axes of human development.

Most patients, on the other hand, experience both illness and wellness through the fuzzier lens of intuition, despite having health care providers who deal with them as if they were as rational as the providers themselves. Understandably, the physicians' tendency to think of disease processes entirely through their intellect does have an effect on those patients who, by dint of their own higher education, are also predisposed to intellectualize problems. This mode of communication can partially serve to lessen the impact of bad news, but the doctor-patient relationship should do more. Regardless of how much more, it remains clear that physicians are largely ignorant of the value of processing life through intuitive, emotive processes.

This narrow vision gives precedence to rigidly informational modes of communication over the personal, emotive ones. Intentionally or not, physicians casually dismiss the possibility that a patient can only truly understand the doctor's communication in emotive terms, as they process major life events, especially traumatic ones, that way. While it is impossible to expect physicians to entirely shift the way they personally think about the matrix of pathologies that constitutes their work, we can, perhaps, ameliorate the problem by keeping what is good about intellectualization while leavening it with a dose of humanistic intuition.

First, medical school selection criteria need to be adjusted to take account of fundamental skills of communication and empathy that most develop innately. This may be something as simple as requiring coursework outside the usual array of basic science courses expected by most medical school admissions committees. The admissions officers could also place much heavier weight on the interview, and on sample patient interactions. Finally, the interviewing process could include explicit psychological testing to assess a candidate's ability to both read and communicate emotion.

Second, the training of future physicians through the medical school and residency systems must focus on identifying those physicians who excel at direct, emotive communications with patients, and help future practitioners model these behaviors. While not everyone may be trained to process illness in an emotive way, future physicians can at least learn to mimic those communication styles that will be more effective in reaching their patients. By having students practice modeling very specific behaviors and approaches to communication within the very first weeks of school, the groundwork can be laid that will have a positive impact on an entire career.

Finally, those physicians currently in practice ought to work, through the current system of Continuing Medical Education (CME) credits to change their communication styles. Mock-clinical interactions can take the place of the ineffectual lecture-style approach to CME credits currently so popular among practitioners. By requiring a certain number of Clinical CMEs each year, state medical boards around the country can quickly begin to change the landscape in which patients currently interact with their doctors: a landscape whose contours are solely defined by the abstract and intellectual.

[Adapted from "Doctor Who? A Model for the Failure of Doctor-Patient Communication" by K. Roo, 2011]

20. The author makes which of the follow underlying assumptions about physicians?
   A) Only people who already filter their life experience through their intellect want to become physicians.
   B) Most of them tend to have less emotional and more intellectual personalities than the average citizen.
   C) Many of them are incapable of understanding their emotional reactions to the illness and death they confront in their work.
   D) Some of them would welcome a more rigorous set of CME requirements that include developing new styles of communication in the clinic.

21. Which of the following most accurately characterizes the author's attitude towards the communication styles most commonly employed by physicians currently?
   A) Supportive
   B) Critical
   C) Vituperative
   D) Cautious

22. The author would most likely support adding which of the following courses to the standard pre-medical curriculum?
   A) Vertebrate Immunology
   B) Critical Media Studies
   C) Psychology of Art
   D) Mathematics

23. If a medical school were to institute a policy requiring all of its faculty to participate in clinical CME courses designed to facilitate more effective communication, the author would:
   A) support the decision, as the faculty of any medical school must stay abreast of the latest developments in their respective fields.
   B) oppose the decision, because it would be a misallocation of the institution's resources and its faculty's time.
   C) support the decision, since more effective communication would require a more intuitive approach than the intellectualization their students typically learn from them.
   D) neither support nor oppose the decision, because he is primarily concerned with adjusting the process by which students are filtered before entering medical school rather than their training once there.

24. The author's main goal behind his suggestion for reform in the selection and development of future doctors is most likely:
   A) to allow doctors and patients to communicate in a way that is comfortable for the patient and more likely to change the patients' behavior.
   B) to redress the author's own failings in his communications with his own patients.
   C) to encourage students in the arts who would otherwise not have considered medical school to bring their more direct, emotive communication styles into medicine.
   D) to push medical schools to alter their curriculum such that the intellectual rigors of the work are suborned to the more useful emotive and communicative ones.

Passage V

Both in Babylonia and Egypt, recent discoveries have thrown light upon periods regarded as prehistoric, and we have lately recovered traditions concerning very early rulers both in the Nile Valley and along the lower Euphrates. On the strength of the latter discovery we note the possibility that future excavation in Babylonia would lay bare stages of primitive culture similar to those we have already recovered in Egyptian soil. Meanwhile the documents from Nippur have shown us what the early Sumerians themselves believed about their own origin, and we trace in their tradition the gradual blending of history with legend and myth.

Now one of the newly published literary texts fills in the gap beyond, for it gives us a Sumerian account of the history of the world from the Creation to the Deluge, at about which point, as we saw, the extant portions of the Dynastic List take up the story.

The Babylonian account of the Deluge, which was discovered by George Smith in 1872 on tablets from the Royal Library at Nineveh, is embedded in a long epic of twelve Books recounting the adventures of the Old Babylonian hero Gilgamesh. Towards the end of this composite tale, Gilgamesh, desiring immortality, crosses the Waters of Death in order to beg the secret from his ancestor Ut-napishtim, who in the past had escaped the Deluge and had been granted immortality by the gods.

The Eleventh Tablet, or Book, of the epic contains the account of the Deluge which Ut-napishtim related to his kinsman Gilgamesh. The close correspondence of this Babylonian story with that contained in Genesis is clear to anyone. In some passages the accounts tally even in minute details, such, for example, as the device of sending out birds to test the abatement of the waters. It is true that in the Babylonian version a dove, a swallow, and a raven are sent forth in that order, instead of a raven and the dove three times. But such slight discrepancies only emphasize the general resemblance of the narratives.

In any comparison it is usually admitted that two accounts have been combined in the Hebrew narrative. I should like to point out that this assumption may be made by any one, whatever his views may be with regard to the textual problems of the Hebrew Bible and the traditional authorship of the Pentateuch. It is immaterial whether we identify the compiler of these Hebrew narratives with Moses himself, or with some later Jewish historian whose name has not come down to us.

[Adapted from *Legends of Babylon in Relation to Hebrew Tradition*, by Leonard W. King, 1918.]

25. History and archaeology both aim to make more a detailed study of events and cultures that have occurred in the past, but the latter discipline focuses on artifacts while the former discipline focuses on written documents of all kinds. Given this, what is the likely significance of the statement in the first paragraph that these "periods [are] regarded as prehistoric"?
    A) These cultures have been primarily studied by historians so far, who set such dividing lines.
    B) The cultures date from more than 2,000 years ago, and are BCE (Before Common Era) instead of CE (that is, AD).
    C) No textual records contemporary to the period and location have thus far been discovered.
    D) The cultures involve primitive, pre-modern humans, who co-existed with mastodon.

26. Which of the following cultures is not mentioned anywhere in the passage?
    A) Prehistoric Egyptians.
    B) Early Gnostic Christians.
    C) Ancient Sumerians.

D) Early Hebrews.

27. Why does the author allude to controversy or uncertainty regarding the authorship of the Hebrew Bible in the last paragraph?

    A) The textual problems open up the possibility of multiple authorship or cultural "borrowing" of the story, strengthening the hypothesis of a Babylonian origin.

    B) The author means to imply that until that question has been settled, it's impossible to definitively connect Hebrew and Babylonian accounts of the Deluge.

    C) The author is rhetorically leading readers through an argument to reach his own implicit conclusion: the Babylonian connection strongly suggests that Moses did not author the Hebrew Bible.

    D) The author is anticipating objections or concerns relating to Biblical authorship and demonstrating that that question is independent of the question of Babylonian influence.

28. The author assumes the story of a Great Flood or Deluge to be:

    A) literal historical fact, as evidenced by at least two isolated cultures reporting on these events.

    B) literal historical fact, as evidenced by the major differences in individual accounts but similarities in events.

    C) a myth or legend, as different cultures telling the story share obvious literary, not historical similarities.

    D) a myth or legend, as the textual problems of Genesis and other books put their authorship and origin in dispute.

29. The author implies that later ancient Babylonian texts:

    A) come in two flavors: fictional-poetic and historical-literal.

    B) do not clearly delineate what actually happened and what is metaphorical.

    C) fail to distinguish mythical and historical portions of their narrative.

    D) were the primary source of the Hebrew Bible's Book of Genesis.

30. Which of the following titles most accurately describes this passage?

    A) Myth Borrowing in Hebrew Tradition.

    B) The Real Deluge: History's Greatest Flood Revealed Through Textual Analysis.

    C) A Comparison of Ancient Origin Myths and Legends.

    D) The Real Bible: The Case Against Genesis and the Pentateuch as Historical Documents.

31. Which of the following, if true, would weaken the passage argument of a Babylonian influence on the Bible?

    A) An intermediate culture known to be the only link between Ancient Babylon and the later Hebrews is found to have no knowledge at all of Gilgamesh's epics.

    B) The basic structure of Babylon's Deluge story is found repeated (with variations) in several other later cultures outside the Hebrews.

    C) New ancient Biblical documents reveal that there really was a single writer in the earliest versions of the Bible, concurrent with the Moses as author hypothesis.

    D) A local but large-scale flood is discovered to have really occurred, but in traditional Hebrew territory and not near Babylonia's lower Euphrates.

Key terms: great myths, poor in myths, Greece, Scandinavia

Contrast: nations great in myths have many and marvellous tales vs. sparse stories from myth-poor nations

Cause-and-effect: myths come from imagination, and therefore reflect psychology and thus history

Opinion: quotations suggest author hesitant to make moral judgment on relative quality of different national mythologies

The Chinese are **not unimaginative**, but their minds did not go on to the construction of any myths which should be **world-great and immortal**, likely because there was not that contact and competition with other peoples which demands brain-work of an active kind as the **alternative of subjugation, inferiority, or extinction**. **Confucius** also later discountenanced discussion about the **supernatural**, and it is probable that this may have nipped in the bud much that might have developed a **vigorous mythology**.

Key terms: world-great, immortal, Confucius, supernatural

Contrast: contact with rival peoples spurring mythos vs. China's isolation; myth-building and culture/nation strengthening vs. subjugation/extinction

Cause-and-effect: lack of spur to myths leads to slower development; Confucian discountenance of supernatural effectively stops additional myth-making

Main Idea: the character of Chinese mythos is a product of its historical origins and attendant psychosocial development of its people

1. Which of the following attributes is not ascribed to Chinese language within the passage?
    A) The written language includes ideograms that can represent animals and plants.
    B) The language is tonal.
    C) **The language is relatively poor in myth and metaphor.**
    D) Recognizably older forms of the language are found in the south of the country.

Although Chinese myth is described as less rich than exemplars of "great myth" culture as found in Greece, nothing is said about the Chinese language family's use of myth or metaphor itself. C does almost sound right, replacing culture with language from an otherwise directly-lifted sentence from the passage, which is why it's important not to pick an answer choice that sounds familiar without checking against the passage itself.

2. It can be inferred from the passage that
    A) **Scandinavia had contact with many rival/enemy cultures throughout its history.**
    B) Examining language structures always provides a definitive answer to questions about ancient societies.
    C) Ancient Greece, as an island, was relatively isolated in the same way as Ancient China.
    D) the Chinese, in the era of globalization, are likely to develop some vigorous modern myths.

The last paragraph theorizes about the circumstances which tend to produce a rich mythology. Since the argument goes that a nation/culture will do so if and only if there is direct contact and competition with rival peoples, it can be inferred that any nation with a strong mythological tradition had those historical contacts. The statement in A is therefore a match. B is much too extreme in the use of the word "always". Ancient Greece, with a rich mythos, must not have been isolated, so C is incorrect. D might be a bit tempting, though it seems a little outlandish. Of course what matters is not whether it seems reasonable in a real-life context, but its possible inference from the passage. Considering context, then, the passage is referring to ancient history when saying that contact with other cultures precipitates myth-making, so it would be a stretch to assume a modern-day society would start making true myths (of the kind actually accepted by the people at large). We can therefore say A is the best match.

3. The reason for the author's discussion of yin-yang in paragraph three is
    A) **to make the point that peoples have equally powerful real and mythical conceptions of themselves.**
    B) to argue the intertwined nature of myth and history, with the former being gradually replaced by the latter.
    C) to underscore the disparity between myth-based cultures and historically-real cultures.
    D) to describe the translational equivalence between myth and true history.

Each statement needs to be examined individually in order to determine the best match to what the author actually wrote. The word dual suggests two things existing simultaneously and side-by-side, with a certain symmetry. If myth and history are dual, they do not appear one at a time, one replacing the other, as in answer choice B, there is no major disparity (whatever the measure) between the two as in answer choice C. This leaves A and B, with the former statement saying they are equally powerful, and the latter saying their meanings are equivalent. The word dual does imply they are equally significant, but not that their meanings are themselves equal. A is therefore the correct answer choice.

4. The author would most likely agree that the Chinese people
    A) immigrated from the west, in accordance with their tightly-held tradition.
    B) arrived in the south and spread northwards, as suggested by the evidence of early tropical settlement.
    C) **arrived from the north in waves, later settlers pushing earlier ones south, in accordance with linguistic evidence.**
    D) have been on their land since ancient pre-history, as implied by their unusually long written history.

Each of these suggestions come from the passage, excepting answer choice D. The question is what the passage author believes, and various key words demonstrate the author's preference for the north-to-south theory, which "better" accounts for the facts and "alleged facts" supporting the south-to-north theory. The western immigration tradition is mentioned but given no additional supporting evidence in the passage.

5. Which of the following, if true, would most strengthen the passage author's argument as to the origins of China's mythological character?
    A) Japan, a younger but equally isolated nation is found to possess a relatively rich mythos.
    B) **The most detailed New World mythologies are found within the warring neighbour nations near the Central American isthmus.**
    C) A study finds that cultures of medium-size (population of 5 000-25 000) during their formative years develop more detailed and cohesive myths than larger or smaller ones of similar historical circumstance.
    D) The nation of Britain's superstitions and traditional stories are found to descend from several different cultural origins, including Germanic and French settlers and indigenous groups such as the Celts.

The statement in A would actually weaken the argument that intercultural contact and competition are required for myth-making. B, however, would strengthen the argument. C and D neither strengthen nor weaken the argument: although D is somewhat tempting due to its referencing the variety of different cultures in historical Britain, no mention is made of the comparative richness of British mythos relative to other cultures as a result of this contact.

6. Which of the following titles most accurately describes the passage?
    A) Comparative World Mythology.
    B) Chinese Culture and Character.
    C) **Myth and History in China.**
    D) Chinese and World History.

All of the titles refer to topics tackled in the passage. The question is which are incidental or in support of the main topic, and which are essential to the main topic. The passage author's main purpose is in explaining the origin of

Chinese myth as a product of its history, with discussion of other nations' myths used for either contrast or as direct evidence of this argument. The title in answer choice C best matches the focus of the passage.

7. Which of the following is not cited as evidence that the people of China immigrated from elsewhere?
    A) Traditional stories and myths describing their people battling wild beasts and working the land.
    B) **Differences in the tonality of Chinese and Indo-Chinese language families.**
    C) Linguistic evidence suggesting different dates of settlement in the north and south of the country.
    D) References to a separate aboriginal group at war with the ancestors of modern Chinese.

In fact it is the similarly tonal nature of both language families mentioned in answer choice B, not the differences, which argue for an immigration hypothesis. B is therefore the incorrect statement.

Passage II Explanation

There are many who acknowledge that the **political structures** of the day have an **influence** on the development of **literature** but vehemently oppose the notion that a subtle **biological evolution of the brain** has anything to do with the matter. Yet consider the difference between the forms of literature created by **pre-literate societies** in ancient times and those made during and **after the Industrial revolution**: each exhibits a **stark contrast** with the other, and the production, consumption, and goals of such literature have a subtle interplay not just with the political ecology in which they were created, but on the **kind of brain** intended to receive the literary message.

Key terms: political structures, industrial revolution

Opinion: Many wouldn't think evolution of brain affects literature

Contrast: pre-literate and industrial societies have differing literature

Pre-literate societies had to transmit their literature **orally**, whereas **industrialized societies** did so in **writing**. The primary mental tool by which **oral literature** is both transmitted and consumed is **memory**, which requires development of the **hippocampus and amygdala**. **Reading** literature, however, triggers a series of mechanical controls for the eyes, and in the brain's **visual processing** centers in the **occipital lobe**, bypassing much of the memory activation centers.

Key terms: amygdala, hippocampus, occipital lob

Contrast: oral literature depends on memory, written literature is more visual

It **may seem absurd** that the biological evolution of the brain influences the sorts of literature produced, and yet when **neuroimaging studies** are done on the brains of present-day peoples whose cultures most nearly approximate ancient ways of living, they reveal **strong differences** in both structural and functional development from contemporary brains.

Key terms: neuroimaging studies

Contrast: the brains of pre-literate and industrial people are different

Surviving for millennia as **hunter-gatherers** required the development a brain with an **astounding spatial memory**. Early humans roved over vast territories in their search for food, and they had to be able to store this data and recall it effortlessly in order to survive. This lifestyle both selected for and subsequently promoted the **neural architecture for memory**. It is unsurprising, then, that the literature developed under such circumstances would depend heavily on memory. This memory-based literature persisted long after agriculture and civilization became the predominant mode of living; the **ancient Greeks** were well known to equate memory with intelligence itself. By contrast, once man developed systems for externalizing memory (first the written word, then later recorded sound and images), the **primary mental virtue became speed of processing** that information. Thus the literature that developed from medieval times onward tended towards **exceptionally lengthy tomes** that the reader would **move through relatively quickly**.

Key terms: hunter-gatherers, spatial memory, ancient Greeks

Contrast: hunter-gatherers depend on excellent memory for survival but literate societies value quick processing over memory

These **differences are not merely technological or cultural**. The neuroimaging studies done on "ancient peoples" were extended to comparing the brains of infants less than **a week old**. Those **children born in industrial** and post-industrial societies **already showed stronger initial development** of visual processing and prefrontal cortical regions whereas infants in pre-agricultural tribal societies (most notably the **Etoro** people of Papua New Guinea and the **Pano** tribe in the Amazon rainforest) had **more well developed hippocampal and amygdalar** architectures.

Passage III Explanation

It will be well to consider, what is the **value of philosophy** and why it ought to be studied. It is the more necessary to consider this question, in view of the fact that many men, under the influence of science or of practical affairs, are inclined to **doubt** whether philosophy is anything better than innocent but useless trifling, hair-splitting distinctions, and controversies on matters concerning which knowledge is impossible.

Key terms: value of philosophy, doubt

Opinion: Many people think studying philosophy is frivolous.

Cause-and-Effect: Because many people think studying philosophy is of little value, the author says it is important to explore the value of philosophy.

This view of philosophy appears to result partly from a wrong conception of the kind of goods which philosophy strives to achieve. **Physical science**, through the medium of inventions, is useful to innumerable people who are wholly ignorant of it; thus the study of physical science is to be recommended, not only, or primarily, because of the effect on the student, but rather because of the effect on mankind in general. Thus **utility** does not belong to philosophy. If the study of philosophy has any value at all for others than students of philosophy, it must be only indirectly, through its effects upon the lives of those who study it. It is in these effects, therefore, if anywhere, that the value of philosophy must be primarily sought.

Key terms: physical science, utility

Contrast: Whereas physical science is indirectly useful to even those who are ignorant of it, philosophy is useful only to those who study it.

But further, if we are not to fail in our endeavour to determine the value of philosophy, we must first free our minds from the prejudices of what are wrongly called **'practical' men**. The 'practical' man, as this word is often used, is one who realizes that men must have food for the body, but is oblivious of the necessity of providing food for the mind. It is exclusively among the **goods of the mind** that the value of philosophy is to be found; and only those who are not indifferent to these goods can be persuaded that the study of philosophy is not a waste of time.

Key terms: practical men, goods of the mind

Cause-and-Effect: Because so-called practical men focus on tangible needs, they are oblivious to the needs, or goods, of the mind – which is what philosophy addresses.

Philosophy, like all other studies, aims primarily at **knowledge**. The knowledge it aims at is the kind of knowledge which gives unity and system to the body of the sciences, and the kind which results from a critical examination of the grounds of our convictions, prejudices, and beliefs. But it cannot be maintained that philosophy has had any very great measure of success in its attempts to provide definite **answers** to its **questions**. There are many questions—and among them those that are of the profoundest interest to our spiritual life—which, so far as we can see, must remain insoluble to the human intellect unless its powers become of quite a different order from what they are now. Has the universe any unity of plan or purpose, or is it a fortuitous concourse of atoms? Is consciousness a permanent part of the universe, giving hope of indefinite growth in wisdom, or is it a transitory accident on a small planet on which life must ultimately become impossible? Are good and evil of importance to the universe or only to man? However slight may be the hope of discovering an answer, it is part of the business of philosophy to continue the consideration of such questions, to make us aware of their importance, to examine all the approaches to them, and to keep alive that speculative interest in the universe which is apt to be killed by confining ourselves to definitely ascertainable knowledge.

Key terms: knowledge, answers, questions

Cause-and-Effect: Although philosophy aims at knowledge, it rarely can definitively answer the questions it raises.

Opinion: It is the role of philosophy to ask profound questions; doing so raises the importance of such issues.

The value of philosophy is, in fact, to be sought largely in its very **uncertainty**. The man who has no tincture of philosophy goes through life imprisoned in the prejudices derived from common sense, from the habitual beliefs of his age or his nation, and from convictions which have grown up in his mind without the co-operation or consent of his deliberate reason. To such a man the world tends to become definite, finite, obvious; common objects rouse no questions, and unfamiliar possibilities are contemptuously rejected. As soon as we begin to philosophize, on the contrary, we find that even the most everyday things lead to problems to which only very incomplete answers can be given. Philosophy, though unable to tell us with certainty what is the true answer to the doubts which it raises, is able to suggest many **possibilities** which enlarge our thoughts and free them from the tyranny of custom. Thus, while diminishing our feeling of certainty as to what things are, it greatly increases our knowledge as to what they may be; and it keeps alive our sense of wonder by showing familiar things in an unfamiliar aspect.

[Excerpted from *The Problems of Philosophy*, by Bertrand Russell, 1912.]

Key terms: uncertainty, possibilities

Opinion: The value of philosophy lies in its uncertainty; philosophizing helps us enlarge the possibilities in our world.

Main Idea: While the study of philosophy does not lead to certain answers, doing so addresses needs of the minds of those who study it.

13. The author cites which of the following as a difference between the study of physical science and the study of philosophy?
    A) Physical science directly benefits those who study it, but the study of philosophy benefits mankind in general.
    B) **Physical science can benefit those who are ignorant of it, whereas philosophy benefits primarily those who study it.**
    C) Physical science aims primarily at knowledge, while philosophy does not.
    D) Unlike philosophy, physical science avoids controversies on matters concerning knowledge.

In paragraph 2, the author discusses physical science in contrast with philosophy. Physical science, he says is useful even to people "wholly ignorant of it." Philosophy, however, is useful only to people who study it. That's choice B.

A: This choice gets the difference backwards.
C: Philosophy aims at knowledge too – see the first line of paragraph 4.
D: The author never discusses whether or not physical science avoids controversy.

14. Which of the following does the author NOT describe as a benefit of the study of philosophy?

    A) Studying philosophy encourages interest in our world.
    B) The study of philosophy helps us see the value of questioning our world.
    C) **By studying philosophy, we are more likely to provide definitive answers to the most profound questions.**
    D) Philosophy enlarges our world by freeing us from our customary ways of thinking.

The only choice that is NOT mentioned is choice C; the author actually says that philosophy isn't so great at providing definitive answers. The other choices are all described as benefits of studying philosophy at the very end of paragraph 4, or in paragraph 5.

15. According to the author, what fault might "practical men" find with the study of philosophy?
    A) **Philosophy is nonessential; it does not contribute to the survival to humankind.**
    B) Philosophy benefits the individual, but not humankind in general.
    C) Philosophy raises questions, but neglects to provide answers.
    D) Philosophy challenges widely held beliefs that are essential to man's survival.

The objections of "practical men" to philosophy is discussed in paragraph 3; practical men, says the author, are focused on the needs of the body, but philosophy exclusively serves the needs of the mind. Choice A captures this.

B: Practical men seem to think that philosophy benefits neither the individual nor society as a whole.
C: The author implies that the practical man sees little value in the entire enterprise of philosophy, not just that it doesn't provide answers.
D: Again, it's the whole enterprise that is not useful, according to practical men.

16. Which of the following might convince a "practical" man of the value of philosophy?
    A) Definitive answers to questions regarding spiritual life
    B) A theory that philosophers are actually likely to answer the questions they raise
    C) **Evidence that students of philosophy are likely to contribute useful goods that benefit society in general**
    D) A revelation that the study of physical science is useful to fewer people than previously thought

The practical man is focused on concrete needs, not airy ideas. Choice C, if true, would appeal to the practical man's priority on usefulness.

A, B: These wouldn't matter much – both still would leave philosophy as a nonessential activity of the mind.
D: Even if this were the case, it would devalue physical science, but not necessarily elevate the importance of philosophy in the mind of the practical man.

17. What is the primary goal of the passage?
    A) To assert that the study of philosophy benefits not just those who study it, but society as a whole
    B) **To explore what value lies in studying philosophy**
    C) To argue that studying philosophy is equally important as studying physical science
    D) To describe the essential questions that philosophy attempts to answer

Look to the first line of this passage for its main goal: the author asks why we should bother studying philosophy, since so many people seem to see it as a waste of time. We get some answers towards the passage's end – it enlarges the minds and lives of those who study it. Choice B reflects this.

A: The author says in paragraph 2 that philosophy only benefits those who study it.
C: While it's likely the author believes this, he makes no argument for this in the passage.
D: Some of those essential questions are described in paragraph 4, but in the service of making a larger point – that philosophy raises profound and largely insolvable questions.

18. The author believes that an individual who excludes the study of philosophy from his/her life risks which of the following consequences?
    A) An overvaluation of the usefulness of physical science

B) A preoccupation with hair-splitting distinctions
C) An inability to reach definite answers to profound questions
D) **<u>Imprisonment in one's own convictions and beliefs</u>**

We get the warning at the beginning of paragraph 5: the man who has "no tincture of philosophy" is imprisoned by his own habits and beliefs, and is tyrannized by custom. That's what choice D says.

19. How does the author address the criticism that philosophy raises questions, but fails to answer them?
    A) By postulating that few disciplines actually answer the questions they raise
    B) **<u>By suggesting that raising questions, not providing answers, is philosophy's chief value</u>**
    C) By emphasizing the value of philosophy to the survival of humankind
    D) By criticizing the idea that seeking answers has value to philosophers

The author admits that philosophy seeks knowledge, but doesn't adequately answer the questions it raises – see paragraph 4. Not a problem, he says, since the value of philosophy is to make us aware of the importance of such questions, to awaken our speculative interest, as choice B correctly states.

A: The only other discipline the author mentions is physical science, which he implies answers some questions, as evidenced by inventions.
C: The author postulates that the study of philosophy is hugely important to humankind – but not essential to our survival.
D: The author is fine with the process of seeking answers, but acknowledges that it's likely that a philosopher can provide definitive answers to the questions raised.

Passage IV Explanation

The **barriers to entry** into the medical field and the **training of physicians** creates a twofold process by which those who end up spending their lives as doctors are those who most strongly filter their experiences through the basic defense mechanism of **intellectualization**. They are expected to **approach diseases** through a **rational analysis** of signs, symptoms, diagnoses and prognoses, **rather than** the raw immediacy of sensation, intuition, **feelings** and family. To even apply to medical school with a realistic hope of matriculating, students must complete coursework that both demands a strong native ability to solve intellectual problems and tends to develop that intellectual capacity at the expense of other axes of human development.

Cause-and-effect: Getting into med school and training as a doctor ensures doctors are rational, not emotional.

Most **patients**, on the other hand, **experience both illness** and wellness through the fuzzier lens of **intuition**, despite having health care providers who deal with them as if they were as rational as the providers themselves. Understandably, the physicians' tendency to think of diseases processes entirely through their intellect does have an effect on those patients who, by dint of their own higher education, are also predisposed to **intellectualize problems**. This mode of communication can partially serve to **lessen the impact of bad news**, but the doctor-patient relationship **should do more**. Regardless of how much more, it remains clear that **physicians are largely ignorant of the value of processing life through intuitive**, emotive processes.

Contrast: Patients are more emotional, Doctors more intellectual

Cause-and-effect: Intellectualization can lessen bad news

Opinion: Author thinks doctor-patient relationship should do more, doctors are ignorant for missing out on emotion.

This **narrow vision** gives precedence to rigidly **informational modes of communication** over the personal, emotive ones. Intentionally or not, physicians casually dismiss the possibility that a **patient can only truly understand the doctor's communication in emotive terms**, as they process major life events, especially traumatic ones, that way. While it is impossible to expect physicians to entirely shift the way they personally think about the matrix of pathologies that constitutes their work, we can, perhaps, **ameliorate the problem** by keeping what is good about intellectualization while leavening it with a dose of **humanistic intuition**.

Cause-and-effect: Doctors narrow view leads to communication that focuses on information

Contrast: Doctors communicate information, but patients understand emotion.

Opinion: Author thinks we can't completely fix problem, but we can make it better.

First, **medical school selection criteria** need to be adjusted to take account of fundamental skills of **communication and empathy** that most develop innately. This may be something as simple as requiring coursework outside the usual array of basic science courses expected by most medical school admissions committees. The admissions officers could also place much heavier weight on the interview, and on sample patient interactions. Finally, the interviewing process could include explicit psychological testing to assess a candidate's ability to both read and communicate emotion.

Opinion: Author thinks the criteria to get into med school should focus on emotion and empathy, offers suggestions

Second, the training of future physicians **through the medical school and residency** systems must focus on identifying those physicians who excel at direct, emotive communications with patients, and **help future**

practitioners model these behaviors. While not everyone may be trained to process illness in an emotive way, future physicians can at least learn to **mimic those communication styles** that will be more effective in reaching their patients. By having students practice modeling very specific behaviors and approaches to communication within the very first weeks of school, the groundwork can be laid that will have a positive impact on an entire career.

Opinion: Author thinks med schools and residencies should actively teach doctors to mimic communication styles that will match patients' emotional understanding.

Finally, those physicians currently in practice ought to work, through the current system of **Continuing Medical Education** (CME) credits to **change their communication styles**. Mock-clinical interactions can take the place of the ineffectual lecture-style approach to CME credits currently so popular among practitioners. By **requiring** a certain number of **Clinical CMEs** each year, state **medical boards** around the country can quickly begin to change the landscape in which patients currently interact with their doctors: a landscape whose contours are solely defined by the abstract and intellectual.

[Adapted from "Doctor Who? A Model for the Failure of Doctor-Patient Communication" by K. Roo, 2011]

Key terms: Continuing Medical Education

Cause-and-effect: State medical boards could change physician behavior by requiring clinical CME's based on communication style.

Main Idea: Doctors are disconnected from patients because they take an informational, rational approach to diseases and to communication whereas patients are emotional and intuitive, thus med schools, residency programs, and state medical boards should take steps to fix this.

20. The author makes which of the follow underlying assumptions about physicians?
    A) Only people who already filter their life experience through their intellect want to become physicians.
    B) **Most of them tend to have less emotional and more intellectual personalities than the average citizen.**
    C) Many of them are incapable of understanding their emotional reactions to the illness and death they confront in their work.
    D) Some of them would welcome a more rigorous set of CME requirements that include developing new styles of communication in the clinic.

The question asks us for something that fits with the author's point of view about physicians. Although the question uses the word "assumption" we must still make sure our answer sticks closely to the author's main idea. Only choice B fits the bill – doctors being more intellectual and less emotional was the author's main point.

A, C: These choices are too extreme. A's "only" and C's "incapable" go beyond what the author asserts.
D: While some doctors might be in favor of clinical CME's we're never given any information about how doctors themselves view the CMEs they must attend.

21. Which of the following most accurately characterizes the author's attitude towards the communication styles most commonly employed by physicians currently?
    A) Supportive
    B) **Critical**
    C) Vituperative
    D) Cautious

The author clearly states his opinion that things need to change. Thus we know he's not a fan of the current intellectual and informational way that doctors talk to their patients. Thus choices A and D are out. Critical is a good match and choice B is the right answer.

C: Vituperative is much too strong. While the author argues strongly in favor of change he doesn't rant about the evils of informational communication styles.

22. The author would most likely support adding which of the following courses to the standard pre-medical curriculum?
   A) Vertebrate Immunology
   B) Critical Media Studies
   C) **Psychology of Art**
   D) Mathematics

The question asks about the coursework future doctors go through, so we should check back in the passage. The author asserts that they should complete coursework outside the usual science classes. Given that the author focuses so much on intuition, empathy, and emotion, the best fit is choice C. A class on psychology and on expression through art would help achieve the author's goals.

A, D: These are the classic "science and math" that make up the current coursework.
B: A class on breaking down the messages found in TV and other media may help future doctors think about communication styles but it missed the mark with the author's focus on emotion and intuition.

23. If a medical school were to institute a policy requiring all of its faculty to participate in clinical CME courses designed to facilitate more effective communication, the author would:
   A) support the decision, as the faculty of any medical school must stay abreast of the latest developments in their respective fields.
   B) oppose the decision, because it would be a misallocation of the institution's resources and its faculty's time.
   C) **support the decision, since more effective communication would require a more intuitive approach than the intellectualization their students typically learn from them.**
   D) neither support nor oppose the decision, because he is primarily concerned with adjusting the process by which students are filtered before entering medical school rather than their training once there.

The author explicitly states in the final paragraph that doctors should go through CME's to help mold their communication styles into something more fitting for their patients. That fits choice C perfectly.

A: While the author would support this decision, his concern is less about "keeping up with developments" than it is about a very specific problem: mismatch in communication styles between doctors and patients.
B, D: The author would strongly support such a decision and so we may eliminate these.

24. The author's main goal behind his suggestion for reform in the selection and development of future doctors is most likely:
   A) **to allow doctors and patients to communicate in a way that is comfortable for the patient and more likely to change the patients' behavior.**
   B) to redress the author's own failings in his communications with his own patients.
   C) to encourage students in the arts who would otherwise not have considered medical school to bring their more direct, emotive communication styles into medicine.
   D) to push medical schools to alter their curriculum such that the intellectual rigors of the work are suborned to the more useful emotive and communicative ones.

A question about the author's main goal should stick with our main idea, and choice A does that – the author is very concerned with how doctors and patients communicate.

B: We don't know if the author herself is unable to communicate well with her own patients.
C, D: While the author may support this, she never suggests getting rid of (or diminishing) the rigorous intellectual training and coursework, only supplementing it

The author mentions this controversy and then states that, whatever your opinion on the question of Biblical authorship, you can still make the same assumption with regards to Babylonian influence. The author is making a point of bringing up the question, just to make clear that it is irrelevant to what is being argued in the passage. D is a match for that. The other answer choices incorrectly assume that the answer to this question actually does matter, either strengthening or weakening or even reversing the argument.

28. The passage author assumes the story of a Great Flood or Deluge to be
    A) literal historical fact, as evidenced by at least two isolated cultures reporting on these events.
    B) literal historical fact, as evidenced by the major differences in individual accounts but similarities in events.
    C) **<u>a myth or legend, as different cultures telling the story share obvious literary, not historical similarities.</u>**
    D) a myth or legend, as the textual problems of Genesis and other books put their authorship and origin in dispute.

The author does not explicitly state an opinion, but an assumption of the Deluge as a myth is necessary to the argument. Since the author comes to the conclusion that the similarities between the stories mean that one influenced the author, the author must assume that these similarities do not come from having independently experienced the same catastrophic event. That eliminates answer choices A and B, but now it's necessary to infer from the passage why the author assumes the Deluge to be a myth, since no time is spent explicitly discussing why this can be assumed to be true. The author does discuss the textual similarities and minor differences between the Babylonian and Hebrew accounts (the birds sent to find land, for example), which implies that these are considered as strong markers of a literary, rather than historical relationship between the two stories, as stated in answer choice C. The explanation in D brings up textual issues in Genesis, which the author brings up as an aside, explicitly stating that this question is unrelated to the question of Babylonian influence.

29. The author implies that later ancient Babylonian texts
    A) come in two flavors: fictional-poetic; historical-literal.
    B) do not clearly delineate what actually happened and what is metaphorical.
    C) **<u>fail to distinguish mythical and historical portions of their narrative.</u>**
    D) were the primary source of the Hebrew Bible's Book of Genesis.

In the first paragraph, the author describes a gradual blend of myth and fact. This gradual blending suggests that enough documents over a period of time have been found that those stories which modern scholars know to be historical records and those stories which are known to be legend start to be combined more and more in later documents. This relationship implies, however, that a single later document does not, in itself, contain any clues as to what is historically true and what is myth. B and C both seem like possible matches, but a closer check on the passage reveals there is actually no discussion of any Babylonian myths being a metaphor for anything. So C is the correct match.

30. Which of the following titles most accurately describes this passage?
    A) **<u>Myth Borrowing in Hebrew Tradition.</u>**
    B) The Real Deluge: History's Greatest Flood Revealed Through Textual Analysis.
    C) A Comparison of Ancient Origin Myths and Legends.
    D) The Real Bible: The Case Against Genesis and the Pentateuch as Historical Documents.

The focus of the passage is in providing evidence for an eventual conclusion relating Hebrew myth to a Babylonian literary origin. A is a good match for this. The passage author does not suggest the Deluge is real history, eliminating B, while the comparison of the legends is a means to supporting an argument, so C doesn't quite cover the real goal of the passage. The title in D comes from a side-note to the main argument so would not be a representative title.

31. Which of the following, if true, would weaken the passage argument of a Babylonian influence on the Bible?

A) **An intermediate culture known to be the only link between Ancient Babylon and the later Hebrews is found to have no knowledge at all of Gilgamesh's epics.**

B) The basic structure of Babylon's Deluge story is found repeated (with variations) in several other later cultures outside the Hebrews.

C) New ancient Biblical documents reveal that there really was a single writer in the earliest versions of the Bible, concurrent with the Moses as author hypothesis.

D) A local but large-scale flood is discovered to have really occurred, but in traditional Hebrew territory and not near Babylonia's lower Euphrates.

Anything suggesting an alternate explanation for the similarity of the two Deluge legends outside of Hebrew familiarity with the Babylonian stories, or anything suggesting that the Hebrews would not have been able to get the stories from the Babylonians would weaken the argument. A fits the bill, as it suggests the story may not have ever been passed on. B actually would strengthen the argument somewhat, as it would show evidence that Babylon's story had indeed been passed on and copied, making it more plausible that the Hebrews had likewise copied it. C and D would neither strengthen nor weaken the argument.

SECTION 3: SKIMMING TECHNIQUE

You may, of course, use any technique you'd like on the following half-section but I strongly recommend that you take this opportunity to begin your timed practice with the skimming technique. Regardless of which technique you use, when working your way through this section, there's only one absolute requirement: **you must time yourself strictly**. Don't set a timer counting down, rather use a stopwatch counting up. You do yourself no favors by casually going through with no awareness of time. The first step to improving your timing is to see exactly where your time is going.

If you would like to get the best practice for the skimming technique, do the following before you start:

1. Get a stopwatch to count up (or a stopwatch app on your phone).
2. Go some place where you won't be interrupted and that is relatively quiet.
3. Get some foam earplugs to block out the noise.

When you start the section, start the stopwatch counting up.

Every time you finish reading a passage, hit the "lap" button on the stopwatch. Every time you finish a set of questions, hit the "lap" button again. At the end of the section you'll have 10 data points showing you how long you took to read each passage and how long for the questions.

With the skimming technique you should spend about 1.5 minutes on the passage and 8.5 minutes on the questions.

Then, when reviewing the explanations afterwards, quickly skim over the **bold** words to see if your skim picked up on the important ideas, and read the **Main Idea** at the bottom to see if you understood the overall gist of the passage.

Passage I

We have to realize the peculiar relations between Europe, ancient and mediaeval, and the great empires of Eastern Asia. The two civilizations had never been in direct contact. Yet in a sense they were always connected. The Greeks and the Romans had at least vague reports of peoples who lived on the far eastern confines of the world, beyond even the conquests of Alexander the Great in Hindustan. It is certain, too, that Europe and Asia had always traded with one another in a strange and unconscious fashion. The spices and silks of the unknown East passed westward from trader to trader, from caravan to caravan, until they reached the Persian Gulf, the Red Sea, and, at last, the Mediterranean.

The journey was so slow, so tedious, the goods passed from hand to hand so often, that when the Phoenician, Greek, or Roman merchants bought them their origin had been forgotten. For century after century this trade continued. When Rome fell, other peoples of the Mediterranean continued the Eastern trade. With the Crusades, all the treasures which the warriors of the Cross brought home, helped to impress on the mind of Europe the surpassing riches of the East.

Gradually a new interest was added. As time went on doubts increased regarding the true shape of the earth. If the earth was really a globe, it might be possible to go round it and to reappear on the farther side of the horizon. Then the East might be reached, not only across the deserts of Persia and Tartary, but also by striking out into the boundless ocean.

It was the stern logic of events which compelled the enterprise. The Turks swept westward. Arabia, Syria, the Isles of Greece, and, at last, in 1453, Constantinople itself, fell into their hands. The Eastern Empire, the last survival of the Empire of the Romans, perished beneath the sword of Mahomet. Then the pathway by land to Asia, to the fabled empires of Cathay and Cipango, was blocked by the Turkish conquest. Commerce, however, remained alert and enterprising, and men's minds soon turned to the hopes of a western passage which should provide a new route to the Indies.

[Adapted from *Chronicles of Canada*, by Stephen Leacock, 1915.]

1. According to the passage, what was the easternmost outpost the Ancient Romans were aware of in detail?
   A) Constantinople
   B) Cipango
   C) Hindustan
   D) Istanbul

2. Which of the following is not cited in the passage as part of the merchant chain that brought Eastern goods to the Europe?
   A) Cathay
   B) Desert caravans across Tartary
   C) The Dead Sea
   D) Phoenician merchants

3. Suppose that Mahomet had been defeated by the Persians, who went on to push eastward and establish high-volume trade routes between the Mediterranean and Far East. Given the information in the passage, how would this likely have affected the search for a western passage to the Indies?
   A) The enterprise likely would have been initiated in Constantinople rather than Western Europe.
   B) The journey would have begun and proceeded in much the way.
   C) The search for a western passage wouldn't have happened until later.
   D) The search for a western passage would have started much earlier.

4. One of the outcomes resulting from European expeditions seeking a westward route to the Indies was European nations becoming aware of the American continents. Which of the following outcomes might have been expected based on the information in the passage?
   A) Spread of unfamiliar diseases caused heavy losses amongst indigenous peoples.
   B) Christian nations sent missionaries and soldiers to conquer and baptize.
   C) Fur offered for trade in Canada led to a heavy increase in Atlantic ship traffic.
   D) American domestic crops transformed European cooking.

5. Given the information in the passage, which of the following, if true, might have resulted in the flow of Eastern goods to Europe prior to the Turkish conquest being less than it actually was?
   A) If Alexander the Great had never been born
   B) If the Phoenician civilization had fallen with the Roman
   C) Harsher travel conditions in the Atlantic
   D) War between Persia and Arabia

Passage II

The best-known examples of metafiction appear abruptly in the 1960's as examples of a fully realized mode of ironic writing without any obvious predecessors. Metafiction is best understood a form of novel in which the author never lets the reader forget that he is reading a novel. Rather than aim for a realistic tone that permits the reader to "lose himself" in the book, metafiction forces the reader to contemplate the physical act of reading itself. Despite features of metafiction that suggest it grew out of earlier trends in Romantic literature, few critics could directly link the style to any particular predecessors. Recently, a potent reevaluation of the work *Jacques the Fatalist and his Master* by Denis Diderot, suggests that this work may bridge the gap between metafiction and earlier writing.

Jacques the Fatalist and his Master was written between 1765 and 1780, although it was not published as a full French version until 1796. At the time, the work was largely unappreciated and received, at best, lukewarm reviews in Germany and elsewhere outside Diderot's homeland. The work centers around the relationship between Jacques and his master, who is unnamed throughout the novel. The master instructs Jacques to regale him with tales of his various romantic affairs to pass the time as they travel. As Jacques speaks, he is continually interrupted by other characters, who are themselves interrupted. Halfway through the work, Diderot even introduces "The Reader" who evinces continual exasperation with the characters and pushes them to get back on track with the tale. Within this fractured structure, the characters are consistently contradictory: one chapter focuses on two best friends who constantly duel each other, dealing grave wounds in the process. Finally, the unwieldy tale includes large sections lifted entirely from the earlier novel *Tristam Shandy*.

The structure of *Jacques* helps demonstrate why metafiction developed the traits that it did. Metafiction's goal is to keep the reader focused on the act of reading itself. It does this by eschewing the usual linear narrative structure. If the reader's expectations are wholly thwarted, he is put in a state of "high alert" that does not permit him to lose himself in the book. Metafiction also plays with the typography and physical layout of the words on the page. By continually shifting the typeface, or laying the words in groups or orientations other than a typical paragraph, the reader's attention is focused on the level of the words on the page itself rather than on the meaning behind those words. Finally, metafiction shifts narrative voice, making use of the second person (e.g. "You open the door.") to address the reader directly.

In *Jacques*, we may see predecessors of many of these traits. In the earliest German translations, which predate even the first full publication in France, the book shifts from traditional paragraphs to the layout more commonly used in scripts and back again, with no seeming relationship between the layout and the content of the story itself. In addition, by including "the Reader" as a character, Diderot anticipated the use of second person by metafiction authors who came two centuries later.

But ultimately it may be the breaking of narrative structure which reveals the most about how and why metafiction developed. As early as the late 1700's, critics spoke of literature as a "dying art". It was believed that everything that could be said had been said. "After [H]omer and Shakespeare," one critic opined, "what [is] left for us to say?" Much of the artistic fervor on the Continent during the time was found in the theater, and it is believed that authors sought to capture the immediacy of live plays, most notably the theater of the absurd. The wild shifts in the narrative of these plays were seen to have great comedic effect, and we can now see that *Jacques* sought to capture that energy and humor. In that regard, we may draw a straight line directly from *Jacques* to the 1960's, in which writers sought to use metafiction to capture the energy of the counter-cultural movement and its chosen form of self-expression: rock and roll music.

[Adapted from "Meta-me and Meta-you" by K. O'Connell-Choate, Sussex County Press, 2011]

6. Why does the author include a discussion of literary critics who felt that literature was a dying art?
    A) To indicate how old the notion is that "everything that could be said ha[s] been said"
    B) To illustrate why metafiction sought to address the reader directly in the second person narrative voice
    C) To argue that the metafiction of the 1960's bears a direct relationship with *Jacques*
    D) To demonstrate that critics are often wrong when they make assessments that bear on the future of an art

7. If it were later discovered that in Diderot's original manuscript of *Jacques* that he included several sections of dialogue written upside down, this would:
    A) demonstrate the sloppiness with which printers approached their art in the 18th century.
    B) further support the author's thesis by providing a link between *Jacques* and later metafiction.
    C) provide a concrete reason why the work was poorly received.
    D) weaken the author's contention that *Jacques* contained features that focused the reader on the physical act of reading.

8. The passage provides information to answer all of the following questions EXCEPT:
    A) What feature of metafiction made the reader focus on the physical act of reading?
    B) The relationship between *Jacques* and the theater of the time is most closely analogous to the relationship between the metafiction of the 1960's and what art?
    C) Did any writers from the 1960's other than writers of metafiction make use of the second person?
    D) Does metafiction have any features that it shares with earlier Romantic fiction?

9. Which of the following, if discovered, would most *weaken* the author's thesis?
    A) No metafiction writers from the 1960's had read, or were even aware of *Jacques*.
    B) Even readers who are reading a traditional narrative maintain some level of attention on the physical act of reading.
    C) Diderot was unaware of developments in arts outside literature.
    D) It was common in the 18th century for novelists to quote entire passages from earlier works.

10. Literary analysts may find themselves discussing the subjects of their inquiry in a less than objective way. Which of the following would the author of this passage most likely have written?
    A) *Tristam Shandy*, by contrast, is a masterful construct that rewards both the casual reader and the most focused literary analyst.
    B) *Jacques* is a trifle of a book, with a quick breezy air that belies its philosophical heft.
    C) Metafiction leaves us feeling like we have read the ultimate expression of the writer's art; we have scaled the intellectual Mount Olympus of writing and come down again the other side, changed, but not perhaps for the better.
    D) Not an easy work to read, *Jacques* goes down less like a smooth glass of wine and more like a sharp medicine that fights you every step of the way.

16. Which of the following would most directly disprove the hypothesis of Mr. John Lea?
  A) Miners encamped in tents downwind of cholera wards in south central Colorado suffered very low incidents of the disease.
  B) Cattle ranchers in Montana contracted cholera only after having moved their herd from the north to the south along the Missouri River.
  C) A number of settlements in Nevada suffered low incidents of cholera even though they had soft water.
  D) A city in New Mexico experienced high incidences of cholera after a group of travelers with cholera visited the city.

17. Which of the following is the best characterization of the author's views on the theory of cholera's transmission via airborne effluvia?
  A) Irruptive
  B) Rebarbative
  C) Supercilious
  D) Solipsistic

This page intentionally left blank.

Passage IV

Said Prof. Pfleiderer to the writer in the winter of 1897: "I am sorry to know that the Japanese are deficient in religious nature." In an elaborate article entitled, "Wanted, a Religion," a missionary describes the three so-called religions of Japan, Buddhism, Confucianism, and Shintoism, and shows to his satisfaction that none of these has the essential characteristics of religion.

The impression that the Japanese people are not religious is due to various facts. The first is that for about three hundred years the intelligence of the nation has been dominated by Confucian thought. The tendency of Confucian ethics is to leave the gods severely alone, although their existence is not absolutely denied. When Confucianism became popular in Japan, the educated part of the nation broke away from Buddhism, which, for nearly a thousand years, had been universally dominant. To them Buddhism seemed superstitious in the extreme. It was not uncommon for them to criticise it severely. For this reason, beyond doubt, has Western agnosticism found so easy an entrance into Japan. Yet this statement implies that agnosticism is new to Japan.

And various other considerations demand our notice. Many Westerns have exceedingly shallow conceptions of the real nature of religion or the part it plays in the development of society and of the individual. But we do not pronounce the West irreligious because of ignorant or irreverent utterances. We must not judge the religious many by the irreligious few.

Particular beliefs and practices of religion have indeed changed and passed away, even in Christianity. But the essentially religious nature of man has re-asserted itself in every case, and the outward expressions of that nature have thereby only become freer from elements of error and superstition. Exactly this is taking place in Japan to-day. The apparent irreligion of to-day is the groundwork of the purer religion of to-morrow.

If the Japanese are emotional and sentimental, we should expect them to be, perhaps more than most peoples, religious. This expectation is not disappointed by a study of their history. The universality of the respect and adoration, not to say love, bestowed throughout the ages of history on the "Kami" (the multitudinous Gods of Shintoism), is a standing witness to the depth of the religious feeling in the Japanese heart. True, it is associated with the sentiments of love of ancestors and country, with filial piety and loyalty; but these, so far from lowering the religion, make it more truly religious?

[Adapted from *Evolution of the Japanese: Social and Psychic*, by Sidney L. Gulic, 1903.]

18. Based on the passage, it can be assumed that one of the reasons Confucianism is not considered a religion is
    A) that it fails to make a definite ruling on the status of the supernatural.
    B) its unfriendliness to established religions such as Buddhism.
    C) that it does not definitely accept the existence of gods.
    D) its interpretation of the Kami.

19. According to the passage, irreligiosity in Japan can be traced at least as far back as
    A) the advent of Shintoism.
    B) the arrival of Western agnosticism.
    C) the first pushback against Christian missionaries.
    D) the arrival of Confucianism.

20. According to the passage, which of the following is a necessary element of true religion?
    A) Superstition.
    B) Consistency in tradition and beliefs.
    C) A strong consensus.
    D) Love.

21. The passage author likely would not agree with which of the following statements about religion?
    A) Religious convictions remain a constant anchor in a changing cultural landscape.
    B) Despite a sometimes vocal and ignorant minority, the West is by and large a religious bastion.
    C) The purest religions have shed their old superstitions.
    D) Religion is integral to the human spirit.

22. In China, a drop-off in religious belief coincided with political changes in the mid-20ᵗʰ century. According to the passage, this could be interpreted as
    A) a natural progression towards agnosticism.
    B) a coincidental result of Confucianism's periodic return to Chinese fashion.
    C) due to the fundamentally irreligious nature of Asian societies reasserting itself.
    D) a transition period to a purer religion, free of outmoded beliefs.

23. Which of the following, if true, would most weaken the author's argument about the "essentially religious nature of man"?
    A) Those countries with the longest traditions of religious belief have the highest rates of religious identification.
    B) A longitudinal study finds that, without regular reinforcement, religious people lose their faith at markedly higher rate than agnostics or atheists spontaneously find faith.
    C) Over time, everyday and household superstitions are found to become less prevalent.
    D) An increase in the worldwide percentage of people with religious faith can be attributed to the two fastest-growing religions.

24. The author would likely agree that, far in the future
    A) religious conviction will be essentially universal.
    B) religion will have become effectively extinct.
    C) today's religious plurality will persist, though the relative frequencies are likely to shift.
    D) beliefs within nations will have homogenized, with blocks of both faithful and atheistic countries.

Passage V

It is not in the Indian experience to seriously consider limits on family size. Yet as early as the 1960's, the exploding Indian population began to surface as a problem, discussed first only in the rarefied atmosphere of a few Indian universities, but eventually in the halls of governmental power. The population control movement made itself felt in a number of ways: the One Child Tax Credit, the subsidization of medical care for women willing to be sterilized, and the encouragement of smaller family size through a number of other economic and cultural approaches.

The major driving force behind the population control movement was a simple concern about food. Government officials tracking the nation's agricultural production had estimated that India's ability to produce enough food to feed its people would be outstripped by the growing population by 1980. Given that the world markets for staple foods was experiencing unprecedentedly high prices through the 1960's, policymakers were understandably concerned. By 1964, Indian production of rice had peaked, and most regions were starting to see declines in production as soil fertility declined.

Attempts to address the overpopulation issue generally fell into two broad categories: economic and cultural. The usual economic approach was to either offer tax credits to married couples who choose to have no children or one child or to levy large increases in taxes on those couples choosing to have more than one. This latter approach was taken, to dramatic effect, by China in the 1970's. Fortunately for the citizens of India, their government did not follow the draconian "One Child Policy" seen in China. Cultural approaches, on the other hand, involve government subsidy of the production of works intended to emphasize the benefits of having fewer children. Such works included direct publication of informational pamphlets (much like "public service announcements" seen on American TV) distributed to doctors' offices and, more indirectly, subsidization of movies and television programs featuring protagonists whose decision to have a small family is presented in a sympathetic light.

At the extreme end of the scale, governments have attempted to control the population through direct medical intervention. Ironically, the greatest practitioner of this approach was the United States. Despite never having an overpopulation problems akin to China or India, both federal and state governments in the U.S. had several policies in the beginning of the 20th century that either encouraged or forced sterilization upon certain people. Almost uniformly, those people were racial minorities, those with psychological problems, or those who encountered the criminal justice system. Such practices were almost entirely halted by the middle of the century, but a few vestiges remain even today.

Despite the expenditure of tremendous amounts of time and money to address the issue, the government's concerns about overpopulation in India were eventually rendered moot. The Green Revolution came late to India, but it eventually came. The combination of plant recombination, carefully planned irrigation, and pesticide use allowed grain production worldwide to skyrocket. Beginning in Mexico in 1948, under the direction of Norman Borlaug, Mexican farmers found they could vastly increase their corn and wheat yields. In the mid 1960's, Borlaug brought his approach to India. By cultivating a particular strain of dwarf rice, Indian farmers found they were able to grow plants that could sustain much higher yields than previously possible. By 1970, the rice output of a single acre of land had doubled, and presently is over triple that ever achieved prior to 1960. By the end of the century, India became the world's most successful rice producer, and exports tons of excess food annually. The Green Revolution is often credited with having saved over a billion people from starving to death, and the greatest portion of that impact was felt in India.

[Adapted from "Three Little Indians" by M.R. Green, 2011.]

25. The author would most likely *disagree* with which of the following assertions?
   A) In large part, the effectiveness of India's efforts to curb overpopulation were irrelevant.
   B) The path to population control taken by India's government was more beneficent than was that taken by China's government.
   C) The Green Revolution brought about an increase in food production that outstripped the food needs of India's exploding population.
   D) The Indian government worked both directly and indirectly to curb the Indian population beginning in the first half of the twentieth century.

26. Which of the following government policies would the author most strongly endorse?

    A) favoring economic approaches over cultural approaches to encouraging smaller family size

    B) linking federal welfare dollars for unwed mothers to a requirement to submit to sterilization

    C) creating federally-owned movie studios to produce films with protagonists with only one child

    D) subsidies for the further development of crop strains that can increase yield per acre

27. An Indian government official who advocates economic incentives to small family size would likely endorse which of the following?

  I. tax credits to married couples who choose to have one child or no children

 II. a negative income tax for adults choosing to remain unmarried and childless

 III. a graduated taxation scale in which families pay taxes that increase slightly with each additional child born

    A) I only

    B) I and II only

    C) I and III only

    D) II and III only

28. The passage information most strongly supports the inference that:

    A) population controls through direct medical intervention were popular throughout Europe.

    B) the level of food production in the United States has generally been adequate for its population.

    C) the horrors of eugenics carried out in certain countries in the mid-20th century led to the total eradication of forced sterilization throughout the world.

    D) the present global average rice production per acre is more than 300% that of the average rice production per acre in the 1950's.

29. If, in the 21st century, the effects of the Green Revolution in India were to both spread to the whole globe and to have had further improvements in their effectiveness, which of the following is most likely?

    A) Increases in the average tax benefit for unmarried childless adults.

    B) Further investment in new genetic engineering technologies to alter crops to be more pest resistant.

    C) Governments would finally end population controls through direct medical intervention.

    D) Government subsidies for cultural works encouraging a small family would decrease or disappear.

30. Suppose that, over the course of a decade, changing climactic conditions lead to decreased crop productivity such that India finds itself with a looming overpopulation problem again. According to the passage information, which of the following is most likely?

    A) Changes to the tax structure at the federal level would take place.

    B) Given the failures of previous population control efforts, no new population control movement would surface in either academia or the government.

    C) Researchers would develop new strains of crops that would allow for a second Green Revolution.

    D) Local government agencies throughout India would be forced to import food staples from the U.S.

31. Which of the following events would likely cause world governments to increase the amounts of tax subsidies given to married couples who have only one child?

    A) The world population rises to a level that outstrips the ability of agricultural producers to create enough food.

    B) China's One Child Policy demonstrates itself to be effective in bringing a nation's population into line with its capacity to grow or purchase food.

    C) Courts around the world determine that engaging in either forced sterilization or coerced sterilization is a violation of basic human rights.

    D) A new technology that can cheaply and quickly create fresh water for crop irrigation is discovered.

Half Section 3: Answer Key and Explanations

Passage 1
1. C
2. C
3. C
4. C
5. D

Passage 2
6. C
7. B
8. C
9. C
10. D

Passage 3
11. C
12. C
13. D
14. D
15. C
16. A
17. C

Passage 4
18. C
19. D
20. D
21. A
22. D
23. B
24. A

Passage 5
25. D
26. D
27. B
28. B
29. D
30. A
31. A

Passage I Explanation

We have to realize the peculiar relations between **Europe**, ancient and mediaeval, and the great empires of **Eastern Asia**. The two civilizations had never been in direct contact. Yet in a sense they were always connected. The **Greeks** and the **Romans** had at least vague reports of peoples who lived on the far eastern confines of the world, beyond even the conquests of **Alexander the Great** in **Hindustan**. It is certain, too, that Europe and Asia **had always traded with one another in a strange and unconscious fashion**. The spices and silks of the unknown East passed westward from trader to trader, from caravan to caravan, until they reached the **Persian Gulf**, the **Red Sea**, and, at last, the **Mediterranean**.

Key terms: Europe, Asia, Greeks, Romans, Alexander the Great, Hindustan, Persian Gulf, Red Sea, Mediterranean

Contrast: lack of knowledge/direct communication between Europe/Asia vs. near continuous but unconscious commercial contact

Cause-and-effect: unbroken line of traders and caravans tie together nations despite ignorance of each other

The journey was so slow, so tedious, the goods passed from hand to hand so often, that when the **Phoenician**, Greek, or Roman merchants bought them their origin had been forgotten. For century after century this trade continued. When **Rome fell**, other peoples of the **Mediterranean continued the Eastern trade**. With the **Crusades**, all the treasures which the warriors of the Cross brought home, helped to **impress on the mind of Europe the surpassing riches** of the East.

Key terms: Phoenician

Cause-and-effect: Rome falls, other peoples take over their role in Eastern trade; Crusades increase European interest in Eastern trade

Gradually a new interest was added. As time went on doubts increased regarding the true shape of the earth. If the **earth was really a globe, it might be possible to go round it** and to reappear on the farther side of the horizon. Then the East might be reached, not only across the deserts of Persia and Tartary, but also by striking out into the boundless ocean.

Contrast: flat Earth vs. globe

Cause-and-effect: belief in round Earth stoked interest in exploratory sea journey to Western ocean

It was the stern logic of events which compelled the enterprise. **The Turks swept westward. Arabia**, **Syria**, the **Isles of Greece**, and, at last, in **1453, Constantinople** itself, fell into their hands. The Eastern Empire, the last survival of the Empire of the Romans, perished beneath the sword of **Mahomet**. Then the **pathway by land to Asia**, to the fabled empires of **Cathay** and **Cipango**, was **blocked by the Turkish conquest**. Commerce, however, remained alert and enterprising, and **men's minds soon turned to the hopes of a western passage** which should provide a new route to the Indies.

[Adapted from *Chronicles of Canada*, by Stephen Leacock, 1915.]

Key terms: Turks, Mahomet, Cathay, Cipango

Cause-and-effect: Turkish conquest prevented land trade between Europe/Mediterranean and Asia; lack of Eastern route increased commercial interest in western sea passage

Main Idea: Trade between Europe and eastern Asia was very slow due to the distances involved and the political turmoil that hampered trade. Ultimately, European traders sought to sail west due to war by the Turks.

1. According to the passage, what was the easternmost outpost the Ancient Romans were aware of in detail?
   A) Constantinople
   B) Cipango
   C) **Hindustan**
   D) Istanbul

The Ancient Greeks and Romans were aware of the easternmost extent of Alexander the Great's conquests, which ended in Hindustan. According to the passage, the peoples beyond this point were vaguely known, and no names are mentioned. C is therefore a match.

A: This was the capital of the Eastern Roman Empire.
B: This is the easternmost of the options listed, but the passage only mentions later Westerners being aware of its existence.
D: This is a city in modern Turkey, not information found in the passage. There's no reason, based on the passage itself, to choose this option.

2. Which of the following is not cited in the passage as part of the merchant chain that brought Eastern goods to the Europe?
   A) Cathay
   B) Desert caravans across Tartary
   C) **The Dead Sea**
   D) Phoenician merchants

The Dead Sea is never mentioned in the passage, although the Red Sea is. It's important to check on a detail-oriented question like this, since memory can be unreliable on such specifics.

A: Cathay is mentioned as one of the Eastern empires providing goods in a later paragraph.
B, D: These are both mentioned as links in the supply chain in different parts of the passage.

3. Suppose that Mahomet had been defeated by the Persians, who went on to push eastward and establish high-volume trade routes between the Mediterranean and Far East. Given the information in the passage, how would this likely have affected the search for a western passage to the Indies?
   A) The enterprise likely would have been initiated in Constantinople rather than Western Europe.
   B) The journey would have begun and proceeded in much the way.
   C) **The search for a western passage wouldn't have happened until later.**
   D) The search for a western passage would have started much earlier.

The passage makes a causal connection between the interruption in trade resulting from the Turkish conquest and the impetus for expeditions seeking a western passage. If land-based trade continued unchecked, or, as here, increased, it follows that these westward sea journeys would not have reason to occur as soon as they did.

A: There's no information in the passage to support this. Given that Constantinople is significantly eastward of Western Europe, however, it seems they would have proportionally less reason to seek a western route. It's not necessary to know any details about Constantinople beyond those given in the passage to make this determination.
B: The passage makes clear that the Turkish conquest was a factor in the search for a western passage.
D: This is the opposite of what should be expected.

4. One of the outcomes resulting from European expeditions seeking a westward route to the Indies was European nations becoming aware of the American continents. Which of the following outcomes might have been expected based on the information in the passage?

    A) Spread of unfamiliar diseases caused heavy losses amongst indigenous peoples.

    B) Christian nations sent missionaries and soldiers to conquer and baptize.

    C) **<u>Fur offered for trade in Canada led to a heavy increase in Atlantic ship traffic.</u>**

    D) American domestic crops transformed European cooking.

All of these statements are factually true, but we're interested in determining what could have been predicted from the passage alone. The passage showed that as long as Eastern and Western nations had something the other wanted, trade would occur unless forcibly interrupted. This implies that contact between Europe and the Americas would also result in a steady flow of goods, given a desired product. The situation C is in line with this.

A: The passage never discusses disease.

B: The passage touches on religious wars but many of the nations mentioned know and care little about each other's cultures or beliefs. Based on the passage alone, religion is implied to be irrelevant more often than not.

D: The effect of goods from a newly discovered trading partner on the culture receiving those goods is not discussed in the passage.

5. Given the information in the passage, which of the following, if true, might have resulted in the flow of Eastern goods to Europe prior to the Turkish conquest being less than it actually was?

    A) If Alexander the Great had never been born.

    B) If the Phoenician civilization had fallen with the Roman.

    C) Harsher travel conditions in the Atlantic.

    D) **<u>War between Persia and Arabia.</u>**

War in the desert countries (but against the Turk invaders) is exactly what interrupted the trade route in real history, so war between Persia and Arabia would surely at least hinder the progress of traders connecting the Eastern nations with the Mediterranean. The specific example we're given of something that hampers trade was war (specifically the conquest by the Turks) so it stands to reason that an earlier war would also have hampered trade.

A: There's no indication, at least in the passage, that Alexander the Great was responsible for stitching together the trade route in the first place, maintaining it, or otherwise affecting trade one way or another.

B: The Phoenicians are mentioned as links in the Mediterranean part of the supply chain. However, they are one of many, and it's implied that when one group disappears (as the Romans did), another will and has stepped in.

C: The Atlantic is irrelevant to this portion of history, wherein the only connection between Europe and Asia was land-based.

Passage II Explanation

The best-known examples of **metafiction appear abruptly in the 1960's** as examples of a fully realized mode of ironic writing **without any obvious predecessors**. Metafiction is best understood a form of novel in which the author never lets the reader forget that he is reading a novel. Rather than aim for a realistic tone that permits the reader to "lose himself" in the book, **meta-fiction forces the reader to contemplate the physical act of reading itself**. Despite features of meta-fiction that suggest it grew out of earlier trends in Romantic literature, **few critics could directly link the style to any particular predecessors**. Recently, a potent reevaluation of the work *Jacques the Fatalist and his Master* **by Denis Diderot**, suggests that this work may **bridge the gap** between metafiction and earlier writing.

Key terms: metafiction, Jacques the Fatalist, Denis Diderot

Opinion: Jacques may help link metafiction to earlier literary traditions

Cause-and-effect: metafiction pushes the reader to think about the physical act of reading

Jacques the Fatalist and his Master was written between 1765 and 1780, although it was not published as a full French version until 1796. **At the time, the work was largely unappreciated** and received, at best, **lukewarm reviews** in Germany and elsewhere outside Diderot's homeland. The work centers around the relationship between Jacques and his master, who is unnamed throughout the novel. The master instructs Jacques to regale him with tales of his various romantic affairs to pass the time as they travel. As Jacques speaks, he is **continually interrupted** by other characters, who are themselves interrupted. Halfway through the work, **Diderot even introduces "The Reader" who evinces continual exasperation** with the characters and pushes them to get back on track with the tale. Within this **fractured structure**, the characters are consistently **contradictory**: one chapter focuses on two best friends who constantly duel each other, dealing grave wounds in the process. Finally, the **unwieldy tale** includes large sections lifted entirely from the earlier novel *Tristam Shandy*.

Key terms: The Reader

Opinion: Author doesn't seem to like the book very much – calls it fractured, unwieldy, lukewarm; critics at the time didn't like it either.

The **structure of *Jacques*** helps demonstrate why metafiction developed the traits that it did. Metafiction's goal is to **keep the reader focused on the act of reading itself**. It does this by eschewing the usual linear narrative structure. If the reader's expectations are wholly thwarted, he is put in a state of "high alert" that does **not permit him to lose himself in the book**. Metafiction also plays with the typography and physical layout of the words on the page. By continually **shifting the typeface**, or laying the words in groups or orientations other than a typical paragraph, the reader's attention is focused on the level of the words on the page itself rather than on the meaning behind those words. Finally, metafiction **shifts narrative voice**, making use of the second person (e.g. "You open the door.") to address the reader directly.

Key terms: structure, typeface

Cause-and-effect: shifting layout, typeface, voice lets metafiction works keep the reader on their toes and focused on the act of reading itself

In *Jacques*, **we may see predecessors** of many of these traits. In the earliest German translations, which predate even the first full publication in France, the **book shifts from traditional paragraphs** to the layout more commonly used in **scripts and back again**, with no seeming relationship between the layout and the content of the story itself. In addition, by including **"the Reader"** as a character, Diderot anticipated the use of second person by metafiction authors who came two centuries later.

Opinion: Author sees connection between Jacques and metafiction

But ultimately it may be the **breaking of narrative structure** which reveals the most about how and why metafiction developed. As early as the late 1700's, critics spoke of **literature as a "dying art"**. It was believed that everything that could be said had been said. "After [H]omer and Shakespeare," one critic opined, "what [is] left for us to say?" Much of the **artistic fervor** on the Continent during the time was **found in the theater**, and it is believed that **authors sought to capture the immediacy of live plays**, most notably the theater of the absurd. The wild shifts in the narrative of these plays were seen to have great comedic effect, and we can now see that ***Jacques sought to capture that energy and humor***. In that regard**, we may draw a straight line** directly from *Jacques* to the 1960's, in which writers sought to use **metafiction to capture the energy** of the counter-cultural movement and its chosen form of self-expression: **rock and roll music**.

[Adapted from "Meta-me and Meta-you" by K. O'Connell-Choate, Sussex County Press, 2011]

Cause-and-effect: Jacques and metafiction used similar techniques to capture the energy of another art form – theater for Jacques and rock music for metafiction.

Main Idea: Despite seeming like it came out of nowhere, metafiction does have connections to earlier literature, most notably Jacques. Both used similar techniques in an effort to capture the energy of another art form into their literature.

6. Why does the author include a discussion of literary critics who felt that literature was a dying art?
    A) To indicate how old the notion is that "everything that could be said ha[s] been said"
    B) To illustrate why metafiction sought to address the reader directly in the second person narrative voice
    C) **To argue that the metafiction of the 1960's bears a direct relationship with *Jacques***
    D) To demonstrate that critics are often wrong when they make assessments that bear on the future of an art

The critics mentioned in the question are discussed in the final paragraph. In that paragraph we see the author's central thesis: that *Jacques*'s relationship to theater is a predecessor and analogue to metafiction's relationship to rock and roll music. That's closest to choice C.

A: The idea that there's nothing new under the sun certainly is an old idea, but the age of that cliché doesn't bear on the author's thesis in the final paragraph.
B: We're told that using the second voice was done in order to keep the reader alert and this is discussed in paragraph three, not the final paragraph.
D: While critics may often be wrong, quoting a single example doesn't prove that they're often wrong, nor does the author try to make that point.

7. If it were later discovered that in Diderot's original manuscript of *Jacques* that he included several sections of dialogue written upside down, this would:
    A) demonstrate the sloppiness with which printers approached their art in the 18th century.
    B) **further support the author's thesis by providing a link between *Jacques* and later metafiction.**
    C) provide a concrete reason why the work was poorly received.
    D) weaken the author's contention that *Jacques* contained features that focused the reader on the physical act of reading.

Having text printed upside down would force the reader to turn the book around. This would be the kind of technique metafiction would use to force the reader to remain focused on the physical act of reading itself. That *Jacques* did such a thing strengthens the author's thesis about the connection between *Jacques* and later metafiction.

A: This is out of scope. The technology for printing books is never discussed.

C: We don't know if readers of the time would have found upside down printing amusing, interesting, or wholly negative.

D: This is the opposite of what the question says. Having to turn the book upside down would force you to be aware of the physical act of reading a book.

8. The passage provides information to answer all of the following questions EXCEPT:
    A) What feature of metafiction made the reader focus on the physical act of reading?
    B) The relationship between *Jacques* and the theater of the time is most closely analogous to the relationship between the meta-fiction of the 1960's and what art?
    C) **Did any writers from the 1960's other than writers of metafiction make use of the second person?**
    D) Does metafiction have any features that it shares with earlier Romantic fiction?

The author doesn't discuss other writers from the 1960's and thus the passage contains no information to answer the question in choice C.

A: This question is answered in paragraph 3.

B: This question is answered in the final paragraph.

D: This is answered in paragraph 1.

9. Which of the following, if discovered, would most *weaken* the author's thesis?
    A) No metafiction writers from the 1960's had read, or were even aware of *Jacques*.
    B) Even readers who are reading a traditional narrative maintain some level of attention on the physical act of reading.
    C) **Diderot was unaware of developments in arts outside literature.**
    D) It was common in the 18th century for novelists to quote entire passages from earlier works.

As our main idea tells us, the author's thesis is that there is a link between metafiction and earlier literature in *Jacques* because both attempted to capture the energy of another art form in their literature. If choice C is true, then Diderot could not have possibly been trying to capture the energy of the "theater of the absurd" since he would have been unaware of it.

A: The author isn't attempting to argue that metafiction writers themselves were directly trying to imitate *Jacques* but rather that there was a literary tradition preceding metafiction that included some of its elements.

B: That metafiction focused almost entirely on the physical act of reading doesn't mean other readers aren't somewhat aware of the act of reading.

D: The fact that *Jacques* quotes from an earlier work is a random supporting detail not directly related to the author's thesis.

10. Literary analysts may find themselves discussing the subjects of their inquiry in a less than objective way. Which of the following would the author of this passage most likely have written?
    A) *Tristam Shandy*, by contrast, is a masterful construct that rewards both the casual reader and the most focused literary analyst.
    B) *Jacques* is a trifle of a book, with a quick breezy air that belies its philosophical heft.
    C) Metafiction leaves us feeling like we have read the ultimate expression of the writer's art; we have scaled the intellectual Mount Olympus of writing and come down again the other side, changed, but not perhaps for the better.
    D) **Not an easy work to read, *Jacques* goes down less like a smooth glass of wine and more like a sharp medicine that fights you every step of the way.**

This question asks us to take the author's general discussion and see which answer choice uses subjective language while still staying within the author's views. He describes *Jacques* as fractured, contradictory, and unpopular. Those words suggest choice D – that *Jacques* is not an easy work to read.

A: We don't see anything in the passage that lets us infer the author's opinion of *Tristam Shandy*.
B: "Quick" and "breezy" don't fit the word choice the author used in describing *Jacques*.
C: "Ultimate" is too strong for what the author has given us.

Passage III Explanation

An **objection** that has repeatedly been made to **the propagation of cholera through the medium of water**, is, that everyone who drinks of the water ought to have the disease at once. This objection arises from **mistaking** the department of **science** to which the communication of cholera belongs, and looking on it as a question of chemistry, **instead of one of natural history**, as it undoubtedly is. It **cannot be supposed** that a morbid poison, which has the property, under suitable circumstances, of reproducing its kind, should **be capable of being diluted indefinitely** in water, like a chemical salt; and therefore it is **not to be presumed that the cholera-poison would be equally diffused through every particle of the water.**

Key Terms: propagation, morbid poison, diluted, diffused

Opinions: Some people think that if cholera is spread through water, everyone who drinks the water should get cholera.

Contrasts: The author contrasts looking at the spread of cholera from a scientific standpoint and from a natural history standpoint.

Cause and Effect: Because cholera can reproduce itself in the right circumstances, there will be unequal amounts of cholera in the water supply.

As regards the morbid matter of cholera, **many other circumstances**, besides the quantity of it which is present in a river at different periods of the epidemic, must influence the chances of its being swallowed, such as its remaining in a butt or other vessel **till it is decomposed or devoured by animalcules**, or its merely **settling to the bottom** and remaining there. In the case of the pump-well in Broad Street, Golden Square, if the cholera poison was contained in the **minute whitish flocculi, visible** on close inspection to the naked eye, **some persons might drink of the water without taking any, as they soon settled to the bottom of the vessel**.

Key Terms: animalcules, flocculi

Cause and Effect: If the cholera decomposes, is eaten by other organisms, or settles to the bottom of the container, the person might not consume it/contract cholera.

It is not necessary to oppose any other theories in order to establish the principles I am endeavoring to explain, for the **field I have entered on was almost unoccupied**. The **best attempt** at explaining the phenomena of cholera, which previously existed, was probably that which supposed that the disease was communicated **by effluvia given off** from the patient into the surrounding air, **and inhaled by others into the lungs**; but this view required its advocates to draw very largely on what is called **predisposition**, in order to account for the numbers who approach near to the patient without being affected, whilst others acquire the disease without any near approach. It also **failed entirely to account for the sudden and violent outbreaks of the disease**, such as that which occurred in the, neighborhood of Golden Square.

Key Terms: effluvia, predisposition

Opinions: Some earlier theories were that cholera was spread through effluvia that are given off by patients into the air and then inhaled by others.

Cause and Effect: According to this theory, the effluvia didn't directly result in cholera but rather "predisposition" someone to contracting cholera.

Another view having a certain number of advocates is that **cholera depends on an unknown something** in the atmosphere which becomes localized, and has **its effects increased by the gases** given off from decomposing animal and vegetable matters. This hypothesis is, however, **rendered impossible** by the motion of the atmosphere, and, even in the absence of wind, **by the laws which govern the diffusion of aeriform bodies**; moreover, the connection between cholera and offensive effluvia is **by no means such as to indicate cause and effect**; even in London, as was before mentioned, many places where offensive effluvia are very abundant have been visited very lightly by cholera, whilst the comparatively open and cleanly districts of Kennington and Clapham have suffered severely. If inquiry were made, a far closer connection would be found to exist between offensive effluvia and the itch, than between these effluvia and cholera; yet as the cause of itch is well known, we are quite aware that **this connection is not one of cause and effect.**

Key Terms: diffusion of aeriform bodies

Opinions: Another opinion of how cholera spreads is via "something" in the atmosphere that is intensified by the gases given off by decaying plants and animals.

Contrasts: The author contrasts the rates of cholera in locations with heavy effluvia and in locations with light effluvia, indicating that the levels of effluvia don't have anything to do with the rates of cholera.

Mr. John Lea, of Cincinnati, has advanced what he calls **a geological theory of cholera**. He supposes that the cholera poison, **which he believes to exist in the air about the sick**, **requires the existence of calcareous or magnesian salts in the drinking-water** to give it effect. He says that, in the western districts of the United States, the cholera passed round the arenacious, and spent its fury on the calcareous regions; and that it **attacked with deadly effect those who use the calcareous water, while it passed by those who used sandstone or soft water**. The connection which Mr. Lea has observed between cholera and the water is highly interesting; although it probably admits of a very different explanation from the one he has given.

Key Terms: geological theory of cholera, arenacious, calcareous water

Opinions: Mr. John Lea thinks that cholera exists in the air about the sick. He also thinks that the cholera in the air needs some other salts in the water in order to take effect.

Cause and Effect: According to Mr. John Lea, drinking hard water causes one to contract cholera.

11. If it had been true that many places where "offensive effluvia" were abundant had been visited severely by cholera, while the comparatively open and cleanly districts had been visited lightly, how would this information affect the author's argument concerning the transmission of cholera?
    A) It would disprove the author's argument.
    B) It would affirm the author's argument.
    C) **It would have no effect on the author's argument.**
    D) It would challenge the author's argument.

In order to answer this question, the reader has to comprehend the difference between correlation and causation. The reader must consider that the author establishes that the correlation between effluvia and the itch did not indicate a cause and effect relationship. The correct choice is choice C because choice C is consistent with the position that correlation does not equal causation. While a correlation between abundant effluvia and high instances of cholera would be worth noting, the correlation would have no effect on the author's argument concerning the transmission of cholera via water.

A, D: These choices suggest that this correlation would somehow weaken or negate the author's argument concerning the transmission of cholera via water. Not only does this information NOT weaken or negate the author's claim, but it also does not prove a cause and effect relationship between abundant effluvia and cholera.
B: This information is not related to the author's argument concerning the transmission of cholera in water; it would also not affirm the author's argument that cholera is not transmitted via effluvia.

12. Earlier in the essay, the author states that "It may therefore be safely concluded that this influence is pretty generally admitted by the profession. It must not be disguised, however, that medical men are not yet generally convinced that the

disease is actually communicated from person to person by the morbid matter being swallowed…" Which of the following concepts from the passage could NOT be plausibly supposed to be the "influence" referred to by the author?

    A) "…the medium of water…"
    B) "…the motion of the atmosphere…"
    C) **"…the sudden and violent outbreaks of the disease…"**
    D) "…effluvia given off from the patient…"

The "influence" in the quote is most likely referring to an external factor that affects the communication of cholera, so the correct choice is choice C because the sudden and violent outbreaks of the disease is not an external factor that could affect the communication of cholera. The "influence" in the quote is most likely something that causes the sudden and violent break out, not the break out itself.

A, B, D: All three of these choices are discussed in the passage as possible external factors that influence or affect the spread of cholera (although some are disproven). So, without knowing what comes in the rest of the passage, it is possible that the author could be talking about any of these factors in the quote.

13. Which of the following study findings would NOT provide support for the influence of sourced water on mortality from cholera?

    A) "There were several instances in which persons, especially maid-servants and young men, died of cholera within a few days after coming from the country to a house supplied with polluted water"
    B) "The outbreak of cholera in the Baltic fleet occurred within forty-eight hours after pollution from sick-wards had been taken on board"
    C) "Nearly all of the persons drinking water from a polluted pump-well…were attacked together, while the population around experience no increase of cholera"
    D) **"In these instances, the evacuations remain the greater part of this time in a dry state on the soiled linen, without undergoing any change."**

In order to answer this question, the reader must evaluate each statement as it relates to water and the transmission of/mortality from cholera and identify the statement that does not support a hypothesis that cholera is spread through water. The correct choice is choice D because the study finding has little to nothing to do with water. Choice D concerns the "evacuations" of a patient and the condition of those stools. This finding does not relate to sourced water or its influence on mortality from cholera.

A, B, C: Each of these choices makes a connection between sourced water and cholera.

14. Based on the information in the passage, which of the following statements would indicate that yellow fever is communicated in the same way as the author believes is true of cholera?

    A) "The fever is more endemic in the high lands and in the desert, than on the low lands on the shores of the Mediterranean."
    B) "Persons are infected with the fever *only* when exposed to secretions and discharges of those who have already contracted the fever, particularly in instances where such exposure is prolonged and frequent."
    C) "The low rate of mortality amongst medical men and undertakers is of notice...there is no reason why these callings should particularly expose persons to the malady."
    D) **"When the fever visited this country, it was most fatal in London, York, Winchester, and certain other towns having a river of fresh water passing through them…it is twice as fatal in districts south of the Thames as in those on the north."**

To answer this question, the reader must first understand that the author believes cholera to be transmitted via water (though the exact mechanism remains unknown), and compare that stated belief with the mechanisms of communication indicated in the answer choices below. The correct choice is D because this choice attributes the spread of yellow fever to the presence of a source of fresh water, which corresponds with the author's theory of the "propagation of cholera through the medium of water."

A: This answer choice makes no statement regarding the method of communicating yellow fever and can therefore not be the correct answer.

B: The author implies a belief in the "propagation of cholera through the medium of water" but makes no explicit connection between the water, and the "secretions and discharges" of those suffering from cholera.

C: The author makes no statements in the passage about physicians and undertakers at all; we can therefore draw no conclusions about the communication of cholera to those populations based on available evidence. This choice is not as good of a choice as D.

15. Based on the information in the passage, which groups of people would those who believe in alternate theories consider most at risk for contracting cholera?
  I. **Nurses who cleanse the bodies of the dead indoors prior to burial**
 II. Barristers at work in a courtroom located in the vicinity of many sufferers of cholera
III. **Rag-pickers scavenging through the homes of those who died**
    A) II only
    B) III only
    C) **I and III only**
    D) I and II only

To answer this question, the reader must know that alternative theories cited by the author involve "offensive effluvia" coming from the bodies of those affected, and an "unknown something" in the air, the effect of which is possibly exacerbated by gases from decomposing living things. Choice C is the correct choice because both I and III are likely to contract cholera according to these alternative theories. Nurses who cleanse the bodies of the dead would be directly exposed to the "offensive effluvia" cited by one alternative theory from the passage and rag-pickers scavenging through the homes of those who died would be exposed to the same gases that the dead would have been, as well as their "offensive effluvia."

A, D: This choice is not the correct choice because II is not true: such barristers would be neither directly exposed to "offensive effluvia" nor the "unknown something in the air", and certainly not the gases given off by decomposing living things cited by another alternate theory from the passage.

B: This choice is not the correct choice because it excludes I which is also true.

16. Which of the following would most directly disprove the hypothesis of Mr. John Lea?
    A) **Miners encamped in tents downwind of cholera wards in south central Colorado suffered very low incidents of the disease.**
    B) Cattle ranchers in Montana contracted cholera only after having moved their herd from the north to the south along the Missouri River.
    C) A number of settlements in Nevada suffered low incidents of cholera even though they had soft water.
    D) A city in New Mexico experienced high incidences of cholera after a group of travelers with cholera visited the city.

B and D: No information provided in these answer choices disproves the notion proposed by Mr. Lea. In fact, the information in D could even be interpreted as supporting, though not conclusive, evidence.

C: Mr. Lea proposes that two factors cause cholera; the presence of one without the other having no effect on the illness's transmission therefore neither proves nor disproves his supposition.

To answer this question, the reader must know that the hypothesis of Mr. John Lea is that cholera is contracted via the combining of two unrelated factors: one, the airborne transmission of something from the body of an affected individual, and the other, the presence in drinking water of certain key minerals. Choice A is the correct choice because miners sharing the same encampment would likely share the same type of water; if miners downwind of cholera wards don't catch the disease that provides evidence against the airborne transmission of one of Mr. Lea's theorized necessary factors.

17. Which of the following is the best characterization of the author's views on the theory of cholera's transmission via airborne effluvia?
    A) Irruptive
    B) Rebarbative
    C) **<u>Supercilious</u>**
    D) Solipsistic

To answer this question correctly, the reader has to have knowledge of the vocabulary words used in the answer choices, as well as infer that the author's tone and attitude towards the stated theory is dismissive or derisive. Choice C is the correct choice because supercilious means dismissive or derisive. This is exactly the author's tone towards the theory (notice the dismissiveness adopted when discussing the concept of "predisposition", for example). Some students may be confused by the author's characterization of the theory as the best of the previous attempts; the author states immediately prior however that previous research was rather thin, off-setting the supposed compliment. C must be the correct answer.

A: Irruptive stems from the verb "irrupt", to hastily enter in a forcible or violent manner. Nothing about the passage's tone indicates that this word would be appropriately used.
B: Rebarbative means "unattractive and objectionable". The author may believe that the theory of airborne effluvia is rebarbative (though the word is rather strong for the otherwise composed tone of the passage), but the word could hardly be used to describe the views of the author themselves.
D: Solipsistic means self-referential. We may conceive of the author's views as solipsistic, but the word isn't an objective way to characterize the author's views, and therefore not appropriate for use here.

Passage IV Explanation

Said **Prof. Pfleiderer** to the writer in the winter of 1897: "I am sorry to know that the **Japanese** are **deficient in religious nature**." In an elaborate article entitled, "**Wanted, a Religion**," a missionary describes the three **so-called** religions of Japan, **Buddhism**, **Confucianism**, and **Shintoism**, and shows to his satisfaction that **none of these has the essential characteristics of religion**.

Key terms: Prof. Pfleiderer, Japanese, Buddhism, Confucianism, Shintoism

Contrast: Japanese religions do not fit the mould of what defines a religion to Westerners

Opinion: Pfleiderer thinks irreligiosity is a deficiency; author and unnamed missionary believe Japanese religions not to be "real" religions

The impression that the Japanese people are not religious is due to various facts. The first is that for about three hundred years the intelligence of the nation has been dominated by **Confucian thought**. The tendency of Confucian ethics is to leave the gods severely alone, although their existence is not absolutely denied. When Confucianism became popular in Japan, the educated part of the nation **broke away from Buddhism**, which, for nearly a thousand years, had been universally dominant. To them Buddhism seemed superstitious in the extreme. It was not uncommon for them to criticise it severely. For this reason, beyond doubt, has **Western agnosticism** found so easy an entrance into Japan. Yet this statement **implies that agnosticism is new to Japan**.

Key terms: Confucian thought, Western agnosticism

Contrast: Confucianism agnostic towards gods vs. Buddhism highly superstitious

Cause-and-effect: introduction of Confucianism caused shift away from Buddhism for educated Japanese; Western agnosticism new to Japan, incorrectly implies that agnosticism as a whole is new

And various other considerations demand our notice. Many **Westerns** have exceedingly **shallow conceptions** of the real nature of religion or the part it plays in the development of society and of the individual. But we do not pronounce the West irreligious because of ignorant or irreverent utterances. We must not judge the religious many by the **irreligious few**.

Key terms: Westerns

Contrast: the West includes irreligious individuals, but a majority are still religious

Particular beliefs and practices of religion have indeed changed and passed away, even in **Christianity**. But the **essentially religious nature of man** has re-asserted itself in every case, and the outward expressions of that nature have thereby only become freer from elements of **error and superstition**. Exactly this is taking place in Japan to-day. The **apparent irreligion** of to-day is the groundwork of the **purer religion** of to-morrow.

Key terms: Christianity

Contrast: religious nature independent of error and superstition

Cause-and-effect: seeming irreligion is a step in the development of purer religion later

Opinion: humans are "essentially" religious; Japan is only apparently irreligious

If the Japanese are **emotional and sentimental**, we should expect them to be, perhaps more than most peoples, religious. This expectation is not disappointed by a study of their history. The universality of the respect and adoration, not to say love, bestowed throughout the ages of history on the "**Kami**" (the multitudinous Gods of Shintoism), is a standing witness to the depth of the religious feeling in the Japanese heart. True, it is associated with the sentiments of **love of ancestors and country**, with filial piety and loyalty; but these, so far from lowering the religion, make it **more truly religious**?

Key terms: emotional, sentimental, Kami

Cause-and-effect: love of Kami associated with love of ancestors and country

Opinion: true heartfelt love is the core of religious feeling, even when the love is not directed towards god(s)

Main Idea: Japanese appear to be irreligious but in fact have deep religious feeling, are in transition period to purer religion

18. Based on the passage, it can be assumed that one of the reasons Confucianism is not considered a religion is
    A) that it fails to make a definite ruling on the status of the supernatural.
    B) its unfriendliness to established religions such as Buddhism.
    C) **that it does not definitely accept the existence of gods.**
    D) its interpretation of the Kami.

The passage discusses Confucian thought in the second paragraph, after stating in paragraph one that it is not a religion. Relative to Buddhism, Confucianism is described as less superstitious, prevalent among the educated, and uninterested in (though neither denying nor affirming the existence of) gods. Confucianism's criticism of superstition is said to be the main reason Western agnosticism was easily accepted in Japan, implying that Confucian thought is itself agnostic due to its non-superstitious mindset (not due to its vendetta against Buddhism, which is incidental). Answer choice C is an imperfect match, but by far the best one available, as the passage never equates superstition with belief in gods. A does not work, because a definite ruling has been made. B is not the defining characteristic of Confucianism but an example of it (its impatience for superstition). The Kami are never discussed with reference to Confucianism, which eliminates D.

19. According to the passage, irreligiosity in Japan can be traced at least as far back as
    A) the advent of Shintoism.
    B) the arrival of Western agnosticism.
    C) the first pushback against Christian missionaries.
    D) **the arrival of Confucianism.**

The passage explicitly states in the second paragraph that Confucianism allowed easy entrance for Western agnosticism, but clarifies that agnosticism in general is not new. Since Confucianism is implied to be agnostic (and its stance on gods is the very definition of the word), we can eliminate the Christian missionaries and Western agnostics who came later. Now the only question is whether Shintoism, predating Chinese Confucianism in Japan, is itself an older source of this apparent irreligiosity. Though it's denied religious status in the first paragraph, this is a quote that the passage itself does not necessarily endorse. In discussion in the last paragraph, Shintoism is described "a standing witness to the depth of religious feeling in the Japanese heart". So, at least according to the passage, it seems Confucianism is the earliest cited source of irreligiosity.

20. According to the passage, which of the following is a necessary element of true religion?
    A) Superstition.
    B) Consistency in tradition and beliefs.
    C) A strong consensus.
    D) **Love.**

The passage explicitly suggests that "true religion" will tend to lose its superstitions, which eliminates both A and B as answer choices (as change in belief is also implied). C is nowhere in the passage, but D, love, is strongly identified as key to religious feeling in the final paragraph of the passage.

21. The passage author likely would not agree with which of the following statements about religion?
    A) **Religious convictions remain a constant anchor in a changing cultural landscape.**
    B) Despite a sometimes vocal and ignorant minority, the West is by and large a religious bastion.
    C) The purest religions have shed their old superstitions.
    D) Religion is integral to the human spirit.

Each statement needs to be examined individually. The statement in A contradicts what is written in paragraph four about practices and beliefs passing away within a religion over time. B, C, and D are all found in the passage.

22. In China, a drop-off in religious belief coincided with political changes in the mid-20th century. According to the passage, this could be interpreted as
    A) a natural progression towards agnosticism.
    B) a coincidental result of Confucianism's periodic return to Chinese fashion.
    C) due to the fundamentally irreligious nature of Asian societies reasserting itself.
    D) **a transition period to a purer religion, free of outmoded beliefs.**

The authors tells us that the lack of religion in Japan is creating the foundation for a "purer" religion to come in the future. If something similar were to have happened in China, the author would likely hold a similar belief - that the irreligious period was simply a transition to a purer religion, as choice D asserts.

23. Which of the following, if true, would most weaken the passage author's argument about the "essentially religious nature of man"?
    A) Those countries with the longest traditions of religious belief have the highest rates of religious identification.
    B) **A longitudinal study finds that, without regular reinforcement, religious people lose their faith at markedly higher rate than agnostics or atheists spontaneously find faith.**
    C) Over time, everyday and household superstitions are found to become less prevalent.
    D) An increase in the worldwide percentage of people with religious faith can be attributed to the two fastest-growing religions.

The author asserts that humans are inherently religious beings. He believes that even when a society expresses no religion, it is simply on its way towards becoming religious again. To weaken that assertion, we would need evidence that humans are not inherently religious. Choice B gives us a good example of that - if religious people spontaneously lose religion more frequently than non-religious people gain it, that suggests that human nature is not inherently religious.

24. The passage author would likely agree that, far in the future
    A) **religious conviction will be essentially universal.**
    B) religion will have become effectively extinct.
    C) today's religious plurality will persist, though the relative frequencies are likely to shift.
    D) beliefs within nations will have homogenized, with blocks of both faithful and atheistic countries.

The author asserts not only the fundamentally religious nature of the human spirit, but that this will "always reassert itself". The author turns this argument to Japan's apparently truly religious identity, arguing its seeming irreligiosity to be a temporary transition period on the way to true religion. Taken to its logical conclusion, the implication is that any non-religious person or society is a temporary thing, so the author should wholeheartedly agree with the statement in answer choice A. B says exactly the opposite, and C and D are nowhere in the passage.

Passage V Explanation

It is not in the **Indian experience to seriously consider limits on family size**. Yet as early as the 1960's, the **exploding** Indian **population** began to surface as a **problem**, discussed first only in the rarefied atmosphere of a few Indian universities, but eventually in the halls of governmental power. The **population control movement** made itself felt in a number of ways: the **One Child Tax Credit**, the subsidization of medical care for women willing to be sterilized, and the encouragement of smaller family size through a number of other economic and cultural approaches.

Key terms: One Child Tax Credit

Opinion: Indian society doesn't seriously consider limiting family size, but the Indian government used a tax subsidy to try to limit family size.

The major driving force behind the population control movement was a simple **concern about food**. Government officials tracking the **nation's agricultural production** had estimated that India's ability to produce enough food to feed its people would be outstripped by the growing population by 1980. Given that the **world markets for staple foods** was experiencing unprecedentedly **high prices through the 1960's**, policymakers were understandably concerned. By 1964, Indian production of rice had peaked, and most regions were starting to see declines in production as soil fertility declined.

Cause-and-effect: Concerns about population are fundamentally a concern about food supply. High prices in food markets had people concerned.

Attempts to address the overpopulation issue generally fell into two broad categories: **economic and cultural**. The usual economic approach was to either offer **tax credits to married couples who choose to have no children** or one child or to **levy large increases in taxes** on those couples choosing to have **more than one**. This latter approach was taken, to dramatic effect, by **China** in the 1970's. **Fortunately** for the citizens of **India**, their government did **not** follow the **draconian "One Child Policy"** seen in China. **Cultural** approaches, on the other hand, involve government **subsidy** of the production of works intended to emphasize the **benefits of having fewer children**. Such works included direct publication of informational pamphlets (much like "**public service announcements**" seen on American TV) distributed to doctors' offices and, more indirectly, subsidization of movies and television programs featuring **protagonists** whose decision to have a **small family is presented in a sympathetic** light.

Key terms: public service announcements

Contrast: China punished people for having more than one child but India rewarded people for only having one child.

Opinion: Author thinks the India approach is much better. Indian government thought it was a good idea to sponsor TV programs showing people only having one child.

At the **extreme** end of the scale, governments have attempted to control the population through **direct medical intervention**. Ironically, the **greatest practitioner** of this approach was the **United States**. Despite **never having an overpopulation problems** akin to China or India, both federal and state governments in the U.S. had several policies in the beginning of the 20th century that either **encouraged or forced sterilization upon certain people**. Almost uniformly, those people were racial **minorities**, those with **psychological problems**, or those who encountered the **criminal justice** system. Such practices were almost entirely halted by the middle of the century, but a few vestiges remain even today.

Opinion: Those in the US thought it was a good idea to force or coerce sterilization. Author thinks this was extreme (and ironic since the US didn't have an overpopulation problem).

Cause-and-effect: Forced sterilization was most often done to minorities, criminals, and people with mental health issues.

Despite the expenditure of tremendous amounts of time and money to address the issue, the **government's concerns** about overpopulation in India were eventually **rendered moot**. The **Green Revolution** came late to India, but it eventually came. The combination of **plant recombination**, carefully planned **irrigation**, and **pesticide** use allowed **grain production** worldwide to **skyrocket**. Beginning in **Mexico** in 1948, under the direction of **Norman Borlaug**, Mexican farmers found they could vastly increase their corn and wheat yields. In the mid 1960's, Borlaug brought his approach to India. By cultivating a particular strain of **dwarf rice**, Indian farmers found they were able to grow plants that could sustain **much higher yields** than previously possible. By 1970, the rice output of a single acre of land had doubled, and presently is over triple that ever achieved prior to 1960. By the end of the century, India became the **world's most successful rice producer**, and **exports tons of excess food annually**. The **Green Revolution** is often credited with having **saved over a billion people from starving to death**, and the greatest portion of that impact was felt in India.

[Adapted from "Three Little Indians" by M.R. Green, 2011.]

Key terms: Green Revolution, Mexico, Norman Borlaug, dwarf rice

Cause-and-effect: Using dwarf plants, pesticides, and irrigation the green revolution vastly increased food yields. Eventually led to India being a rice exporter.

Main Idea: Population control fundamentally stems from a concern over food supply, and can take the form of monetary rewards, monetary punishments, or forced sterilization, but by far the preferred choice is monetary rewards. Population control was eventually rendered moot by the Green Revolution.

25. The author would most likely *disagree* with which of the following assertions?
    A) In large part, the effectiveness of India's efforts to curb overpopulation were irrelevant.
    B) The path to population control taken by India's government was more beneficent than was that taken by China's government.
    C) The Green Revolution brought about an increase in food production that outstripped the food needs of India's exploding population.
    D) **The Indian government worked both directly and indirectly to curb the Indian population beginning in the first half of the twentieth century.**

The author asserts in the final paragraph that the population control efforts were rendered moot by the Green Revolution. That's choice A. The author calls China's policies draconian and says that the Indians were fortunate that their government didn't take that approach (choice B). The author also says in the final paragraph that India now exports food, meaning their increases in food production were greater than their population increase, so he would agree with choice C. That leaves choice D as the correct answer.

26. Which of the following government policies would the author most strongly endorse?
    A) favoring economic approaches over cultural approaches to encouraging smaller family size
    B) linking federal welfare dollars for unwed mothers to a requirement to submit to sterilization
    C) creating federally-owned movie studios to produce films with protagonists with only one child
    D) **subsidies for the further development of crop strains that can increase yield per acre**

The author ends the passage by telling us that concerns over a population too large for the available food supply were eventually rendered moot by the Green Revolution. Thus further increases in yield per acre would help allay any future fears about overpopulation, and the author would likely support them. Thus choice D is correct.

27. An Indian government official who advocates economic incentives to small family size would likely endorse which of the following?

   I. **tax credits to married couples choose to have one child or no children**

  II. **a negative income tax for adults choosing to remain unmarried and childless**

 III. a graduated taxation scale in which families pay taxes that increase slightly with each additional child born

      A) I only

      B) **I and II only**

      C) I and III only

      D) II and III only

The passage tells us that India took an approach of rewarding people who chose not to have more than one child, rather than punish those with more children. Thus I and II fit India's approach and choice B is correct. III would fit the approach China took.

28. The passage information most strongly supports the inference that:

      A) population controls through direct medical intervention were popular throughout Europe.

      B) **the level of food production in the United States has generally been adequate for its population.**

      C) the horrors of eugenics carried out in certain countries in the mid-20th century lead to the total eradication of forced sterilization throughout the world.

      D) the present global average rice production per acre is more than 300% that of the average rice production per acre in the 1950's.

We're told that the population control efforts in the US were ironic because it never had an overpopulation problem the way other countries did. Since "overpopulation" means overpopulation relative to food production, we can infer that the US has always been able to produce enough food to feed itself and therefore choice B is correct.

29. If, in the 21st century, the effects of the Green Revolution in India were to both spread to the whole globe and to have had further improvements in their effectiveness, which of the following is most likely?

      A) Increases in the average tax benefit for unmarried childless adults.

      B) Further investment in new genetic engineering technologies to alter crops to be more pest resistant.

      C) Governments would finally end population controls through direct medical intervention.

      D) **Government subsidies for cultural works encouraging a small family would decrease or disappear.**

With a further spread and increased success of the Green Revolution, we can imagine that governments would no longer fear overpopulation, since they would have enough food to feed everyone. If that were the case, there would be no need to subsidize any cultural intervention to encourage people to have fewer children.

30. Suppose that, over the course of a decade, changing climactic conditions lead to decreased crop productivity such that India finds itself with a looming overpopulation problem again. According to the passage information, which of the following is most likely?

      A) **Changes to the tax structure at the federal level would take place.**

      B) Given the failures of previous population control efforts, no new population control movement would surface in either academia or the government.

      C) Researchers would develop new strains of crops that would allow for a second Green Revolution.

      D) Local government agencies throughout India would be forced to import food staples from the U.S.

If overpopulation re-emerged as a problem, the most likely consequence would be government officials trying once again to address the problem the same way they did last time. That's choice A.

31. Which of the following events would likely cause world governments to increase the amounts of tax subsidies given to married couples who only have one child?

A) **The world population rises to a level that outstrips the ability of agricultural producers to create enough food.**

B) China's One Child Policy demonstrates itself to be effective in bringing a nation's population into line with its capacity to grow or purchase food.

C) Courts around the world determine that engaging in either forced sterilization or coerced sterilization is a violation of basic human rights.

D) A new technology that can cheaply and quickly create fresh water for crop irrigation is discovered.

If governments are subsidizing the decision to have only one child, then that would mean they are once again worried about overpopulation. Overpopulation is fundamentally defined as having too many people and not enough food, so choice A would likely lead to the tax subsidies discussed in the question.

CHAPTER 5.
Timed Section Practice
53 Questions, 90 Minutes

SECTION 1: HIGHLIGHTING TECHNIQUE

You can certainly use any technique you'd like on the following timed section, but I strongly recommend you use this as a chance to get full, timed section practice with the highlighting technique. When working your way through this section, there's only one absolute requirement: **<u>you must time yourself strictly</u>**. You do yourself no favors by sneaking in a few extra minutes, or stopping for breaks, etc. You can only get better at the MCAT by simulating Test Day.

If you would like to get the best practice for the highlighting technique, do the following before you start:

1. Get a stopwatch to count up and a timer to count down (many phones can do both at once).
2. Get a yellow highlighter.
3. Go some place where you won't be interrupted and that is relatively quiet.
4. Get some foam earplugs to block out the noise.

When you start the section, start by hitting the count-down timer. Then start the stopwatch counting up.

Every time you finish reading a passage, hit the "lap" button on the stopwatch. Every time you finish a set of questions, hit the "lap" button again. At the end of the section you'll have 18 data points showing you how long you took to read each passage and how long for the questions.

With the highlighting technique you should spend $4 - 4.5$ minutes on the passage and $5.5 - 6$ minutes on the questions.

Then, when reviewing the explanations afterwards, look to the **bold text** as a guide for what we suggest you highlight. You will also see notes between paragraphs to help guide your understanding of the passage.

Passage I

Sir John Lubbock's ties to Darwin are exceedingly easy to trace: not only was he a member of the "X Club," a dining club of scientific gentleman who banded together to support and defend Darwin's theories after the 1859 publication of *The Origin of Species*, but he was a close personal friend of the older scientist; he grew up near Darwin's Down House and received comments on several of his works from him before publication. Yet, as George Stocking argues, it is appropriate to consider the bulk of Victorian anthropologists (or, to be historically accurate, ethnologists), "Darwinistic" if not "Darwinian." By this, Stocking means that while many of the theories espoused in the anthropology of the day might not have been "explicit or directly implied in *The Origin*," there were a range of "metaphysical, moral, or ideological notions deriving from other sources that were intermingled with Darwinism," including the raising of "new questions which had not been relevant in other contexts" (146). Thus Victorian anthropology can be linked to a new approach to science fueled by, if not entirely cohesive with, Darwin's ideas.

The Darwinistic elements of approaches such as Lubbock's are most obvious in terms of two seemingly contradictory claims about human culture: the uniformity of cultural development and the idea that natural selection created favored groups. Like other social evolutionists of his time, Lubbock rejected the notion that all human groups began at an advanced level of civilization (exemplified, for proponents of the devolution theory, by Western European men), but certain "savage" groups "unlearned" that high level of civilization. Instead, proponents of an evolutionary anthropology argued for a progressive sequence of development. As Sir Edward Tylor, one of Lubbock's contemporaries, wrote,

> the condition of culture among the various societies of mankind…is a subject apt for the study of laws of human thought and action. On the one hand, the uniformity which so largely pervades civilization may be ascribed, in great measure, to the uniform action of uniform causes; while on the other hand its various grades may be regarded as stages of development or evolution, each the outcome of previous history, and about to do its proper part in shaping the history of the future" (1).

Lubbock's own particular contribution to this theory included his coining of the terms "Paleolithic" and "Neolithic" in his examinations of the characteristics of particular stages of development and arguing that contemporary "primitive" cultures represented European man's prehistoric state.

Yet despite an insistence that all groups theoretically move through the same stages, Lubbock, as did many of his cohorts, saw the modern-day existence of "primitive" cultures as evidence of their evolutionary unfitness. While Europeans had advanced through the stages of civilization, he argued, the groups that had not failed to do so because they lacked fitness. While humans shared a general physical fitness, variation existed in mental fitness to develop and, Lubbock wrote, "the great principle of natural selection. . . in man affects the mind and has little influence on the body" (491). In arguing thusly, Bruce Trigger argues, Lubbock introduced an element of biological fitness to utilize culture. "What was new," writes Trigger, "was Lubbock's ... insistence that, as a result of natural selection, human groups had become different from each other, not only culturally, but also in their biological capacities to utilize culture" (116).

[Adapted from "Lubbock and Darwin" by R. Grubbs, 1911.]

1. Based on the passage, proponents of the devolution theory believed that:
    A) uniform natural laws indicate the likeliness of the entropy of social structures.
    B) cultural development only occurred in groups with the proper mental fitness.
    C) Western Europeans inevitably decline from the heights of their cultural evolution.
    D) it was possible for a group to move backwards through stages of civilization.

2. Which of the following conclusions about Lubbock's beliefs about natural selection can be inferred from the passage?
    A) He believed that it was more likely to operate somatically than psychologically in humans.
    B) He believed that it was more likely to operate psychologically than somatically in humans.
    C) He had severe doubts as to whether natural selection's precepts applied to humans.
    D) He argued that it was the sole factor that led to variation between human groups.

3. The author quotes Tylor in order to:
    A) highlight Lubbock's insistence that human groups had varying amounts of cultural fitness.
    B) argue that uniformitarian views served to illustrate and defend Darwin's views.
    C) explain the origin of terms such as "Paleolithic" and "Neolithic."
    D) demonstrate that many Victorian anthropologists linked laws of species and human development.

4. Based on the passage, with which of the following stances would Lubbock be most likely to agree?
    A) The metaphysical and moral elements of Darwin's theories proved far more useful to anthropologists than the physical aspects of his ideas.
    B) Neolithic humans proved to be more affected by natural selection than those of Paleolithic times.
    C) Human civilization has evolved through recognizable stages, but certain groups do not have the biological fitness to develop culturally.
    D) Most human cultures began at advanced stages of civilization but struggled under natural forces.

5. Suppose that a Victorian textbook on ethnology was discovered that focused on what it termed "primitive" cultures. This would most lend credence to the passage's claim that:
    A) members of the X Club had been successful in disseminating Darwin's theories.
    B) anthropologists such as Lubbock understood some cultures to be representative of the prehistoric stages of development.
    C) Paleolithic and Neolithic stages were actually far more advanced than earlier anthropologists had given them credit for.
    D) anthropology corrected many of the misapprehensions of ethnology.

6. All of the following approaches might be termed "Darwinistic" EXCEPT:
    A) one that insisted that human evolution did not occur through natural selection, as claimed in *The Origin*.
    B) one based on the writings of Herbert Spencer, a Victorian who espoused evolutionary ideas.
    C) an ethnology text that raised questions about the fitness of various groups to evolve culturally.
    D) an article that applied the moral questions raised in *The Origin* to religious questions of the time period.

7. Based on the passage, which of the following models of human development would Lubbock find likely?
    A) A culture begins with simple tools, evolves physically to develop more complex devices, and ultimately rises to a high level of civilization.
    B) A culture bypasses the Paleolithic stage, evolves mentally to develop more complex devices, and ultimately rises to a high level of civilization.
    C) A culture begins with simple tools, evolves mentally to develop more complex devices, and ultimately falls from its previous high level of civilization.
    D) A culture begins with simple tools, evolves mentally to develop more complex devices, and ultimately rises to a high level of civilization.

Passage II

In Hopi Indian culture, the house belongs to the woman. She literally builds it, and she is the head of the family, but the men help with the lifting of timbers, and now-a-days often lay up the masonry if desired; the woman is still the plasterer. The ancestral home is very dear to the Hopi heart, men, women, and children alike.

The women bring water, clay, and earth, and mix a mud mortar, which is used sparingly between layers of stone. Walls are from eight to eighteen inches thick and seven or eight feet high, above which rafters or poles are placed and smaller poles crosswise above these, then willows or reeds closely laid, and above all reeds or grass holding a spread of mud plaster. When thoroughly dry, a layer of earth is added and carefully packed down. All this is done by the women, as well as the plastering of the inside walls and the making of the plaster floors.

Now the women proceed to plaster the interior, to which, when it is dry, a coat of white gypsum is applied (all with strokes of the bare hands), giving the room a clean, fresh appearance. In one corner of the room is built a fireplace and chimney, the latter often extended above the roof by piling bottomless jars one upon the other, a quaint touch, reminding one of the picturesque chimney pots of England.

The roofs are finished flat and lived upon as in Mediterranean countries, particularly in the case of one-story structures built against two-story buildings, the roof of the low building making the porch or roof-garden for the second-story room lying immediately adjacent.

Formerly, the house was practically bare of furniture save for the fireplace and an occasional stool, but the majority of the Hopi have taken kindly to American small iron cook stoves, simple tables and chairs, and some of them have iron bedsteads. Even now, however, there are many homes, perhaps they are still in the majority, where the family sits in the middle of the floor and eats from a common bowl and sleeps on a pile of comfortable sheep skins, rolled up when not in use.

In the granary, which is usually a low back room, the ears of corn are often sorted by color and laid up in neat piles, red, yellow, white, blue, black, and mottled, a Hopi study in corn color. Strings of native peppers add to the colorful ensemble.

[Adapted from *The Unwritten Literature of the Hopi*, by Hattie Greene Lockett, 1933.]

8. Which of the following best describes the author's attitude to Hopi living conditions?
    A) Simple, clean and attractive
    B) Crude and somewhat garish, but functional
    C) Charmingly backwards
    D) Aesthetically attractive and seductively opulent

9. Which of the following titles most accurately describes this passage?
    A) How to Construct a Traditional Hopi House
    B) Hopi Architecture, Then and Now
    C) The Hopi House and its Social Implications
    D) An Overview of the Traditional Hopi Home

10. Which of the following home-building tasks is, according to the passage, often assigned to men?
    A) Laying and attaching of timbers
    B) Plastering
    C) Masonry
    D) Application of gypsum

11. According to the passage, until recently, Hopi homes normally did NOT include:
    A) any furniture, even the smallest stool.
    B) a gypsum coating.
    C) timber building materials.
    D) iron-made furnishings.

12. The passage implies that male children of a family:
    A) will live outdoors, as the house is for women only.
    B) gain their adult home only by marrying a woman.
    C) are able to inherit their ancestral home only if they are eldest, not automatically.
    D) are responsible for the day-to-day upkeep and structural integrity of their home as children.

Passage IV

The roots of journalism lie in two very distinct camps: first, with the brute attempt to control the flow of information and thereby cudgel the public into acceptance of the elite's version of events; second, with the attempt only to entertain, to bring "news" in the forms of stories and songs from distant places sung by traveling entertainers who thought only to provide diversion for their audiences. As literacy became widespread through the 19th century, the modern form of the newspaper emerged, although it would take until well into the 20th century for a system of professional journalistic ethics to emerge. By the middle of the 20th century, journalism had evolved into a respectable profession with its own norms, rules, and mechanisms for the censure of those violating them. Advertising is at the very beginning of this progression.

Advertising can most clearly contribute to the advancement of civilized society not through a further crowding of society's communicative spaces with ever more raucous, shock- and entertainment-driven messages. Instead, advertising must seek to develop a balance between meeting the commercial goals of the advertisers, the informational needs of the consumer, and the professional ethics that all meaningful human occupations should strive for. Due to the increasing sophistications of market research through the 1970's and 80's, we have only come to think of advancement in advertising as mere technical precision that allows advertisers to achieve the commercial goals of their clients with greater and greater success. But mere financial gain and technical mastery do not a profession make.

The notion of a profession arose most distinctly in the case of medicine. In that context, practitioners were expected to provide their patients with information, to have a certain level of technical mastery in their trade, and to make a healthy living while practicing their profession. Doctors were not expected to starve in service of a noble goal; in nearly every society we have studied, those practicing what the society recognizes as "healing arts" have actually been among the richest or most powerful. Thus it is a false dichotomy to oppositionally juxtapose money and professionalism. Yet it is this very dichotomy that leads those in advertising to blithely dismiss any notions of advertising-as-profession as the most naive of assertions. Even worse, much of the public seems to have accepted, if not outright celebrated, the primacy of financial success for all marketplace transactions. The idea that advertising would even begin to truthfully communicate information is seen as a raucous joke. In a recent film, the plot was driven by the simple question, "what if there were no such thing as lying?" and the better part of the film's humor derived from showing advertisements that were simple, straightforward communications of a product's advantages and disadvantages. Rather than appreciate them as representations of what advertising could be, the audience is meant to laugh.

To free ourselves from the bind of a finance-first view of advertising, there must be a fundamental shift in how consumers view advertising. At present, we react with either passive consumption or cynical acceptance of their manipulations. We must instead demonstrate that we value honesty and clear communication by rewarding those businesses that use such tactics, and sharply punishing those that are disingenuous. A single week-long boycott of a company's services would send a clearer message than any political posturing by ineffectual elected officials.

As the bulk of our commercial activity moves online, consumers and advertisers in technologically developed countries are confronted with a new opportunity: either reproduce the same old cycle of technically brilliant manipulations and cynical reactions, or generate a new advertising professionalism that seeks to engage with consumers in an information exchange in the way that a journalist engages with readers, a doctor with patients, or a teacher with students.

[Adapted from, "Ethics in Advertising: Impossible Possibilities" by R. Carriero, 2011.]

20. The author's argument would be most *weakened* if which of the following were true?
   A) A boycott of a company's products would motivate that company to engage in less truthful and more manipulative advertising practices.
   B) Consumers tend to be happier with purchases when they believe the advertising that motivated them to make the purchase was largely truthful.
   C) Consumers tend to less happy with purchases when they believe the advertising that motivated them to make the purchase was largely truthful.
   D) The roots of medical professionalism are inseparable from its origins as a semi-religious field practiced by people who were both doctor and priest.

21. The author would NOT agree that which of the following behaviors is an acceptable part of professional advertising?
   A) Constructing a billboard that lists the three major advantages of a new surgical technique while failing to mention possible side effects, instead referring potential patients to a website for full information
   B) Filming a commercial that provides a side-by-side comparison between two products to demonstrate the superiority of one company's product
   C) Writing an advertisement for use in a legal journal read exclusively by attorneys touting the advantages of a new online web research system that includes several paragraphs of relatively small text at the bottom of the ad that provide technical details of how the service works
   D) Recording a radio ad that uses high-volume and potentially offensive language to grab the attention of drivers who would otherwise ignore the ad

22. The author makes which of the following assumptions regarding the nature of the advertising business?
   A) Companies that spend a proportionally larger portion of their revenues on advertising will capture most business.
   B) Advertisers have been so successful with past models of raucous shock-driven messaging that they are unlikely to change in the future.
   C) Advertising itself is a profession, much like medicine or journalism or education.
   D) Advertisers are aware of and respond to consumer attitudes about the tone and content of the messages being advertised.

23. The author believes that society will impose pressure on advertisers to change their behavior as a result of:
   A) a paradigm shift in the values that make up a profession.
   B) increased trust in advertisers to express honest opinions.
   C) a failure of journalism to live up to its professional standards.
   D) an increased valuation of candor in communications.

24. As used in the passage, *dichotomy* (paragraph 3) most nearly means:
   A) choice to meet two goals at once.
   B) choice between two mutually exclusive ends.
   C) placement of two ideas next to each other.
   D) an incorrect assumption about a choice.

25. The author implies that the relationship between financial success and being honest with consumers is:
   A) one with tension, albeit tension that can be responded to in a way that achieves both ends.
   B) one with a long history in the practice of medicine in which medical practitioners have demonstrated that they are mutually incompatible.
   C) a false relationship, since making money and behaving professionally are largely irrelevant to each other.
   D) that trust in the honesty of a professional is what leads to the financial success of the professional.

Passage V

The nature of the universe itself is at once the simplest and most important story mankind has been telling itself since time immemorial. Unlike simple children's tales meant to entertain, cosmological myths start, not as mere stories, but rather as "true myths" whose proponents believe represent an accurate accounting of the universe. These myths speak of a vast, wondrous (often infinite) universe, in which the Earth, Sun and Moon occupy a privileged position. Today, however, we have developed long past such anthropocentric immaturity. We now know that the universe was not spat out by some all-powerful gods, nor rested on a turtle's back by a great eagle god, or any of a myriad of other fantastical tales. To address ourselves to the real questions about the nature and fate of the universe by referring to the supernatural is like answering questions of complex economic issues with Aesop's fables. Simple constructs are simply inadequate in the face of the universe's stunning complexity.

The history of the development of modern cosmology is, in essence, a tale of trading childish stories for harsh and humbling truths. If the historiographer Leopold von Ranke is right, then the life of a scientific discipline is not unlike the life of a single person, in which the discipline begins with an infant's blind groping, progresses to a toddler's first shaky steps, through the exuberance of adolescence and finally arriving at the measured wisdom of a full age.

The maturation of cosmology can be seen to have started, in its very earliest stages, with the Greek philosopher Anaxagoras in 500 BC. Anaxagoras, surrounded by contemporaries who still clung to childish notions of a universe overseen by a bevy of gods and goddesses who had placed Earth at the center of things, dared to suggest that the universe was simply an infinite void filled with indivisible particles called atoms. Anaxagoras suggested two key ideas that proved shockingly prescient: that all of the happenings in the cosmos, from a falling rock to the motions of distant stars, could be understood by learning the simple rules of these atoms, and that once we understood those rules, there would be no place left in the universe for the like of Zeus or Hera.

If the history of a maturing cosmology features Anaxagoras as the one who knocked the gods off their throne, the award for knocking man off of his goes to Philolaus in 410 BC. Philolaus played a central role in the development of the Pythagorean universe, which is widely credited with being the first cosmology to have a non-geocentric model of the Universe. Philolaus developed a model that bears a striking resemblance to our modern conception of the Milky Way galaxy. He posited that there was a "central fire" to the universe which would be analogous to the supermassive black hole that sits at the center of the Milky Way. He correctly guessed that the Sun, Earth, and Moon all orbit the same central object and even more impressive, guessed that the rising and setting of the Sun was not because the Sun orbited the Earth, but rather because the Earth revolved with respect to the Sun.

Cosmology ultimately reveals more about how humanity is perceived than about the nature of the universe itself. When early civilizations presumed that mankind was the superlative being, closer to the gods than to other animals they constructed a cosmology that was fitting. Both our physics and biology have proceeded to increasingly minimize and marginalize our place in the universe. It was self-evident to Darwin and those that followed in his footsteps that humans were just another animal, simply an especially clever type of great ape. Darwin's ideas took hold at the end of the 19th century and paved the way for us to understand, and more importantly, to accept the notion that the universe also did not hold us in any special regard.

We have, finally, shed our childish stories about the universe and our place in it. Painful though it may be, this liberates us to appreciate the truly breathtaking majesty of the universe as it actually is.

[Adapted from "Growing Universe, Shrinking Gods" by J.K.S. Davidoski, 2011.]

26. The author's main point about cosmology is that:
    A) it developed in a way analogous to the development of a person.
    B) geocentric models of the universe were understandable at the time.
    C) the development of cosmology has demonstrated the decreasing importance of humanity in the universe.
    D) the workings of the cosmos are based on the behavior of atoms.

27. Someone who accepts the author's views as presented in the passage would reasonably expect:
    A) religious leaders to object to future developments in cosmology even more strenuously than they have to the current state of the science.
    B) humanity to revert to earlier, simpler tales that placed people at the center of creation.
    C) the influence of Philolaus's work to increase.
    D) that future developments in cosmology will broaden our understanding of the universe and continue to reflect our perceptions of ourselves.

28. Anaxagoras differed with his contemporaries in that:
    A) he sought to mature the science of cosmology.
    B) he asserted that there was no room for Zeus between the atoms that made up the universe.
    C) he believed the universe was infinite.
    D) he did not believe in the literal reality of the gods.

29. The author's attitude towards early cosmological myths is most aptly described as:
    A) condescending.
    B) appreciative.
    C) wondrous.
    D) pained.

30. The passage suggests that both Anaxagoras and Philolaus:
    A) met with disapproval from their contemporaries.
    B) contributed to cosmological models that properly set aside notions of the centrality of humanity in the universe.
    C) had a greater understanding of the physical universe than others at the time.
    D) believed in material, rather than religious, explanations for the workings of the cosmos.

Passage VI

Speech is so familiar a feature of daily life that we rarely pause to define it. It seems as natural to man as walking, and only less so than breathing. Yet it needs but a moment's reflection to convince us that this naturalness of speech is but an illusory feeling. The process of acquiring speech is, in sober fact, an utterly different sort of thing from the process of learning to walk. The normal human being is predestined to walk, not because his elders will assist him to learn the art, but because his organism is prepared from birth, or even from the moment of conception, to take on all those expenditures of nervous energy and all those muscular adaptations that result in walking.

Not so language. Eliminate society and it is certain that a new-born individual will never learn to talk. Or remove him from the social environment into which he has come and transplant him to an utterly alien one. His speech will be completely at variance with the speech of his native environment.

Interjections are among the least important of speech elements. But their discussion is valuable mainly because it can be shown that even they, avowedly the nearest of all language sounds to instinctive utterance, are only superficially of an instinctive nature. Were it therefore possible to demonstrate that the whole of language is traceable, in its ultimate historical and psychological foundations, to the interjections, it would still not follow that language is an instinctive activity.

But, as a matter of fact, all attempts so to explain the origin of speech have been fruitless. There is no tangible evidence, historical or otherwise, tending to show that the mass of speech elements and speech processes has evolved out of the interjections. These are a very small and functionally insignificant proportion of the vocabulary of language; at no time and in no linguistic province that we have record of do we see a noticeable tendency towards their elaboration into the primary warp and woof of language. They are never more, at best, than a decorative edging to the ample, complex fabric.

The way is now cleared, then, for a serviceable definition of language. Language is a purely human and non-instinctive method of communicating ideas, emotions, and desires by means of a system of voluntarily produced symbols. There is no discernible instinctive basis in human speech as such, and such human or animal communication, if "communication" it may be called, as is brought about by involuntary, instinctive cries is not, in our sense, language at all.

[Adapted from *An Introduction to the Study of Speech*, by Edward Sapir, 1921.]

31. The author would likely agree with which of the following?
    A) Human language and non-verbal communication have very little overlap.
    B) If interjections were truly instinctive, the possibility of an instinctive component in language could not be completely dismissed.
    C) If raised outside of human society, it is unlikely a child can ever run.
    D) Non-human animals do not possess even the rudiments of language.

32. Which of the following would *weaken* the author's argument about animal communication?
    A) Ant communication can be described as emergent behavior, arising from a series of simple rules, unconsciously followed by individual ants.
    B) Gorillas trained in sign-language will create novel sentences from known words.
    C) Parrots can be trained to carry out simple scripted conversations, learning to give an appropriate response to certain recognized phrases in exchange for a food reward.
    D) Studies show patients with damage to particular parts of the brain sometimes lose the ability to process or use verbs, but not nouns.

33. According to the passage, an individual develops language:
    A) as naturally as walking, and only less so than breathing.
    B) through the slow building up of involuntary cries and learned interjections.
    C) when immersed in a language-using society.
    D) automatically when the brain reaches a certain level of development.

34. Alan Turing created a thought experiment considered highly influential in the field of artificial intelligence. Dubbed the Turing test, a human converses with both other humans and a programmed artificial device, via text displays only. If the artificial device cannot be reliably distinguished from real humans based on conversation only, it has passed the test. Some argue that passing the Turing test is equivalent to understanding language. Which of the following would the author likely believe?
    A) The machine, because it is taught the rules by humans, can be considered language-using.
    B) A machine can only truly use language if it can pass the Turing test.
    C) A failure of the Turing test does not preclude true language use by a machine if it is sufficiently advanced.
    D) A machine that passes the Turing test is not an example of true language use.

35. According to the passage, which of the following is NOT true of interjections?
    A) They are the only examples of language sounds found to be of instinctive utterance.
    B) They are not significant aspects of language.
    C) There is no evidence that interjections have ever evolved into speech elements or processes.
    D) They are distinct from involuntary animal cries.

Passage VII

While there is no such thing as "elder poetry", at the end of the 20th century a number of publishers started to release small collections of poems by both young and old writers that specifically addressed themselves to the experiences of elderly people. While these poems struggled with the experiences of older citizens, it is essential to distinguish them from the over-simplified label "elder poetry", which would suggest that American culture is split into "young" and "old". While the day-to-day experiences of both such groups diverge from each other (especially at the ends of the spectrum), the salient fact is less their divergence than their overlap. The renowned expert on aging, Donald Leigh, correctly put it thus:

> Elderly poets ought not be analyzed as a wholly separate group on the grounds of the false notion that they are all alike, or that they even follow similar lyrical or stylistic patterns that somehow reflect their senescence. But, in our increasingly youth-obsessed culture, the elderly to have a special literary place that can be described. Such description must, perforce, include the ever increasing marginalization of elderly voices in our society, the isolation felt as a consequence of that marginalization, the gradual diminishment of both personal, that is to say mental, and political, that is economic, power.

A decade into the 21st century, there is by now a sizable body of poetic works that focus on these personal and public experiences of the elderly. That the public experiences of a youth oriented culture inform the private sphere is axiomatic. The youth orientation fundamentally means any society whose dominant mode is a capitalist marketplace is one in which the marketplace focuses nearly all of its energy in appealing to younger consumers (in the understandable paradigm that it is better to capture the brand loyalty of the young, thereby creating a lifetime of purchasing habits).

One example of an elder poet reflecting on these experiences is found in Michelle Rood's collection *December Speaks*. In the first poem, Rood reflects on young lovers who are kept apart only by the intransigence of the nearly-senile elder patriarch of the young woman's family. To fulfill their romance, the patriarch serves only as an obstacle that must be circumvented or destroyed. The lovers here represent the dynamism of the public sphere of life, and the patriarch is, perhaps, a stand-in for Rood herself.

In societies in which the elderly are still accorded some fuller measure of respect, the poetry produced by their literary emeriti reflect the potent spark that can be produced when a lifetime of experience is melded both with the calming of passions that comes with age, and the sublimated horror of impending death. The 95 year old Lebanese poet Farid Rafiq writes in *The Olive Grove* of a successful farmer approaching his one hundredth birthday (demonstrating, perhaps, that no matter how old we become, "old" is always someone older than us). The farmer sees his children as the powerful elder statesmen of the community who still come to him for advice, his grandchildren as the leaders of the family who sometimes come to pay their respects, and his great-grandchildren as the rambunctious youth who, filled with the mindless energy of their age, ignore him entirely. Rafiq presents us with the man's meditations through a series of poignant images reflecting the man's gradual surrender of all that mattered to him. By the time his birthday arrives, the man has retreated into total dementia, not as an unwilling victim of a disease, but as a voluntary choice of one seeking a final shelter from the crushing losses that have built up in his mind.

[Adapted from, "Old Writers, Young Voices" by B. Leigh, 2011.]

36. The passage discussion of the experience of young and old writers assumes that:
    A) the experience of younger poets is wholly distinct from that of older poets.
    B) there is a degree of similarity between the experience of young and old poets.
    C) the experience of rambunctious youth is inferior to the experience of literary emeriti.
    D) elder poets influence younger poets through their choice of imagery.

37. According to the passage, many elder poets write poetry that:
    A) focuses on their isolation in a culture that is obsessed with youth.
    B) they show distinctly lyrical patterns that mark them as elder poets.
    C) present the voices of the elderly through the lens of youth.
    D) portray the elderly as an impediment to the dynamism of youth.

38. In the final paragraph, the author asserts that:
    A) elder poetry of higher quality is produced when society accords respect to its older citizens.
    B) poets who feel at least some connection to their grandchildren and great-grandchildren produce work that is more respectful of the elderly than those who are isolated.
    C) senility and dementia serve different literary functions based on the position of the poet in society.
    D) Rafiq treats dementia less seriously than he should.

39. The author implies that the relationship between elderly family members with ailing mental faculties and younger people:
    I. serves primarily as a barrier to happiness for younger people in Rafiq's poetry.
    II. reflects the experiences of the elder poet in the larger society.
    III. is fundamentally detrimental to the elderly.
    A) I only
    B) II only
    C) II and III only
    D) I, II, and III

40. According to the passage, capitalist societies:
    A) are youth oriented because of their economic structure.
    B) marginalize the voices of the elderly because their lyrical and stylistic patterns are unique to them.
    C) have, in the 21st century, shifted into a youth orientation.
    D) encourage day-to-day experiences that are widely divergent between the young and old.

Passage VIII

If Bach is the mathematician of music, as has been asserted, Beethoven is its philosopher. In his work the philosophic spirit comes to the fore. To the genius of the musician is added in Beethoven a wide mental grasp, an altruistic spirit, that seeks to help humanity on the upward path. He addresses the intellect of mankind.

Up to Beethoven's time musicians in general (Bach is always an exception) performed their work without the aid of an intellect for the most part; they worked by intuition. In everything outside their art they were like children. Beethoven was the first one who had the independence to think for himself—the first to have ideas on subjects unconnected with his art.

He it was who established the dignity of the artist over that of the simply well-born. His entire life was a protest against the pretensions of birth over mind. His predecessors, to a great extent subjugated by their social superiors, sought only to please. Nothing further was expected of them. This mental attitude is apparent in their work. The language of the courtier is usually polished, but will never have the virility that characterizes the speech of the free man.

As with all valuable things, however, Beethoven's music is not to be enjoyed for nothing. We must on our side contribute something to the enterprise, something more than simply buying a ticket to the performance. No other composer demands so much of one; no other rewards the student so richly for the effort required. The making a fact the subject of thought vitalizes it. It is as if the master had said to the aspirant: "I will admit you into the ranks of my disciples, but you must first prove yourself worthy." An initiation is necessary; somewhat of the intense mental activity which characterized Beethoven in the composition of his works is required of the student also. There is a tax imposed for the enjoyment of them.

Like Thoreau, Beethoven came on the world's stage "just in the nick of time," and almost immediately had to begin hewing out a path for himself. He was born in the workshop, as was Mozart, and learned music simultaneously with speaking. Stirring times they were in which he first saw the light, and so indeed continued with ever-increasing intensity, like a good drama, until nearly his end. The American Revolution became an accomplished fact during his boyhood. Nearer home, events were fast coming to a focus, which culminated in the French Revolution. The magic words, Liberty, Equality, Fraternity, and the ideas for which they stood, were everywhere in the minds of the people. The age called for enlightenment and spiritual growth.

[Adapted from *Beethoven*, by George Alexander Fischer, published by Dodd, Mead and Company, 1905.]

41. Which of the following best characterizes the author's view on philosophy?
    A) Philosophy is a separate domain from the creation of art.
    B) Philosophy is uplifting to the human spirit.
    C) Philosophy stands for liberty, quality, and fraternity.
    D) Philosophy is intellectually taxing.

42. What does the author mean when writing in the second paragraph, "Bach is always an exception"?
    A) Bach does not fit the same emotional, philosophic mould as Beethoven.
    B) Bach was possessed of a deep, purposeful intellect his peers lacked.
    C) While most musicians worked from intuition, Bach lacked a visceral feel for melodic structure.
    D) As with da Vinci, Bach's mathematical interests set him apart from the artistic crowd.

43. According to the author, among the following who would gain the most enjoyment from listening to music?
    A) An innocent child hearing nursery tunes, ignorant of the political pretensions of composition
    B) An untrained ear, hearing Beethoven for the first time
    C) A dedicated student, analyzing the carefree compositions of popular musicians
    D) A skilled musicologist, deeply focused on one of Beethoven's most complex pieces

44. How would the author likely characterize Beethoven's style?
    A) Marked by a practiced poise and flourish
    B) Highly analytical, with a deep, but not immediately obvious structural beauty
    C) Powerful, honest, and unrestrained
    D) Disjointed and non-traditional

45. Which of the following would best summarize the author's opinion of Beethoven?
    A) Technically great, but lacking in soul
    B) Deeply intuitive and impossible to analyze structurally
    C) Admirable for his dedication to the cause of political freedom and social revolution
    D) The greatest musician since Bach

46. Which of the following best expresses the author's meaning when he asserts that Beethoven was born "just in the nick of time"?
    A) Beethoven was born at approximately the same historical period as Thoreau.
    B) Beethoven was born into a time period whose context was particularly fitting for his style of music.
    C) The time period was one of political upheaval.
    D) Beethoven was born to a mother who became infertile immediately after giving birth.

47. Elsewhere, the author has written, "it is in the best interests of fiction writers to know their place. Those who would seek payment for spinning fantasies on the pages of pulp fiction novels must be aware that it is their betters who control the purse-strings, and as such it is their betters who have the final editorial say." This view would:
    A) be irrelevant to the author's discussion about Beethoven.
    B) contradict a view the author expresses about Beethoven.
    C) refute the author's discussion of Beethoven's value.
    D) provide further support for the author's argument.

Passage IX

As early as 1900, the American consciousness was already solidifying around a cowboy myth that reflected a vision of the Wild West frontier that has never existed. Recreations of the western frontier – in books, movies, stage-shows and all other manner of media – rely for their effectiveness on including at least some elements of reality, while carefully masking others.

The Wild West image was divorced from reality precisely because it was only the most outlandish, attention-grabbing events which were reported back east. These events made their way into depictions of the Wild West and were repeated so frequently they came to be perceived as the usual course of affairs in the Wild West. Notably, the level of conflict and bloodshed was vastly different than that typically depicted. Wagon trains rarely, if ever came into violent conflict with Indian tribes. Outlaws did not rampage through towns, robbing banks on a daily basis. And most starkly of all – the "cowboy" itself is not an American invention, but a Mexican one. They didn't wear cowboy hats (at least as we envision the modern Stetson hat) nor pack six-shooters at their hip.

As one typical example of the kind of re-creation embodying all of these myths, the tourist destination Old Tucson stages "re-enactments" in which actors portray supposedly historical events that were thought to be emblematic of the Wild West. In each case, the event being depicted exclusively features white, male actors portraying either criminals, lawmen hunting down the criminals, or cowboys pressed into service as agents of justice. Every character depicted is armed with the expected revolver and Stetson cowboy hat and problems are all resolved not just with a gun fight, but one in which the malefactors are killed by gunfire. While this makes for good drama, it serves as terrible history.

The reality of life in the Arizona territory (or any American frontier territory) was quite different. Few, if any, people would have owned or used a revolver. The six-shooters produced in the mid 19th century had a tendency to misfire, were accurate to less than 50 feet, and fired bullets with so little power that they could be stopped by something as simple as heavy leather clothing. Overwhelmingly, people made use of rifles, when they carried weapons at all; towns of any size were routinely banning the carrying of firearms in town as early as the 1860's. The famous gunfight it Tombstone, Arizona, is believed to have started because one group of men refused to follow the town's strict no-firearms law. Not only were weapons themselves less common, but so was violence. Fewer people died from violent clashes (either with criminals or Indians) than from any other cause. As is the case today, things like disease, old age, and accidents were the real dangers.

In the case of the six-shooter, it was at least possible for people of the time to carry one. In the case of the classic Stetson cowboy hat, it would have been literally impossible for someone in the Wild West to be wearing such a hat. Although the Stetson company existed and made hats at the time, they only produced something that looked more like a small sombrero. In fact, photographs taken in the fronter territories in the 19th century show that, although men almost universally wore hats, they overwhelmingly wore much smaller bowler hats.

The most stark contrast between the image of the Wild West and the reality comes with the cowboy himself. Mexican *vaqueros* had been working in the territories moving cattle from pasture to slaughter for literally centuries before white settlers showed up. The styles of horse back riding, lasso work, chaps, and other images and activities we associate with white male cowboys were all long since in use by the *vaqueros*. In fact, well into the start of the 20th century, 40-50% of those working as cowboys are believed to have been Mexican *vaqueros*, Indians, or black freedmen.

[Adapted from *Do's and Don'ts in the Not-So-Wild West*, by Liberty Valance, 1978.]

48. A photo taken of actual cowboys in 1862 is LEAST likely to include which of the following?

    A) A six-shooter

    B) Men wearing hats

    C) One or more rifles

    D) A *vaquero*

49. Which of the following changes to an Old Tucson performance would the author believe would most add to the authenticity of the performance?

    A) The inclusion of non-white actors

    B) Removing firearms from the violent clashes used to resolve disputes

    C) Removing horses since so few actually rode them

    D) The alteration of apparel to include carrying rifles instead of six-shooters

50. The author asserts that people refrained from using six-shooters for which of the following reasons?

    A) Frequent clashes with Indian tribes necessitated weapons with more stopping power.

    B) Six-shooters made at the time were inaccurate.

    C) One was likely to injure oneself when a cartridge blew upon misfire.

    D) Most towns had ordinances prohibiting their sale.

51. The passage provides NO information relevant to which of the following questions?

    A) In what way does the image of the cowboy inaccurately reflect the actual clothing and equipment used by cowboys?

    B) Why were only certain stories and events recounted back east about happenings in the Wild West?

    C) Which elements of the *vaquero* culture were not adopted by white cowboys?

    D) For approximately how long did the cowboy exist in the western territories before Mexican and Indian men began doing similar work?

52. An irony described in the passage about the depictions of the Wild West is that:

    A) women are almost always excluded and yet they were more likely to have been victims of violence.

    B) the interactions between white settlers and Indians would have been more likely to involve violence being done by the white settlers rather than violence being done to them.

    C) events which were portrayed precisely because they were outlandish and rare came to be seen as what had been normal at the time.

    D) a cowboy selected at random in the 19th century would more likely have been non-white than white.

53. The author's primary purpose is to:

    A) explain and clarify some historical inaccuracies in depictions of the Wild West.

    B) argue for an alteration of Wild West depictions to make them more historically accurate.

    C) demonstrate the deleterious effect that racism has had on the cowboy image.

    D) develop a historically accurate description of the kind of equipment used by cowboys.

Timed Section 1 Answer Key

Passage 1
1. D
2. B
3. D
4. C
5. B
6. A
7. D

Passage 2
8. A
9. D
10. C
11. D
12. B

Passage 3
13. C
14. B
15. B
16. C
17. B
18. D
19. A

Passage 4
20. A
21. D
22. D
23. D
24. B
25. A

Passage 5
26. C
27. D
28. D
29. A
30. B

Passage 6
31. D
32. B
33. C
34. D
35. A

Passage 7
36. B
37. A
38. A
39. B
40. A

Passage 8
41. B
42. B
43. D
44. C
45. D
46. B
47. B

Passage 9
48. A
49. A
50. B
51. C
52. C
53. A

Passage I Explanation

Sir John Lubbock's ties to **Darwin** are exceedingly easy to trace: not only was he a member of the "X Club," a dining club of scientific gentleman who banded together to support and defend Darwin's theories after the 1859 publication of *The Origin of Species*, but he was a close personal friend of the older scientist; he grew up near Darwin's Down House and received comments on several of his works from him before publication. Yet, as **George Stocking** argues, it is appropriate to consider the bulk of Victorian anthropologists (or, to be historically accurate, ethnologists), "**Darwinistic**" if not "Darwinian." By this, Stocking means that while many of the theories espoused in the anthropology of the day might not have been "explicit or directly implied in *The Origin*," there were a range of "metaphysical, moral, or ideological notions deriving from other sources that were intermingled with Darwinism," including the raising of "new questions which had not been relevant in other contexts" (146). Thus **Victorian anthropology** can be linked to a new approach to science fueled by, if not entirely cohesive with, Darwin's ideas.

Key terms: Sir John Lubbock, Darwin, George Stocking, "Darwinistic," Victorian anthropology

Opinions: George Stocking argues that Victorian anthropologists should be understood as Darwinistic

Cause-and-Effect: The publication of The Origin of Species led to changes in the kinds of approaches and questions anthropologists asked about human society.

The Darwinistic elements of approaches such as Lubbock's are most obvious in terms of two seemingly contradictory claims about human culture: the **uniformity of cultural development** and the idea that natural selection created **favored groups**. Like other social evolutionists of his time, Lubbock rejected the notion that all human groups began at an advanced level of civilization (exemplified, for proponents of the devolution theory, by Western European men), but certain "savage" groups "unlearned" that high level of civilization. Instead, proponents of an evolutionary anthropology argued for a progressive sequence of development. As **Sir Edward Tylor**, one of Lubbock's contemporaries, wrote,

> the condition of culture among the various societies of mankind…is a subject apt for the study of laws of human thought and action. On the one hand, the uniformity which so largely pervades civilization may be ascribed, in great measure, to the uniform action of uniform causes; while on the other hand its various grades may be regarded as stages of development or evolution, each the outcome of previous history, and about to do its proper part in shaping the history of the future" (1).

Lubbock's own particular contribution to this theory included his coining of the terms "Paleolithic" and "Neolithic" in his examinations of the characteristics of particular stages of development and arguing that contemporary "primitive" cultures represented **European man's** prehistoric state.

Key terms: Uniformity of cultural development, favored groups, Sir Edward Tylor, European man

Opinions: Tylor, like Lubbock, argued that human culture was subject to uniform natural laws

Contrast: uniformity of cultural development versus preservation of favored groups

Cause-and-Effect: contemporary "primitive" cultures, according to Lubbock, are equivalent to prehistoric cultures and a way to study them

Yet despite an insistence that all groups theoretically move through the same stages, Lubbock, as did many of his cohorts, saw the modern-day existence of "primitive" cultures as evidence of their **evolutionary unfitness**. While Europeans had advanced through the stages of civilization, he argued, the groups that had not failed to do so because they lacked fitness. While humans shared a general physical fitness, variation existed in **mental fitness** to develop and, Lubbock wrote, "the great principle of natural selection. . . in man affects the mind and has little influence on the body" (491). In arguing thusly, **Bruce Trigger** argues, Lubbock introduced an element of biological fitness to utilize culture. "What

had not been relevant in other contexts.'" Thus choice B, which draws from an intermingled source, and choices C and D, which both apply issues from *The Origin* to other contexts are "Darwinistic." This leaves choice A as the one that does not fit the description, because it argues against Darwin's ideas, and is thus the credited answer.

7. Based on the passage, which of the following models of human development would Lubbock find likely?
- A) A culture begins with simple tools, evolves physically to develop more complex devices, and ultimately rises to a high level of civilization.
- B) A culture bypasses the Paleolithic stage, evolves mentally to develop more complex devices, and ultimately rises to a high level of civilization.
- C) A culture begins with simple tools, evolves mentally to develop more complex devices, and ultimately falls from its previous high level of civilization.
- D) **<u>A culture begins with simple tools, evolves mentally to develop more complex devices, and ultimately rises to a high level of civilization.</u>**

The passage depicts Lubbock's beliefs that culture developed progressively and that natural selection worked on mental, rather than physical attributes, in humans. Thus choice D is the credited answer.

A: stresses physical rather than mental evolution.
B: there is no evidence in the passage that a stage can be bypassed, eliminating choice B.
C: Lubbock did not believe in devolution, eliminating choice C.

Passage II Explanation

In **Hopi Indian** culture, the house belongs to the woman. She **literally builds it**, and she is the **head of the family**, but the men help with the lifting of timbers, and now-a-days often lay up the masonry if desired; the woman is still the plasterer. The ancestral home is very dear to the Hopi heart, men, women, and children alike.

Key terms: Hopi Indian

Cause-and-effect: Hopi women built and own the house, implied to be tied to her head-of-family status

The women bring water, clay, and earth, and mix a **mud mortar,** which is used sparingly between layers of stone. Walls are from **eight to eighteen inches thick** and **seven or eight feet high**, above which rafters or poles are placed and smaller poles crosswise above these, then willows or reeds closely laid, and above all **reeds or grass holding a spread of mud plaster**. When thoroughly dry, a layer of earth is added and carefully packed down. All this is done by the women, as well as the plastering of the inside walls and the making of the **plaster floors**.

Cause-and-effect: stone, wood, and reed base of walls and roofs are underlying structure upon which plaster is laid

Now the women proceed to plaster the interior, to which, when it is dry, a coat of **white gypsum is applied** (all with strokes of the bare hands), giving the room a clean, fresh appearance. In one corner of the room is built a fire-place and chimney, the latter often extended above the roof by piling bottomless jars one upon the other, **a quaint touch**, reminding one of the **picturesque chimney pots of England**.

Key terms: England

Contrast: similarity in appearance of Hopi and English chimneys

Cause-and-effect: final coat of gypsum makes inner house very fresh- and clean-looking

Opinion: passage author is fond of the Hopi piled-jar chimneys, and also of English chimney pots

The roofs are finished **flat and lived upon as in Mediterranean countries**, particularly in the case of one-story structures built against two-story buildings, the roof of the low building making the **porch or roof-garden for the second-story room** lying immediately adjacent.

Key terms: Mediterranean

Contrast: Hopi roofs similar in form and function to Mediterranean roofs

Cause-and-effect: one-story house roof used as balcony for second-story house

Formerly, the house was practically bare of furniture save for the fireplace and an occasional stool, but the majority of the Hopi have taken kindly to American **small iron cook stoves**, **simple tables and chairs**, and some of them have **iron bedsteads**. Even now, however, there are many homes, **perhaps they are still in the majority**, where the family sits in the middle of the floor and eats from a common bowl and sleeps on a pile of comfortable sheep skins, rolled up when not in use.

Contrast: traditional austerity of interior decoration versus modern furnishings

Cause-and-effect: influence of European-American culture on furnishing, but author not sure whether modern furnishings are more common than traditional style

In the **granary**, which is usually a low back room, the ears of corn are often **sorted by color and laid up in neat piles**, red, yellow, white, blue, black, and mottled, a Hopi study in corn color. **Strings of native peppers add to the colorful ensemble**.

Key terms: granary

Contrast: low back food storage room a beautiful artistic display

Cause-and-effect: organization of food by color has unexpected aesthetic

Opinion: author finds even food storage charming and aesthetically pleasing

Main Idea: To give an overview of Hopi Indian houses: construction, design, use

8. Which of the following best describes the passage author's attitude to Hopi living conditions?
    A) **Simple, clean and attractive**
    B) Crude and somewhat garish, but functional
    C) Charmingly backwards
    D) Aesthetically attractive and seductively opulent

The statement in answer choice A best matches the tone of the author, which is to say appreciative and aesthetically-inclined towards Hopi sensibilities. The comments in B and C are mixed, offering compliments mixed with criticisms not found in the passage. D is positive, but the description does not match the Hopi style as described, which is simple and clean, not opulent.

9. Which of the following titles most accurately describes this passage?
    A) How to Construct a Traditional Hopi House
    B) Hopi Architecture, Then and Now
    C) The Hopi House and its Social Implications
    D) **An Overview of the Traditional Hopi Home**

The goal of the passage is not to make an argument, but simply to describe the basic structure of a Hopi house, the way it is built, decorated, and lived in. Answer choice A suggests a step-by-step instruction manual, but the goal isn't to get a detailed understanding of how to build one of these homes. B suggests a focus on comparing traditional to newer Hopi homes, but the only change mentioned is that some homes now use American furnishings, and this is not the focus of the passage as a whole. C does not represent the neutral, informational focus of the passage, implying instead of a specific argument. D matches the tone and goal of the passage.

10. Which of the following home-building tasks is, according to the passage, often assigned to men?
    A) The laying and attaching of timbers
    B) Plastering
    C) **Masonry**
    D) Application of gypsum

Answer choice A will be very tempting, but a closer read only reveals that the men often lift the timbers, with no mention of whether they physically attach them or merely hold them in place for the women to attach. The only other option, then, is choice C, and indeed, the passage says that "nowadays", men will "often" do the masonry, if so desired. The phrasing implies that this type of masonry is new to the building of Hopi homes and not always used, but when used, men might be assigned to it. So answer choice C is a match.

11. According to the passage, until recently, Hopi homes normally did NOT include:
    A) any furniture, even the smallest stool.
    B) a gypsum coating.
    C) timber building materials.
    D) **iron-made furnishings.**

A will be a tempting answer, but a closer read of the passage reveals that this statement is slightly off. Prior to some Hopi adopting American-style furnishings such as cooking stoves and iron bedsteads, it was uncommon to have any more than a chimney and occasional small stool as furniture. That leaves D as the logical choice, and indeed, there is no mention of anything iron-made other than the stoves and bedsteads which have been adopted only of late.

12. The passage implies that male children of a family:
    A) will live outdoors, as the house is for women only.
    B) **gain their adult home only by marrying a woman.**
    C) are able to inherit their ancestral home only if they are eldest, not automatically.
    D) are responsible for the day-to-day upkeep and structural integrity of their home as children.

Since it is clearly stated that homes are built by and belong to a female head of the family, it's implied that a woman's mate will not have a home of his own until he marries (or otherwise becomes bonded to) a woman. It's not clear whether they will build the house together or if the woman will initially live alone and a man will join her later, but it is logically implied that, since he cannot own real estate, the man will live with first his mother (or perhaps older sisters) from childhood, and then move in with a woman who will be his wife. There seems to be no room for male bachelor pads in this society's traditions. The home, though it belongs to the female head of the household, is however said to be important to the entire family, so it's not reasonable to assume that male children will live outside without shelter.

Passage III Explanation

The distinctive features of Millet's art are so marked that the most inexperienced observer easily identifies his work. As a painter of **rustic** subjects, he is unlike any other artists who have entered the same field. We get at the heart of the matter when we say that Millet derived his art directly from **nature**. His pictures […] have a peculiar quality of **genuineness** beside which all **other rustic art seems forced and artificial**.

Key terms: rustic, genuineness

Opinion: Millet's distinctive paintings of rustic subjects are particularly genuine and natural.

Contrast: Similar paintings seem artificial in contrast to Millet's genuine-looking works.

The **human side of life** touched him most deeply, and in many of his **earlier pictures, landscape was secondary**. Gradually he grew into the larger conception of a **perfect harmony between man and his environment. Henceforth landscape ceased to be a mere setting** or background in a figure picture, and became an **organic part of the composition**. As a critic once wrote of *The Shepherdess*, "the earth and sky, the scene and the actors, all answer one another, all hold together, belong together."

Key terms: landscape, harmony

Opinion: over time, landscape became as important as human figures to Millet.

Contrast: early Millet is focused on human side; later works stress landscape as well as human.

In figure painting Millet sought neither grace nor beauty, but **expression**. The **leading characteristic** of his art is **strength**, and he distrusted the ordinary elements of **prettiness** as taking something from the total effect he wished to produce. It was always his first aim to make his people look as if they **belonged** to their station. His was the **genuine peasant** of field and farm, **no imaginary denizen** of the poets' Arcady.

Key terms: expression, strength, genuine

Opinion: Millet aimed to paint genuine, not idealized, peasants; author claims that his art is characterized by strength.

While Millet's art is, in its entirety, quite unique, there are certain interesting points of **resemblance** between his work and that of some **older masters**. He is akin to **Rembrandt** both in his **indifference to beauty** and in his intense **love of human nature**. Millet's indifference to beauty is the more remarkable because in this he **stood alone** in his day and generation, while in the northern art of the seventeenth century, of which Rembrandt is an exponent, beauty was never supreme.

Key terms: Rembrandt, indifference to beauty

Opinion: like Rembrandt, Millet did not focus on beauty but on human nature.

As a lover of human nature, Millet's **sympathies**, though no less intense than Rembrandt's, were **less catholic**. His range of observation was **limited to peasant life**, while **the Dutch master painted all classes** and conditions of men. Yet both alike were profound **students of character** and regarded **expression** as the chief element of beauty. **Rembrandt**, however, sought expression principally in the **countenance**, and **Millet** had a fuller understanding of the expressiveness of the **entire body**.

Key terms: catholic

Contrast: Millet stuck to peasants while Rembrandt painted all classes; Rembrandt focused on faces while Millet saw expressiveness of the entire body.

Millet's instinct for **pose was that of a sculptor**. Many of the figures for his pictures were first carefully modeled in wax or clay. Transferred to canvas they are drawn in the **strong simple outlines** of a statue. It is no extravagant flight of fancy which has likened him to **Michelangelo**. In the **strength** and seriousness of his conceptions, the bold sweep of his lines, and, above all, in the **impression of motion** which he conveys, he has much in common with the great Italian master. Like Michelangelo, Millet gives first preference to the **dramatic moment** when action is imminent.

Key terms: sculptor, Michelangelo, motion

Opinion: author thinks that elements of Millet's paintings share qualities with Michelangelo's sculptures.

When Millet represents **repose** it is as an interval of **suspended action**, not as the end of completed work. The Shepherdess **pauses but a moment** in her walk and will immediately move on again. The man and woman of *The Angelus* rest only for the prayer and then resume their work. The Man with the Hoe snatches but a brief respite from his labors.

Key terms: suspended action

Opinion: author says that Millet's figures look like they are at momentary rest, not fixed pose.

To the qualities which are reminiscent of Michelangelo Millet adds another in which he is allied to the **Greeks**. This is his **tendency towards generalization**. It is the **typical rather than the individual** which he strives to present. "My dream," he once wrote, "is **to characterize the type**." So his figures, like those of Greek sculpture, reproduce **no particular model**, but are the **general** type deduced from the study of many individuals.

[Excerpted from *Jean Francois Millet*, by Estelle M. Hurll, 1900.]

Key terms: Greeks, generalization

Contrast: Millet strives to portray a generalized type rather than the individual.

Main Idea: Millet's paintings of rustic subjects strive towards genuineness; they integrate landscape with human subject. His work shares elements with Rembrandt (indifference to beauty and expressiveness), Michelangelo (a sense of action about to happen), and the Greeks (tendency to generalize).

13. An appropriate title for this essay might be:
      A) Millet, Rembrandt, and Michelangelo: Painters of the Rustic
      B) The Expressive Landscapes of Jean Millet
      C) **Jean Millet: Expressions of the Genuine**
      D) The Idealized Peasant: The Works of Jean Millet

Asking for a good title is basically asking for the main idea of a passage. What's the main idea here? First and foremost, that Millet's paintings aim to portray genuine peasant life – choice C.

A: This is wrong because while the author mentions Rembrandt and Michelangelo sharing qualities with Millet, neither are painters of rustic life.
B: The author tells us that Millet's landscape becomes more important and in harmony with his figure painting; but this answer omits the key element of Millet's work – his human figures.
D: This answer confuses a detail from the final paragraph, which says that Millet aims to generalize; this answer, though, says his peasants are idealized – which is not the same thing.

14. Which statement best capture's the author's description of Millet's portrayal of landscape?
   A) In his early works, landscape was an organic part of the composition.
   B) **Over time, landscape became less background and more important to the overall composition.**
   C) As Millet's paintings became more sculptural, his landscapes became less important.
   D) Because Millet loved human nature, he cared less for the natural world.

Look to Paragraph 2, which talks about the relationship between figure and landscape in Millet's work. There, the author says that over time landscape and figure grew more harmonious, which is what choice B. says.

A: This choice gets it backwards – in the early works, landscape was not as important to the overall composition.
C: The author talks about the sculptural elements of Millet's works in paragraphs 6 – 8, but no theory is put forth about the relationship between sculpture and landscape.
D: Quite the opposite; the author says in paragraph 2: Millet loved the human side of life, but grew to see the landscape as important to integrate in the whole picture.

15. What does the author most likely mean by the statement that Millet's peasant is "no imaginary denizen of the poet's Arcaday"?
   A) Rather than invent his subjects, Millet's peasants were actual people the artist knew.
   B) **Rather than idealize the peasant, Millet aimed to portray his subjects as they actually appeared.**
   C) Millet preferred to paint peasants because they did not have "ordinary elements of prettiness."
   D) Millet's peasants, though not beautiful, were truly poetic.

This quote comes at the end of paragraph 3, where the author is talking about Millet's focus on expression rather than beauty. Even if the wording of the quote is a little obscure, you can get the gist that the author is saying that Millet's peasants are not poeticized. Choice B says that.

A: This choice distorts the idea of not idealizing peasants – they were realistic, not real.
C: We learn earlier in this paragraph that the painter distrusted ordinary prettiness – but that refers to his refusal to idealize his subjects, not that his subjects were not attractive.
D: This distorts the quote – Millet's peasants may or may not have been beautiful, but they were not idealized or portrayed as "poetic."

16. Suppose a previously unknown 19th century painting were discovered. It depicts three figures picking potatoes; they look as if they are statues, posed against an indistinct background. Critics decide that the work is *not* attributed to Millet for all of the following reasons EXCEPT:
   A) Millet's paintings exhibited great harmony between figure and background, and this work does not.
   B) Millet's subjects, rather than looking posed, seem to be taking a short pause from their activities, while these seem unmoved.
   C) **A painting with such sculptural qualities would be more likely attributed to Michelangelo than to Millet.**
   D) Expressiveness of landscape was important to Millet.

The subject of this newly-discovered painting seems typical for Millet, but critics see several key problems. All of the choices except choice C hit elements of Millet's art. Choice C distorts the comparison to Michelangelo.

17. Which of the following most accurately describes the author's comparison of the work of Millet with that of Rembrandt?

    A) Rembrandt's paintings tend to more religious themes than those of Millet.

    B) **<u>Millet primarily painted peasants, whereas Rembrandt's subjects were more diverse.</u>**

    C) Millet was less interested in physical beauty than was Rembrandt.

    D) While both Rembrandt and Millet were students of character, Rembrandt was more interested in expressions of beauty.

In paragraphs 4 and 5 the author talks about several aspects in which Millet's works resemble Rembrandt's; one of which is that while both were interested in human nature, Millet focused on peasants while Rembrandt had a broader range of subjects. That's choice B.

A: This mistakes the word "catholic" – which means "wide ranging" here – for "Catholic," meaning pertaining to Catholicism. Nothing about religion in this passage.

C: Neither painter was particularly interested in portraying physical beauty, says our author.

D: Both were students of character; Rembrandt was focused on expressions of character in the face, while Millet saw expressiveness in the entire body. But as in choice C, neither was intent on portraying beauty per se.

18. The passage attributes which of the following to the works of Millet?

  I. **<u>An expression of harmony between humans and their surroundings</u>**

  II. **<u>An ability to portray expression in the body and not just the face</u>**

  III. **<u>A tendency to present the typical rather than the individual</u>**

    A) I only

    B) I and II only

    C) I and III only

    D) **<u>I, II, and III</u>**

Choice D is correct here. All three Roman Numeral choices are true according to the passage. Roman Numeral I is expressed in paragraph 2; Roman Numeral II, in paragraph 5; and Roman Numeral III, in paragraph 8.

19. The author cites which of the following as evidence of Millet's kinship with sculptors such as Michelangelo?

    A) **<u>The impression of suspended motion in Millet's work</u>**

    B) Millet's tendency towards generalization

    C) The resemblance of Millet's sculptures to Greek models

    D) Millet's early works in wax and clay

In paragraph 6, the author tells us that above all, it's the sense of action that is about to happen that Millet's paintings share with the works of Michelangelo – choice A.

B: Millet's tendency towards generalization exemplifies his similarity to Greek sculpture, not to Michelangelo.

C: According to the passage, Millet was a painter, never a sculptor.

D: Millet's models in wax or clay were simply to help him compose his paintings.

Passage IV Explanation

The roots of **journalism** lie in two very distinct camps: first, with the brute attempt to **control the flow of information** and thereby cudgel the public into acceptance of the elite's version of events; second, with the attempt only to **entertain**, to bring "news" in the forms of stories and songs from distant places sung by traveling entertainers who thought only to provide diversion for their audiences. As **literacy** became widespread through the **19th century**, the modern form of the **newspaper** emerged, although it would take until well into the **20th century** for a system of professional **journalistic ethics** to emerge. By the middle of the 20th century, journalism had evolved into a **respectable profession with its own norms, rules**, and mechanisms for the censure of those violating them. **Advertising is at the very beginning** of this progression.

Key terms: journalism, newspaper, literacy

Opinion: Author thinks journalism has become a respectable profession because it has norms and rules

Contrast: Journalism is now a profession but advertising isn't

Advertising can most clearly contribute to the **advancement** of civilized society **not** through a further crowding of society's communicative spaces with ever more **raucous, shock- and entertainment-driven** messages. Instead, advertising must seek to develop a **balance** between meeting the **commercial goals** of the advertisers, the **informational needs of the consumer**, and the **professional ethics** that **all meaningful human occupations should strive for**. Due to the increasing sophistications of market research through the 1970's and 80's, we have only come to think of **advancement** in advertising as **mere technical precision** that allows advertisers to achieve the commercial goals of their clients with greater and greater success. But mere financial gain and technical mastery does **not a profession** make.

Key terms: advancement, commercial goals, informational needs

Opinion: Author thinks advertising should avoid shock and entertainment driven messages and should seek a professional balance between informing customers and making money.

Contrast: Advertising has advanced but only in technical sense, not a professional sense.

The **notion of a profession** arose most distinctly in the case of **medicine**. In that context, practitioners were expected to provide their patients with **information**, to have a certain level of **technical mastery** in their trade, and to **make a healthy living** while practicing their profession. Doctors were not expected to starve in service of a noble goal; in nearly **every society** we have studied, those practicing what the society recognizes as "**healing arts**" have actually been among the **richest** or most powerful. Thus it is a **false dichotomy** to oppositionally juxtapose **money and professionalism**. Yet it is this very dichotomy that leads those in advertising to blithely dismiss any notions of advertising-as-profession as the most naive of assertions. Even worse, much of the **public seems to have accepted**, if not outright celebrated, the primacy of financial success for all marketplace transactions. The **idea that advertising** would even begin to **truthfully** communicate information is seen as a **raucous joke**. In a recent film, the plot was driven by the simple question, "what if there were no such thing as lying?" and the better part of the film's humor derived from showing advertisements that were simple, straightforward communications of a product's advantages and disadvantages. Rather than appreciate them as representations of what advertising could be, the audience is meant to laugh.

Cause-and-effect: The whole idea of a profession arose with medicine

Opinion: Author thinks that medicine shows us that you can be professional and still make lots of money. Author says public is cynical and views honesty in advertising as a joke.

To **free ourselves** from the bind of a **finance-first view of advertising**, there must be a **fundamental shift in how consumers view advertising**. At present, we react with either passive consumption or cynical acceptance of their manipulations. We must instead **demonstrate that we value honesty** and clear communication by **rewarding those businesses** that use such tactics, and sharply punishing those that are disingenuous. A single week-long boycott of a company's services would send a clearer message than any political posturing by ineffectual elected officials.

Cause-and-effect: A shift in public opinion where the public demands honest advertising would create a shift towards advertising as a profession.

As the **bulk of our commercial activity moves online**, consumers and advertisers in technologically developed countries are confronted with a new opportunity: either **reproduce the same old cycle** of technically brilliant manipulations and cynical reactions, or **generate a new advertising professionalism** that seeks to engage with consumers in an information exchange in the way that a journalist engages with readers, a doctor with patients, or a teacher with students.

[Adapted from, "Ethics in Advertising: Impossible Possibilities" by R. Carriero, 2011.]

Key terms: online

Opinion: Author thinks the move to online commerce is another chance to create a profession of advertising.

Main Idea: Advertising is not yet a profession because it only serves financial needs rather than balancing the needs of consumers and society vs. making money, but other professions like medicine show it's possible to make plenty of money while still behaving professionally.

20. The author's argument would be most *weakened* if which of the following were true?
    A) **A boycott of a company's products would motivate that company to engage in less truthful and more manipulative advertising practices.**
    B) Consumers tend to be happier with purchases when they believe the advertising that motivated them to make the purchase was largely truthful.
    C) Consumers tend to less happy with purchases when they believe the advertising that motivated them to make the purchase was largely truthful.
    D) The roots of medical professionalism are inseparable from its origins as a semi-religious field practiced by people who were both doctor and priest.

The author's argument about creating a profession of honest advertising suggests that a week-long boycott would send a clear message. If choice A were true, such a boycott would backfire and only create more dishonest advertising.

B, C: The author is not concerned with happiness.

21. The author would NOT agree that which of the following behaviors is an acceptable part of professional advertising?
    A) Constructing a billboard that lists the three major advantages of a new surgical technique while failing to mention possible side effects, instead referring potential patients to a website for full information
    B) Filming a commercial that provides a side-by-side comparison between two products to demonstrate the superiority of one company's product
    C) Writing an advertisement for use in a legal journal read exclusively by attorneys touting the advantages of a new online web research system that includes several paragraphs of relatively small text at the bottom of the ad that provide technical details of how the service works
    D) **Recording a radio ad that uses high-volume and potentially offensive language to grab the attention of drivers who would otherwise ignore the ad**

The author makes a specific point about saying that advertising that is shock and entertainment driven is not helpful or professional. Thus choice D is an example of an ad the author would not agree is professional.

22. The author makes which of the following assumptions regarding the nature of the advertising business?
    A) Companies that spend a proportionally larger portion of their revenues on advertising will capture most business.
    B) Advertisers have been so successful with past models of raucous shock-driven messaging that they are unlikely to change in the future.
    C) Advertising itself is a profession, much like medicine or journalism or education.
    D) **Advertisers are aware of and respond to consumer attitudes about the tone and content of the messages being advertised.**

The author's argument hinges on the notion that advertising would serve the informational needs of consumers and the financial needs of businesses, and that something like a boycott would generate good results. For a boycott to work, advertisers must be aware of the consumers' attitudes and be willing to shift in response to them.

23. The author believes that society will impose pressure on advertisers to change their behavior as a result of:
    A) a paradigm shift in the values that make up a profession.
    B) increased trust in advertisers to express honest opinions.
    C) a failure of journalism to live up to its professional standards.
    D) **an increased valuation of candor in communications**.

In paragraph 4, the author tells us that the shift depends on a change in how consumers view advertising and what they demand of advertisers. If consumers value honesty and candor and reward those businesses that use it, that will create a shift in advertising.

24. As used in the passage, *dichotomy* most nearly means:
    A) choice to meet two goals at once.
    B) **choice between two mutually exclusive ends**.
    C) placement of two ideas next to each other.
    D) an incorrect assumption about a choice.

The author presents the choice between being professional and making money as a "false dichotomy". Meaning he thinks you can do both. Thus "dichotomy" is being used to mean a choice between two mutually exclusive options, which is choice B.

25. The author implies that the relationship between financial success and being honest with consumers is:
    A) **one with tension, albeit tension that can be responded to in a way that achieves both ends.**
    B) one with a long history in the practice of medicine in which medical practitioners have demonstrated that they are mutually incompatible.
    C) a false relationship, since making money and behaving professionally are largely irrelevant to each other.
    D) that trust in the honesty of a professional is what leads to the financial success of the professional.

The author clearly understands that advertisers are successful using their manipulative or dishonest techniques and that they have become increasingly sophisticated in doing so. But he describes the choice between financial success and professionalism as a "false dichotomy" meaning he clearly thinks both can be achieved.

Passage V Explanation

The **nature of the universe** itself is at once the simplest and **most important story** mankind has been telling itself since time immemorial. Unlike simple child's tales meant to entertain, cosmological myths start, not as mere stories, but rather as "**true myths**" whose **proponents believe represent an accurate** accounting of the universe. These myths speak of a vast, wondrous (often infinite) universe, in which the **Earth**, Sun and Moon occupy a **privileged position**. Today, however, we have developed **long past such anthropocentric immaturity**. We now know that the universe was not spat out by some all-powerful gods, nor rested on a turtle's back by a great eagle god, or any of a myriad of other fantastical tales. To address ourselves to the real questions about the nature and fate of the universe by referring to the supernatural is like answering questions of **complex economic issues** with **Aesop's fables**. **Simple constructs** are simply **inadequate** in the face of the universe's stunning complexity.

Key terms: true myth, Aesop's fables

Opinion: Author thinks myths are immature and over-simplified

Contrast: Early myths put Earth in a special position but now we've moved past that

The history of the development of modern cosmology is, in essence, a tale of **trading childish stories for harsh and humbling truths**. If the historiographer **Leopold von Ranke** is right, then the life of a scientific discipline is not unlike the life of a single person, in which the discipline begins with an infant's blind groping, progresses to a toddler's first shaky steps, through the exuberance of adolescence and finally arriving at the measured wisdom of a full age.

Key terms: Leopold von Ranke

Opinion: Author again calls early cosmology childish and says today's beliefs are true and are humbling.

The **maturation of cosmology** can be seen to have started, in its very earliest stages, with the Greek philosopher **Anaxagoras** in 500BC. Anaxagoras, surrounded by contemporaries who still clung to **childish notions** of a universe overseen by a bevy of **gods** and goddesses who had placed Earth at the center of things, dared to suggest that the universe was simply an **infinite void filled with indivisible particles called atoms**. Anaxagoras suggested two key ideas that proved shockingly prescient: that **all of the happenings** in the cosmos, from a falling rock to the motions of distant stars, could be understood by learning the **simple rules** of these atoms, and that once we understood those rules, there would be no place left in the universe for the like of Zeus or Hera.

Key terms: Anaxagoras, gods, atoms

Opinion: Anaxagoras thought the whole universe was only made of atoms and there were no gods, author thinks believing in gods is childish.

If the history of a maturing cosmology features Anaxagoras as the one who knocked the gods off their throne, the award for **knocking man off of his** goes to **Philolaus** in 410BC. Philolaus played a central role in the development of the **Pythagorean universe**, which is widely credited with being the first cosmology to have a **non-geocentric model** of the Universe. Philolaus developed a model that bears a striking resemblance to our modern conception of the **Milky Way** galaxy. He posited that there was a "**central fire**" to the universe which would be analogous to the supermassive black hole that sits at the center of the Milky Way. He correctly guessed that the Sun, Earth, and Moon all orbit the same central object and even more impressive, **guessed that the rising and setting of the Sun** was not because the Sun orbited the Earth, but rather because the **Earth revolved with respect to the Sun**.

Key terms: Philolaus, Pythagorean, Milky Way, central fire

Opinion: Philolaus thought the Earth revolved around the sun and that Earth was not at the center of the universe.

Cosmology ultimately **reveals more about how humanity is perceived** than about the nature of the universe itself. When early civilizations presumed than **mankind was the superlative being**, closer to the gods than to other animals they constructed a **cosmology that was fitting**. Both our physics and biology have proceeded to increasingly **minimize and marginalize our place in the universe**. It was self-evident to **Darwin** and those that followed in his footsteps that **humans were just another animal**, simply an especially clever type of great ape. Darwin's ideas took hold at the end of the 19th century and paved the way for us to understand, and more importantly accept, the notion that **the universe also did not hold us in any special regard**.

Key terms: superlative being, Darwin

Opinion: author thinks cosmology reveals how we view ourselves, that humans aren't special in the universe

Contrast: we used to think man was above other animals but now we know we're just another animal

We have, finally, **shed our childish stories about the universe** and our place in it. Painful though it may be, this liberates us to appreciate the truly **breathtaking majesty of the universe as it actually is**.

[Adapted from "Growing Universe, Shrinking Gods" by J.K.S. Davidoski, 2011.]

Opinion: Author reiterates again that our old notions were childish, thinks the universe "as it actually is" is breathtaking and majestic.

Main Idea: Our cosmology of the universe has changed over time away from a childish notion of the earth or humans being special to a harsh truth that we're not special (just another animal) but that this truth lets us see the majestic universe as it really is.

26. The author's main point about cosmology is that:
    A) it developed in a way analogous to the development of a person.
    B) geocentric models of the universe were understandable at the time.
    C) **the development of cosmology has demonstrated the decreasing importance of humanity in the universe.**
    D) the workings of the cosmos are based on the behavior of atoms.

The author indicates that we've moved away from thinking that the Earth has a special place in the universe and from thinking that humans are anything more than just another animal. Thus over time, we've come to see ourselves as less and less important, which is choice C.

A, B, D: These are all mentioned in the passage as supporting ideas but fail to capture the overall main idea.

27. Someone who accepts the author's views as presented in the passage would reasonably expect:
    A) religious leaders to object to future developments in cosmology even more strenuously than they have to the current state of the science.
    B) humanity to revert to earlier, simpler tales that placed people at the center of creation.
    C) the influence of Philolaus's work to increase.
    D) **that future developments in cosmology will broaden our understanding of the universe and continue to reflect our perceptions of ourselves.**

The author shows how the various cosmologies over time have reflected how humanity views itself. When Darwin came along and showed man was just another animal, that went hand-in-hand with a cosmology that relegated us to a relatively unimportant position. Presumably this relationship would continue into the future and choice D is correct.

28. Anaxagoras differed with his contemporaries in that:
    A) he sought to mature the science of cosmology.
    B) he asserted that there was no room for Zeus between the atoms that made up the universe.
    C) he believed the universe was infinite.
    D) **he did not believe in the literal reality of the gods.**

The author tells us that Anaxagoras was surrounded by childish contemporaries who still believed in the gods. Thus choice D is correct and he was unique for not believing in the literal reality of the gods.

29. The author's attitude towards early cosmological myths is most aptly described as:
    A) **condescending.**
    B) appreciative.
    C) wondrous.
    D) pained.

The author repeatedly calls myths childish and immature. That's choice A: condescending.

30. The passage suggests that both Anaxagoras and Philolaus:
    A) met with disapproval from their contemporaries.
    B) **contributed to cosmological models that properly set aside notions of the centrality of humanity in the universe.**
    C) had a greater understanding of the physical universe than others at the time.
    D) believed in material, rather than religious, explanations for the workings of the cosmos.

The author thinks that our diminished sense of our own importance is true, albeit a harsh truth. He presents both Anaxagoras and Philolaus as people who made important first steps in shedding those myths – first by dismissing the gods and second by recognizing that the Earth is not the center of the universe. Thus choice B is correct.

Passage VI Explanation

Speech is so familiar a feature of daily life that we rarely pause to define it. **It seems as natural to man as walking**, and only less so than breathing. Yet it needs but a moment's reflection to convince us that this naturalness of speech is but an illusory feeling. **The process of acquiring speech is, in sober fact, an utterly different sort of thing from the process of learning to walk**. The normal human being is predestined to walk, not because his elders will assist him to learn the art, but because his organism is prepared from birth, or even from the moment of conception, to take on all those expenditures of nervous energy and all those muscular adaptations that result in walking.

Key terms: speech

Contrast: speech feels as natural as walking, but the process of learning is utterly different

Not so language. **Eliminate society and it is certain that a new-born individual will never learn to talk**. Or remove him from the social environment into which he has come and **transplant him to an utterly alien one. His speech will be completely at variance** with the speech of his native environment.

Cause-and-effect: eliminating or changing society will eliminate or alter speech

Interjections are among the least important of speech elements. But their discussion is valuable mainly because it can be shown that even they, avowedly the nearest of all language sounds to **instinctive utterance**, are only superficially of an instinctive nature. Were it therefore possible to demonstrate that the **whole of language is traceable,** in its ultimate historical and psychological foundations**, to the interjections,** it would still **not follow that language is an instinctive** activity.

Key terms: interjections, instinct

Contrast: interjections seem instinctive, actually are not

Cause-and-effect: interjections are not instinctive, if all language is built up from interjections, language is still not instinctive

But, as a matter of fact, all attempts so to explain the origin of speech have been fruitless. There is **no tangible evidence,** historical or otherwise, tending to show that the mass of **speech** elements and speech processes **has evolved** out of the **interjections**. These are a very small and functionally insignificant proportion of the vocabulary of language; at no time and in no linguistic province that we have record of do we see a noticeable tendency towards their elaboration into the primary warp and woof of language. **They are** never more, at best, than a **decorative edging** to the ample, complex fabric.

Contrast: interjections are simple, but do not evolve; interjections seem fundamental, are insignificant edging

The way is now cleared, then, for a serviceable definition of language. **Language is a purely human and non-instinctive** method of communicating ideas, emotions, and desires by means of a system of **voluntarily produced symbols**. There is no discernible instinctive basis in human speech as such, and such human or animal communication, if **"communication" it may be called, as is brought about by involuntary, instinctive cries is not, in our sense, language at all**.

[Adapted from *An Introduction to the Study of Speech*, by Edward Sapir, 1921.]

Key terms: language, communication

Contrast: true language is voluntary and non-instinctive, animal communication is involuntary

Cause-and-effect: ideas/emotions are communicated by voluntary symbols

Opinion: referring to instinctive cries as "communication" is questionable

Main Idea: Language is a very human activity but is not instinctive because even interjections, the most nearly instinctive kind of speech, are just "decorative edging" to language. Rather language is a human system of learning to use symbols to communicate.

31. The author would likely agree with which of the following?
    A) Human language and non-verbal communication have very little overlap.
    B) If interjections were truly instinctive, the possibility of an instinctive component in language could not be completely dismissed.
    C) If raised outside of human society, it is unlikely a child can ever run.
    D) **Non-human animals do not possess even the rudiments of language.**

In the final paragraph, the author defines language and clearly states both that language is "purely human" and that animal cries are part of an entirely separate, non-overlapping category from true speech. Answer choice D might seem a little extreme, but in this case, extreme is what fits the author's argument.

A: Actually, the author states there is no overlap – none at all.
B: This is the opposite of what the author states in paragraph four, that even if interjections were instinctive, they are not the basis for language anyway.
C: This is the opposite of what the passage states about walking, which is that all humans are pre-adapted to do it even without instruction.

32. Which of the following would *weaken* the author's argument about animal communication?
    A) Ant communication can be described as emergent behavior, arising from a series of simple rules, unconsciously followed by individual ants.
    B) **Gorillas trained in sign-language will create novel sentences from known words.**
    C) Parrots can be trained to carry out simple scripted conversations, learning to give an appropriate response to certain recognized phrases in exchange for a food reward.
    D) Studies show patients with damage to particular parts of the brain sometimes lose the ability to process or use verbs, but not nouns.

The author characterizes animal communication as instinctual, entirely separate from language (described as a purely human phenomenon), which requires purposeful and voluntary use of symbols of known meaning. Any evidence of an animal using language, as defined by the author, or of known animal communication revealing language-like aspects, would weaken his argument. B is a clear example of true language by the author's definition.

A: This instinctive, unconscious behavior strengthens the author's argument.
C: Since there is no apparent understanding on the part of the parrot, this does not weaken the author's argument.
D: This is not relevant to the author's argument about animal communication.

33. According to the passage, an individual develops language:
    A) as naturally as walking, and only less so than breathing.
    B) through the slow building up of involuntary cries and learned interjections.
    C) **when immersed in a language-using society.**
    D) automatically when the brain reaches a certain level of development.

The passage states that language is not instinctual and is socially-dependent.

A: The passage states that language only appears to be as natural as walking; this apparent naturalness is illusory.
B: This contradicts the passage, which states that language is not formed up of these things.
D: This is nowhere in the passage.

34. Alan Turing created a thought experiment considered highly influential in the field of artificial intelligence. Dubbed the Turing test, a human converses with both other humans and a programmed artificial device, via text displays only. If the artificial device cannot be reliably distinguished from real humans based on conversation only, it has passed the test. Which of the following statements would the author likely agree with?
    A) The machine, because it is taught the rules by humans, can be considered language-using.
    B) A machine can only truly use language if it can pass the Turing test.
    C) A failure of the Turing test does not preclude true language use by a machine if it is sufficiently advanced.
    D) **A maching that passes the Turing test is not an example of true language use.**

The author states that language communication is exclusively human, and that it requires the use of voluntarily-produced symbols to express ideas, emotions, or desires. It's not clear what would constitute voluntary behavior for a programmed machine with set rules, but since it's not human, it can be discounted and there's no need to ruminate any further on the nature of free will and consciousness. Thus choice D is correct, as the other choices suggest or imply that a non-human machine could truly use language.

A, B, C: Both thought experiments have been shown, by the author's definition, to fall short of true language.

35. According to the passage, which of the following is NOT true of interjections?
    A) **They are the only examples of language sounds found to be of instinctive utterance.**
    B) They are not significant aspects of language.
    C) There is no evidence that interjections have ever evolved into speech elements or processes.
    D) They are distinct from involuntary animal cries.

The passage states that interjections are the "avowedly the nearest" to being instinctive utterances, but then goes on to say that this only appears to be true superficially. In fact, they are not instinctive at all, which makes the statement in answer choice A false, and thus the correct answer to the question.

B, C: These are both stated in the passage much the same way as expressed here.
D: This is not explicitly stated in the passage, but must be true by implication. Interjections are definitely stated to be non-instinctive, while animal cries are instinctive. The statement in answer choice D must therefore be correct.

Passage VII Explanation

While there is no such thing as "**elder poetry**", at the end of the 20th century a number of publishers started to release **small collections of poems** by both young and old writers that specifically addressed themselves to the **experiences of elderly people**. While these poems struggled with the experiences of older citizens, it is essential to distinguish them from the **over-simplified label "elder poetry**", which would suggest that American culture is split into "young" and "old". While the day-to-day experiences of both such groups diverge from each other (especially at the ends of the spectrum), **the salient fact is less their divergence than their overlap**. The renowned expert on aging, **Donald Leigh**, correctly put it thus:

Key terms: elder poetry, Donald Leigh

Opinion: Author thinks that elder poetry isn't its own category and that the similarities between poets is more important than their differences.

> Elderly poets ought **not be analyzed** as a **wholly separate group** on the grounds of the false notion that they are all alike, or that they even follow similar lyrical or stylistic patterns that somehow reflect their senescence. But, in our **increasingly youth-obsessed culture**, the elderly to have **a special literary place** that can be described. Such description must, perforce, include the ever **increasing marginalization** of elderly voices in our society, the **isolation** felt as a consequence of that marginalization, the gradual **diminishment of** both personal, that is to say mental, and political, that is economic, **power**.

Opinion: Leigh thinks that elder poets are not a separate category but deserve a "special place" in that they address the marginalization of older people in a youth-obsessed culture.

A decade into the 21st century, there is by now a sizable **body of poetic works** that focus on these **personal** and **public experiences of the elderly**. That the public experiences of a youth oriented culture inform the private sphere is axiomatic. The **youth orientation** fundamentally means any society whose dominant mode is a **capitalist marketplace** is one in which the marketplace focuses nearly all of its energy in **appealing to younger consumers** (in the understandable paradigm that it is better to capture the brand loyalty of the young, thereby creating a lifetime of purchasing habits).

Cause-and-effect: Capitalism means that the public sphere become youth obsessed since companies want to capture young customers.

Contrast: There are private and public experiences of the elderly (but the public influences the private)

One example of an elder poet reflecting on these experiences is found in **Michelle Rood's** collection **December Speaks**. In the first poem, Rood reflects on young lovers who are kept apart only by the intransigence of the nearly-senile elder patriarch of the young woman's family. To fulfill their romance, the **patriarch serves only as an obstacle** that must be circumvented or destroyed. The **lovers** here represent the **dynamism of the public sphere of life**, and the patriarch is, perhaps, a stand-in for Rood herself.

Key terms: Michelle Rood, December Speaks

Opinion: Author says the old person is a symbol for the elderly author and the young lovers are a symbol of the youth-obsessed culture.

In **societies** in which the elderly are still accorded some **fuller measure of respect**, the **poetry** produced by their literary emeriti reflect the **potent spark** that can be produced when a lifetime of experience is melded both with the calming of passions that comes with age, and the sublimated horror of impending death. The 95 year old Lebanese poet **Farid Rafiq** writes in **The Olive Grove** of a successful farmer approaching his one hundredth birthday (demonstrating, perhaps, that no matter how old we become, "old" is always someone older than us). The **farmer sees his**

children as the powerful elder statesmen of the community who still come to him for advice, his grandchildren as the leaders of the family who sometimes come to pay their respects, and his great-grandchildren as the rambunctious youth who, filled with the mindless energy of their age, ignore him entirely. Rafiq presents us with the man's meditations through a series of poignant images reflecting the **man's gradual surrender** of all that mattered to him. By the time his birthday arrives, the man has retreated into **total dementia**, not as an unwilling victim of a disease, but as a voluntary choice of one **seeking a final shelter** from the crushing losses that have built up in his mind.

[Adapted from, "Old Writers, Young Voices" by B. Leigh, 2011.]

Key terms: Rafiq, Olive Grove, dementia

Opinion: Author sees that in a culture that respects the elderly the poetry they produce has a "potent spark". Rafiq shows us an older man who is dying and slipping into dementia.

Main Idea: Elder poets address the concerns of the elderly in both their private concerns and their interactions with public life, but you can't separate out "elder poetry" as its own category. The author seems to think the poetry made in societies that respect the elderly is better.

36. The passage discussion of the experience of young and old writers assumes that:
    A) the experience of younger poets is wholly distinct from that of older poets.
    B) **there is a degree of similarity between the experience of young and old poets.**
    C) the experience of rambunctious youth is inferior to the experience of literary emeriti.
    D) elder poets influence younger poets through their choice of imagery.

Right in the very beginning, the author tells us in the first paragraph that the similarities are more important than the differences in the poetry produced, and the author explicitly rejects the notion that there is a label "elder poetry" that can be applied to writers. That fits choice B.

37. According to the passage, many elder poets write poetry that:
    A) **focuses on their isolation in a culture that is obsessed with youth.**
    B) they show distinctly lyrical patterns that mark them as elder poets.
    C) present the voices of the elderly through the lens of youth.
    D) portray the elderly as an impediment to the dynamism of youth.

In the second paragraph the author quotes Leigh who tells us that the elderly are marginalized in a youth-obsessed culture. Then in the fourth paragraph we get an example of a poem in which the elderly person is simply viewed as an obstacle. This matches choice A.

38. In the final paragraph, the author asserts that:
    A) **elder poetry of higher quality is produced when society accords respect to its older citizens.**
    B) poets who feel at least some connection to their grandchildren and great-grandchildren produce work that is more respectful of the elderly than those who are isolated.
    C) senility and dementia serve different literary functions based on the position of the poet in society.
    D) Rafiq treats dementia less seriously than he should.

The author uses the phrase "potent spark" to describe the poetry produced by elder poets in those societies that still have some measure of respect for the elderly. Thus choice A is correct.

39. The author implies that the relationship between elderly family members with ailing mental faculties and younger people:
   I. served primarily as a barrier to happiness for younger people in Rafiq's poetry.
  II. **reflects the experiences of the elder poet in the larger society.**
 III. is fundamentally detrimental to the elderly
        A) I only
        B) **II only**
        C) II and III only
        D) I, II, and III

The passage gives us two examples of the relationships between the elderly and young people. In the youth-obsessed society, the elder poet writes of the elderly person being seen as a barrier to the dynamic energy of youth. However in Rafiq's society, where the elderly are still given a measure of respect, the speaker in the poem is able to look over his children and grand-children and see that they come to him for advice and respect his wisdom. Thus II is true and choice B is correct.

40. According to the passage, capitalist societies:
        A) **are youth oriented because of their economic structure.**
        B) marginalize the voices of the elderly because their lyrical and stylistic patterns are unique to them.
        C) have, in the 21st century, shifted into a youth orientation.
        D) encourage day-to-day experiences that are widely divergent between the young and old.

At the end of paragraph 2 the author tells us that capitalism, with its obsession over capturing young consumers, ends up creating a public sphere that is youth-obsessed and youth-dominated. That matches choice A.

Passage VIII Explanation

If **Bach is the mathematician** of music, as has been asserted, **Beethoven is its philosopher**. In his work the **philosophic spirit** comes to the fore. To the genius of the musician is added in Beethoven a **wide mental grasp**, an **altruistic spirit**, that seeks to help humanity on the **upward path**. He addresses the intellect of mankind.

Key terms: Bach, Beethoven, philosophy

Contrast: Bach the mathematician vs. Beethoven the philosopher

Cause-and-effect: the philosophic spirit implies wide mental grasp and altruism

Opinion: the author believes Beethoven is a gifted musician who seeks the betterment of humanity

Up to Beethoven's time musicians in general (**Bach is always an exception**) performed their work without the aid of an **intellect** for the most part; they worked by **intuition**. In everything outside their art they were like children. Beethoven was the first one having the independence to think for himself—the first to have **ideas on subjects unconnected with his art**.

Key terms: intellect, intuition

Contrast: most musicians are intuitive with limited intellects, Beethoven broadly brilliant

Opinion: Bach is also exceptional amongst musicians

He it was who established the **dignity of the artist** over that of the **simply well-born**. His entire life was a protest against the **pretensions of birth over mind**. His predecessors, to a great extent **subjugated** by their social superiors, **sought only to please**. Nothing further was expected of them. This mental attitude is apparent in their work. The language of the **courtier is usually polished**, but will never have the **virility** that characterizes the speech of the free man.

Contrast: a courtier has style, lacks power of speech/ideas of "free man"

Cause-and-effect: subjugated artists reflected in empty art

Opinion: suggests being "simply well-born" is not a virtue; Beethoven's musical predecessors were courtier-like, not free to express themselves honestly

As with all **valuable things**, however, Beethoven's music is not to be enjoyed for nothing. We must on our side contribute something to the enterprise, something more than simply buying a ticket to the performance. No other composer **demands so much** of one; no other **rewards the student** so richly for the **effort** required. The making a fact the subject of thought vitalizes it. It is as if the master had said to the aspirant: "I will admit you into the ranks of my disciples, but you must first prove yourself worthy." An initiation is necessary; somewhat of the intense mental activity which characterized Beethoven in the composition of his works is required of the student also. There is a tax imposed for the enjoyment of them.

Key terms: effort

Contrast: other music is more easily enjoyed than Beethoven's, other music is ultimately less satisfying and meaningful than Beethoven's

Opinion: Beethoven's music is more worthwhile than typical fare

Like **Thoreau**, Beethoven came on the world's stage "just in the nick of time," and almost immediately had to begin hewing out a path for himself. He was **born in the workshop**, as was **Mozart**, and learned music simultaneously with speaking. **Stirring times they were in which he first saw the ligh**t, and so indeed continued with ever-increasing intensity, like a good drama, until nearly his end. The **American Revolution** became an accomplished fact during his boyhood. Nearer home, events were fast coming to a focus, which culminated in the **French Revolution**. The magic words, **Liberty, Equality, Fraternity**, and the ideas for which they stood, were everywhere in the minds of the people. The age called for **enlightenment** and **spiritual growth**.

[Adapted from *Beethoven*, by George Alexander Fischer, published by Dodd, Mead and Company, 1905.]

Key terms: Thoreau, American Revolution, French Revolution

Cause-and-effect: born to music, Beethoven had a special fluency; revolutionary ideas in the air, influenced enlightenment nature of Beethoven's work

Opinion: these were times of progress and greatness

Main Idea: Beethoven and his music elevated the status of musicians over mere courtiers. His music is deep, philosophical and intensely rewarding for the student willing to study and appreciate it.

41. Which of the following best characterizes the author's view on philosophy?
    A) Philosophy is a separate domain from the creation of art.
    B) **Philosophy is uplifting to the human spirit.**
    C) Philosophy stands for liberty, quality, and fraternity.
    D) Philosophy is intellectually taxing.

The author identifies Beethoven as a philosopher and supports this by saying, amongst other things, he will help humanity on an upward path.

A, C, D: Statements with surface similarities to these appear throughout the passage, but none of them are addressing what the author suggests are the defining features of philosophy.

42. What does the passage author mean when writing in the second paragraph, "Bach is always an exception"?
    A) Bach does not fit the same emotional, philosophic mould as Beethoven.
    B) **Bach was possessed of a deep, purposeful intellect his peers lacked.**
    C) While most musicians worked from intuition, Bach lacked a visceral feel for melodic structure.
    D) As with da Vinci, Bach's mathematical interests set him apart from the artistic crowd.

This is the second time in as many paragraphs Bach has been set apart from other musicians, although the passage is really about Beethoven. In context, the passage author says most musicians lack intellect and are child-like, excepting Bach from this (and then Beethoven). B is a clear match to that.

A: This paragraph was not about the differences between Beethoven and Bach but how both of them differed from other musicians.
C, D: These do not appear in the passage, although Bach is described as a mathematician metaphorically.

43. According to the passage author, whom amongst the following would gain the most enjoyment from listening to music?
    A) An innocent child hearing nursery tunes, ignorant of the political pretensions of composition
    B) An untrained ear, hearing Beethoven for the first time
    C) A dedicated student, analyzing the carefree compositions of popular musicians
    D) **A skilled musicologist, deeply focused on one of Beethoven's most complex pieces**

The passage states that Beethoven requires effort to appreciate but that the effort is very rewarding, and implies that other music, while easier to enjoy is ultimately less enjoyable. A student of music effortfully listening to Beethoven, as in D, is a good match for this question.

A, B, C: Each of these is missing at least one of these two critical elements, the effort on the part of the student or the caliber of music listened to.

44. How would the passage author most likely characterize Beethoven's style?
    A) Marked by a practiced poise and flourish
    B) Highly analytical, with a deep, but not immediately obvious structural beauty
    C) **Powerful, honest, and unrestrained**
    D) Disjointed and non-traditional

Paragraph three likens Beethoven to a "free man", contrasting him with his courtier-like predecessors, with flowery prose but lacking both power and honesty. C is a good match to a description of, at least, the emotional and intellectual content of Beethoven in the author's view.

A: Sounds familiar from the passage, but in context it referred to courtier-like musicians.
B: Not found anywhere in the passage. (Though it does sound suspiciously like a description of Bach.)
D: Again, not supported by the passage.

45. Which of the following would best summarize the author's opinion of Beethoven?
    A) Technically great, but lacking in soul
    B) Deeply intuitive and impossible to analyze structurally
    C) Admirable for his dedication to the cause of political freedom and social revolution
    D) **The greatest musician since Bach**

The author's admiration of Beethoven is clear. The main argument is that Beethoven is not only different from, but better than the musicians whom came before him. However, the author does carefully exempt Bach from any criticism that is laid upon other musicians in contrast to Beethoven. Whether Beethoven is considered an equal, inferior, or superior (the author does not rank them against each other explicitly) D is the best match.

A: The passage never criticizes Beethoven.
B: This is not supported by the passage.
C: The passage does connect revolutionary ideas with Beethoven's musical and intellectual output, but this answer choice suggests a more explicitly political agenda that the passage does not support. The discussion of political revolution is also part of a supporting paragraph, not the overall argument of the passage.

46. Which of the following best expresses the author's meaning when he asserts that Beethoven was born "just in the nick of time"?
    A) Beethoven was born at approximately the same historical period as Thoreau.
    B) **Beethoven was born into a time period whose context was particularly fitting for his style of music.**
    C) The time period was one of political upheaval.
    D) Beethoven was born to a mother who became infertile immediately after giving birth.

After the quote mentioned in the question, the author goes on to discuss the various exciting political changes occurring in the world at that time, and notes that Beethoven hewed out a path for himself. Thus the author implies that Beethoven's work was particularly well-suited to the time period. Thus choice B is correct.

A: The author says that Thoreau was also born in the nick of time but we won't know if that refers to the same time period for both men.
C: The author mentions upheaval, but the political upheaval itself is not what makes Beethoven's birth noteworthy, but rather his place in it.
D: This is not mentioned in the passage.

47. Elsewhere, the author has written, "it is in the best interests of fiction writers to know their place. Those who would seek payment for spinning fantasies on the pages of pulp fiction novels must be aware that it is their betters who control the purse-strings, and as such it is their betters who have the final editorial say." This view would:

    A) be irrelevant to the author's discussion about Beethoven.

    B) **contradict a view the author expresses about Beethoven.**

    C) refute the author's discussion of Beethoven's value.

    D) provide further support for the author's argument.

In paragraph 3 the author makes a point of celebrating the fact that Beethoven upheld the dignity of the artist over his supposed betters. This quote expresses the opposite opinion – that the artist should defer to his social "betters". Thus this quote contradicts one of the author's opinions and choice B is correct.

Passage IX Explanation

As early as 1900, the **American consciousness** was already solidifying around a **cowboy myth** that reflected a vision of the **Wild West** frontier that has **never existed**. Recreations of the western frontier – in books, movies, stage-shows and all other manner of media – rely for their effectiveness on including at least **some elements of reality**, while carefully masking others.

Key terms: American consciousness, Wild West

Opinion: author thinks the cowboy myth never existed but has some elements of reality

The Wild West image was divorced from reality precisely because it was **only the most outlandish**, attention-grabbing events which **were reported back east**. These events made their way into depictions of the Wild West and were repeated so frequently they **came to be perceived as the usual course of affairs** in the Wild West. Notably, the level of conflict and bloodshed was vastly different than that typically depicted. Wagon trains rarely, if ever came into violent conflict with Indian tribes. Outlaws did not rampage through towns, robbing banks on a daily basis. And most starkly of all – the **"cowboy" itself is not an American invention, but a Mexican one**. They didn't wear cowboy hats (at least as we envision the modern Stetson hat) nor pack six-shooters at their hip.

Contrast: "cowboy" as an American idea vs a Mexican one

Cause and effect: reporting of attention-grabbing events created the idea that such events were normal

As one typical example of the kind of **re-creation embodying all of these myths**, the tourist destination **Old Tucson** stages "re-enactments" in which actors portray **supposedly historical** events that were thought to be emblematic of the Wild West. In each case, the event being depicted exclusively features **white, male actors** portraying either criminals, lawmen hunting down the criminals, or cowboys pressed into service as agents of justice. Every character depicted is armed with the **expected revolver and Stetson cowboy hat** and problems are all resolved not just with a gun fight, but one in which the malefactors are killed by gunfire. While this makes for good drama, it serves as **terrible history**.

Key terms: Old Tucson, Stetson cowboy hat

Opinion: author thinks recreations focusing on violence and only showing white male actors are terrible history

The **reality** of life in the Arizona territory (or any American frontier territory) was **quite different**. Few, if any, people would have owned or used a revolver. The **six-shooters** produced in the mid 19th century had a tendency to **misfire**, were accurate to less than 50 feet, and fired bullets with so little power that they could be stopped by something as simple as heavy leather clothing. Overwhelmingly, people made use of **rifles**, when they carried weapons at all; towns of any size were routinely **banning the carrying of firearms** in town as early as the 1860's. The famous gunfight it **Tombstone**, Arizona, is believed to have started because one group of men refused to follow the town's strict no-firearms law. Not only were weapons themselves less common, but so was violence. Fewer people died from violent clashes (either with criminals or Indians) than from any other cause. As is the case today, **things like disease, old age, and accidents were the real dangers**.

Contrast: firearms were much less common and people used rifles not six-shooters; people died from disease and old age not violent conflict

Cause and effect: the poor stopping power, unreliability, and inaccuracy of six-shooters made them a poor choice

In the case of the six-shooter, it was at least possible for people of the time to carry one. In the case of the classic **Stetson cowboy hat, it would have been literally impossible** for someone in the Wild West to be wearing such a hat. Although the Stetson company existed and made hats at the time, they only produced something that looked more like a small sombrero. In fact, photographs taken in the fronter territories in the 19th century show that, although men almost universally wore hats, they overwhelmingly **wore much smaller bowler hats**.

Cause and effect: Stetson didn't make what we think of as "cowboy" hats during the time of the Wild West

Contrast: men didn't wear cowboy hats they wore bowler hats

The **most stark contrast** between the image of the Wild West and the reality comes with the **cowboy himself**. Mexican *vaqueros* had been working in the territories moving cattle from pasture to slaughter for literally centuries before white settlers showed up. The styles of horse back riding, lasso work, chaps, and other **images and activities we associate with white male cowboys** were all **long since in use by the *vaqueros***. In fact, well into the start of the 20th century, 40-50% of those working as cowboys are believed to have been Mexican *vaqueros*, Indians, or black freedmen.

Contrast: the look and activities we think of as "cowboy" originated with Mexican *vaqueros*

Main Idea: The popular image of the Wild West includes a number of ideas that are not historically accurate, including the types of guns and hats worn by cowboys, the white male image of the cowboy, and the supposed frequency of violence; these inaccuracies come, in part, from the fact that only the rare attention-grabbing events got reported.

48. A photo taken of actual cowboys in 1862 is LEAST likely to include which of the following?
   A) A six-shooter
   B) Men wearing hats
   C) One or more rifles
   D) A *vaquero*

In the fourth paragraph, we read that few people actually used six-shooters and that rifles were the preferred firearm of the time.

49. Which of the following changes to an Old Tucson performance would the author believe would most add to the authenticity of the performance?
   A) The inclusion of non-white actors
   B) Removing firearms from the violent clashes used to resolve disputes
   C) Removing horses since so few actually rode them
   D) The alteration of apparel to include carrying rifles instead of six-shooters

In the final paragraph the author tells us that the starkest contrast between reality and depictions of the Wild West was that the "cowboy" image is actually derived in large part from the Mexican *vaquero*. To bring a depiction more in line with historical accuracy, then, we would need to see non-white actors.

50. The author asserts that people refrained from using six-shooters for which of the following reasons?
   A) Frequent clashes with Indian tribes necessitated weapons with more stopping power.
   B) Six-shooters made at the time were inaccurate.
   C) One was likely to injure oneself when a cartridge blew upon misfire.
   D) Most towns had ordinances prohibiting their sale.

In the fourth paragraph, the author mentions that six-shooters in the 19th century were only accurate to a short distance, giving this as one reason why people did not favor them as weapons.

51. The passage provides NO information relevant to which of the following questions?
    A) In what way does the image of the cowboy inaccurately reflect the actual clothing and equipment used by cowboys?
    B) Why were only certain stories and events recounted back east about happenings in the Wild West?
    C) Which elements of the *vaquero* culture were not adopted by white cowboys?
    D) For approximately how long did the cowboy exist in the western territories before Mexican and Indian men began doing similar work?

The passage discusses inaccuracies, especially with the six-shooter and the cowboy hat, which eliminates choice A. The second paragraph tells us that certain stories and events were recounted because they were particularly attention-grabbing and outlandish, which eliminates choice B. Finally, the passage tells us that the *vaqueros* actually pre-date white cowboys, which answers choice D. Thus by process of elimination the correct answer must be choice C.

52. An irony described in the passage about the depictions of the Wild West is that:
    A) women are almost always excluded and yet they were more likely to have been victims of violence.
    B) the interactions between white settlers and Indians would have been more likely to involve violence being done by the white settlers rather than violence being done to them.
    C) events which were portrayed precisely because they were outlandish and rare came to be seen as what had been normal at the time.
    D) a cowboy selected at random in the 19th century would more likely have been non-white than white.

The passage never mentions violence being done to Indians or women, meaning choices A and B can be eliminated right off the bat. Choice C describes the irony presented at the start of the second paragraph. Events that were discussed because they were rare got discussed so often that they were perceived as commonplace, creating an ironic outcome. Choice D can be eliminated because the passage only speculates that 40-50% of cowboys were non-white.

53. The author's primary purpose is to:
    A) explain and clarify some historical inaccuracies in depictions of the Wild West.
    B) argue for an alteration of Wild West depictions to make them more historically accurate.
    C) demonstrate the deleterious effect that racism has had on the cowboy image.
    D) develop a historically accurate description of the kind of equipment used by cowboys.

Throughout the text, the author takes a very factual, cut-and-dry tone in which he explains facets of the Wild West image portrayed in popular accounts and contrasts those images with the realities of life in the frontiers of America. Thus he is explaining and clarifying throughout the passage and choice A is correct.

Timed Section Practice
53 Questions, 90 Minutes

SECTION 2: NOTE-TAKING TECHNIQUE

You can certainly use any technique you'd like on the following timed section, but I recommend very strongly that you use this as an opportunity to get a full timed section of practice with the note-taking technique. When working your way through this section, there's only one absolute requirement: **you must time yourself strictly**. You do yourself no favors by sneaking in a few extra minutes, or stopping for breaks, etc. You can only get better at the MCAT by simulating Test Day.

If you would like to get the best practice for the note-taking technique, do the following before you start:

1. Get a stopwatch to count up and a timer to count down (many phones can do both at once).
2. Get separate scratch paper to take notes on and two pencils.
3. Go some place where you won't be interrupted and that is relatively quiet.
4. Get some foam earplugs to block out the noise.

When you start the section, start by hitting the count-down timer. Then start the stopwatch counting up.

Every time you finish reading a passage, hit the "lap" button on the stopwatch. Every time you finish a set of questions, hit the "lap" button again. At the end of the section you'll have 18 data points showing you how long you took to read each passage and how long for the questions.

With the note-taking technique you should spend 5.5 - 7 minutes on the passage and 3 - 4.5 minutes on the questions.

Then, when reviewing the explanations afterwards, look to the notes underneath each paragraph for a guide about what sorts of things you should take note of. You'll also see **bold** notations in the passage itself to point out key phrases and words to help your understanding of the passage.

Please note, the notes between paragraphs are not a literal transcription of what you should write on your scratch paper. Your own notes are going to be abbreviated, much shorter, and probably only make sense to you. Our notes are there to guide you to the sorts of ideas that are worth paying attention to. The exact words you need to jot down are up to you.

Passage I

When the Herakleopolite dominion was finally overthrown, in spite of the valiant resistance of the princes of Asyût, and the Thebans assumed the Pharaonic dignity, thus founding the XIth Dynasty, the Theban necropolis was situated in the great bay in the cliffs, immediately north of Shêkh Abd el-Kûrna, which is known as Dêr el-Bahari. In this picturesque part of Western Thebes, in many respects perhaps the most picturesque place in Egypt, the greatest king of the XIth Dynasty, Neb-hapet-Râ Mentuhetep, excavated his tomb and built for the worship of his ghost a funerary temple, which he called *Akh-aset*, "Glorious-is-its- Situation," a name fully justified by its surroundings. This temple is an entirely new discovery, made by Prof. Naville and Mr. Hall in 1903. The results obtained up to date have been of very great importance, especially with regard to the history of Egyptian art and architecture, for our sources of information were few and we were previously not very well informed as to the condition of art in the time of the XIth Dynasty.

The actual tomb of the king has not yet been revealed, although that of Neb-hetep Mentuhetep, who may have been his immediate predecessor, was discovered by Mr. Carter in 1899. It was known, however, and still uninjured in the reign of Ramses IX of the XXth Dynasty. Then, as we learn from the report of the inspectors sent to examine the royal tombs, which is preserved in the Abbott Papyrus, they found the *pyramid-tomb* of King Xeb-hapet-Râ which is in Tjesret (the ancient Egyptian name for Dêr el-Bahari); it was intact. We know, therefore, that it was intact about 1000 B.C. The description of it as a pyramid-tomb is interesting, for in the inscription of Tetu, the priest of Akh-aset, who was buried at Abydos, Akh-aset is said to have been a pyramid. That the newly discovered temple was called Akh-aset we know from several inscriptions found in it. And the most remarkable thing about this temple is that in its centre there was a pyramid. This must be the pyramid-tomb which was found intact by the inspectors, so that the tomb itself must be close by. But it does not seem to have been beneath the pyramid, below which is only solid rock. It is perhaps a gallery cut in the cliffs at the back of the temple.

The pyramid was then a dummy, made of rubble within a revetment of heavy flint nodules, which was faced with fine limestone. It was erected on a pyloni-form base with heavy cornice of the usual Egyptian pattern. This central pyramid was surrounded by a roofed hall or ambulatory of small octagonal pillars, the outside wall of which was decorated with coloured reliefs, depicting various scenes connected with the *sed-heb* or jubilee-festival of the king, processions of the warriors and magnates of the realm, scenes of husbandry, boat-building, and so forth, all of which were considered appropriate to the chapel of a royal tomb at that period. Outside this wall was an open colonnade of square pillars. The whole of this was built upon an artificially squared rectangular platform of natural rock, about fifteen feet high. To north and south of this were open courts. The southern is bounded by the hill; the northern is now bounded by the Great Temple of Hat-shepsu, but, before this was built, there was evidently a very large open court here. The face of the rock platform is masked by a wall of large rectangular blocks of fine white limestone, some of which measure six feet by three feet six inches. They are beautifully squared and laid in bonded courses of alternate sizes, and the walls generally may be said to be among the finest yet found in Egypt. We have already remarked that the architects of the Middle Kingdom appear to have been specially fond of fine masonry in white stone. The contrast between these splendid XIth Dynasty walls, with their great base-stones of sandstone, and the bad rough masonry of the XVIIIth Dynasty temple close by, is striking. The XVIIIth Dynasty architects and masons had degenerated considerably from the standard of the Middle Kingdom.

[Adapted from *Egypt's Dynasties* by Casey Choate, 2011.]

1. Based on the passage, the Thebans were preceded by the:
    A) Neb-hetep Mentuhetep.
    B) Asyût.
    C) Herakelopites.
    D) Shêkh Abd el-Kûrna.

2. Suppose that a pyramid was found in a newly discovered temple of the XIth Dynasty. The author would most likely argue that:
    A) the pyramids served a religious purpose which is not yet clear to archeologists.
    B) the many deaths of the Herakleopolite rebellion necessitated a larger necropolis.
    C) the tombs were relocated to galleries at a later date.
    D) such details may be less rare than previously believed.

3. The author discusses the Abbott Papyrus in order to:
    A) begin to trace the period in which knowledge of Akh-aset faded from history.
    B) suggest that inspectors failed in their task in keeping the tomb intact.
    C) demonstrate the paucity of information available about the XIth dynasty.
    D) contrast the architectural choices made by those in the XIIth and XXth dynasties.

4. According to the passage, the discovery of the temple of Neb-hapet-Râ Mentuhetep is most important due to the fact that it:
    A) establishes the standards of masonry and decoration that endured after the Middle Period.
    B) sheds light upon the brutal battle of succession between the Herakleopolite and the princes of Asyût.
    C) contrasts the building style of the Great Temple of Hat-shepsu.
    D) reveals important details about the art and architecture of the XIth dynasty.

5. Suppose that an archeologist discovered a tomb from the time of Neb-hetep Mentuhetep shortly after this report was written. The writer of the report would most likely be:
    A) pleased to gain a new source of information about the building techniques of the period.
    B) surprised that any tombs remained intact after the battle raged by the princes of Asyût in 1000 B.C.
    C) doubtful that any edifice could reach the picturesque splendor of Dêr el-Bahari.
    D) certain that it could be differentiated from earlier pyramid tombs and funerary temples.

6. Which of the following can be definitively stated about Akh-aset?
    I. It was intact in 1000 B.C.
   II. It consists of a solid rock pyramid with a galley in the back.
  III. It was destroyed by Hat-Shepsu.
    A) I only
    B) III only
    C) I and II only
    D) II and III only

7. All of the following are assumed to be features of XIth dynasty architecture EXCEPT:
    A) large, rough cut rocks.
    B) colored reliefs.
    C) sandstone based masonry.
    D) small octagonal pillars.

Passage II

To European architects brought up on the traditions of stone and brick construction, our Japanese method of building with wood and bamboo seems scarcely worthy to be ranked as architecture. It is but quite recently that a competent student of Western architecture has recognized and paid tribute to the remarkable perfection of our great temples. Such being the case as regards our classic architecture, we could hardly expect the outsider to appreciate the subtle beauty of the tea-room, its principles of construction and decoration being entirely different from those of the West.

The tea-room (the Sukiya) does not pretend to be other than a mere cottage—a straw hut, as we call it. The original ideographs for Sukiya mean the Abode of Fancy. Latterly the various tea-masters substituted various Chinese characters according to their conception of the tea-room, and the term Sukiya may signify the Abode of Vacancy or the Abode of the Unsymmetrical. It is an Abode of Fancy inasmuch as it is an ephemeral structure built to house a poetic impulse. It is an Abode of Vacancy inasmuch as it is devoid of ornamentation except for what may be placed in it to satisfy some aesthetic need of the moment. It is an Abode of the Unsymmetrical inasmuch as it is consecrated to the worship of the Imperfect, purposely leaving some thing unfinished for the play of the imagination to complete. On account of the extreme simplicity and chasteness of its scheme of decoration, it appears to foreigners almost barren.

The Sukiya consists of the tea-room proper, designed to accommodate not more than five persons, an anteroom (mid-suya) where the tea utensils are washed and arranged before being brought in, a portico (machiai) in which the guests wait until they receive the summons to enter the tea-room, and a garden path (the roji) which connects the machiai with the tea-room.

The tea-room is unimpressive in appearance. It is smaller than the smallest of Japanese houses, while the materials used in its construction are intended to give the suggestion of refined poverty. Yet we must remember that all this is the result of profound artistic forethought, and that the details have been worked out with care perhaps even greater than that expended on the building of the richest palaces and temples. A good tea-room is more costly than an ordinary mansion, for the selection of its materials, as well as its workmanship, requires immense care and precision. Indeed, the carpenters employed by the tea-masters form a distinct and highly honoured class among artisans, their work being no less delicate than that of the makers of lacquer cabinets.

The simplicity and purism of the tea-room resulted from emulation of the Zen monastery. A Zen monastery differs from those of other Buddhist sects inasmuch as it is meant only to be a dwelling place for the monks. We have already said that it was the ritual instituted by the Zen monks of successively drinking tea out of a bowl before the image of Bodhi Dharma, which laid the foundations of the tea-ceremony. We might add here that the altar of the Zen chapel was the prototype of the Tokonoma,—the place of honour in a Japanese room where paintings and flowers are placed for the edification of the guests.

[Adapted from *The Book of Tea*, by Kakuzo Okakura, 1906]

8. In the prairies in what is now Central Canada, early European settlers frequently made use of sod houses, constructed into the side of hills and built from sections of cut sections of soil and grass. In contrast, Ancient Mesoamerican peoples built vast, long-lasting stone cities, with no Western influence. Based on the passage, one would expect Western architects to rate which style more highly?

    A) They would favor the sod houses since they follow a European tradition.

    B) They would favor the sod houses because of their simpler aesthetics.

    C) They would favor the stonework out of a craving for exotic design.

    D) They would favor the stonework for independently hitting on Western design ideals.

9. The passage operates under the assumption that Zen Buddhist monks

    A) live ascetic, practical lives.

    B) appreciate beauty and ornate craftsmanship.

    C) live in deceptively simple, incredibly costly dwellings.

    D) drink far less tea than is popularly believed.

10. Which statement *contradicts* the passage's description of tea rooms?

    A) They are built to exist briefly but beautifully.

    B) They give the impression of restrained wealth.

    C) They are tributes to the flawed reality of life.

    D) They are possessed of a comely simplicity.

11. The first line of the second paragraph, "The Sukiya does not pretend to be other than a . . . straw hut," is intended to

    A) clarify the goals and values of a tea-room in contrast to those of Western architecture.

    B) argue against the notion that tea-rooms match monastic aesthetics.

    C) provide evidence of the tea-room's emulation of the Zen monastery.

    D) discredit the praise of tea-room enthusiasts.

Passage III

At the outset, a key difference must be understood: that between the actual creative act of making a sculpture and the subsequent questions of criticism that allow us to understand a given piece of sculpture and place it in a larger framework. The first is a raw creative expression that requires mastery over the physical act of chiseling away stone; the other an academic topic more akin to history or literary study. Needless to say, some have attempted to meld the two. A common misconception of the early nineteenth century was that all lovers and critics of sculpture must attempt to hew meaning from blank rock themselves before they could offer insight or criticism. And even more distressingly, several major art schools have recently started suggesting that their apprentice sculptors must achieve a mastery of the history of sculpture before ever picking up the chisel.

As intellectually edifying as it may be to memorize an endless list of the names of sculptors and works and artistic movements, the job of the young sculptor is completely different. The young creative person must learn to summon and harness the particular madness that takes over the successful sculptor: at once the creator must be an obsessive, ensuring surgical precision with each hammer-blow, lest the work be ruined by a single errant strike, and at the same time the creator must allow the mind to flow smoothly, freely, and be open to inspiration.

The problem of how to bring the novice sculptor into the right state of mind is one that has gotten no easier to answer with modern materials and techniques. One approach currently in vogue is that sculptors should look to the methods of dance, which need only be modified to fit the work of the sculptor. The sculptor may model his own working process on that of the dancer in several different ways. The first would be for the sculptor to treat his chisel and hammer as if they were simply extensions of his body, to be controlled with the precision that a dancer controls his arms and legs. Another is to emulate the dancers' notions of expression through position. The creative act of sculpture itself would then become the work of art, rather than the final product. Often sculptors who attempt this approach take from dancers their basic method of mastery through repetition and practice. These artists will craft the same sculpture over and over until they get it right. Finally, some will take the dancers' use of music as a way to create the proper mindset and set their sculpting to a soundtrack.

Although it has not yet been recognized generally, this basic emulation of dancers has largely failed to live up to the enthusiasm with which it was initially embraced. No doubt, as its proponents loudly declaim, there is a large area in which the basic approaches of the sculptor and the dancer are similar, or perhaps even exactly the same. Such overlap would include things like evoking emotion, non-literal self-expression, and an awareness of basic spatial composition. But such ideas are common to sculpture, dance, painting, film – any visual art and perhaps even any art in general. Ultimately, we must recognize the simplicity of the answer is this: sculpture is its own distinct avenue of artistic expression with its own methods and approaches. The problem of getting the young sculptor into the right mindset lies in teaching the young sculptor how to sculpt and how to invite the free-flowing obsessiveness needed for that art. Turning to dance as a shortcut is no shortcut at all.

It is only a particularly myopic vision of the creative mindset that excludes the actual practice of sculpting as a possible approach. This myopia is likely driven by fear rather than a striving for success. When months of work may be irretrievably ruined by a single mistake, the novice sculptor understandably seeks solutions outside his field.

[Adapted from: "Let's Get Physical: Sculpt by Sculpting" by Juliana O'Connell, 2011.]

12. The author's overall purpose in writing the passage is to:
    A) assert that those artists who study both dance and sculpture are more fully able to succeed in making sculpture than others.
    B) describe the features of dance and sculpture that are similar.
    C) argue that the creative process of sculpting is its own enterprise distinct from either dance or artistic criticism of sculpture.
    D) demonstrate that art schools have failed their young sculptors by focusing on the history of sculpture rather than the process of creating sculpture.

13. According to the author, the task of a novice sculptor is to:
  I. discover a way to engender the free-flowing obsessiveness needed to create sculpture.
 II. learn to place their own work in the larger framework of art history.
III. meld the methods of other physically expressive activities such as dance into the act of sculpting.
>   A) I only
>   B) II only
>   C) I and II only
>   D) I and III only

14. Assume that a journeyman sculptor is about to begin work on a new piece. The author would likely state that the most important task to be performed is:
>   A) clarifying how the new piece will fit into the larger historical framework of sculpture.
>   B) adopting a mindset that permits the sculptor to control the hammer and chisel as extensions of her own body.
>   C) understanding that the piece will be flawed and will require repetition to produce mastery.
>   D) finding the right attitude to permit creative sculpting.

15. The author could best clarify the sentence, "It is only a particularly myopic vision of the creative mindset that excludes the actual practice of sculpting as a possible approach," by doing which of the following?
>   A) Offering a definition of "myopic vision"
>   B) Explaining more fully what a creative mindset is and how that relates to the actual practice of sculpting
>   C) Demonstrating how dancers exhibit their approach to the creative mindset
>   D) Giving an example of an art historian who does not have such a myopic vision

16. The author thinks that teaching young sculptors how to sculpt is important because:
>   A) it allows them to be more successful in their work by melding the physical approaches of dance and sculpture.
>   B) there is no meaningful overlap between sculpture and other art forms, thus requiring young sculptors to eschew any potential shortcuts.
>   C) it is by developing both careful precision and flowing inspiration that a sculptor finds the motivation to succeed in the work.
>   D) the actual practice of sculpting is the way to learn how to invite the "particular madness" that results in successful sculpture.

17. Assume that an art school hired a new Director to oversee its sculpture department and the Director had all new students take dance classes in addition to their sculpture work. If several such students then went on to produce exemplary works of sculpture, this would:
  I. be consistent with the author's main point.
 II. refute the author's assertion that "[t]urning to dance as a shortcut is no shortcut at all."
III. provide evidence suggesting that dance is one means to help sculptors develop the right mental attitude needed to succeed at sculpting.
>   A) II only
>   B) III only
>   C) I and III only
>   D) II and III only

18. In another work, the author of the passage stated that "a painting of a sculpture is no sculpture at all" and that "dancers who attempt to 'sculpt' space in their work are misguided, at best". These statements have what relevance to the passage?
>   A) The first is irrelevant whereas the second refutes the author's argument about the relationship between dance and sculpture.
>   B) They support the author's general contention that sculpture has its own unique approach to the creative process.
>   C) They support the notion that emotion, non-literal self-expression, and spatial composition are common to all visual arts.
>   D) They weaken the author's assertion that historical context is relevant to the creative process.

Passage V

I have seldom felt so proud of being a representative of the people as now, when it gives me an opportunity to advocate a cause which cannot be represented or defended in this chamber by those directly and particularly affected by it, owing to the leven of prejudice that the beliefs and ideas of the past have left in the mind of modern man. The cause of female suffrage is one sure to strike a sympathetic chord in every unprejudiced man, because it represents the cause of the weak who, deprived of the means to defend themselves, are compelled to throw themselves upon the mercy of the strong.

But it is not on this account alone that this cause has my sympathy and appeals to me. It has, besides, the irresistible attraction of truth and justice, which no open and liberal mind can deny. If our action as legislators must be inspired by the eternal sources of right, if the laws passed here must comply with the divine precept to give everybody his due, then we cannot deny woman the right to vote, because to do otherwise would be to prove false to all the precepts and achievements of democracy and liberty which have made this century what may be properly called the century of vindication.

Female suffrage is a reform demanded by the social conditions of our times, by the high culture of woman, and by the aspiration of all classes of society to organize and work for the interests they have in common. We cannot detain the celestial bodies in their course; neither can we check any of those moral movements that gravitate with irresistible force towards their center of attraction: Justice. The moral world is governed by the same laws as the physical world, and all the power of man being impotent to suppress a single molecule of the spaces required for the gravitation of the universe, it is still less able to prevent the generation of the ideas that take shape in the mind and strive to attain to fruition in the field of life and reality.

It is an interesting phenomenon that whenever an attempt is made to introduce a social reform, in accordance with modern ideas and tendencies and in contradiction with old beliefs and prejudices, there is never a lack of opposition, based on the maintenance of the *status quo*, which it is desired to preserve at any cost. As was to be expected, the eternal calamity howlers and false prophets of evil raise their fatidical voices on this present occasion, in protest against female suffrage, invoking the sanctity of the home and the necessity of perpetuating customs that have been observed for many years.

Frankly speaking, I have no patience with people who voice such objections. If this country had not been one of the few privileged places on our planet where the experiment of a sudden change of institutions and ideals has been carried on most successfully, without paralyzation or retrogression, disorganization or destruction, I would say that the apprehension and fears of those who oppose this innovation might be justified.

But in view of the fruitful results of our own revolutions, and what those new institutions of liberty and democracy have brought to our country; and considering the marked progress made by us, thanks to these same institutions, in all the orders of national life, in spite of a few reactionists and ultra-conservatives, who hold opinions to the contrary and regret the past, I do not and cannot, understand how there still are serious people who seriously object to the granting of female suffrage, one of the most vivid aspirations now agitating modern society.

[Adapted from *The Woman and the Right to Vote*, Rafael Palma, 1919.]

26. It can be inferred from the passage that the author:
    A) has personally experienced prejudice of the kind described in the text.
    B) does not self-identify as politically liberal.
    C) considers women's suffragists as having relatively little political power on their own behalf.
    D) sees equal rights for women as impossible without a major sociopolitical shake-up.

27. What is the significance of the author's reference to the physical law of gravitation in the third paragraph?
    A) It's an analogy for the idea that one good deed leads to another, like pieces of rock accreting into a planet.
    B) It means that moral rightness is an inevitable and irresistible as processes governed by physical laws.
    C) It contrasts with social and moral change, which, unlike the movement of planets, is uncertain and inexactly predicted.
    D) It's meant to illustrate that inevitability is an illusion of hindsight, as no social circumstance is truly inevitable.

28. The author implies that those who oppose the female suffrage movement:
    A) are protecting their own economic interests.
    B) do so out of gender prejudice.
    C) fear a backlash from standing out from the crowd politically.
    D) have never really thought about why they hold the views they do.

29. Which of the of the following, if true, would most strengthen the main argument of the passage?
    A) Social reform is often followed by a brief economic recession.
    B) Gender diversity in the workplace tends to lead to employee reorganization.
    C) Other nations pushing back against the female right to vote tend to have a higher agricultural base.
    D) Other nations that have granted full voting rights to women have suffered no social backlash or ill effects.

30. Which of the following titles most accurately describes this passage?
    A) Time for Change
    B) Life of a Woman
    C) The Reform Process
    D) The History of Female Suffrage

Passage VI

News of the completion of the transcontinental railroad came to the Southern Paiute peoples in what would become the state of Arizona at a time when they were slowly beginning to return to the quiet agrarian life that had sustained them for millennia, after a disastrous attempt by Chief Kwiumpus to turn the Paiutes into a conquering, slave-owning society similar to the nearby Navajo. News came slowly to the Southern Paiutes, as the twin barriers of desert and language helped isolate them both from ever-expanding populations of whites as well as from other Indian tribes.

At the bottom on the Southern Paiute power structure sat the foundation of its conservatism: children. Any child, even those of the most powerful chiefs, were considered to be beneath those adults who had successfully completed their Rite of Adulthood. Proper instruction of children in the traditional ways of the tribe was considered the sacred duty of every Paiute. Combined with children's natural inclination towards stable, simple structures both in life and in story-telling, the relationship that Paiute adults had with the tribe's children created a core of conservatism that lasts even to the present day. At the top of the Southern Paiute hierarchy sat the holy women who served as a combination of healer, diplomat, advisor to the chiefs, and conduit to the heavens. These priestesses were reliably protective of the tribe's old ways, despite the increasing incursions of change from whites and other tribes.

Between these two ends of the totem pole, however, hid a small minority of dissidents, primarily young braves who had had the most contact with the outside, actively traded with whites and other tribes, sought to explore new methods of hunting and agriculture, learned English, and, most scandalously, began following the tenets of Christianity.

To these priestesses, these children, and these dissident young braves came the shocking news of the whites' new development: an iron trail with a great iron horse that would bring newcomers in an unstoppable wave even larger than the steady river brought by the wagon trains of the past. A few recklessly defiant tribesmen openly rejoiced; they spoke of riding the "iron horse" of the transcontinental railroad themselves, and seeing the great nation of the white man for themselves. They thought to learn the ways of these men that came in such numbers. As more missionaries built their churches closer and closer to Paiute lands, some began openly joining their services and speaking of what they heard when they returned to their villages.

Within two decades of the completion of the railroad, new settlements by whites had encroached into the territory of a nearby Northern Paiute nation. Violence inevitably erupted, with the resultant destruction and displacement of the entire Pakwidocade tribe. The fury of the Southern Paiute chieftains and holy women turned on the dissidents and, by extension, any of the young men who had taken to interacting overmuch with the whites. The Kuyuidokado family, who had largely converted to Christianity, was wiped out in a single night of bloody conflict. The one chieftain to actively encourage trading with the whites, Chief Pogidukadu, was stripped of his rank and exiled with his sons. And the entire tribe of Kutzakika'a peoples were attacked for no sin greater than having a holy woman who sought to include Jesus Christ as one of the many children of the Earth Goddess in the Paiute pantheon.

Ultimately, the conflict between the expanding borders of the United States and the widely scattered Southern Paiute tribes ended as all such conflicts eventually ended, although the Paiutes were able to hold on much longer than most, simply by virtue of inhabiting land that was not deemed desirable by the settlers who came streaming into the Arizona territory.

[Adapted from *Conservatism in the Tribal Peoples* by Connell Choate, 1945.]

31. Which of the following groups of people played a role in preserving the traditional societal structures in the Southern Paiutes?

 I. Children of tribal chieftains
 II. Traders who interacted with outsiders
III. Diviners who interpreted signs from the gods

   A) I only
   B) II only
   C) III only
   D) I and III only

32. It may be inferred from the passage that the Southern Paiutes may have survived longer as a distinct cultural entity if they had:

   A) partially embraced the new cultural ideas brought in by the whites.
   B) joined with a larger, more powerful tribe such as the Navajo.
   C) been located further south, farther away from the transcontinental railroad.
   D) succeeded in their attempt to become a conquering, slave-owning society.

33. Which of the following consequences would have been likely, had more than one chieftain been supportive of the Christian church's attempts to convert the Southern Paiutes?

   A) The entire Southern Paiute nation would have converted to Christianity.
   B) Interactions between the Southern Paiutes and the whites would have allowed the Southern Paiutes to maintain themselves as an independent nation to the present day.
   C) More children would have been taught English and the basic tenets of Christianity.
   D) The chiefs who also supported the missionaries would also have been either stripped of power or wiped out.

34. Which of the following facts from the passage supports the notion that the braves who favored adopting the ways of the whites were in a minority?

   A) The wise women served as the mediators of the Southern Paiute's relationship with their gods.
   B) The children and those who taught them reinforced the simple, traditional cultural norms.
   C) Those who actively traded with the whites were more likely to adopt their ways.
   D) When violent conflict erupted between the Northern Paiutes and the whites, the Southern Paiutes reacted by attacking those among them who favored turning to the ways of the white settlers.

35. Which of the following facts most likely *weakens* the author's contention that the holy women were powerful supporters of the traditional culture?

   A) To be selected to become a holy woman, a girl must display mastery of several traditional female arts.
   B) After selection, a young woman endures a rigorous month-long ritual in which all assumptions about herself and her world are stripped away.
   C) Less than one in six young women selected to become a holy woman can survive the training process.
   D) After achieving full status as a holy woman, new priestesses are expected to apprentice to an elder holy woman for a decade or more.

36. The author suggests that the young braves who began adopting white ways were rejecting traditional cultural values and norms. It is equally possible that:

   A) the braves felt resentment towards the exclusive power the holy women had in interceding with the gods.
   B) frequent and prolonged exposure to a new group of people led the braves to adapt to their new surroundings.
   C) a desire to overthrow the structure of traditional Southern Paiute culture lead the braves to seek out new avenues to power.
   D) whites forcibly converted the braves to Christianity.

Passage VII

Miguel de Cervantes y Saavedra was born in 1547 at Alcala de Hénarès. His family belonged to the class of impoverished gentlefolk, poor but intensely proud of their descent from one of those hardy mountaineers the Saavedras, who, five centuries before, so heroically defended the northern portion of Spain against the Moors. While the hereditary possessions were growing less and less, the heads of the family would endeavor to compensate for present privations, by relating to their children the noble deeds and the great estates of their ancestors.

Whether debarred by poverty or negligence, the last an unlikely supposition, Cervantes did not graduate at the University of Alcala or any other, a circumstance that occasioned him much fortification in his manhood and advanced age. Émile Chasles thus expresses himself on this subject:

"The graduated took their revenge. When Cervantes acquired celebrity they recollected that he had taken no degree. When he sought an employ they applied to him by way of iron brand the epithet, Ingenio Lego, 'He is not of ours,' said they; 'he is not a cleric.' The day when he attracted the attention of all Europe their anger was excessive towards the writer who possessed talent without permission, and genius without a diploma. Cervantes gaily replied, that he admired their pedantic learning, their books bristling with quotations, the complements they paid each other in Greek, their erudition, their marginal notes, their doctors' degrees, but that he himself was naturally lazy, and did not care to search in authors for what he was able to say without them; and finally, that when there is a dull or foolish thing to be expressed, it will do in Spanish as well as in Latin."

He was smarting under the contempt of the learned asses of his day when writing the preface to his Don Quixote:

"Alas, the story of Don Quixote is as bare as a rush! Ah, if the author could do as others,—cite at the head of the book a litany of authorities in alphabetic order, commencing with Aristotle and ending with Xenophon or Zoilus! But the poor Cervantes can find nothing of all this. There he sits, paper before him, the pen behind his ear, his elbow on the table, his cheek in his hand, and himself all unable to discover pertinent sentences or ingenious trifles to adorn his subject."

[Adapted from "Miguel de Cervantes y Saavedra", published in *The Catholic World*, March, 1867.]

37. Chasles uses the phrase, "talent without permission", in order to
    A) imply that Cervantes' critics were resentful of a man of his class having greater ability.
    B) bolster the image of Cervantes as a willful outsider.
    C) contrast Cervantes artistic achievements with his educational lack.
    D) establish Cervantes as anti-establishment in his time.

38. Which of the following verbal attacks does Cervantes not make on "the graduated" in the passage?
    A) Implying that they utilize learned quotes to compensate for an inability to express their own thoughts
    B) Sarcastically dismissing their written Greek and Latin as pointless posturing
    C) Referring to them as learned asses
    D) Mocking them for the praise they give each other

39. Which of the following best matches Chasles' opinion of Cervantes, based on the passage?
    A) A tragically under-appreciated genius
    B) A plainspoken but powerful writer
    C) A brilliant, unpretentious artist
    D) A mercilessly incisive linguist

40. Which of the following assumptions can be attributed to the author?
    A) Honest poverty is noble.
    B) Material wealth is a source of pride.
    C) Higher degrees are pretentious.
    D) Formal education and creativity are mutually exclusive.

Passage VIII

Children are great geniuses of creativity, but their creativity serves no purpose that is directly visible to the adult mind. In fact, the notion of "purpose" itself is a construct of the adult mind. With that construct comes the inevitable effort to turn the effort into the purpose itself.

Creativity's wellsprings are the twin engines of recombination and the happy mistake. In the first, we see children dash heedlessly ahead, combining and recombining ideas, words, and images in endless, effortless, and nearly thoughtless ways. This mad dash forward also opens children up to the second: the happy mistake. By not watching every footfall in their rush to create, children risk a misstep that may twist an ankle, but also open themselves up to the possibility that the misstep will lead them in a wholly new and unanticipated direction. Yet adults, in their attempts to replicate the creativity of childhood, sever both of these from underlying joie de vivre that impels children forward.

A conscious effort to recombine ideas in a particular way creates, at best, a sterile laboratory in which progress is slowed to a crawl and creativity's gush of ideas reduced to a glacial progression of pale, obviously derivative notions. The adult organizes creativity into work, destroying the joy that is the source of the child's success. The adult mind asks itself a series of questions: "What if I combine A with B? What if I combine A with C? What if I combine A with D?" whose end result is less progress in a month of work than a child achieves in an hour. Whether painter, musician, businessman or scientist, the adult's efforts at creativity are stymied by an insistence on organized recombination rather than the child's chaotic throwing together of ideas.

If organization slows the adult's creativity to a crawl, fear paralyzes it entirely. Mistakes are not merely bumps on the road to creative success, they are the cobblestones that make up the road itself. Ninety nine mistakes may be problems that frustrate and hinder, but it's the one-hundredth that lets true genius show. The history of nearly all human endeavors show that it is the happy mistake, the serendipitous accident that provides the great breakthrough. The unexpected not only solves the problem, but shows that the way forward is even more open, more exciting, and more successful that had even been thought possible. Children easily take advantage of the happy mistake simply by virtue of being willing to make mistakes–lots of them. Adults, by dint of their fear of failure, fear of looking foolish, or fear of mistake itself, leave themselves closed to the only meaningful avenue for advancement.

Mother nature is constrained by no such fear. Nature itself is, perhaps, the single most powerful creative force around us. This is no new-age philosophical metaphysic, but instead an evaluation of the creative power of life in its relentless ability to harness the same powers of creativity as the human mind. The genetic blueprint by which the architecture of life is built engages in a recombination of "ideas" – genes – at its very core. The vast success of sexual reproduction over asexual in every environment on Earth is due to the fact that sexual reproduction is a process of recombination. By shuffling the genetic deck, life opens itself up to new and interesting combinations that can lead to success. Such combinations can also lead to failure, but nature fears failure not.

Nature's happy accidents can be seen in the mutations which spring up over and over again in the genetic code. Like the serendipitous creativity of the artist, most mistakes will prove useless or harmless, but it is the rare beneficial mutation which provides such an overwhelming advantage of one species over another that the balance of the entire environment can be shifted. Evolution, then, is the model for human creativity. Our minds are an ecosystem of ideas, and we must allow those ideas to come and go with the same careless rapidity with which Mother Nature allows individual life forms, or even whole species to emerge, live, and disappear.

[Adapted from "Creating Creativity" by Kristen O'Connell, 2011.]

41. The author's main point is that:
    A) the structure of the adult mind makes it impossible for adults to be truly creative.
    B) fear of mistakes closes adults off from an important source of creativity.
    C) creativity depends on factors harnessed easily by children and nature but not adults.
    D) recombination of ideas or genes is the true essence of creativity.

42. Which of the following would most strongly *weaken* the author's argument about creativity?
    A) Adults can, with practice, learn to recombine ideas in a manner similar to children's.
    B) Thomas Edison, renowned for his creativity in engineering, is often quoted as saying that invention is "one percent inspiration and ninety-nine percent perspiration."
    C) The cellular machinery that controls genes spends a vast amount of time and effort correcting genetic mutations and carefully controlling genetic recombination during sexual reproduction.
    D) Mistakes made during creative endeavors are often quite destructive and serve as significant setback to the work being attempted.

43. Suppose that Nobel Prize-winning scientists are often looked down upon by their immediate peers for being "sloppy, thoughtless scientists". The author would point out that:
    A) luck plays such an overwhelming role in having great breakthroughs that their sloppiness is irrelevant.
    B) the Nobel committee is itself somewhat sloppy and thoughtless in deciding who to award.
    C) the sloppier one is in one's work, the more slowly one is able to recombine ideas in a search for something new.
    D) it is their willingness to be somewhat sloppy that lets them have the serendipitous accidents that create success.

44. Which of the following assertions from the passage might it be possible to *refute* with clear counterexamples?
 I. Children's creativity serves no purpose.
 II. The idea of purpose causes us to transform efforts themselves into purposes.
III. Recombination leads to the vast success of sexual reproduction.
    A) II only
    B) III only
    C) I and III only
    D) II and III only

45. Suppose a study of the process by which poets write their poems demonstrates that a methodical recombination of linguistic ideas creates more serendipitous discoveries than otherwise. What relevance would this have to the author's thesis?
    A) It weakens the author's contention about the relationship between the method of recombination and creativity.
    B) It disproves the author's central argument about creativity.
    C) It strengthens the connection between a childlike process of recombination and creativity.
    D) It neither helps nor hurts the passage's argument as it is irrelevant to the author's contentions.

46. The author's attitude towards mistakes can best be described as:
    A) enthusiastic about their positive effects.
    B) a balance of positive regard for their effects on creativity and worry about their negative consequences.
    C) trepidation.
    D) concern that mistakes can interrupt the flow of recombination.

47. Which of the following best exemplifies the type of creativity the author celebrates?
    A) A computer program creates a novel recipe for Baltic Apple Pie by testing billions of ingredient recombinations in microseconds.
    B) A highly successful author consistently creates best-sellers by writing variations on the same theme for each novel.
    C) A celebrated jazz pianist with over six decades of experience playing music performs original improvisations each night by throwing together musical ideas from across the decades with a haphazard disregard for the boundaries between different types of jazz.
    D) A performance artist films himself painting and as soon as he makes a single errant brushstroke in the work, he violently destroys the canvas, at the end of which he displays both the final perfect painting and video screen showing himself destroying every painting with even a single mistake.

Passage IX

The history of Great Britain is the one with which we are in general the best acquainted, and it gives us many useful lessons. We may profit by their experience without paying the price which it cost them. Although it seems obvious to common sense that the people of such an island should be but one nation, yet we find that they were for ages divided into three, and that those three were almost constantly embroiled in quarrels and wars with one another. Notwithstanding their true interest with respect to the continental nations was really the same, yet by the arts and policy and practices of those nations, their mutual jealousies were perpetually kept inflamed, and for a long series of years they were far more inconvenient and troublesome than they were useful and assisting to each other.

Should the people of America divide themselves into three or four nations, would not the same thing happen? Would not similar jealousies arise, and be in like manner cherished? Instead of their being "joined in affection" and free from all apprehension of different "interests," envy and jealousy would soon extinguish confidence and affection, and the partial interests of each confederacy, instead of the general interests of all America, would be the only objects of their policy and pursuits. Hence, like most other BORDERING nations, they would always be either involved in disputes and war, or live in the constant apprehension of them.

The most sanguine advocates for three or four confederacies cannot reasonably suppose that they would long remain exactly on an equal footing in point of strength, even if it was possible to form them so at first; but, admitting that to be practicable, yet what human contrivance can secure the continuance of such equality? Independent of those local circumstances which tend to beget and increase power in one part and to impede its progress in another, we must advert to the effects of that superior policy and good management which would probably distinguish the government of one above the rest, and by which their relative equality in strength and consideration would be destroyed. For it cannot be presumed that the same degree of sound policy, prudence, and foresight would uniformly be observed by each of these confederacies for a long succession of years.

Whenever, and from whatever causes, it might happen, and happen it would, that any one of these nations or confederacies should rise on the scale of political importance much above the degree of her neighbors, that moment would those neighbors behold her with envy and with fear. Both those passions would lead them to countenance, if not to promote, whatever might promise to diminish her importance; and would also restrain them from measures calculated to advance or even to secure her prosperity. Much time would not be necessary to enable her to discern these unfriendly dispositions. She would soon begin, not only to lose confidence in her neighbors, but also to feel a disposition equally unfavorable to them. Distrust naturally creates distrust, and by nothing is good-will and kind conduct more speedily changed than by invidious jealousies and uncandid imputations, whether expressed or implied.

Let candid men judge, then, whether the division of America into any given number of independent sovereignties would tend to secure us against the hostilities and improper interference of foreign nations.

[Adapted from *The Federalist Papers: No. 5*, John Jay, 1787.]

48. The author would likely *disagree* with which of the following statements?

    A) Though newly-sovereign US states would initially be on an equal footing, inequality would creep in eventually.

    B) Isolated island nations are less likely to live under the shadow of war, all other things being equal.

    C) Jealousy will tend to erode relations between any near nations.

    D) A unified country with a strong federal government will ultimately benefit every American state.

49. Based on paragraph three, the author assumes that good government:

    A) is a natural consequence of a mature society.

    B) leads to more good government, becoming more difficult to disrupt over time.

    C) is a balancing act, with longer periods of success being less and less likely.

    D) is entirely dependent on the actions of one's governmental neighbors.

50. The author would argue for which of the following nations as being better served amalgamating under one government?

    A) The former British colonies of Singapore and Hong Kong, separated by 1600 miles of ocean

    B) Tibet and Nepal, geographically close and divided by the mostly impassable Himalayan mountain range

    C) The Republic of Ireland and Northern Ireland, both on the same violently-contested land mass in the British Isles

    D) The United Arab Emirates and Saudi Arabia, their undefined border falling somewhere within several hundred miles of inhospitable, empty desert

51. What is the author's reason for discussing "the effects of that superior policy and good management which would probably distinguish the government of one above the rest" in paragraph three?

    A) To support the argument that good government must be the first priority of any new nation

    B) To illustrate the capricious and accidental nature of successful government policy

    C) To describe the most likely cause of one nation rising above its neighbors

    D) To argue the inevitability of a disparity in the strength of nations, whatever their starting points

52. The author implies that independent nations:

    A) are a temporary historical contrivance, with world government being inevitable.

    B) are justified when sufficient geographic separation exists between regions.

    C) are justified when population size would be unwieldy in a single unified nation.

    D) are preferred, as unification leads to forced proximity of culturally dissimilar groups.

53. Which of the following titles best describes this passage?

    A) The Case for US State Sovereignty

    B) One Banner Under God

    C) Federal Administration and State Rights

    D) The Danger of Rogue States

Timed Section 2 Answer Key

Passage 1	Passage 6
1. C	31. D
2. D	32. C
3. A	33. D
4. D	34. B
5. A	35. B
6. A	36. B
7. A	

Passage 2	Passage 7
8. D	37. A
9. A	38. C
10. B	39. C
11. A	40. B

Passage 3	Passage 8
12. C	41. C
13. A	42. D
14. D	43. D
15. D	44. C
16. D	45. A
17. B	46. A
18. B	47. C

Passage 4	Passage 9
19. C	48. A
20. A	49. C
21. D	50. C
22. A	51. D
23. C	52. B
24. C	53. B
25. D	

Passage 5
26. C
27. B
28. B
29. D
30. A

Passage I Explanation

When the Herakleopolite dominion was finally overthrown, in spite of the valiant resistance of the princes of Asyût, and the **Thebans** assumed the Pharaonic dignity, thus founding the **XIth Dynasty**, the Theban necropolis was situated in the great bay in the cliffs, immediately north of Shêkh Abd el-Kûrna, which is known as Dêr el-Bahari. In this picturesque part of Western Thebes, in many respects perhaps the most picturesque place in Egypt, the greatest king of the XIth Dynasty, **Neb-hapet-Râ Mentuhetep**, excavated his tomb and built for the worship of his ghost a funerary temple, which he called *Akh-aset*, "Glorious-is-its- Situation," a name fully justified by its surroundings. This temple is an entirely new discovery, made by **Prof. Naville** and **Mr. Hall** in **1903**. The results obtained up to date have been of very great importance, especially with regard to the history of Egyptian art and architecture, for our sources of information were few and we were previously not very well informed as to the condition of art in the time of the XIth Dynasty.

Key terms: Thebans; XIth Dynasty; Neb-hapet-Râ Mentuhetep; Akh-aset; Prof Naville; Mr. Hall; 1903

Cause-and-Effect: the ascension of the Thebans as pharaohs led to founding a necropolis in a beautiful part of Egypt; finding Neb-hapet-Râ Mentuhetep's tomb led to greater knowledge about art and architecture of XIth dynasty

The actual tomb of the king has not yet been revealed, although that of **Neb-hetep Mentuhetep**, who may have been his immediate predecessor, was discovered by Mr. Carter in 1899. It was known, however, and still uninjured in the reign of Ramses IX of the **XXth Dynasty**. Then, as we learn from the report of the inspectors sent to examine the royal tombs, which is preserved in the **Abbott Papyrus**, they found the pyramid-tomb of King Xeb-hapet-Râ which is in Tjesret (the ancient Egyptian name for Dêr el-Bahari); it was intact. We know, therefore, that it was intact about **1000 B.C.** The description of it as a pyramid-tomb is interesting, for in the inscription of Tetu, the priest of Akh-aset, who was buried at Abydos, Akh-aset is said to have been a pyramid. That the newly discovered temple was called **Akh-aset** we know from several inscriptions found in it. And the most remarkable thing about this temple is that in its centre there was a pyramid. This must be the pyramid-tomb which was found intact by the inspectors, so that the tomb itself must be close by. But it does not seem to have been beneath the pyramid, below which is only solid rock. It is perhaps a gallery cut in the cliffs at the back of the temple.

Key terms: Neb-hetep Mentuhetep; XXth Dynasty; Abbott Papyrus; 1000 B.C.; Akh-Aset

Contrast: tomb was uninjured/not lost in the XXth dynasty vs current time when it has not been found

Cause-and-Effect: details from the Abbott Papyrus prove that pyramid-tomb was intact in 1000 B.C. and newly discovered temple has pyramid in its center, suggesting they are the same; also it is known that discovered temple was called Akh-aset because of inscriptions on it

The pyramid was then a dummy, made of rubble within a revetment of heavy flint nodules, which was faced with fine limestone. It was erected on a pyloni-form base with heavy cornice of the usual Egyptian pattern. This central pyramid was surrounded by a roofed hall or ambulatory of small octagonal pillars, the outside wall of which was decorated with coloured reliefs, depicting various scenes connected with the sed-heb or jubilee-festival of the king, processions of the warriors and magnates of the realm, scenes of husbandry, boat-building, and so forth, all of which were considered appropriate to the chapel of a royal tomb at that period. Outside this wall was an open colonnade of square pillars. The whole of this was built upon an artificially squared rectangular platform of natural rock, about fifteen feet high. To north and south of this were open courts. The southern is bounded by the hill; the northern is now bounded by the Great Temple of **Hat-shepsu**, but, before this was built, there was evidently a very large open court here. The face of the rock platform is masked by a wall of large rectangular blocks of fine white limestone, some of which measure six feet by three feet six inches. They are beautifully squared and laid in bonded courses of alternate sizes, and the walls generally may be said to be among the finest yet found in Egypt. We have already remarked that the architects of the Middle Kingdom appear to have been specially fond of fine masonry in white stone. The contrast between these splendid XIth Dynasty walls, with their great base-stones of sandstone, and the bad rough masonry of the XVIIIth Dynasty temple close by, is striking. The XVIIIth Dynasty architects and masons had degenerated considerably from the standard of the Middle Kingdom.

[Adapted from *Egypt's Dynasties* by Casey Choate, 2011.]

Key terms: Hat-shepsu

Contrast: well cut and designed architecture of XIth dynasty vs rougher work of XVIII dynasty

Main Idea: The passage describes a XIth dynasty tomb which is the only of the period to be discovered in modern times. It reveals a great deal about the art and architecture of the time.

1. Based on the passage, the Thebans were preceded by the:
    A) Neb-hetep Mentuhetep.
    B) Asyût.
    C) **Herakelopites.**
    D) Shêkh Abd el-Kûrna.

The first paragraph states that "When the Herakleopolite dominion was finally overthrown…the Thebans assumed the Pharaonic dignity," making choice C the credited answer.

A, B, D: These names are mentioned at other points in the passage, but were not the group who came before the Thebans.

2. Suppose that a pyramid was found in a newly discovered temple of the XIth Dynasty. The author would most likely argue that:
    A) the pyramids served a religious purpose which is not yet clear to archeologists.
    B) the many deaths of the Herakleopolite rebellion necessitated a larger necropolis.
    C) the tombs were relocated to galleries at a later date.
    D) **such details may be less rare than previously believed.**

In the second paragraph the author states that "the most remarkable thing about this temple is that in its centre there was a pyramid." This suggests that pyramids within tombs were rare, since finding one makes it clear that this site is Akh-aset. Finding another would lessen the rarity, as in choice D.

A, C: the passage does not discuss either religious purposes or relocating tombs.
B: While the passage starts by discussing the overthrow of the Herakleopolites, it does not connect the building of pyramids with this event.

3. The author discusses the Abbott Papyrus in order to:
    A) **begin to trace the period in which knowledge of Akh-aset faded from history.**
    B) suggest that inspectors failed in their task in keeping the tomb intact.
    C) demonstrate the paucity of information available about the XIth dynasty.
    D) contrast the architectural choices made by those in the XIIth and XXth dynasties.

The Abbott Papyrus is the "report of the inspectors sent to examine the royal tombs" during the XXth Dynasty. They reported on the tomb, so, the author of the passage concludes, "We know, therefore, that it was intact about 1000 B.C." Since the tomb has been recently rediscovered, it must have been lost for some years and the Abbott papyrus is a means to trace that history, as in choice A.

B: The passage states that the inspectors were ordered to "examine" the tombs, not protect them as in choice B.

C: The Abbott Papyrus is from the XXth Dynasty, eliminating choice C.

D: There is no discussion of whether the Abbott Papyrus describes architectural details, eliminating choice D.

4. According to the passage, the discovery of the temple of Neb-hapet-Râ Mentuhetep is most important due to the fact that it:

    A) establishes the standards of masonry and decoration that endured after the Middle Period.

    B) sheds light upon the brutal battle of succession between the Herakleopolite and the princes of Asyût

    C) contrasts with the building style of the Great Temple of Hat-shepsu.

    D) **<u>reveals important details about the art and architecture of the XIth dynasty.</u>**

The passage as a whole focuses on the way that the discovery of Akh-aset, which was the temple of Neb-hapet-Râ Mentuhetep, adds new information about the aesthetics and architecture of the XIth dynasty, a period about which relatively little was known, as in choice D.

A: The passage suggests masonry and decoration changed throughout time, eliminating choice A, which suggests they remain the same.

B: there is no information on the battle as in choice C.

C: Hat-shepsu is discussed in terms of location, not style.

5. Suppose that an archeologist discovered a tomb from the time of Neb-hetep Mentuhetep shortly after this report was written. The writer of the report would most likely be:

    A) **<u>pleased to gain a new source of information about the building techniques of the period</u>**

    B) surprised that any tombs remained intact after the battle staged by the princes of Asyût in 1000 B.C.

    C) doubtful that any edifice could reach the picturesque splendor of Dêr el-Bahari.

    D) certain that it could be differentiated from earlier pyramid tombs and funerary temples.

In the first paragraph, the author states that "the results obtained up to date have been of very great importance, especially with regard to the history of Egyptian art and architecture, for our sources of information were few and we were previously not very well informed as to the condition of art in the time of the XIth Dynasty." Thus choice A is the answer.

B: there is no evidence that all tombs were destroyed.

C: Dêr el-Bahari is a location, not a building, as in choice C.

D: the passage does not state that tombs from the time are clearly differentiable from earlier ones, eliminating choice D.

6. Which of the following can be definitively stated about Akh-aset?

  I. **<u>It was intact in 1000 B.C.</u>**

  II. It consists of a solid rock pyramid with a galley in the back.

  III. It was destroyed by Hat-Shepsu

    A) **<u>I only</u>**

    B) III only

    C) I and II only

    D) II and III only

I: In the passage, we are told that the tomb "was known….and still uninjured in the reign of Ramses IX of the XXth Dynasty... We know, therefore, that it was intact about 1000 B.C.," meaning this is supported.

II: the passage states that the tomb is "perhaps a gallery cut in the cliffs at the back of the temple," but it is not certain, eliminating choice II.

III: Hat-Shepsu was built later than Akh-aset.

7. All of the following are assumed to be features of XIth dynasty architecture EXCEPT:
    A) <u>**large, rough cut rocks.**</u>
    B) colored reliefs.
    C) sandstone based masonry.
    D) small octagonal pillars.

The passage states that the walls of the XIth dynasty temple had "great base-stones" in contrast to the "bad rough masonry of the later temple," meaning choice A is not a feature of XIth dynasty architecture.

B, C, D: Colored reliefs, sandstone, and pillars are all listed, eliminating choices B,C, and D.

Passage II Explanation

To **European** architects brought up on the traditions of **stone and brick** construction, our Japanese method of building with **wood and bamboo** seems scarcely worthy to be ranked as architecture. It is but quite recently that a competent student of **Western architecture** has recognized and paid tribute to the **remarkable perfection** of our great temples. Such being the case as regards our classic architecture, we could hardly expect the outsider to appreciate the **subtle beauty** of the tea-room, its principles of construction and decoration **being entirely different** from those of the West.

Key terms: European architects, Japanese method, Western architecture

Contrast: European/Western architecture is stone/brick, Japanese is wood/bamboo; principles of construction are completely different in each tradition

Cause-and-effect: due to unfamiliarity with Japanese traditions, most Westerners lack frame of reference to appreciate its architecture

Opinion: tea-rooms have subtle beauty, temples achieve remarkable perfection

The **tea-room (the Sukiya)** does not pretend to be other than a **mere cottage**—a straw hut, as we call it. The original ideographs for Sukiya mean the **Abode of Fancy**. Latterly the various tea-masters substituted various **Chinese characters** according to their conception of the tea-room, and the term Sukiya may signify the **Abode of Vacancy** or the **Abode of the Unsymmetrical**. It is an Abode of Fancy inasmuch as it is an ephemeral structure built to house a **poetic impulse**. It is an Abode of Vacancy inasmuch as it is devoid of ornamentation except for what may be placed in it to satisfy some **aesthetic need** of the moment. It is an Abode of the Unsymmetrical inasmuch as it is consecrated to the worship of the **Imperfect**, purposely leaving some thing unfinished for the play of the imagination to complete. On account of the extreme simplicity and chasteness of its scheme of decoration, it appears to foreigners almost barren.

Key terms: tea-room (Sukiya), Chinese characters

Contrast: Sukiya referred to as both fancy and unsymmetrical, fancy and empty

Opinion: the tea-room is unfamiliar to foreigners, but is exactly what it means to be

The Sukiya consists of the **tea-room proper**, designed to accommodate not more than five persons, an **anteroom (midsuya)** where the tea utensils are washed and arranged before being brought in, a **portico (machiai)** in which the guests wait until they receive the summons to enter the tea-room, and a **garden path (the roji)** which connects the machiai with the tea-room.

Key terms: anteroom (midsuya), portico (machiai), garden path (the roji)

The tea-room is unimpressive in appearance. It is **smaller** than the **smallest of Japanese houses**, while the materials used in its construction are intended to give the suggestion of **refined poverty**. Yet we must remember that all this is the result of **profound artistic forethought**, and that the details have been worked out with care perhaps even greater than that expended on the building of the **richest palaces and temples**. A good tea-room is **more costly than an ordinary mansion**, for the selection of its materials, as well as its workmanship, requires immense care and precision. Indeed, the carpenters employed by the tea-masters form a distinct and highly honoured class among artisans, their work being no less delicate than that of the makers of **lacquer cabinets**.

Contrast: appearance of refined poverty belies incredible care and cost involved

Cause-and-effect: care and precision, quality of materials, highly-trained carpenters all contribute to extremely high cost for a tiny tea-room

Passage III Explanation

At the outset, a key difference must be understood: that between the **actual creative act of making a sculpture** and the subsequent questions of **criticism** that allow us to understand a given piece of sculpture and place it in a larger framework. The first is a raw creative expression that requires mastery over the physical act of chiseling away stone; the other an academic topic more akin to history or literary study. Needless to say, **some have attempted to meld the two**. A common misconception of the early nineteenth century was that all lovers and critics of sculpture must attempt to hew meaning from blank rock themselves before they could offer insight or criticism. And even more **distressingly**, several major art schools have recently started suggesting that **their apprentice sculptors must achieve a mastery of the history** of sculpture before ever picking up the chisel.

Opinion: some think being a critic requires learning sculpture or being a sculptor requires learning art criticism, but the author rejects this, calls it "distressing".

As intellectually edifying as it may be to memorize an endless list of the names of sculptors and works and artistic movements, the job of the young sculptor is completely different. The **young creative person must learn to summon and harness the particular madness** that takes over the successful sculptor: at once the creator must be an **obsessive**, ensuring **surgical precision** with each hammer-blow, lest the work be ruined by a single errant strike, and at the same time the creator must allow **the mind to flow smoothly, freely, and be open** to inspiration.

Opinion: Author thinks it's the job of a young sculptor to learn to get into the sculpting mindset, which is both free flowing and obsessive.

The **problem of how to bring the novice sculptor into the right state of mind** is one that has gotten **no easier to answer** with modern materials and techniques. One approach currently in vogue is that sculptors should look to the **methods of dance**, which need only be modified to fit the work of the sculptor. The sculptor may model his own working process on that of the dancer in several different ways. The first would be for the **sculptor to treat his chisel and hammer as if they were simply extensions of his body**, to be controlled with the precision that a dancer controls his arms and legs. Another is to **emulate** the dancers' notions of **expression through position**. The creative act of sculpture itself would then become the work of art, rather than the final product. Often sculptors who attempt this approach take from dancers their **basic method of mastery through repetition and practice**. These artists will craft the same sculpture over and over until they get it right. Finally, some will take the **dancers' use of music** as a way to create the proper mindset and set their sculpting to a soundtrack.

Cause-and-effect: Some try to help sculptors get into the right mindset by taking one of several different approaches used in dance.

Although it has not yet been recognized generally, **this basic emulation of dancers has largely failed** to live up to the enthusiasm with which it was initially embraced. No doubt, as its proponents loudly declaim, there is a large area in which the basic approaches of the sculptor and the dancer are similar, or perhaps even exactly the same. Such **overlap would include things like evoking emotion, non-literal self-expression, and an awareness of basic spatial composition**. But such ideas are **common to** sculpture, dance, painting, film – any visual art and perhaps even **any art in general**. Ultimately, we must recognize the simplicity of the answer is this: **sculpture is its own distinct avenue** of artistic expression with its own methods and approaches. The problem of getting the young sculptor into the right mindset lies in **teaching the young sculptor how to sculpt** and how to invite the free-flowing obsessiveness needed for that art. Turning to dance as a shortcut is no shortcut at all.

Opinion: Author thinks using dance has failed and that any overlap between dance and sculpture is just the basic overlap common to all arts. Author thinks sculptors learn by sculpting.

It is only a particularly myopic vision of the creative mindset that excludes the actual practice of sculpting as a possible approach. This myopia is likely **driven by fear** rather than a striving for success. When months of work my be irretrievably ruined by a single mistake, **the novice sculptor understandably seeks solutions outside his field**.

[Adapted from: "Let's Get Physical: Sculpt by Sculpting" by Juliana O'Connell, 2011.]

Cause-and-effect: Fear of failure drives young sculptors to seek shortcuts from outside sculpture.

Main Idea: Sculpture is its own distinct form of expression and you learn to sculpt by sculpting. Sculptors shouldn't need to, or have to, turn to first learning art history or dance or some other field.

12. The author's overall purpose in writing the passage is to:
    A) assert that those artists who study both dance and sculpture are more fully able to succeed in making sculpture than others.
    B) describe the features of dance and sculpture that are similar.
    C) **argue that the creative process of sculpting is its own enterprise distinct from either dance or artistic criticism of sculpture**.
    D) demonstrate that art schools have failed their young sculptors by focusing on the history of sculpture rather than the process of creating sculpture.

The author considers and rejects the ideas that sculptors should be required to master art history and art criticism or other art forms such as dance. She thinks the best way to learn to be a sculptor is to actually sculpt. Thus choice C is correct.

13. According to the author, the task of a novice sculptor is to:
 I. **discover a way to engender the free-flowing obsessiveness needed to create sculpture**.
 II. learn to place their own work in the larger framework of art history.
 III. meld the methods of other physically expressive activities such as dance into the act of sculpting.
    A) **I only**
    B) II only
    C) I and II only
    D) I and III only

The author explicitly rejects the notions that sculptors should be required to study art history or dance, thus making II and III false. Thus choice A is correct.

14. Assume that a journeyman sculptor is about to begin work in a new piece. The author of the passage would likely state that the most important task to be performed is:
    A) clarifying how the new piece will fit into the larger historical framework of sculpture.
    B) adopting a mindset that permits the sculptor to control the hammer and chisel as extensions of her own body.
    C) understanding that the piece will be flawed and will require repetition to produce mastery.
    D) **finding the right attitude to permit creative sculpting.**

The author makes a point of saying that young sculptors need not master art history first, thus eliminating choice A. In refuting the notion that dance is the means to becoming a sculptor, she would reject choices B and C, which are described as a part of dance. Thus by process of elimination we're left with choice D.

15. The author could best clarify the sentence, "It is only a particularly myopic vision of the creative mindset that excludes the actual practice of sculpting as a possible approach." by doing which of the following?

A) Offering a definition of "myopic vision"

B) Explaining more fully what a creative mindset is and how that relates to the actual practice of sculpting

C) Demonstrating how dancers exhibit their approach to the creative mindset

D) **Giving an example of an art historian who does not have such a myopic vision**

The author tells us that art must, of course, include sculpture as its own separate, valid technique. To explain her point further she could offer support from other writers, including art historians. Thus choice D is correct.

16. The author thinks that teaching young sculptors how to sculpt is important because:

A) it allows them to be more successful in their work by melding the physical approaches of dance and sculpture.

B) there is no meaningful overlap between sculpture and other art forms, thus requiring young sculptors to eschew any potential shortcuts.

C) it is by developing both careful precision and flowing inspiration that a sculptor finds the motivation to succeed in the work.

D) **the actual practice of sculpting is the way to learn how to invite the "particular madness" that results in successful sculpture**.

The author's main idea is that sculpture is its own valid art form with its own valid techniques and that you learn to be a sculptor by sculpting. She thinks that success in sculpture requires the "particular madness" referred to in choice D, thus it is correct.

A, B: These both contradict statements in the passage.

C: The author doesn't discuss "motivation" and thus this is outside the scope of the passage.

17. Assume that an art school hired a new Director to oversee its sculpture department and the Director had all new students take dance classes in addition to their sculpture work. If several such students then went on to produce exemplary works of sculpture, this would:

I. be consistent with the author's main point.

II. refute the author's assertion that "[t]urning to dance as a shortcut is no shortcut at all."

III. **provide evidence suggesting that dance is one means to help sculptors develop the right mental attitude needed to succeed at sculpting.**

A) II only

B) **III only**

C) I and III only

D) II and III only

The author thinks that sculpture requires a combination of obsessiveness and free-flowing mental state that permit the act of sculpting to happen. The question shows us that dance may be one way to achieve that right mental state. Thus III is true and choice B is correct.

I: The question is not entirely consistent with the author's main point. She does seem to think that dance and sculpture are unique, so the situation described doesn't exactly fit.

II: The question doesn't refute the author. It's entirely possible that the art program in question already routinely produced gifted sculptors even before the new director had students taking dance.

18. In another work, the author of the passage stated that "a painting of a sculpture is no sculpture at all" and that "dancers who attempt to 'sculpt' space in their work are misguided, at best". These statements have what relevance to the passage?

    A) The first is irrelevant whereas the second refutes the author's argument about the relationship between dance and sculpture.

    B) **They support the author's general contention that sculpture has its own unique approach to the creative process.**

    C) They support the notion that emotion, non-literal self-expression, and spatial composition are common to all visual arts.

    D) They weaken the author's assertion that historical context is relevant to the creative process.

This question shows the author sounding a consistent theme. She acknowledges that all art shares certain facets of self-expression, but then thinks that sculpture has its own unique way of doing this. If she also thinks painting and dance have their own approaches to take, that would be consistent with her overall theme.

Passage IV Explanation

Research suggests that schools have an essential role to play in **local community cohesion and development**, a trend that has gained currency among urban and rural school advocates alike. A growing body of theory views the support of local schools as an **essential community development practice**. Historically, local schools sought to utilize school facilities as social development tools to turn around blighted urban neighborhoods. America's school-houses acted as a **crucible for emerging concepts such as social capital.**

Key Terms: community cohesion, community development, social capital

Cause and Effect: It is implied that if local school facilities are used as social development tools, blighted urban neighborhoods can be turned around.

Yet there are those who view the retention of local schools as a barrier to **progress, professionalism, and efficiency**. The school of thought that favors large, **centralized schools** is built on the theoretical heritage of **modernity**, including faith in **progress, scientific approaches and objective quantitative analysis** as the basis for **rational decision-making. Technocratic knowledge** is privileged over **community knowledge**, thereby greatly increasing the agency of the bureaucracy to consolidate schools. Arguments around social cohesion are overpowered by the officialdom's logical-sounding entreaties for parents to accept new, enlarged, superior communities for the betterment of their children, rather than "clinging to the past."

Key Terms: progress, professionalism, efficiency, centralized schools, scientific approaches, objective quantitative analysis, rational decision-making, technocratic knowledge, community knowledge.

Contrast: The author specifically contrasts technocratic knowledge with community knowledge, but the entire paragraph establishes that there is a contrast between the ideological and epistemological viewpoints of those who support centralized schools with the viewpoints of those who support local schools.

Opinion: It is the opinion of those who support centralized schools that parents who are supporters of local schools are clinging to the past, to outdated and outmoded models of education. This opinion is based on their beliefs that centralized schools are more professional and efficient

Cause and Effect: Because technocratic knowledge is privileged over community knowledge in debate concerning school consolidation, the bureaucracy has more power to affect change (close schools).

But a growing research consensus reveals that **students fare better in smaller schools academically and socially**. Among the consistent findings are that larger consolidated schools tend to have higher rates of violence, lower parental and student involvement, lower academic achievement and higher drop-out rates at the high school level. Additionally, **consolidation has the greatest consequences for the poorest members of the community**. Economically and socially disadvantaged communities appear to find greater advantage in small school environments in close proximity to the community served, as opposed to larger, geographically distant consolidated schools. There is also well developed theorizing around the essential role schools play in promoting healthy community development, yet **none of this seems to make any difference once a school is cited for closure**. Despite the strong body of research to back parents' claims that school consolidation negatively impacts children and their communities, their local schools still close.

Key Terms: economically and socially disadvantaged communities

Contrast: In this paragraph, the author highlights the negative aspects of large consolidated schools, contrasting these with local schools that do not suffer from the same issues of violence, lower parental and student involvement, lower academic achievement and higher drop-out rates. The author also contrasts the consequences of school consolidation between socioeconomic groups. The economically and socially disadvantaged suffer more than other, less disadvantaged populations.

Cause and Effect: At the end of the paragraph, the author suggests that a cause and effect relationship has somehow been corrupted. The expectation is that because of all of the research supporting local schools, local school supporters would be more successful in saving their schools from consolidation. However, the author notes that this expected effect is not actually coming to fruition.

Convincing educators to support schools as **tools of community survival** remains an unrealized goal. Despite decades of rhetorical support for schools as centers of community, actual implementation remains stymied by a brick wall of **education planning** that appears to actively prevent schools from migrating beyond the domain of education into the domain of community life. Advocates tend to expend great effort on gathering and communicating data to decision-makers, almost always to no avail. School boards, driven by **neoliberal frameworks of rationalization, standardization and professionalism**, are not in a position to receive and act on community-generated qualitative information that arises from a radically different framework.

Key Terms: tools of community survival, education planning, neoliberal frameworks of rationalization, standardization and professionalism

Contrast: The author contrasts what has been said about schools as centers for community and what has been done relating to schools as being centers for community. "Despite" signals that although there is a lot of talk about using schools as centers for community, the actual use of schools in this way has been "stymied by a brick wall." So although there has been talk, there has been no actual action to support this talk. Also, the author contrasts the frameworks that school boards and community activists are using, suggesting that these frameworks are irreconcilable.

Opinion: The author's opinion is that education planning is actively trying to prevent schools from being used as centers of community life.

Cause and Effect: The author suggests that because school boards are coming at the issue from a radically different framework than community members, they are unable or incapable of receiving and acting on information that the community brings forward.

If it is necessary to step outside the system in order to seriously challenge it, we must become more aware, then, that when the **educational bureaucracy** conjures up community, the understandings and approaches come from a different place. In brief, knowing consolidation has negative consequences is not enough to win the battle. Knowing the **theoretical differences and power dynamics** behind the process may not be enough either but, at the very least, such readings push activists to re-assess their traditional approach of trying to convince a **recalcitrant bureaucracy** through argument, and to instead capitalize on their strengths in communications, networking, local knowledge, and community action. From this point, school advocates may break through to larger social movements.

Key Terms: educational bureaucracy, theoretical differences and power dynamics, recalcitrant bureaucracy

Contrast: The educational bureaucracy's notion of community is different from activists' notions of community because these notions come from different theoretical places.

Opinion: The author's opinion is that activists must first understand the theoretical differences and power dynamics that are involved in debates concerning school consolidation. Then, the author believes that after understanding these aspects of the debate, activists can determine more effective methods for advocating for their schools and affecting change.

[Adapted from "School Consolidation" by P. Elliot, Review of Literature. *In Education*, 2012.]

19. Based on the context and contents of the passage, what does social capital most likely mean?
- A) The collective real estate and personal property of a group of people that belong to a social network
- B) The social configurations in society that evolve from the actions of the individuals
- C) **The collective value of social networks and the positive attributes, such as those of goodwill, fellowship, and mutual sympathy that exist among a group of individuals and families who make up a social network**
- D) The durable goods and other financial assets that people may exchange within their social networks for other goods and services

In order to answer this question, the reader must infer what the term social capital means from the context of the passage. Given the content and the focus on the author's argument, the correct choice is C. C is the correct choice because the emphasis of the passage is on the ability of local schools to be tools of community cohesion, development and survival. While the author does mention that economically disadvantaged communities suffer the most from school consolidation, the majority of the article is not focused on the economic aspects of school consolidation but rather the social aspects, and particularly the positive social aspects. Choice C is the choice that includes positive social aspects.

A, D: They both suggest that "capital" in the term "social capital" is a tangible good or asset.
B: While it addresses the "social" aspect of "social capital," it does not include anything concerning the "capital" aspect of "social capital."

20. Which of the following claims would most *weaken* the author's claim that the support of local schools is an essential community development practice?
- A) **Community and place are irrelevant in the discussion of school closures because community can exist anywhere and, indeed, may never exist at all as a tangible entity due to the digital nature of contemporary life**
- B) Consolidation has the greatest consequences for the poorest members of the community because their fragile social ties and limited mobility are boosted by the presence of neighborhood schools.
- C) Social cohesion is not something generated solely by communities in isolation from government policy.
- D) Schools have been clearly shown to contribute greatly to cohesive and supportive community life, simultaneously fostering stability and new opportunities.

In order to answer this question, the reader must consider what the author means by "the support of local schools" being an "essential community development practice." Given the content of the passage, the reader needs to determine that these theories suggest that communities develop cohesion by supporting their local schools – and that without local schools to support, community development will suffer. The reader must also determine which of the following choices are harmful to or could disprove this particular claim. Choice A is the correct choice because it calls into question the author's assumptions about community. According to choice A, traditional ideas of community are being reevaluated and redefined, but the author does not seem to address these changing notions of community. The author's claim that local schools are needed in order for community development is seriously called into question if traditional manifestations of community are in fact extinct.

B, C, D: Each of these choices could be used to support the author's claim rather than challenge the author's claim.

21. Which of the following sentences from the passage most reveals the author's attitude concerning educators and educational policy makers?
- A) Convincing educators to support schools as tools of community survival remains an unrealized goal.
- B) Arguments around social cohesion are overpowered by the officialdom's logical-sounding entreaties for parents to accept new, enlarged, superior communities for the betterment of their children, rather than "clinging to the past."
- C) School boards, driven by neoliberal frameworks of rationalization, standardization and professionalism, are not in a position to receive and act on community-generated qualitative information that arises from a

radically different framework.

D) **Despite decades of rhetorical support for schools as centers of community, actual implementation remains stymied by a brick wall of education planning that appears to actively prevent schools from migrating beyond the domain of education into the domain of community life.**

In order to answer this question, the reader must infer from the content, from word choice, and from other stylistic tools, what the author's position is specifically as it relates to educators and education policy makers. The author's attitude towards educators and education policy makers may also be inferred from the author's attitude toward school consolidation, as she aligns educators and policy makers as being markedly in the camp of school consolidation. Then, once the reader has established the author's attitude towards educators and policy makers, the reader must evaluate each choice, determining which choice is most aligned with the author's attitude. The correct choice is choice D. Choice D includes the most explicit characterization of educators and policy makers, describing them as a "brick wall" that blocks the implementation of schools as center of community. The author claims that education planning is "actively prevent[ing]" schools from moving into the domain of community life, which characterizes educators and policy makers as antagonistic. These characterizations align with the author's attitude toward educators and policy makers.

A: The tone or attitude of this sentence is more one of frustration and/or dismay with the ineffectiveness of activists' efforts rather than frustration or dismay with the educators themselves.

B: This choice hints at the author's contempt of educator's *arguments* that school consolidation is progress, which should be valued above all else, rather than revealing the author's attitude towards the actors (educators and policy makers) themselves.

C: This sentence has a neutral tone or attitude as it relates to the framework of school boards, educators and policy makers. Rather than insinuating that the framework of school boards is *wrong*, the author asserts that the framework is *different* (and incompatible with) the framework of community activists.

22. Which dichotomy does the author's discussion seem the most concerned with?
    A) **Bureaucracy and democracy**
    B) Quantitative and qualitative
    C) Modern and traditional
    D) Professional and unprofessional

In order to answer this question, the reader must be able to identify content within the text that relates to each of these dichotomies and then determine which dichotomy receives the most attention from the author in the passage. The correct choice is choice A because throughout the article, the author continually contrasts the positions of the school board, policy makers, etc (bureaucracy) with the positions of the community activists (democracy).

B, C, D: Although each of these dichotomies is mentioned or alluded to at some point within the text, each of these dichotomies' roles is in support of the larger discussion of bureaucracy and democracy. The bureaucracy is associated with quantitative research methods, modernism and professionalism. The community activists (the democracy) are associated with qualitative methods and are characterized by supporters of consolidation as holding onto outdated traditions.

23. Which of the following would the author be LEAST likely to promote as a school-based community development initiative?
    A) Coordinating the development of affordable housing and public schools
    B) Engaging schools in community economic development strategies
    C) **Occasionally sharing school space with government and service agencies**
    D) Including student entrepreneurial projects as part of standard curriculum

In order to answer this question, the reader must be able to infer potential concrete initiatives for community development from the somewhat abstract discussion of how local schools can facilitate community development. The author does not provide concrete examples of how schools can be tools of community cohesion, development and survival, but based on the concepts presented in the passage, the reader can infer which of the choices would be the least likely to facilitate community cohesion, development and survival. Choice C is the correct choice because this choice would be the least likely to facilitate community cohesion, development and survival, and would therefore be the choice the author would be the least likely to support. From the passage, the reader can infer that the author is interested in more permanent initiatives and efforts, but choice C is only suggesting occasional sharing of school space – rather than a more permanent, cooperative or collaborative sharing of school space.

A, B, D: Each of these initiatives could facilitate community cohesion, development and survival in a more long lasting and collaborative way than choice C. The author would most likely support each of these initiatives.

24. The primary intended audience for this passage consists of:
  I. School board officials and educators
 II. Teachers and parents
III. Community advocates
      A) I only
      B) II only
      C) **III only**
      D) I, II and III

In order to answer this question, the reader can consider a number of aspects of the passage including the content itself, the style of the piece (whether it is informal or formal, etc.), the tone, the word choice and the level of technical terms or jargon. The reader may even consider where the piece was originally published (which is mentioned in the source attribution at the end of the passage). Choice C is the correct choice. While the content includes an overview of both sides of the school consolidation debate, there are indications throughout that the information is intended to benefit community advocates. For example, the author mentions, "Arguments around social cohesion are overpowered…" which suggests she is addressing those making these arguments about social cohesion. Then, the final two paragraphs specifically address the intended audience of community advocates. The author states, "If it is necessary to step outside the system in order to seriously challenge it, *we* must become more aware . . . ." This is a call to action and the plural pronoun *we* groups the reader with the author. The author is certainly advocating for local schools as a community advocate.

A. The passage is not attempting to convince school boards and educators to change their position, nor is the passage trying to inform school boards or educators of the positions of community advocates. The way the author addresses school boards and educators throughout the passage suggests that she is not intending or expecting this audience to read the passage.
B: While the author does address parents' roles in advocating for local schools ("Despite the strong body of research to back parents' claims that school consolidation negatively impacts children and their communities, their local schools still close."), the main intended audience is community activists, which could potentially include parents. But since there is no choice that includes BOTH teachers and parents AND community activists, choice C is the best choice.
D: Choice D includes school board officials and educators, which we have already established are not the intended audience for this passage.

25. Which paragraph most clearly reveals the author's purpose?
      A) The second paragraph
      B) The third paragraph
      C) The fourth paragraph
      D) **The fifth paragraph**

In order to answer this question, the reader must determine the function of each paragraph and how that function relates to the author's purpose. While the entire passage works cohesively to accomplish the author's purpose, each paragraph on its own may be more directly or indirectly related to that purpose. Choice D is the correct choice because the author's argument is structured inductively. The author continues to build her argument from one paragraph to the next until the final paragraph, the fifth paragraph, in which she ties each of the previous paragraphs together. The author's purpose is stated in the fifth paragraph. The author intends to help community advocates understand the educational bureaucracy's theoretical framework – and the theoretical differences and power dynamics that are at play in the issue of school consolidation – so that advocates can reevaluate and improve upon their approaches. Ultimately, the author is issuing a call to action to advocates – to revise their tactics to be more effective.

A, B: These paragraphs function to contrast the educational bureaucracy's framework with that of community activists. While contrasting these frameworks is important, it is only one part of accomplishing the purpose of helping advocates understand these differences in order to improve upon their approaches.

C: The fourth paragraph primarily functions as a summation of the obstacles that advocates have faced. Ultimately, the author's purpose is a call to action to advocates. That call to action doesn't happen until the fifth paragraph.

Passage V Explanation

I have seldom felt so **proud** of being a representative of the people as now, when it gives me an opportunity to advocate a cause which **cannot be represented or defended in this chamber by those directly and particularly affected by it**, owing to the leven of prejudice that the beliefs and ideas of the past have left in the mind of modern man. The cause of **female suffrage** is one sure to **strike a sympathetic chord in every unprejudiced man**, because it represents the cause of the weak who, deprived of the means to defend themselves, **are compelled to throw themselves upon the mercy of the strong**.

Key terms: female suffrage

Cause-and-effect: the women who lack equal rights lack means to rectify this, so advocacy by the strong with a voice is necessary; women lack power of men because of ancient beliefs and prejudices

Opinion: the plight of the weak and mistreated is intrinsically compelling

But it is not on this account alone that this cause has my sympathy and appeals to me. It has, besides, **the irresistible attraction of truth and justice, which no open and liberal mind can deny**. If our action as legislators must be inspired by the eternal sources of right, if the laws passed here must comply with the divine precept to give everybody his due, then **we cannot deny woman the right to vote, because to do otherwise would be to prove false to all the precepts and achievements of democracy and liberty which have made this century what may be properly called the century of vindication.**

Contrast: sympathy for the weak independent of support for the side of justice

Cause-and-effect: unequal rights for women are inconsistent with liberty and democracy

Opinion: justice and truth are appealing, particularly to the liberal-minded

Female suffrage is a reform demanded by the social conditions of our times, by the high culture of woman, and by the **aspiration of all classes of society to organize and work for the interests they have in common**. We cannot detain the celestial bodies in their course; neither can we check any of those moral movements that gravitate with irresistible force towards their center of attraction: Justice. **The moral world is governed by the same laws as the physical world, and all the power of man being impotent to suppress a single molecule** of the spaces required for the gravitation of the universe, it is still less able to prevent the generation of the ideas that take shape in the mind and strive to attain to fruition in the field of life and reality.

Contrast: unalterable movement of heavens similar to unalterable course of social change

Cause-and-effect: justice and moral ideas provide an irresistible force, remade society is a foregone conclusion

It is an interesting phenomenon that whenever an attempt is made to introduce a social reform, **in accordance with modern ideas and tendencies and in contradiction with old beliefs and prejudices**, there is never a lack of opposition, based on the maintenance of the *status quo*, which it is desired to preserve at any cost. As was to be expected, **the eternal calamity howlers and false prophets of evil raise their fatidical voices on this present occasion**, in protest against female suffrage, invoking the sanctity of the home and the necessity of perpetuating customs that have been observed for many years.

Contrast: social reform fits modern ideas but contradicts old prejudices

Opinion: author doubts legitimacy of concerns raised by opponents of suffrage

Frankly speaking, I have no patience with people who voice such objections. If this country had not been one of the few privileged places on our planet where **the experiment of a sudden change of institutions and ideals has been carried on most successfully**, without paralyzation or retrogression, disorganization or destruction, I would say that the apprehension and fears of **those who oppose this innovation might be justified**.

Contrast: worry-mongering of those opposing change vs. reality of previous successful social change

Cause-and-effect: previous social changes have gone over very well

Opinion: these concerns are not valid or defensible

But in view of the fruitful results of our own revolutions, and what those new institutions of liberty and democracy have brought to our country; and considering the marked progress made by us, thanks to these same institutions, in all the orders of national life, in spite of a few reactionists and ultra-conservatives, who hold opinions to the contrary and regret the past, I do not and **cannot, understand how there still are serious people who seriously object to the granting of female suffrage, one of the most vivid aspirations now agitating modern society**.

Cause-and-effect: previous success makes it impossible rationally to censure female suffrage

Opinion: previous social changes have done unfettered good

Main Idea: equal rights for women are morally necessary, inevitable, desirable, beneficial, and those opposing have only prejudice as a reason

26. It can be inferred from the passage that the author:
    A) has personally experienced prejudice of the kind described in the text.
    B) does not self-identify as politically liberal.
    C) **considers women's suffragists as having relatively little political power on their own behalf.**
    D) sees equal rights for women as impossible without a major sociopolitical shake-up.

The author clearly indicates that the individuals experiencing this prejudice are unable to represent themselves and therefore need an advocate, eliminating A. The author implies having liberal leanings, eliminating B. Answer choice D is the opposite of what is stated, which is that previous social upheavals occurred without a hitch, and giving women the vote should be easily accomplished. Answer choice C is a match. The author states in the first paragraph that advocating for the female vote is of value because it is like defending the weak from the strong, implying that the women suffering from discrimination and battling it have little power compared to the author as advocate.

27. What is the significance of the author's reference to the physical law of gravitation in the third paragraph?
    A) It's an analogy for the idea that one good deed leads to another, like pieces of rock accreting into a planet.
    B) **It means that moral rightness is an inevitable and irresistible as processes governed by physical laws.**
    C) It contrasts with social and moral change, which, unlike the movement of planets, is uncertain and inexactly predicted.
    D) It's meant to illustrate that inevitability is an illusion of hindsight, as no social circumstance is truly inevitable.

Reading the paragraph, the analogy clearly allies justice with the sun, as producing a force as irresistible as gravity. The analogy also suggests that doing the right thing when the stars are aligned is inevitable and should not be struggled against. B is a match, while C and D contradict the idea of this paragraph, and A is irrelevant to the analogy as discussed in the passage.

28. The author implies that those who oppose the female suffrage movement:
    A) are protecting their own economic interests.
    B) **do so out of gender prejudice.**
    C) fear a backlash from standing out from the crowd politically.
    D) have never really thought about why they hold the views they do.

The author sarcastically refers to these individuals as calamity howlers, paraphrasing the concerns they raise while implying a complete lack of belief that the concerns are genuine. Since the author implies these are not the real reasons, and elsewhere states that the unprejudiced can only support female suffrage, it can be inferred that the passage author simply feels these individuals are prejudicial, matching answer choice B. None of the other statements are implied or directly supported by the passage.

29. Which of the of the following, if true, would most strengthen the main argument of the passage?
    A) Social reform is often followed by a brief economic recession.
    B) Gender diversity in the workplace tends to lead to employee reorganization.
    C) Other nations pushing back against the female right to vote tend to have a higher agricultural base.
    D) **Other nations that have granted full voting rights to women have suffered no social backlash or ill effects.**

The passage author has already stated that previous social reforms in this country have gone on without a hitch, but every cause and revolution is different. Evidence that the exact same type of reform, women's voting rights, had occurred in other countries without difficulties, makes the passage argument in its favor even stronger. A, contradicting this idea, would, if true, weaken the argument. B and C neither strengthen nor weaken the argument, being irrelevant to its given evidence and conclusion.

30. Which of the following titles most accurately describes this passage?
    A) **Time for Change**
    B) Life of a Woman
    C) The Reform Process
    D) The History of Female Suffrage

A is a little vague, though it gets at the main idea, obliquely. The author is certainly agitating for change. Leave this answer choice aside for now. B is not a good fit, being far too broad and not getting at women's rights at all. C sounds very informational, but the author is clearly arguing for a particular conclusion. D, likewise, sounds too objective, since the passage is arguing a particular point of view and a straightforward history would not do that. So, A, the imperfect first option turns out to be the best fit. It is the only title suggesting a point of view, an argument, which the passage definitely contains. And it references that argument, albeit in vague terms. In advocating the vote for women, the author is indeed saying that it is time for change.

Passage VI Explanation

News of the completion of the **transcontinental railroad** came to the **Southern Paiute** peoples in what would become the state of Arizona at a time when they were slowly beginning to return to the **quiet agrarian life** that had sustained them for millennia, after a **disastrous** attempt by **Chief Kwiumpus** to turn the Paiutes into a **conquering, slave-owning society** similar to the nearby **Navajo**. News came slowly to the Southern Paiutes, as the twin barriers of **desert and language helped isolate** them both from ever-expanding populations of whites as well as from other Indian tribes.

Key terms: transcontinental railroad, Southern Paiute, Chief Kwiumpus, Navajo

Opinion: Chief Kwiumpus's efforts were bad

Cause-and-effect: Desert and language isolated them, leading them to get news slowly.

At the bottom on the Southern Paiute power structure sat the **foundation of its conservatism: children**. Any child, even those of the most powerful chiefs, were considered to be beneath those adults who had successfully completed their Rite of Adulthood. **Proper instruction of children in the traditional ways** of the tribe was considered the **sacred duty of every Paiute**. Combined with children's natural inclination towards stable, simple structures both in life and in story-telling, the relationship that Paiute **adults had with the tribe's children** created a **core of conservatism** that lasts even to the present day. At the top of the Southern Paiute hierarchy sat the **holy women** who served as a combination of healer, diplomat, advisor to the chiefs, and conduit to the heavens. These priestesses were **reliably protective of the tribe's old ways**, despite the increasing incursions of change from whites and other tribes.

Key terms: holy women

Cause-and-effect: Conservatism in Paiute culture was supported by children and holy women

Between these two ends of the totem pole, however, hid a **small minority of dissidents**, primarily **young braves** who had had the **most contact with the outside**, actively traded with whites and other tribes, sought to explore new methods of hunting and agriculture, learned English, and, **most scandalously**, began following the tenets of **Christianity**.

Opinion: Young braves with outside contact believed in the new ways including Christianity

To these priestesses, these children, and these dissident young braves came the **shocking news** of the whites' new development: an iron trail with a **great iron horse** that would **bring newcomers in an unstoppable wave** even larger than the steady river brought by the wagon trains of the past. A few recklessly defiant tribesmen openly rejoiced; they spoke of riding the "iron horse" of the transcontinental railroad themselves, and seeing the great nation of the white man for themselves. **They thought to learn the ways of these men that came in such numbers**. As more missionaries built their churches closer and closer to Paiute lands, **some began openly joining their services** and speaking of what they heard when they returned to their villages.

Cause-and-effect: New railroad brought more whites and led some Paiutes to join them.

Within two decades of the completion of the railroad, **new settlements by whites had encroached** into the territory of a nearby Northern Paiute nation. **Violence** inevitably erupted, with the resultant destruction and **displacement of the entire Pakwidocade** tribe. The **fury** of the Southern Paiute chieftains and holy women **turned on the dissidents** and, by extension, any of the young men who had taken to interacting overmuch with the whites. The **Kuyuidokado** family, who had largely converted to Christianity, was wiped out in a single night of bloody conflict. The one chieftain to actively encourage trading with the whites, **Chief Pogidukadu**, was stripped of his rank and exiled with his sons. And the entire tribe of **Kutzakika'a** peoples were attacked for no sin greater than having a holy woman who sought to include Jesus Christ as one of the many children of the Earth Goddess in the Paiute pantheon.

Cause-and-effect: New settlements encroached on land, led to violence, and Southern Paiutes retaliated by attacking those in the tribe who supported the new ways of the white men.

Key terms: Pakwidocade, Kuyuidokado, Pogidukadu, Kutzakika'a

Ultimately, **the conflict** between the expanding borders of the United States and the widely scattered Southern Paiute tribes **ended as all such conflicts eventually ended**, although the **Paiutes** were able to **hold on much longer** than most, simply by virtue of inhabiting **land that was not deemed desirable** by the settlers who came streaming into the Arizona territory.

[Adapted from *Conservatism in the Tribal Peoples* by Connell Choate, 1945.]

Cause-and-effect: Conflict ended way it always did, having less-desirable land let Paiutes hold on longer than most.

Main Idea: Most of Paiute society was conservative. But changes to Paiute society brought by the white men led some members of the tribes to embrace the new ways, but violence between whites and neighboring Northern Paiutes created a backlash of violence against those supporting the new ways of the whites, primarily Christianity.

31. Which of the following groups of people played a role in preserving the traditional societal structures in the Southern Paiutes?
   I. **Children of tribal chieftains**
  II. Traders who interacted with outsiders
 III. **Diviners who interpreted signs from the gods**
      A) I only
      B) II only
      C) III only
      D) **I and III only**

I and III are mentioned directly in the second paragraph as being a source of traditional conservatism in the tribes. II is mentioned as being a part of the new ways.

32. It may be inferred from the passage that the Southern Paiutes may have survived longer as a distinct cultural entity if they had:
      A) partially embraced the new cultural ideas brought in by the whites.
      B) joined with a larger, more powerful tribe such as the Navajo.
      C) **been located further south, farther away from the transcontinental railroad.**
      D) succeeded in their attempt to become a conquering, slave-owning society.

The author tells us that they survived relatively long because they were separated by desert and occupied land that was deemed undesirable. Had they been even further away, they likely would have survived longer.

33. Which of the following consequences would have been likely had more than one chieftain been supportive of the Christian church's attempts to convert the Southern Paiutes?
      A) The entire Southern Paiute nation would have converted to Christianity.
      B) Interactions between the Southern Paiutes and the whites would have allowed the Southern Paiutes to maintain themselves as an independent nation to the present day.

C) More children would have been taught English and the basic tenets of Christianity.

D) **<u>The chiefs who also supported the missionaries would also have been either stripped of power or wiped out.</u>**

The passage tells us that those in the tribe who started adopting new ways were violently attacked. Had another chief adopted such ways, he would likely also have been attacked, as choice D says.

A, B: These are too extreme.

C: This may have happened, but we don't know if the additional chieftain who supported the Christians would have allowed them to proselytize to the children nor teach them English.

34. Which of the following facts from the passage supports the notion that the braves who favored adopting the ways of the whites were in a minority?

A) The wise women served as the mediators of the Southern Paiute's relationship with their gods.

B) **<u>The children and those who taught them reinforced the simple, traditional cultural norms.</u>**

C) Those who actively traded with the whites were more likely to adopt their ways.

D) When violent conflict erupted between the Northern Paiutes and the whites, the Southern Paiutes reacted by attacking those among them who favored turning to the ways of the white settlers.

We're told that the braves who adopted the new ways were in the minority, but this question asks us to identify a fact that makes it clear that they were a minority group. So we need a fact that makes it clear that the majority of the culture was oriented towards conservatism. The discussion in the passage tells us that all children and those who instructed children (which is seen as the duty of all tribe members) were inclined towards conservatism. This makes it clear that the overwhelming majority of the society was conservative. Thus those favoring the new ways must have been in the minority. Thus choice B is correct.

A: We don't know how many wise women there were. Although they were conservative, this fact tells us nothing about the minority status of those who wanted to adopt new ways.

C: This also aligns with the passage, but does not tell us anything about the number of such people.

D: Again, this does come from the passage but doesn't tell you which group was in the majority and which was in the minority.

35. Which of the following facts most likely *weakens* the author's contention that the holy women were powerful supporters of the traditional culture?

A) To be selected to become a holy woman, a girl must display mastery of several traditional female arts.

B) **<u>After selection, a young woman endures a rigorous month-long ritual in which all assumptions about herself and her world are stripped away.</u>**

C) Less than one in six young women selected to become a holy woman can survive the training process.

D) After achieving full status as a holy woman, new priestesses are expected to apprentice to an elder holy woman for a decade or more.

The author asserts that the holy women were protective of the old ways. To weaken that contention, we would want an answer choice that suggests that the holy women were not a force for stability and conservatism – something that suggested they were open to change. Choice B fits, since stripping away all previous assumptions would make one more open to new ideas and change.

A, D: These would strengthen the tie between conservative, old ways and the holy women.

C: How selective or dangerous the process is doesn't tell you anything about whether the holy women were inclined towards the old ways or towards change.

36. The author suggests that the young braves who began adopting white ways were rejecting traditional cultural values and norms. It is equally possible that:

    A) the braves felt resentment towards the exclusive power the holy women had in interceding with the gods.

    B) **frequent and prolonged exposure to a new group of people lead the braves to adapt to their new surroundings.**

    C) a desire to overthrow the structure of traditional Southern Paiute culture lead the braves to seek out new avenues to power.

    D) whites forcibly converted the braves to Christianity.

The passage tells us that the braves were adopting the ways of new people and suggests they were being "defiant" by rejecting the old ways. However, an alternative explanation would be that they were simply adapting to the new surroundings they found themselves in – in the company of whites and dealing with Christians. Rather than a rejection of the old, they could have been embracing the new. That's choice B and the right answer.

A, C: This would support the original contention in the passage. If the young men felt resentment towards those in power, they may have been defiant of it and sought to overthrow it.

Passage VII Explanation

Miguel de Cervantes y Saavedra was born in **1547** at **Alcala de Hénarès**. His family belonged to the class of impoverished gentlefolk, poor but intensely proud of their descent from one of those hardy mountaineers the **Saavedras**, who, five centuries before, so heroically defended the northern portion of **Spain** against the **Moors**. While the hereditary possessions were growing less and less, the heads of the family would **endeavor to compensate** for present privations, by relating to their children the noble deeds and the great estates of their ancestors.

Key terms: Cervantes, Alcale de Hénarès, Saavedras, Spain, Moors

Contrast: Cervantes' people were poor, yet proud

Cause-and-effect: as wealth decreased, pride increased

Opinion: Saavedras were heroic and descendants are admirable

Whether debarred by poverty or negligence, the last an unlikely supposition, Cervantes did not graduate at the **University of Alcala** or any other, a circumstance that occasioned him much fortification in his manhood and advanced age. **Émile Chasles** thus expresses himself on this subject:

"The graduated took their revenge. When Cervantes acquired celebrity they recollected that he had taken no degree. When he sought an employ they applied to him by way of iron brand the epithet, **Ingenio Lego**, 'He is not of ours,' said they; 'he is not a cleric.' The day when he attracted the attention of all Europe their anger was excessive towards the writer who **possessed talent without permission, and genius without a diploma**. Cervantes gaily replied, that he admired their pedantic learning, their books bristling with quotations, the complements they paid each other in Greek, their erudition, their marginal notes, their doctors' degrees, but that he himself was naturally lazy, and did not care to **search in authors for what he was able to say without them**; and finally, that when there is a dull or foolish thing to be expressed, **it will do in Spanish as well as in Latin**."

Key terms: University of Alcala, Émile Chasles, Ingenio Lego,

Contrast: diploma vs. genius; scholarship vs. originality; pretension vs. clarity

Cause-and-effect: Cervantes' success attracts jealousy and enmity of higher classes

Opinion: passage author thinks barrier to education likely to be poverty, not negligence; Chasles believes Cervantes talented, unfairly targeted for petty reasons

He was smarting under the contempt of the **learned asses** of his day when writing the preface to his **Don Quixote**:

"Alas, the story of **Don Quixote is as bare as a rush! Ah, if the author could do as others,—cite at the head of the book a litany of authorities** in alphabetic order, commencing with **Aristotle** and ending with **Xenophon** or **Zoilus**! But the poor Cervantes can find nothing of all this. There he sits, paper before him, the pen behind his ear, his elbow on the table, his cheek in his hand, and himself all unable to discover pertinent sentences or ingenious trifles to adorn his subject."

[Adapted from "Miguel de Cervantes y Saavedra", unattributed, published in *The Catholic World*, March, 1867.]

Key terms: Don Quixote, Aristotle, Xenophon, Zoilus

Contrast: other writers characterized as derivative and pompous, Cervantes is original and unaffecting

Cause-and-effect: criticism of Cervantes inspires biting response in preface of Quixote

Opinion: describes Cervantes' critics as learned asses; Cervantes is legitimately talented

37. Chasles uses the phrase, "talent without permission", in order to
　　A) **imply that Cervantes' critics were resentful of a man of his class having greater ability.**
　　B) bolster the image of Cervantes as a willful outsider.
　　C) contrast Cervantes artistic achievements with his educational lack.
　　D) establish Cervantes as anti-establishment in his time.

In the context of the passage, Cervantes' critics are described as excessively angry at a newly famous compatriot whose education was less than their own. The phrasing, which was said another way, "genius without a diploma", suggests the combination of his lesser education and greater ability was the source of their ire. Answer choice A refers to a class difference rather than an educational difference, but information elsewhere in the passage supports the idea that the two things are connected, so A is still a good match.

B: Though he is happy to respond in kind, the passage does not support a reading of Cervantes as an outsider by choice.
C: The passage never states that Cervantes' achievements were in spite of his lack of education.
D: This is not supported by the passage.

38. Which of the following verbal attacks does Cervantes not make on "the graduated" in the passage?
　　A) Implying that they utilize learned quotes to compensate for an inability to express their own thoughts
　　B) Sarcastically dismissing their written Greek and Latin as pointless posturing
　　C) **Referring to them as learned asses**
　　D) Mocking them for the praise they give each other

The description of the graduated as learned asses comes directly from the author.

A, B, D: Each of these can be found in the passage in a quote or paraphrase of Cervantes' writings.

39. Which of the following best matches Chasles' opinion of Cervantes, based on the passage?
　　A) A tragically under-appreciated genius
　　B) A plainspoken but powerful writer
　　C) **A brilliant, unpretentious artist**
　　D) A mercilessly incisive linguist

Each of these descriptions holds some truth. Since the question stem asks of Chasles' opinion, the answer lies in the quotation of his found in paragraph two. He recounts the story of the graduated taking their revenge, and one of the few things that is not a quotation or paraphrasing of the critics or Cervantes is Chasles' characterization of their "excessive anger" towards Cervantes, for having "talent without permission". He also notes that this all occurred when Cervantes had acquired celebrity throughout Europe. Cervantes response, as told by Chasles, is of a biting and precise attack on their hollow pretenses. Chasles presents this without comment of his own, unlike his qualification of the critics as excessively angry for petty reasons, suggesting a degree of tacit agreement with Cervantes' response. The description of Cervantes as brilliant and unpretentious is thus a good match.

A: Despite these criticisms, it's clear that Cervantes was not under-appreciated in Europe as a whole. This is also a bit extreme.
B: The only support for this is in Cervantes' choice to write in Spanish instead of Latin. Writing in a living language is less pretentious, but doesn't necessarily equate to plainspokenness.
D: The reader might read Cervantes' verbal repartee as merciless incisive, but Chasles makes no such judgment, paraphrasing the writer's words without additional comment of his own.

40. Which of the following assumptions can be attributed to the passage author?
    A) Honest poverty is noble.
    B) **Material wealth is a source of pride.**
    C) Higher degrees are pretentious.
    D) Formal education and creativity are mutually exclusive.

In the first paragraph the author describes the fierce pride of Cervantes' people, and, further, that it was necessary to compensate for their decreasing wealth by increasing their ancestral pride. This pride in their ancestors is attributed to their noble deeds and, again, their own supposed material wealth. It's assumed here, then, that the simple possession of wealth is itself a point of pride, even for those with none.

A: Though the author exhibits a tone of admiration, it's not dependent on the assumption that the poverty is itself a virtue.

C: Certainly the author and those he quotes often consider some individuals with advanced degrees to be pretentious, but there's no reason to attribute to the passage author the assumption that all who possess such degrees are pretentious.

D: There's no indication that the author feels Cervantes' educational limitations actually were necessary to his creative gifts.

Passage VIII Explanation

Children are great geniuses of creativity, but their creativity serves **no purpose** that is directly visible to the adult mind. In fact, the notion of "**purpose**" itself is a construct of the **adult mind**. With that construct comes the inevitable effort to turn the effort into the purpose itself.

Opinion: children are creative, but not creative for any purpose

Creativity's wellsprings are the **twin engines of recombination and the happy mistake**. In the first, we see children dash heedlessly ahead, **combining and recombining ideas**, words, and images in endless, effortless, and nearly thoughtless ways. This mad dash forward also opens children up to the second: the **happy mistake**. By not watching every footfall in their rush to create, children risk a misstep that may twist an ankle, but also open themselves up to the possibility that the misstep will lead them in a wholly new and unanticipated direction. Yet **adults**, in their attempts to replicate the creativity of childhood, **sever** both of these from underlying **joie de vivre** that impels children forward.

Cause-and-effect: Recombination and the happy mistake lead to creativity

Contrast: Adults sever the joy from creativity when they try to recreate the creativity of childhood.

A **conscious effort to recombine** ideas in a particular way creates, at best, a **sterile laboratory** in which progress is slowed to a crawl and creativity's gush of ideas reduced to a glacial progression of pale, obviously derivative notions. The **adult organizes** creativity into work, **destroying the joy** that is the source of the child's success. The adult mind asks itself a series of questions: "What if I combine A with B? What if I combine A with C? What if I combine A with D?" whose end result is less progress in a month of work than a child achieves in an hour. Whether painter, musician, businessman or scientist, the **adult's efforts at creativity** are **stymied** by an insistence on **organized recombination** rather than the child's chaotic throwing together of ideas.

Contrast: Adults attempt to recombine in an organized way whereas children do it quickly and joyfully

Opinion: Adult attempts to organize recombination creates sterility and slows down creativity

If organization slows the adult's creativity to a crawl, **fear paralyzes it entirely. Mistakes** are not merely bumps on the road to creative success, they are the cobblestones that **make up the road itself**. Ninety nine mistakes may be problems that frustrate and hinder, but it's the one-hundredth that lets true genius show. The history of nearly all human endeavors show that it is the **happy mistake**, the serendipitous accident that **provides the great breakthrough**. The unexpected not only solves the problem, but shows that the way forward is even more open, more exciting, and more successful that had even been thought possible. **Children** easily take advantage of the **happy mistake** simply by virtue of being **willing to make mistakes—lots of them**. Adults, by dint of their fear of failure, fear of looking foolish, or fear of mistake itself, leave themselves **closed to** the only meaningful avenue for **advancement**.

Contrast: Adults are paralyzed by a fear of mistakes but children rush ahead and are willing to make lots and lots of mistakes

Opinion: Author sees mistakes as vitally important – the only means to advancement.

Mother nature is constrained by no such fear. Nature itself is, perhaps, the **single most powerful creative** force around us. This is no new-age philosophical metaphysic, but instead an evaluation of the creative power of life in its relentless ability to harness the same powers of creativity as the human mind. The genetic blueprint by which the architecture of life is built engages in **a recombination of "ideas" – genes** – at its very core. The vast success of sexual reproduction over asexual in every environment on Earth is due to the fact that sexual reproduction is a process of recombination. By shuffling the genetic deck, life opens itself up to new and interesting combinations that can lead to success. Such combinations can also lead to failure, but nature fears failure not.

Opinion: Author thinks nature is a good example of powerful creativity coming out of recombination.

Nature's happy accidents can be seen in the **mutations** which spring up over and over again in the genetic code. Like the serendipitous creativity of the artist, **most mistakes will prove useless or harmless**, but it is the **rare beneficial mutation** which provides such an **overwhelming advantage** of one species over another that the balance of the entire environment can be shifted. Evolution, then, is the model for human creativity. **Our minds are an ecosystem of ideas**, and we must allow those ideas to **come and go with the same careless rapidity** with which Mother Nature allows individual life forms, or even whole species to emerge, live, and disappear.

[Adapted from "Creating Creativity" by Kristen O'Connell, 2011.]

Opinion: Author sees nature as willing to make lots and lots of mistakes – mutations – which then occasionally lead to huge payouts. Author thinks we should cultivate the ideas in our minds.

Main Idea: creativity, as demonstrated by children and nature, springs from a willingness to make lots of mistakes and a willingness to throw together ideas in new recombinations, but adults are paralyzed by fear of mistakes and a sterile, methodical approach to new recombinations.

41. The author's main point is that:
    A) the structure of the adult mind makes it impossible for adults to be truly creative.
    B) fear of mistakes closes adults off from an important source of creativity.
    C) **creativity depends on factors harnessed easily by children and nature but not adults.**
    D) recombination of ideas or genes is the true essence of creativity.

The author discusses two key factors: willingness to make mistakes and a fast, free-flowing recombination as the keys to creativity. He tells us that children and nature demonstrate these factors but not adults. That matches choice C.

42. Which of the following would most strongly *weaken* the author's argument about creativity?
    A) Adults can, with practice, learn to recombine ideas in a manner similar to children's.
    B) Thomas Edison, renowned for his creativity in engineering, is often quoted as saying that invention is "one percent inspiration and ninety-nine percent perspiration."
    C) The cellular machinery that controls genes spends a vast amount of time and effort correcting genetic mutations and carefully controlling genetic recombination during sexual reproduction.
    D) **Mistakes made during creative endeavors are often quite destructive and serve as significant setback to the work being attempted.**

The core of the authors argument rests on the notion that it's okay to make mistakes, and that being willing to rush headlong into lots and lots of mistakes generates the freedom necessary to find the "happy mistake" or that moment of serendipity which is the only path forward. If, in fact, mistakes are actively destructive to the creative process and are a huge setback, then the author's argument would be severely weakened. Thus choice D is correct.

43. Suppose that Nobel Prize-winning scientists are often looked down upon by their immediate peers for being "sloppy, thoughtless scientists". The author would point out that:
    A) luck plays such an overwhelming role in having great breakthroughs that their sloppiness is irrelevant.
    B) the Nobel committee is itself somewhat sloppy and thoughtless in deciding who to award.
    C) the sloppier one is in ones work, the more slowly one is able to recombine ideas in a search for something new.
    D) **it is their willingness to be somewhat sloppy that lets them have the serendipitous accidents that create success.**

The author strongly emphasizes a willingness to rush forward and not worry about mistakes as a key part of the creative process. If a scientist has won the Nobel prize, that clearly demonstrates a high level of success, and such success may very likely be caused by a certain "sloppiness" that leaves them open to the happy accident that creates success. Thus the author would point out choice D.

44. Which of the following assertions from the passage might it be possible to *refute* with clear counterexamples?
  I. **Children's creativity serves no purpose.**
  II. The idea of purpose causes us to transform efforts themselves into purposes.
  III. **Recombination leads to the vast success of sexual reproduction.**
      A) II only
      B) III only
      C) **I and III only**
      D) II and III only

We're asked for which assertions could have clear counter-examples. Here both I and III could possibly be refuted with counter-examples. A scientist could study the differences between sexual and asexual reproduction and discover that, in fact, some factor other than recombination leads to success for species that reproduce sexually. Similarly, a psychologist could study children engaged in creative play and find that their creativity does serve some purpose.

However, there can be no clear counter-example to II since it is more of an abstract philosophical statement, rather than a concrete empirical statement that could be studied. Thus choice C is correct.

45. Suppose a study of the process by which poets write their poems demonstrates that a methodical recombination of linguistic ideas creates more serendipitous discoveries than otherwise. What relevance would this have to the author's thesis?
      A) **It weakens the author's contention about the relationship between the method of recombination and creativity.**
      B) It disproves the author's central argument about creativity.
      C) It strengthens the connection between a childlike process of recombination and creativity.
      D) It neither helps nor hurts the passage's argument as it is irrelevant to the author's contentions.

The author asserts that the methodical recombination of adults is sterile and slow and does not lead to real creativity, whereas the creativity of children is a mad rush forward with ideas and words thrown together almost "thoughtlessly". If a study showed that methodical recombination were actually more successful, it would weaken the author's connection between the *type* of recombination and creativity. Thus choice A is correct.

46. The author's attitude towards mistakes can best be described as:
      A) **enthusiastic about their positive effects.**
      B) a balance of positive regard for their effects on creativity and worry about their negative consequences.
      C) trepidation.
      D) concern that mistakes can interrupt the flow of recombination.

The author calls mistakes the happy accidents that are the only path towards success. His overall tone towards creativity, mistakes, and recombination is overwhelmingly positive. Thus choice A is correct.

47. Which of the following best exemplifies the type of creativity the author celebrates?
      A) A computer program creates a novel recipe for Baltic Apple Pie by testing billions of ingredient recombinations in microseconds.
      B) A highly successful author consistently creates best-sellers by writing variations on the same theme for each novel.
      C) **A celebrated jazz pianist with over six decades of experience playing music performs original improvisations each night by throwing together musical ideas from across the decades with a haphazard disregard for the boundaries between different types of jazz.**

D) A performance artist films himself painting and as soon as makes a single errant brushstroke in the work, he violently destroys the canvas, at the end of which he displays both the final perfect painting and video screen showing himself destroying every painting with even a single mistake.

We need an answer choice that demonstrates the two factors that the author says lead to creativity: a willingness to make mistakes, and reckless recombination. Only choice C fits.

A: The author explicitly says that this sort of methodical, rigid recombination can never be a wellspring of real creativity.

B: This would be the opposite of creativity.

D: Reacting in a violently negative way to mistakes would be the opposite of the author's attitude.

Passage IX Explanation

The history of **Great Britain** is the one with which we are in general the best acquainted, and it gives us many useful lessons. We may profit by their experience without **paying the price which it cost them**. Although it seems **obvious to common sense** that the people of such an island should be but one nation, yet we find that they were for ages divided into three, and that those three were almost constantly embroiled in quarrels and wars with one another. Notwithstanding their **true interest with respect to the continental nations was really the same**, yet by the arts and policy and practices of those nations, their mutual **jealousies were perpetually kept inflamed**, and for a long series of years they were far more inconvenient and troublesome than they were useful and assisting to each other.

Key terms: Great Britain

Contrast: nations of Britain had similar aims yet worked against each other

Cause-and-effect: Britain's history of nations full of mistakes, author's country could avoid those mistakes; nations of Britain remained divided because their politics actively kept them at each other's throats

Opinion: fractured mini-nations are inefficient and irrational, unification is obviously preferable

Should the people of **America** divide themselves into three or four nations, **would not the same thing happen**? Would not similar jealousies arise, and be in like manner cherished? Instead of their being "joined in affection" and free from all apprehension of different "interests," envy and jealousy would soon extinguish confidence and affection, and the **partial interests of each confederacy, instead of the general interests of all America, would be the only objects of their policy** and pursuits. Hence, like **most other BORDERING nations, they would always be either involved in disputes and war**, or live in the constant apprehension of them.

Key terms: America

Cause-and-effect: separation of US into multiple smaller nations would likewise be of disadvantage to each of them; separate nations by their nature do not consider the greater good of all nations; bordering nations tend to struggle with disputes

Opinion: political differences and international disputes are to be avoided

The most sanguine advocates for three or four confederacies **cannot reasonably suppose that they would long remain exactly on an equal footing in point of strength, even if it was possible to form them so at first**; but, admitting that to be practicable, yet what human contrivance can secure the continuance of such equality? Independent of those **local circumstances which tend to beget and increase power in one part and to impede its progress in another**, we must advert to the effects of that superior policy and good management which would probably distinguish the government of one above the rest, and by which their relative equality in strength and consideration would be destroyed. For **it cannot be presumed that the same degree of sound policy, prudence, and foresight would uniformly be observed by each of these confederacies for a long succession of years**.

Cause-and-effect: with so many random factors, some degree of political and economic disparity between near-nations is a certainty

Opinion: author assumes an initial equal footing for the sake of argument, but doubts both initial equality and sufficient similarity in regional opportunity; author considers exact equality an unnatural, contrived situation, not a naturally-occurring balance

Whenever, and from whatever causes, it might happen, and happen it would, **that any one of these nations or confederacies should rise on the scale of political importance much above the degree of her neighbors, that moment would those neighbors behold her with envy and with fear**. Both those passions would lead them to countenance, if not to promote, whatever might promise to diminish her importance; and would also restrain them from measures calculated to advance or even to secure her prosperity. Much time would not be necessary to enable her to discern these unfriendly dispositions. She would soon begin, not only to lose confidence in her neighbors, but also to feel a disposition equally unfavorable to them. **Distrust naturally creates distrust, and by nothing is good-will and kind conduct more speedily changed than by invidious jealousies and uncandid imputations, whether expressed or implied**.

Cause-and-effect: a disparity in strength will occur, and this will lead to envy and fear; distrust leads to more distrust, so hostilities of some kind are inevitable

Let candid men judge, then, **whether the division of America into any given number of independent sovereignties would tend to secure us against the hostilities and improper interference of foreign nations**.

Opinion: several fractured states are more relatively vulnerable, e.g. foreign threats

Main Idea: separate bordering nations will always be weaker individually than a unified state, because they will work against each other

48. The author would likely *disagree* with which of the following statements?
  A) **Though newly-sovereign US states would initially be on an equal footing, inequality would creep in eventually.**
  B) Isolated island nations are less likely to live under the shadow of war, all other things being equal.
  C) Jealousy will tend to erode relations between any near nations.
  D) A unified country with a strong federal government will ultimately benefit every American state.

At first glance, each of these statements seem compatible with the passage. B and D are both somewhat tempting, as the language is different from that of the passage. However, the statement in B is implied by the statements about border-nations and war, and the statement in D is also a rehash of the argument for a single nation rather than several, with the several sovereignties and single nation being discussed instead as states and the federal government. A, however, though seemingly lifted directly from the passage, includes the statement that these sovereign states would start on an equal footing. In fact, this was a hypothetical which the author's tone showed clear skepticism of, assumed for the sake of argument only.

49. Based on paragraph three, the author assumes that good government:
  A) is a natural consequence of a mature society.
  B) leads to more good government, becoming more difficult to disrupt over time.
  C) **is a balancing act, with longer periods of success being less and less likely.**
  D) is entirely dependent on the actions of one's governmental neighbors.

The author writes that it is unlikely for multiple nations to observe good and successful government for a long period of time, which seems to assume that good government is at least partially based on chance and that an eventual mistake disrupting a successful streak is inevitable. Were good government a natural state of things according to the author, it would not be considered impossible that several nations would achieve a similar state of permanently well-administered and strong, stable nations (as in A and B), rather than inevitable disparities leading to equally inevitable distrust and disputes (the consequence of C). The author also seems to assume that the governments of the nations can be considered in isolation as independent of each other, considering their relations only after the disparity has occurred (which eliminates D).

50. The author would argue for which of the following nations as being better served amalgamating under one government?
    A) The former British colonies of Singapore and Hong Kong, separated by 1600 miles of ocean
    B) Tibet and Nepal, geographically close and divided by the mostly impassable Himalayan mountain range
    C) **The Republic of Ireland and Northern Ireland, both on the same violently-contested land mass in the British Isles**
    D) The United Arab Emirates and Saudi Arabia, their undefined border falling somewhere within several hundred miles of inhospitable, empty desert

The author argued that bordering nation-states will tend to be in dispute, at war, or in constant threat of those things. This does imply that non-bordering countries might reasonably remain independent. Of the four pairs of nations listed in the answer choices, only the one listed in answer choice C mentions no geographic region for their separation. And indeed, the note of the land being "violently-contested" is one of the author's points of argument in favor of unification, rather than a reason against it.

51. What is the author's reason for discussing "the effects of that superior policy and good management which would probably distinguish the government of one above the rest" in paragraph three?
    A) To support the argument that good government must be the first priority of any new nation
    B) To illustrate the capricious and accidental nature of successful government policy
    C) To describe the most likely cause of one nation rising above its neighbors
    D) **To argue the inevitability of a disparity in the strength of nations, whatever, their starting points**

Reading the sentence in context eliminates answer choices A and B. The surrounding sentences discuss how several neighboring nations will likely end up being of differing strength. In fact, the author makes a multi-step argument, skeptically assuming that several nations could be of the same initial conditions to begin with, then considering whether the varying advantages of their region (unspecified, but presumably natural resources would be one consideration) would tend to favor one state over another, assuming it wouldn't for the sake of argument (but clearly doubting this), then finally stating that even if all other things were equal, the intricate series of guesswork involved in government policy would also certainly see varying levels of success, with this initial disparity simply tending to increase over time. No matter what the initial conditions, one nation achieving superiority is thus shown to be inevitable, matching D. C, on the other hand, is a poorer match, as the author does not suggest government is the most likely cause of a disparity (nor the least likely), but one more example that will tend to disrupt the precarious and unnatural situation of equal strength across nations.

52. The author implies that independent nations:
    A) are a temporary historical contrivance, with world government being inevitable.
    B) **are justified when sufficient geographic separation exists between regions.**
    C) are justified when population size would be unwieldy in a single unified nation.
    D) are preferred, as unification leads to forced proximity of culturally dissimilar groups

The author argued for unification, but was specific in the circumstances mentioned. It's obvious that a single island should have a single nation, according to the author, especially given that border-states tend to live under the shadow of war. The argument was not extended to (nor did it imply) the necessity or desirability of a world government. The focus was on geography and borders rather than cultural similarity or population size (neither of which were mentioned explicitly). Based on this, the only implication that can be drawn from the passage as to the situations in which separate nations ought to exist is geographic in nature.

2. Suppose an oil painting done near the end of the Renaissance, in the general style of Renaissance portraiture, includes particularly strong emotions, and depicts one of the subject's hands coming slightly "out of frame" at the edge of the painting. The author would likely assert that:

    A) the person commissioning the painting had particularly daring taste in art.

    B) the painting itself was an example of a heroic act in breaking with tradition.

    C) the painter was forward-looking by embracing new Baroque trends.

    D) the elements of the painting were somewhat conservative by the standards of the time.

3. By the turn of the century, only art critics in America routinely assert that Michelangelo's David is the finest of the Renaissance sculptures of David. Compared to their counterparts in Europe, these critics:

    A) likely misunderstand the significance of the historical story of David and Goliath.

    B) over-emphasize the value of the extreme popularity of Michelangelo's David.

    C) are harshly disapproving of sculptures that depict their subjects stepping outside the proper boundaries of the sculpture.

    D) probably place greater emphasis on the masterful execution of the heroic male nude than on depicting the specific heroism of David.

4. Suppose that an art historian discovers that Michelangelo's David was actually originally intended as part of a larger installation that included two other sculptures: one sculpture that depicted Goliath before the fight and a third depicting David standing triumphantly over Goliath's corpse. This would:

    A) have no relevance to a discussion of David sculptures.

    B) make it unambiguously clear that Michelangelo's full representation would have been the definitive example of Renaissance sculpture.

    C) suggest that the author's interpretation of Michelangelo's artistic vision was less plausible.

    D) strengthen the author's assertion that Bernini's work engages with earlier representations of David.

5. According to the author, which of the following details demonstrate Bernini's break with earlier traditions?

  I. Bernini's strikingly young age when he received the commission

  II. The mastery necessary to make the first free-standing marble sculpture of the Baroque period

  III. The strong emotions depicted plainly on David's face

    A) I only

    B) III only

    C) II and III only

    D) I, II, and III

6. What is the significance of the author's assertion that Bernini's David is "no longer self-contained"?

    A) It introduces the author's view of several interesting aspects of Bernini's sculpture.

    B) It contrasts the highly emotional depiction in Bernini's sculpture with the lack of emotion in Michelangelo's.

    C) It emphasizes the technical mastery of Bernini's piece that parallels the technical achievement in Donatello's bronze David.

    D) It reveals that the author finds Bernini's David to be the finest artistic representation of David from the Renaissance period.

7. Which of the following statements, if true, would *weaken* the author's assertions about the significance of Bernini's David?

    A) Donatello's David was sculpted with one of the arms jutting slightly out over the base of the statue.

    B) The level of painstaking work required to depict strong facial emotions in marble required such skill that no sculptor was able to replicate Bernini's feat for nearly 75 years.

    C) Early in his career, Bernini's work was a collaboration between himself and two apprentices who went on to become Masters in their own right.

    D) Within three to four decades after Donatello's David, sculptors routinely began depicting Catholic saints in the throes of great ecstasy.

Passage II

Students of behavioral economics have shown that much of the economic behavior that people exhibit follows fairly simple principles of reward and punishment. When explaining microeconomic changes, they look simply to the basic rewards (more money) and punishments (less money) present in a system, and attempt to model the behavior of people or companies as if they were rational actors simply trying to maximize their utility. Recently, however, a major shift has occurred in these analyses which begins to acknowledge that human behavior does not always follow such simple rational patterns. This new form of analysis has even been summed up in a recently coined phrase to describe human behavior: predictably irrational.

Despite these shifts in microeconomic analyses, the underlying framework hasn't changed. The assumption is still that people will always seek to maximize gain and minimize loss, with the added layer of acknowledging that humans are particularly bad at estimating those gains or losses. In a typical example, if offered a sum of money right now (say $100) or another sum of money a year later whose value vastly outstrips the current sum plus the time value of money (say $150), most respondents will make the "irrational" first choice for the lesser sum. Thus, they are making a mathematically "incorrect" choice, even though they would assert that they're maximizing their utility; they want that money *now*.

Yet even this supposedly empirical approach to economics flies in the face of another fundamental macroeconomic model used around the world: the basic income. In those states with a basic income system, every citizen is guaranteed some minimum payment of money, regardless of any condition aside from citizenship. Unlike welfare systems commonly used in Western nations that only provide money to single mothers, or the disabled, or the elderly, the basic income is paid to all citizens. Closely related to the basic income is the guaranteed annual income. Under these systems, each citizen is guaranteed some basic income level. If a person is totally unemployed, the government simply writes a check for a certain amount. If a citizen earns a bit of money, then the government check is reduced by however much the citizen earned.

The implementation of these systems seems to fly in the face of the microeconomic models that explain people's behavior. After all, if the government is simply going to write you a check that's enough to cover your needs, who would possibly choose to work? The reward-to-work ratio of being unemployed under such a system is literally infinite. Yet the famous case of the "Mincome" demonstrated that, perhaps, peoples' behavior is controlled by much more than simple utility maximization.

From 1974 to 1979 the town of Dauphin, Manitoba in Canada provided a guaranteed minimum income for all of its residents. Regardless of age, gender, living situation or physical ability, every adult in the city was given a minimum salary to cover basic needs. Every microeconomic model would have predicted a drastic plummeting of the employment rates in the city. And yet the changes were minor: employment only decreased 1% among men and 3% among married women. The only two groups to show significant decreases in their employment rates were teenagers and mothers of infants. The participants in the study made it clear that they valued time home with their infant children much more than the rewards of having a job. Teenagers, as well, were able to stop looking for low paying menial jobs to help contribute to the home since their minor additional income was unnecessary. The benefits of the system were startling: hospital visits decreased dramatically, high school graduation rates increased, and violent crime ceased almost entirely.

Yet for most of the men in the city who served as primary breadwinners for their households, nothing changed. They continued to work. This result has yet to be explained by any economic model, "rational" or otherwise.

[Adapted from *If You Pay Them, They Will Come* by Kristen O'Connell, 2011.]

8. Which of the following best states the author's main idea?
   A) When rational actor economic models are updated to account for the predictably irrational behavior of people, economists can accurately predict human behavior.
   B) Even when guaranteed a certain minimum income, married women largely continued working, thus demonstrating the inadequacy of classic behavioral economics.
   C) Minimum income programs demonstrate that human economic behavior is not accurately modeled by systems presupposing utility-maximizing rationality.
   D) Economic modeling will always fail to adequately describe the irrational aspects of human behavior.

9. Suppose a province in a European nation chooses to institute a guaranteed minimum income system. The author implies that which of the following people would be *least* likely to stop working?
   A) Man S, a middle-aged unmarried man supporting a teenage daughter and a son in college
   B) Man Q, a high school senior who has been earning minimum wage working as a busboy at a local diner for the past three years
   C) Woman T, a married woman supporting two children, one a toddler and the other an infant, who worked a number of temporary positions over the previous five years
   D) Woman P, an unmarried woman supporting a teenage child, whose yearly income somewhat exceeds the amount offered by the government

10. The author apparently believes that irrational behavior:
   A) accounts for much of the boom and bust cycle found in most economies.
   B) is adequately described by current models of behavioral economics.
   C) would cease if more governments would implement a basic income.
   D) is exhibited when someone fails to maximize their rewards.

11. Suppose an experimenter offers subjects a choice between receiving a mildly painful electric shock now, or a slightly more painful electric shock during a second experiment to be conducted in one month. The author implies that most people would elect:
   A) to receive the less-painful shock now to avoid greater shock in the future.
   B) to receive no shock at all and would withdraw from the experiment.
   C) to receive no shock now and get the greater shock in the future.
   D) to receive whichever shock they perceived as maximizing their utility.

12. According to the author, why have more recent economic models shifted how they analyze human behavior?
   A) Studies have demonstrated that human behavior does not follow the patterns predicted by rational models.
   B) The results of the Mincome experiment needed to be incorporated into their economic models.
   C) Labor markets are unaffected by the presence of a guaranteed basic income for all citizens.
   D) Behavioral economists have adequately shown that much of human behavior can be predicted by looking at basic reward and punishment systems.

13. The author implies that which of the following from the "Mincome" demonstrates the value of a basic income system?
   A) The labor market for men was almost completely unaffected by a guaranteed minimum income.
   B) A minimum income for all citizens protects them from the consequences of irrational decision-making.
   C) Changes in social behavior lead to positive social outcomes for individuals living in Dauphin at the time.
   D) The effect of a minimum income system on a particular citizen in Dauphin depended heavily on that citizen's age and gender.

Passage III

Adult basic education (ABE) and ESL programs, authorized by the Workforce Investment Act and also funded with state and local funds, are designed to assist students in their efforts to acquire literacy and language skills by providing instruction through local education agencies, community colleges, and community-based organizations. The content of instruction within ESL classes varies widely. It is often designed to assist students in their efforts to acquire literacy and language skills by providing a combination of oral language, competency-based work skills, and literacy instruction (Condelli, Wrigley, Yoon, Cronen, & Seburn, 2003). There is, however, little rigorous research that identifies effective instruction. A comprehensive review of published research studies on the effects of literacy interventions for ABE and adult ESL learners (Condelli & Wrigley, 2004) found that out of 17 adult education studies that used a rigorous methodology (i.e., quasi-experimental or randomized trials), only 3 included adult ESL learners (Diones, Spiegel, & Flugman, 1999; St. Pierre et al., 1995; St. Pierre et al., 2003). Furthermore, among the 3 studies that included adult ESL learners, only 1 presented outcomes for those learners, and that study experienced substantial methodological problems that limited the validity of the findings (e.g., a 40 percent overall attrition rate and different attrition rates in the intervention vs. control groups; Diones et al., 1999).

To help improve research-based knowledge of effective instruction for low-literate ESL learners, the National Center for Education Evaluation and Regional Assistance of ED's Institute of Education Sciences contracted with the American Institutes of Research (AIR) to conduct a Study of the Impact of a Reading Intervention for Low-Literate Adult ESL Learners. The intervention studied was the basal reader *Sam and Pat*, Volume I, published by Thomson-Heinle (2006). The goal of this study was to test a promising approach to improving the literacy skills of low-literate adult ESL students under real-world conditions. In their review of the research on ESL instruction in related fields, including adult second language acquisition, reading and English as a foreign language instruction, Condelli & Wrigley (2004) concluded that instruction based on a systematic approach to literacy development was a promising intervention for low-literate adult ESL learners that would be valuable to study (Brown et al., 1996; Cheek & Lindsay, 1994: Chen & Graves, 1995; Carrell, 1985; Rich & Shepherd, 1993; Roberts, Cheek & Mumm, 1994). Specifically, the factors identified as defining a systematic approach to literacy development included: (1) a comprehensive instructional scope that includes direct instruction in phonics, fluency, vocabulary development and reading comprehension, (2) a strategic instruction sequence, (3) a consistent instructional format, (4) easy-to-follow lesson plans, and (5) strategies for differentiated instruction.

Sam and Pat was selected as the focus of the study because it offers an approach to literacy development that is systematic, direct, sequential, and multi-sensory. It also includes multiple opportunities for practice with feedback. Consistent with characteristics identified as promising by Condelli & Wrigley (2004), *Sam and Pat* provides opportunities for cooperative learning, real world tasks, and an explicit focus on reading. In addition, the text was developed for and had been used by the developers with students similar to the study population (literacy level ESL learners).

The impact study used an experimental design to test the effectiveness of *Sam and Pat* in improving the reading and English language skills of adults enrolled in 66 ESL literacy classes at 10 sites. The study addressed three key research questions:

1. How effective is instruction based on the *Sam and Pat* textbook in improving the English reading and language skills of low-literate adult ESL learners compared to instruction normally provided in adult ESL literacy classes?

2. Is *Sam and Pat* effective for certain subgroups of students (e.g., native Spanish speakers)?

3. Is there a relationship between the amount of instruction in reading or English language skills and reading and English language outcomes?

[Adapted from http://www.edpubs.gov/document/ed005180p.pdf?ck=788]

14. Upon which of the following groups does the impact study focus?
    A) ABE learners who have been successful in the workforce
    B) Adult learners with multi-sensory disabilities that inhibit learning
    C) Adult non-native speakers with low literacy levels
    D) ESL learners from specific linguistic subgroups

15. It can be inferred from the passage that many ESL classrooms combine various modes of instruction in order to:
    A) maximize the acquisition of literacy and language skills.
    B) ensure viability in obtaining the skills employers consider essential.
    C) allow for various metrics of evaluation to ascertain effectivity.
    D) prevent the over-emphasis of oral fluency above basic literacy.

16. The author assumes which of the following when asserting *Sam and Pat* is a good choice for the study of increased literacy outcomes?
    A) The reader focuses on the real-world conditions faced by two recent immigrants.
    B) Adult ESL learners prefer basal approaches to other modes of intervention.
    C) Phonics and fluency must precede global reading comprehension.
    D) The reader allows for a systematic approach to literacy instruction.

17. Based on the passage, the Study of the Impact Low-Literate Adult ESL Learners seeks to assess what sort of learning?
    A) Lessons that focus primarily on grammar, phonemes and pronunciation to increase oral fluency and confidence
    B) Ones that proceed in a methodical manner and offer opportunities to work in groups on real world problems
    C) Basal approaches that focus on workforce investment in order to encourage greater participation in the national economy
    D) Those that privilege reading and written texts over spoken language as a means to introduce multi-sensory environments

18. Suppose that an instructor of adult ESL learners sought a researcher to help design a rigorous measurement tool to gauge the effectiveness of her instruction. The writer of the passage would most likely be:
    A) enthusiastic, because such research increases the effectiveness of instruction and the resulting outcomes.
    B) doubtful that such methodologies would serve any purpose due to the high attrition rates in such classes.
    C) surprised that a class was going to be subject to assessment, since that tends to be the exception to the rule.
    D) pleased that the instructor recognized that methodologies for ESL and ABE students involved similar methodologies.

19. All of the following are defined as factors in systematic literacy development EXCEPT:
    A) covering a variety of topics including understanding texts.
    B) varying the strategies by which information is delivered.
    C) differentiating the format in respect to different learning styles.
    D) creating lesson plans that students can easily understand.

20. Suppose that the researchers found that more reading instruction was observed in *Sam and Pat* classes, while more English language instruction was observed in control classes. Based on the passage, the researchers would expect that the students in the *Sam and Pat* class to have:
    A) higher levels of success due to a more systematic integration of literacy and reading.
    B) higher levels of success due to the focus on reading development.
    C) lower levels of success because of a lack of integration of oral and written learning tasks.
    D) lower levels of success because of a dearth of opportunities for cooperative learning experiences.

Passage IV

It is clear that virtue is divided into two sorts: one pertaining to thinking, and the other to character. For the most part, excellence of thinking is the result of teaching, and therefore has need of experience and time, whereas excellence of character comes into being as a result of habit. It is also clear that virtues of character do not come into being in us by nature, because none of the things that are by nature can be habituated to be other than they are. For example, a stone falls downward by nature and it cannot be habituated to fall upward, even if it were to be thrown upward thousands of times. Likewise, fire cannot move downward, just as no thing that happens in nature can be habituated to happen in another way. Therefore, virtues of character come into being neither by nature nor contrary to nature, but rather, they come into being in us who are of a nature to take them on, and they are brought to completion by means of habit.

Before receiving those things that belong to us by nature, we are provided with the potencies for them. In return, we produce the being-at-work of them. This is clear in the case of the senses: it is not from repeatedly seeing or hearing that we took those senses, but rather, having them, we used them. We did not get them by using them. However, we do acquire virtues by first being at work with them, just as is the case of the arts: house builders learn to build houses by building houses and harpists learn to play the harp by playing the harp.

Likewise, we become just by doing things that are just, temperate by doing things that are temperate, and courageous by doing things that are courageous. The work of the lawmaker gives evidence to this, because lawmakers make the citizens of a city good and virtuous by habituating them. Because this is the intention of all lawmakers, those that do it well are successful and those that do it poorly are failures, and in this way, one government differs from another as a good one or a poor one.

Furthermore, every virtue comes into being or is destroyed by means of the same things, and this is true also with the arts, for people become both good and bad harpists by playing the harp and house builders become either good or bad at their art by building well or poorly. If it were otherwise, there would be no need for teachers and all people would have been born either good or bad at particular arts.

It is the same way in the case of the virtues: by acting in our dealings with other people and things, some of us become just and some of us unjust, and by acting in frightening situations and becoming habituated either to being fearful or confident under pressure, some of us become courageous and some of us become cowards. It is just the same way with desires and angry impulses: some will turn themselves one way in these situations and become temperate and gentle, while others will turn themselves the other way and become spoiled an irritable. So, active states like courage and cowardice, justice and injustice, come into being from us being at work at them in similar ways, and therefore, for us to cultivate the virtues in ourselves, it is necessary for us to make our ways of being at work of a certain sort, that is, of the best sort. Therefore, being habituated this way or that straight from childhood makes not a small difference, but an enormous one, or rather, it makes all the difference.

[Adapted from Book II, Chapter 1 of Aristotle's *Nichomachean Ethics*]

21. According to the passage, why are virtues of character not naturally inherent to people?
   A) Because they require a great deal of experience and time to cultivate
   B) Because one must receive the potencies for virtues of character before the virtues themselves
   C) Because every virtue of character comes into being by means of the same things
   D) Because virtue of character is a matter of habit, and natural things cannot be habituated

22. Based upon the passage, the author most likely agrees with which of the following statements?
   A) The most just person is constantly working at acting justly.
   B) People that were habituated to be cowards can become courageous if they work hard enough at it.
   C) The lawmaker is the most virtuous person in a society.
   D) Virtues of character are more important than virtues of thinking.

23. The author makes several references to the harpist and the house builder in order to:
   A) demonstrate how much practice goes into developing virtue of thought.
   B) demonstrate how virtue of character depends upon being at work in a certain way.
   C) give examples of virtuous professions that only the most virtuous people can excel at.
   D) prove that the pursuit of virtue is a more important endeavor than the pursuit of the arts.

24. Based upon the passage, it can be inferred that the author believes the best way for lawmakers to habituate citizens is to:
   A) make laws that require a certain amount of practice at useful arts like house making and pleasurable arts like harp playing.
   B) make laws that allot resources to the education of those with a natural capacity for virtue.
   C) makes laws that require intensive education for all citizens from a very early age.
   D) make laws that encourage citizens to act justly and temperately.

25. Suppose the parents of a newborn boy want him to become a great trumpet player. According to the rationale of the passage, what two things are necessary for this to happen?
   A) He has to have the best teacher and a desire to play well.
   B) He has to practice well and be habituated to behaving like a trumpet player.
   C) He has to have been born with natural talent and practice well.
   D) He has to have been born with natural talent and a desire to play well.

26. According to the passage, all of the following statements are true EXCEPT:
   A) people become just or unjust by behaving justly or unjustly.
   B) for the most excellent and inherently virtuous people, there is no need of teachers.
   C) the senses of sight and sound were not developed by seeing and hearing.
   D) a good government is the one run by lawmakers that properly habituate the people.

27. According to the passage, which of the following will make a person just?
   I. Acting justly in day to day encounters
   II. Studying the nature of justice
   III. Being born with the capacity for justice
   A) I only
   B) III only
   C) I and III
   D) I, II, and III

Passage V

During the early days of World War II, two groups of high-level officers began meeting regularly in Washington, D.C. One group was led by General Brehon Somervell, a politically well-connected officer who provided the major motive power behind the construction of the Pentagon. Those officers who met with Somervell were primarily interested in creating a streamlined military structure that would reduce chains of command between the lowest soldier and the President, but would still have enough flexibility to allow small, quasi-independent groups the freedom necessary to engage in the kind of risk-taking necessary for innovation in any organization. One of the major goals of Somervell's group was to create working papers that could be presented to the President and Congress to convince them to do the necessary reorganization.

Somervell's group began meeting at the very end of 1939, and shortly thereafter another group of retired, semi-retired and reserve officers, centered on Major General William Donovan, began to have meetings. Donovan, the only veteran to have received the four highest awards in the United States (the Medal of Honor, the Distinguished Service Cross, the Distinguished Service Medal, and the National Security Medal), was primarily concerned with shortcomings in America's foreign intelligence apparatus. He sought to revive programs that had been effective during his active service during World War I.

Both of these groups of men consisted largely of anti-establishment thinkers. While they were strongly patriotic, they felt that the bureaucratic structures that had built up around the Presidency to manage the United States' national security had fossilized into an architecture of positions that prevented the country from responding swiftly to new threats, especially that posed by Nazi Germany.

Clearly the urgency created by Hitler's meteoric rise to prominence and his aggression towards his continental neighbors was a more potent force than the conservatism of those who were then holding the reins of military power. The nation as a whole did not share the level of ambivalence about Nazi Germany that many high level government officials did, as Audrey O'Connell convincingly demonstrated in her recent study of the daily tabloid papers that made up most of the media diet of everyday citizens. She soundly refutes the notion that fascist nationalism was a serious thread in the American cultural tapestry of the 1930's and demonstrates that average American citizens overwhelmingly feared Hitler and favored opposition.

FDR, as a man of wide-ranging intellectual engagement, took at least a passing interest in the organizational reforms put forth by groups like Somervell's and Donovan's. But he cannot have been strongly supportive of the work of men who largely hailed from the Republican party, or other anti-Democrat foundations. Among those officers who were the key architects of Department of Defense reform, and the formation of what would become the Office of Special Services (later the CIA), the majority were either active members of the Republican party, or had strong affiliations with those who were.

Nonetheless, FDR ultimately provided the seal of presidential approval to the efforts of Donovan's group; Somervell would have to wait until the end of World War II and the Eisenhower administration to see his plans come to fruition. FDR's statements of approval for reorganizing the military were strong, but saw no action under his watch. And despite the many successes of the OSS in obtaining key intelligence behind enemy lines in Nazi occupied France and Poland and in neutral Turkey, we must not forget that, at first, FDR's support was merely nominal: he allowed the OSS to form, but required that both its manpower and its budget be drawn from existing military structures.

[Adapted from *Inside Outsiders* by Richard Choate, 2011.]

37. Which of the following can reasonably be inferred from David Hume's argument as quoted in the passage?

    A) Unlimited cosmetic surgery for all members of the population should lead to increased physical similarity.

    B) Straight lines and soft color hues are consistent markers of beauty.

    C) Two individuals with the exact same life experiences will lack the usual aesthetic vitiations.

    D) Improvement is unlimited, thus there is no ceiling on beauty.

38. One modern study of the psychology of beauty discovered that perceptions of facial beauty were based on previous experience. Faces that were closer to an average of what the viewer had been used to seeing were considered more beautiful than those faces which deviated from the norm of their experiences. The conclusion was that perception of beauty was heavily influenced by experience rather than being entirely inborn. Based on the passage, whose argument is most weakened by this study?

    A) Plato

    B) Voltaire

    C) Hume

    D) Burke

39. Which of the following quotations about beauty best exemplifies what Voltaire writes in paragraph two?

    A) Love is blind.

    B) Familiarity breeds contempt.

    C) Beauty is in the eye of the beholder.

    D) True beauty transcends personal taste.

40. Plato spoke of ideal forms as existing in another, higher realm, separate from the physical universe. For example, he had argued that any circle drawn by a human hand would be merely an approximation, with small imperfections in the curve, et cetera, compared to the true idea of a circle as mathematically defined. The author would likely agree that:

    A) Hume's work on beauty merely retreads Plato's thinking, his idea of a sound state adding nothing new.

    B) Voltaire misunderstood Plato, missing the most relevant contributions of the great philosopher.

    C) Burke's work is inconsistent with Plato, but the former should be favored.

    D) Hume's similar work on the question of beauty was nevertheless superior to Plato's glancing contribution.

Passage VIII

The rack, the thumbscrew, and the knout are still with us; so are the convict's garb and the social wrath, all conspiring against the spirit that is serenely marching on. Anarchism could not hope to escape the fate of all other ideas of innovation. Indeed, as the most revolutionary and uncompromising innovator, Anarchism must needs meet with the combined ignorance and venom of the world it aims to reconstruct.

The strange phenomenon of the opposition to Anarchism is that it brings to light the relation between so-called intelligence and ignorance. And yet this is not so very strange when we consider the relativity of all things. The ignorant mass has in its favor that it makes no pretense of knowledge or tolerance. Acting, as it always does, by mere impulse, its reasons are like those of a child. "Why?" "Because." Yet the opposition of the uneducated to Anarchism deserves the same consideration as that of the intelligent man.

What, then, are the objections? First, Anarchism is impractical, though a beautiful ideal. Second, Anarchism stands for violence and destruction, hence it must be repudiated as vile and dangerous. Both the intelligent man and the ignorant mass judge not from a thorough knowledge of the subject, but either from hearsay or false interpretation.

A practical scheme, says Oscar Wilde, is either one already in existence, or a scheme that could be carried out under the existing conditions; but it is exactly the existing conditions that one objects to, and any scheme that could accept these conditions is wrong and foolish. The true criterion of the practical, therefore, is not whether the latter can keep intact the wrong or foolish; rather is it whether the scheme has vitality enough to leave the stagnant waters of the old, and build, as well as sustain, new life. In the light of this conception, Anarchism is indeed practical. More than any other idea, it is helping to do away with the wrong and foolish; more than any other idea, it is building and sustaining new life.

Destruction and violence! How is the ordinary man to know that the most violent element in society is ignorance; that its power of destruction is the very thing Anarchism is combating? Nor is he aware that Anarchism, whose roots, as it were, are part of nature's forces, destroys, not healthful tissue, but parasitic growths that feed on the life's essence of society. It is merely clearing the soil from weeds and sagebrush, that it may eventually bear healthy fruit.

Someone has said that it requires less mental effort to condemn than to think. The widespread mental indolence, so prevalent in society, proves this to be only too true. Rather than to go to the bottom of any given idea, to examine into its origin and meaning, most people will either condemn it altogether, or rely on some superficial or prejudicial definition of non-essentials. Anarchism urges man to think, to investigate, to analyze every proposition.

Anarchism is the great liberator of man from the phantoms that have held him captive; it is the arbiter and pacifier of the two forces for individual and social harmony. To accomplish that unity, Anarchism has declared war on the pernicious influences which have so far prevented the harmonious blending of individual and social instincts, the individual and society.

[Adapted from *Anarchism and Other Essays*, Emma Goldman, 1910.]

41. Which of the following definitions of the word "practical" best fits the view of the author?
    A) A scheme is practical if it assumes the current conditions as less than ideal.
    B) A scheme is proved practical once it's successfully been executed.
    C) A practical scheme makes things better, rather than wasting energy on the status quo.
    D) A practical scheme is one whose aims are easily achievable.

42. It can be inferred from the passage that the author considers the apparently violent nature of anarchism:
    A) a pervasive myth.
    B) a necessary evil in combating the forces that corrupt society.
    C) no more violent in reality than a doctor's removal of a cancerous tumor.
    D) a necessary response to the equally violent nature of society's ignorant quarters.

43. Based on the passage description, the philosophy of anarchism can best be described as:
    A) one of incremental, palatable changes summing to wholesale social restructuring.
    B) resting on a few uncompromising, unquestioned propositions that can only lead to complete revolution.
    C) essentially non-violent, intellectually honest and destructive of ignorance and intellectual indolence.
    D) a predominantly rational philosophy with the aim of improving society by considering nothing immune to scrutiny.

44. Which of the following, if true, would most *weaken* the passage's argument in favor of anarchism?
    A) Personality tests suggests anarchists are the group least willing to change their views in light of evidence.
    B) Anarchists are found to be statistically more likely to deface public property or become violent at protests.
    C) Anarchists tend to be amongst the least happy in societies with incompatible political and cultural mores.
    D) A comprehensive review of the anarchist literature suggests that anarchists are the least likely to be bullied into recanting.

45. Based on the sixth paragraph, the author takes for granted that:
    A) it's in human nature to cling to one's prejudices.
    B) most people will tend to take the path of least resistance.
    C) introspection comes naturally, but so does rationalization.
    D) anarchism forces people to confront some difficult truths.

46. The title that best represents the views of this passage is:
    A) The Argument for Anarchism.
    B) A History of Anarchism.
    C) Anarchism: A Call to Action.
    D) Anarchism: Strengths and Weaknesses.

47. Based on the passage, what does the author believe to be at the root of most societal problems?
    A) Rumor and hearsay
    B) Intellectual laziness
    C) Selfishness
    D) Pernicious dogma

Passage IX

Psychology as the behaviorist views it is a purely objective experimental branch of natural science. Its theoretical goal is the prediction and control of behavior. Introspection forms no essential part of its methods, nor is the scientific value of its data dependent upon the readiness with which they lend themselves to interpretation in terms of consciousness. The behaviorist, in his efforts to get a unitary scheme of animal response, recognizes no dividing line between man and brute. The behavior of man, with all of its refinement and complexity, forms only a part of the behaviorist's total scheme of investigation.

It has been maintained by its followers generally that psychology is a study of the science of the phenomena of consciousness. It has taken as its problem, on the one hand, the analysis of complex mental states (or processes) into simple elementary constituents, and on the other the construction of complex states when the elementary constituents are given. The world of physical objects (stimuli, including here anything which may excite activity in a receptor), which forms the total phenomena of the natural scientist, is looked upon merely as means to an end. That end is the production of mental states that may be 'inspected' or 'observed'. The psychological object of observation in the case of an emotion, for example, is the mental state itself. The problem in emotion is the determination of the number and kind of elementary constituents present, their loci, intensity, order of appearance, etc. It is agreed that introspection is the method par excellence by means of which mental states may be manipulated for purposes of psychology. On this assumption, behavior data (including under this term everything which goes under the name of comparative psychology) have no value per se. They possess significance only in so far as they may throw light upon conscious states. Such data must have at least an analogical or indirect reference to belong to the realm of psychology.

Indeed, at times, one finds psychologists who are skeptical of even this analogical reference. Such skepticism is often shown by the question which is put to the student of behavior, 'what is the bearing of animal work upon human psychology?' I used to have to study over this question. Indeed it always embarrassed me somewhat. I was interested in my own work and felt that it was important, and yet I could not trace any close connection between it and psychology as my questioner understood psychology. I hope that such a confession will clear the atmosphere to such an extent that we will no longer have to work under false pretenses. We must frankly admit that the facts so important to us which we have been able to glean from extended work upon the senses of animals by the behavior method have contributed only in a fragmentary way to the general theory of human sense organ processes, nor have they suggested new points of experimental attack. The enormous number of experiments which we have carried out upon learning have likewise contributed little to human psychology. It seems reasonably clear that some kind of compromise must be affected: either psychology must change its viewpoint so as to take in facts of behavior, whether or not they have bearings upon the problems of 'consciousness'; or else behavior must stand alone as a wholly separate and independent science. Should human psychologists fail to look with favor upon our overtures and refuse to modify their position, the behaviorists will be driven to using human beings as subjects and to employ methods of investigation which are exactly comparable to those now employed in the animal work.

[Adapted from "Psychology as the Behaviorist Views It", *Psychological Review*, John B. Watson, 1913.]

48. What is the significance of the quotation in the third paragraph, "what is the bearing of animal work upon human psychology"?
    A) The author is asking a rhetorical question as a lead in to the many and broad applications of animal behavior studies.
    B) The passage's detailed description of the roundabout connections between these studies and theories of human psychology is given as evidence of the many-faceted and interconnected nature of the discipline.
    C) The author is providing evidence of psychologists' exclusive interest in mental states and dismissal of behavior data as being valuable in itself.
    D) The author is making an argument against further animal research as irrelevant to important psychological questions.

49. At the end of the passage, what does the author imply will be the result if psychologists will not reconsider their stance on what constitutes psychology?
    A) Behaviorists and psychologists will work in isolation, limiting insights into human nature on the whole.
    B) Human testing will be the only recourse for behavioral science to move forward.
    C) Behaviorism will be forced to adapt by developing theoretical mental models of their own.
    D) Behaviorists will redefine psychology themselves, contesting the psychological view.

50. Which of the following statements best corresponds to the author's views on behaviorism and psychology?
    A) Behaviorism can offer great insights into human consciousness but the work is less well-regarded than it should be.
    B) Traditional psychologists unfairly dominate the professional conversation, dismissing the value of behavioral research.
    C) Behaviorism and traditional psychology should stand as separate sciences since their goals do not overlap.
    D) Traditional psychology is at a dead-end and will be completely superseded by behaviorism.

51. What does the author mean in the third paragraph when mentioning working under false pretenses?
    A) The author is implying that psychologists are unaware that behaviorists are no longer working towards the same goals as those in traditional psychology.
    B) The author is alluding to misreported or "fudged" data.
    C) The author is implying that behaviorists are being misleading when they don't explicitly note their research focus in the results of their work.
    D) The author is providing evidence of the exploitative use of behavioral scientists by the field of psychology.

52. Which of the following differences between behaviorism and traditional psychology is NOT mentioned in the passage?
    A) Behaviorism is purely interested in predicting behavior, not understanding consciousness.
    B) Psychology is focused on predicting mental states from elementary constituents or determining constituents from states.
    C) Psychology considers human consciousness qualitatively different from the working of animal minds.
    D) Behaviorism is quantitative while psychology is more often qualitative.

53. It can be assumed from the passage that traditional psychology, in the author's view, is:
    A) complementary in its theoretical trappings to the experimental data of behaviorism.
    B) perhaps overvalued, but absolutely necessary to providing a unifying model for behavioral processing.
    C) no more objective than behaviorism, though admittedly less speculative.
    D) more subjective than behaviorism, owing to its focus on interpretation of data.

Timed Section 3 Answer Key

Passage 1	Passage 6
1. B	33. D
2. C	34. C
3. D	35. B
4. C	36. B
5. B	
6. A	Passage 7
7. D	37. A
	38. D
Passage 2	39. C
8. C	40. D
9. A	
10. D	Passage 8
11. C	41. C
12. A	42. C
13. C	43. D
	44. A
Passage 3	45. B
14. C	46. A
15. A	47. B
16. D	
17. B	Passage 9
18. C	48. C
19. C	49. A
20. B	50. B
	51. A
Passage 4	52. D
21. D	53. D
22. A	
23. B	
24. D	
25. C	
26. B	
27. C	

Passage 5
28. D
29. A
30. D
31. A
32. A

Passage I Explanation

It is often widely assumed that **Donatello's first sculpture of David** was originally meant as a depiction of **Isaiah**, but was **hastily reworked** at the last minute. Such revisionist notions have then **inappropriately** been **applied to his second David** – this time sculpted in bronze rather than marble – leading critics to suggest that Donatello was attempting to depict anything from the Greek god Hermes to one of Donatello's lovers to a member of the Medici family.

Key terms: Donatello, David, Isaiah

Opinion: People are wrong to think Donatello's second David was intended as anything but David.

Donatello's **second David is remarkable in several respects**. It is the **first unsupported standing bronze** statue made during the Renaissance, and the **first freestanding nude male sculpture** made **since antiquity**. The statute depicts a **particularly young David** just after vanquishing Goliath, with his foot resting on Goliath's head. Commissioning the piece was a **daring move** by the **Medici** family, as they had been **ejected from the city of Florence** years earlier and David had long been claimed as a **symbol of that city-state**. By prominently displaying Donatello's bronze David, the Medicis were making a public statement about their intention to "**reclaim**" **their Florentine interests**.

Key terms: Medici, Florence

Opinion: Medicis were being daring by displaying a sculpture representing a city they'd been ejected from.

Cause-and-effect: Being a freestanding nude male sculpture and an unsupported bronze makes Donatello's David remarkable

Over **sixty years later**, **Michelangelo** crafted his vision of David. While it is arguably the **most well-known sculpture in the world**, it represents something of a **low point** in the sculptural exploration of the **David myth**. It is undoubtedly a **masterpiece**, but aside from the sling the figure carries over his left shoulder, the work could be **any classical image of the heroic male nude** that has been repeated countless times over the millennia. Michelangelo's decision to remove Goliath from the picture entirely, to place David in a relaxed pose and to only hint at the coming violence in the pinched expression on David's face turns the statue into a **generic, if masterfully executed, vision of male beauty**. **Gone is the true heroism** of the young man who would one day become one of Israel's greatest kings.

Key terms: Michelangelo, David myth, masterpiece, generic

Opinion: Michelangelo's David is a low point since it fails to actually depict the David and Goliath myth and instead is just a beautiful male nude sculpture.

Two decades on, the **heroism would return with Bernini's David**. **By far the most striking** sculptural representation of David to emerge throughout the Renaissance and Baroque periods, Bernini's David was commissioned by **Cardinal Scipione Borghese** (who would later become **Pope Urban VIII**), even though Bernini himself was only 23 years old at the time. Bernini's work engages with the earlier representations done by Donatello, Verrocchio, and Michelangelo, but **creates a strong break with them by embracing the emerging Baroque trends in the arts**.

Key terms: Bernini, Cardinal Scipione Borghese, Baroque

Opinion: Author thinks Bernini's David is the best and it embraces emerging trends in the new Baroque art movement.

Bernini's work is no longer self-contained. By capturing **David in the middle of his action** of hurling the stone that would seal Goliath's fate, the viewer is no longer required to simply stand in front of the sculpture and view it in a proscribed way. Taking in the entire piece demands that **the viewer walk around it**, examining the work from multiple aspects. The figure also literally **oversteps the "proper" boundaries** of sculpture, as Bernini crafted one of David's feet as projecting over the base of the statue. Finally, the work sheds the reserve that characterized earlier sculpture. David's face is **wrought with emotion**, displaying the full measure of what the young hero must have been feeling in his most fateful moment. **What is remarkable** about Bernini's representation is less the sheer technical mastery necessary to accurately render such emotion in marble and more his **willingness to make such a daring break** with earlier artistic traditions.

[Adapted from "Teenage Marble Neat-o Sculpture" by M. Splinter, 2011.]

Opinion: Author notes that Bernini's David oversteps the base, requires viewing from all sides, and that Bernini is daring for being willing to show extreme emotion on David's face.

Main Idea: David has been depicted in sculpture by a number of artists, and although Donatello's was remarkable and Michelangelo's was a generic, but beautiful masterpiece, Bernini's is the best since it showed artistic daring in embracing Baroque and depicting lots of emotion.

1. The author calls Michelangelo's David "generic" because:
    A) it fails to capture Michelangelo's true talent at depicting male beauty.
    B) **although beautiful, it does not engage meaningfully with the Goliath myth.**
    C) it has been copied so often that it fails to evoke any particular reaction in the viewer.
    D) the heroism of the statue is undercut by the fact that it must be viewed from one proscribed angle.

The author criticizes Michelangelo's David for failing to depict the heroism of the David and Goliath myth. He says it is a masterful depiction of male beauty. Thus he likely calls it "generic" because it could be any male nude, not just David. Choice B is therefore correct.

2. Suppose an oil painting done near the end of the Renaissance, in the general style of Renaissance portraiture, includes particularly strong emotions, and depicts one of the subject's hands coming slightly "out of frame" at the edge of the painting. The author would likely assert that:
    A) the person commissioning the painting had particularly daring taste in art.
    B) the painting itself was an example of a heroic act in breaking with tradition.
    C) **the painter was forward-looking by embracing new Baroque trends.**
    D) the elements of the painting were somewhat conservative by the standards of the time.

In the next to last paragraph, the author tells us that Bernini's David broke with tradition and embraced emerging Baroque trends. This question describes features in a painting similar to features in Bernini's David. Thus this painter likely also embraced these new Baroque trends, and choice C is correct.

3. By the turn of the century, only art critics in America routinely assert that Michelangelo's David is the finest of the Renaissance sculptures of David. Compared to their counterparts in Europe, these critics:
    A) likely misunderstand the significance of the historical story of David and Goliath.
    B) over-emphasize the value of the extreme popularity of Michelangelo's David
    C) are harshly disapproving of sculptures that depict their subjects stepping outside the proper boundaries of the sculpture.
    D) **probably place greater emphasis on the masterful execution of the heroic male nude than on depicting the specific heroism of David**.

We're told that Michelangelo's David is a particularly good execution of the male nude, but that the author doesn't like it because it fails to engage with the David and Goliath myth. If American art critics still preferred Michelangelo's David, they must have cared more about the beauty of the sculpture itself rather than depicting the myth. Thus choice D is correct.

4. Suppose that an art historian discovers that Michelangelo's David was actually originally intended as part of a larger installation that included two other sculptures: one sculpture that depicted Goliath before the fight and a third depicting David standing triumphantly over Goliath's corpse. This would:

    A) have no relevance to a discussion of David sculptures.

    B) make it unambiguously clear that Michelangelo's full representation would have been the definitive example of Renaissance sculpture.

    C) **suggest that the author's interpretation of Michelangelo's artistic vision was less plausible.**

    D) strengthen the author's assertion that Bernini's work engages with earlier representations of David.

The author criticizes Michelangelo's depiction of David because it's a generic, pretty sculpture of a male nude. If the sculpture was part of a planned installation that directly depicted the larger David and Goliath myth, then the author is wrong for asserting that Michelangelo chose to completely disregard the myth.

5. According to the author, which of the following details demonstrate Bernini's break with earlier traditions?

  I. Bernini's strikingly young age when he received the commission

  II. The mastery necessary to make the first free-standing marble sculpture of the Baroque period

III. **The strong emotions depicted plainly on David's face**

    A) I only

    B) **III only**

    C) II and III only

    D) I, II, and III

Near the end of the final paragraph, the author discusses how Bernini's willingness to depict strong emotion represented a break with earlier tradition. Thus III is true and choice B is correct.

6. What is the significance of the author's assertion that Bernini's David is "no longer self-contained"?

    A) **It introduces the author's view of several interesting aspects of Bernini's sculpture**.

    B) It contrasts the highly emotional depiction in Bernini's sculpture with the lack of emotion in Michelangelo's.

    C) It emphasizes the technical mastery of Bernini's piece that parallels the technical achievement in Donatello's bronze David.

    D) It reveals that the author finds Bernini's David to be the finest artistic representation of David from the Renaissance period.

Going back to the passage, we see the quote about being self-contained at the start of the final paragraph. This is where the author speaks at length about his analysis of what makes Bernini's sculpture so great. Thus choice A best captures this context.

7. Which of the following statements, if true, would *weaken* the author's assertions about the significance of Bernini's David?

    A) Donatello's David was sculpted with one of the arms jutting slightly out over the base of the statue.

    B) The level of painstaking work required to depict strong facial emotions in marble required such skill that no sculptor was able to replicate Bernini's feat for nearly 75 years.

    C) Early in his career, Bernini's work was a collaboration between himself and two apprentices who went on to become Masters in their own right.

    D) **Within three to four decades after Donatello's David, sculptors routinely began depicting Catholic saints in the throes of great ecstasy**.

The author assert's that Bernini's David is especially significant because Bernini was willing to break with earlier artistic traditions and depict David expressing great emotion. Choice D says that not long after Donatello's David (and well before Bernini), painters were already depicting great emotion routinely. This would make Bernini's choice much less of a break with artistic tradition. Thus choice D weakens the author's view.

Passage II Explanation

Students of **behavioral economics** have shown that much of the economic behavior that people exhibit follows **fairly simple principles** of reward and punishment. When explaining microeconomic changes, they look simply to the basic rewards (more money) and punishments (less money) present in a system, and attempt to model the behavior of people or companies **as if they were rational actors** simply trying to **maximize their utility**. Recently, however**, a major shift has occurred** in these analyses which begins to acknowledge that **human behavior does not always follow such simple rational** patterns. This new form of analysis has even been summed up in a recently coined phrase to describe human behavior: **predictably irrational**.

Key terms: behavioral economics, maximize utility, predictably irrational

Opinion: behavioral economics models human behavior as rational utility maximizing actions

Contrast: Now, economists are acknowledging that people behave irrationally

Despite these shifts in microeconomic analyses, the **underlying framework hasn't changed**. The assumption is still that **people will always seek to maximize gain** and minimize loss, with the added layer of acknowledging that **humans are particularly bad at estimating** those gains or losses. In a typical example, if offered a sum of money right now (say $100) or another sum of money a year later whose value vastly outstrips the current sum plus the time value of money (say $150), most respondents will make the "irrational" first choice for the lesser sum. Thus, they are making a **mathematically "incorrect" choice**, even though they would assert that they're maximizing their utility; they want that money *now*.

Opinion: Author thinks this "new" analysis hasn't really changed and that it still views humans as maximizing utility but just being bad at doing so.

Yet even this **supposedly empirical approach** to economics flies in the face of another fundamental macroeconomic model used around the world: **the basic income**. In those states with a basic income system, **every citizen is guaranteed some minimum payment of money**, regardless of any condition aside from citizenship. Unlike welfare systems commonly used in Western nations that only provide money to single mothers, or the disabled, or the elderly, the **basic income is paid to all citizens**. Closely related to the basic income is the **guaranteed annual income**. Under these systems, each citizen is guaranteed some basic income level. If a person is totally unemployed, the government simply writes a check for a certain amount. If a citizen earns a bit of money, then the government check is reduced by however much the citizen earned.

Key terms: Basic income, guaranteed annual income

Contrast: Basic income systems don't seem to fit with the utility-maximizing view.

The implementation of **these systems** seems to **fly in the face of the microeconomic models** that explain people's behavior. After all, if the government is simply going to write you a check that's enough to cover your needs, who would possibly choose to work? **The reward-to-work ratio of being unemployed** under such a system is **literally infinite**. Yet the famous case of the "Mincome" demonstrated that, perhaps, **peoples' behavior is controlled by much more than simple utility maximization**.

Key terms: microeconomic models, reward-to-work ratio

Contrast: economic models would predict no reason to work under basic income systems yet this doesn't actually happen.

Opinion: Author thinks people's behavior is controlled by more than utility maximization.

From 1974 to 1979 the town of **Dauphin, Manitoba** in Canada provided a **guaranteed minimum income for all of its residents**. Regardless of age, gender, living situation or physical ability, every adult in the city was given a minimum salary to cover basic needs. Every microeconomic **model would have predicted** a drastic **plummeting of the employment rates** in the city. And yet the changes were minor: employment only decreased 1% among men and 3% among married women. The only two groups to show significant **decreases in their employment** rates were **teenagers** and **mothers of infants**. The participants in the study made it clear that they valued time home with their infant children much more than the rewards of having a job. Teenagers, as well, were able to stop looking for low paying menial jobs to help contribute to the home since their minor additional income was unnecessary. The **benefits of the system** were startling: **hospital visits decreased** dramatically, **high school graduation rates increased**, and **violent crime ceased** almost entirely.

Key terms: Dauphin, Manitoba

Cause-and-effect: the guaranteed minimum income only significantly decreased employment among teenagers and mothers with infants. Men and single women kept working. The Mincome also had a number of positive social effects.

Yet for most of the **men** in the city who served as primary breadwinners for their households, nothing changed. They **continued to work**. **This result has yet to be explained** by any economic model, "rational" or otherwise.

[Adapted from *If You Pay Them, They Will Come* by Kristen O'Connell, 2011.]

Opinion: Author thinks the fact that men continued to work cannot be explained by economic models.

Main Idea: Economic models that predict human behavior based on maximizing utility can be based on behavior that is rational or irrational but in either case they fail to adequately explain why unemployment didn't drop that much in the Mincome experiment.

8. Which of the following best states the author's main idea?
    A) When rational actor economic models are updated to account for the predictably irrational behavior of people, economists can accurately predict human behavior.
    B) Even when guaranteed a certain minimum income, married women largely continued working, thus demonstrating the inadequacy of classic behavioral economics.
    C) **Minimum income programs demonstrate that human economic behavior is not accurately modeled by systems presupposing utility-maximizing rationality.**
    D) Economic modeling will always fail to adequately describe the irrational aspects of human behavior.

The author starts by describing both rational and somewhat irrational models of human behavior as maximizing utility. He then goes on to discuss the basic income systems that don't seem to generate behavior that is rational. This contrast between expected behavior and what actually happened when a basic income was attempted is the author's main idea and is best described by choice C.

9. Suppose a province in a European nation chooses to institute a guaranteed minimum income system. The author implies that which of the following people would be *least* likely to stop working?
    A) **Man S, a middle-aged unmarried man supporting a teenage daughter and a son in college**
    B) Man Q, a high school senior who has been earning minimum wage working as a busboy at a local diner for the past three years
    C) Woman T, a married woman supporting two children, one a toddler and the other an infant, who worked a number of temporary positions over the previous five years
    D) Woman P, an unmarried woman supporting a teenage child, whose yearly income somewhat exceeds the amount offered by the government

The passage tells us that 99% of men kept working, especially those that were the sole breadwinner of the household. Choice A best fits the description of someone who would be least likely to stop working.

10. The author apparently believes that irrational behavior:
    A) accounts for much of the boom and bust cycle found in most economies.
    B) is adequately described by current models of behavioral economics.
    C) would cease if more governments would implement a basic income.
    D) **is exhibited when someone fails to maximize their rewards.**

The author starts by defining rational actors as people who behave in a way to maximize their rewards (money) and then goes on suggest that people usually behave irrationally. As an example of that irrationality he points to a person taking $100 now versus $150 in the future. That failure to maximize rewards is presented as irrational, thus choice D is correct.

11. Suppose an experimenter offers subjects a choice between receiving a mildly painful electric shock now, or a slightly more painful electric shock during a second experiment to be conducted in one month. The author implies that most people would elect:
    A) to receive the less-painful shock now to avoid greater shock in the future.
    B) to receive no shock at all and would withdraw from the experiment.
    C) **to receive no shock now and get the greater shock in the future.**
    D) to receive whichever shock they perceived as maximizing their utility.

The author says that people choose a lesser sum of money now rather than delay gratification and get a bigger sum of money in the future. This inability to delay gratification would suggest that people would choose no shock now and not think about the bigger shock coming in the future.

12. According to the author, why have more recent economic models shifted how they analyze human behavior?
    A) **Studies have demonstrated that human behavior does not follow the patterns predicted by rational models.**
    B) The results of the Mincome experiment needed to be incorporated into their economic models.
    C) Labor markets are unaffected by the presence of a guaranteed basic income for all citizens.
    D) Behavioral economists have adequately shown that much of human behavior can be predicted by looking at basic reward and punishment systems.

The author says that the classical studies discussed at the start of the first paragraph have shifted and then goes on to tell us that economists have modeled human behavior as "predictably irrational". That's answer choice A.

D: This is the classic rational model which economists have moved away from, sine people don't behave rationally.

13. The author implies that which of the following from the "Mincome" demonstrates the value of a basic income system?
    A) The labor market for men was almost completely unaffected by a guaranteed minimum income.
    B) A minimum income for all citizens protects them from the consequences of irrational decision-making.
    C) **Changes in social behavior lead to positive social outcomes for individuals living in Dauphin at the time.**
    D) The effect of a minimum income system on a particular citizen in Dauphin depended heavily on that citizen's age and gender.

The author indicates at the end of the passage that the effects on the Mincome were startling. He then gives us a number of positive social outcomes. Choice C captures this best.

Passage III Explanation

<u>**Adult basic education (ABE)**</u> and <u>**ESL**</u> programs, authorized by the Workforce Investment Act and also funded with state and local funds, are designed to assist students in their efforts to acquire <u>**literacy and language skills**</u> by providing instruction through local education agencies, community colleges, and community-based organizations. The content of instruction within ESL classes varies widely. It is often designed to assist students in their efforts to acquire literacy and language skills by providing a combination of oral language, competency-based work skills, and literacy instruction (Condelli, Wrigley, Yoon, Cronen, & Seburn, 2003). There is, however, little rigorous research that identifies effective instruction. A comprehensive review of published research studies on the effects of literacy interventions for ABE and adult ESL learners (Condelli & Wrigley, 2004) found that out of 17 adult education studies that used a rigorous methodology (i.e., quasi-experimental or randomized trials), only 3 included adult ESL learners (Diones, Spiegel, & Flugman, 1999; St. Pierre et al., 1995; St. Pierre et al., 2003). Furthermore, among the 3 studies that included adult ESL learners, only 1 presented outcomes for those learners, and that study experienced substantial methodological problems that limited the validity of the findings (e.g., a 40 percent overall attrition rate and different attrition rates in the intervention vs. control groups; Diones et al., 1999).

Key terms: Adult basic education (ABE); ESL; Literacy and Language Skills

Opinions: Condelli, Wrigley, Yoon, Cronen, & Seburn: instruction in ESL and ABE often uses a variety of instructions; Condelli & Wrigley: many ABE courses with rigorous methodology did not address ESL

Contrast: Goals of ABE ESL literacy and lack of research to ascertain if instruction was effective

Cause-and-Effect: focusing on oral language, competency based work skills and literacy instruction will lead to greater literacy and language skills

To help improve research-based knowledge of effective instruction for low-literate ESL learners, the National Center for Education Evaluation and Regional Assistance of ED's Institute of Education Sciences contracted with the American Institutes of Research (AIR) to conduct a Study of the Impact of a Reading Intervention for Low-Literate Adult ESL Learners. The intervention studied was the basal reader ***Sam and Pat,* Volume I**, published by Thomson-Heinle (2006). The goal of this study was to test a promising approach to improving the literacy skills of low-literate adult ESL students under real-world conditions. In their review of the research on ESL instruction in related fields, including adult second language acquisition, reading and English as a foreign language instruction, Condelli & Wrigley (2004) concluded that instruction based on a systematic approach to literacy development was a promising intervention for low-literate adult ESL learners that would be valuable to study (Brown et al., 1996; Cheek & Lindsay, 1994: Chen & Graves, 1995; Carrell, 1985; Rich & Shepherd, 1993; Roberts, Cheek & Mumm, 1994). Specifically, the factors identified as defining a systematic approach to literacy development included: (1) a comprehensive instructional scope that includes <u>**direct instruction**</u> in phonics, fluency, vocabulary development and reading comprehension, (2) a <u>**strategic instruction sequence**</u>, (3) a <u>**consistent instructional format,**</u> (4) easy-to-follow <u>**lesson plans**</u>, and (5) strategies for <u>**differentiated instruction**</u>.

Key terms: Sam and Pat Vol 1; direct instruction; strategic instruction sequence; consistent instructional format; lesson plans; differentiated instruction

Opinions: Condelli & Wrigley: low literate adult ESL learners may do better with a systematic approach to literacy development

Cause-and-Effect: studying the impact of a reading intervention will lead to better research-based knowledge; a specific set of practices will lead to greater literacy development

Sam and Pat was selected as the focus of the study because it offers an approach to literacy development that is <u>**systematic, direct, sequential, and multi-sensory**</u>. It also includes multiple opportunities for practice with feedback.

Consistent with characteristics identified as promising by Condelli & Wrigley (2004), Sam and Pat provides opportunities for **cooperative learning, real world tasks**, and an explicit **focus on reading**. In addition, the text was developed for and had been used by the developers with students similar to the study population (literacy level ESL learners).

The impact study used an experimental design to test the effectiveness of *Sam and Pat* in improving the reading and English language skills of adults enrolled in 66 ESL literacy classes at 10 sites. The study addressed three key research questions:

1. How effective is instruction based on the *Sam and Pat* textbook in improving the English reading and language skills of **low-literate** adult ESL learners compared to instruction normally provided in adult ESL literacy classes?

2. Is *Sam and Pat* effective for **certain subgroups** of students (e.g., native Spanish speakers)?

3. Is there a relationship between the **amount of instruction** in reading or English language skills and reading and English language outcomes?

Key terms: systematic, direct, sequential, multi-sensory, cooperative learning, real world tasks, focus on reading, low literate, certain subgroups, amount of instruction

Cause-and-Effect: the study seeks to discover if systematic, direct, sequential, and multi-sensory instruction with a focus on cooperative learning, real world tasks, and an explicit focus on reading is effective on low literate adult ESL learners and those in certain subgroups, and if the amount of instruction affects the outcome.

Main Idea: The passage focuses on teaching adult ESL students and the lack of research as to what effectively teaches them. It suggests that systematic, direct, sequential, and multi-sensory instruction with a focus on cooperative learning, real world tasks, and an explicit focus on reading may lead to better outcomes.

14. Upon which of the following groups does the impact study focus?
   A) ABE learners who have been successful in the workforce
   B) Adult learners with multi-sensory disabilities that inhibit learning
   C) **Adult non-native speakers with low literacy levels**
   D) ESL learners from specific linguistic subgroups

One of the questions the study seeks to answer is "how effective is instruction based on the *Sam and Pat* textbook in improving the English reading and language skills of low-literate adult ESL learners compared to instruction normally provided in adult ESL literacy classes." Thus ESL learners with low literacy are a focus of the study, as in choice C.

A, B: There is no mention of success in the workforce or multi-sensory disabilities in the passage.
D: The passage focuses on adult learners, eliminating D which does not discuss the age of the learners.

15. It can be inferred from the passage that many ESL classrooms combine various modes of instruction in order to:
   A) **maximize the acquisition of literacy and language skills.**
   B) ensure viability in obtaining the skills employers consider essential.
   C) allow for various metrics of evaluation to ascertain effectivity.
   D) prevent the over-emphasis of oral fluency above basic literacy.

Based on the passage, "assist[ing] students in their efforts to acquire literacy and language skills" can be aided "by providing a combination of oral language, competency-based work skills, and literacy instruction (Condelli, Wrigley, Yoon, Cronen, & Seburn, 2003)." Thus choice A is the credited answer.

B: the passage does not focus on work readiness as an outcome, as in choice B.

C: while evaluation is a focus of the study, it is a means to increasing literacy, not an end as in choice C.

D: preventing oral fluency is not discussed in the passage.

16. The author assumes which of the following when asserting *Sam and Pat* is a good choice for the study of increased literacy outcomes?
   A) The reader focuses on the real-world conditions faced by two recent immigrants.
   B) Adult ESL learners prefer basal approaches to other modes of intervention.
   C) Phonics and fluency must precede global reading comprehension.
   D) **The reader allows for a systematic approach to literacy instruction.**

The passage discusses the reasons the intervention uses *Sam and Pat*, including the fact that the study creators seek "instruction based on a systematic approach to literacy development." Thus choice D is the credited answer.

A, B: There is no discussion of the content of *Sam and Pat* or the preferences of the learners in the passage.

C: The passage does not discuss the order in which literacy occurs, eliminating choice C.

17. Based on the passage, the Study of the Impact Low-Literate Adult ESL Learners seeks to assess what sort of learning?
   A) Lessons that focus primarily on grammar, phonemes and pronunciation to increase oral fluency and confidence
   B) **Ones that proceed in a methodical manner and offer opportunities to work in groups on real world problems**
   C) Basal approaches that focus on workforce investment in order to encourage greater participation in the national economy
   D) Those that privilege reading and written texts over spoken language as a means to introduce multi-sensory environments

The passage suggests that systematic, direct, sequential, and multi-sensory instruction with a focus on cooperative learning, real world tasks, and an explicit focus on reading may lead to better outcomes, supporting choice B.

A: While the passage suggests "direct instruction in phonics, fluency, vocabulary development and reading comprehension" is a component of instruction, it is not the primary focus as in choice A.

C, D: the national economy and multi-sensory environments are not a factor in the passage, as in choices C and D.

18. Suppose that an instructor of adult ESL learners sought a researcher to help design a rigorous measurement tool to gauge the effectiveness of her instruction. The writer of the passage would most likely be:
   A) enthusiastic, because such research always increases the effectiveness of instruction and the resulting outcomes.
   B) doubtful that such methodologies would serve any purpose due to the high attrition rates in such classes.
   C) **surprised that a class was going to be subject to assessment, since that tends to be the exception to the rule.**
   D) pleased that the instructor recognized that methodologies for ESL and ABE students involved similar methodologies.

According to the passage, "there is…little rigorous research that identifies effective instruction," supporting choice C.

A: there is no proof that research always increases effectivity, as in choice A.

B: while attrition rates are mentioned as a reason research has been unsuccessful, that does not mean they have no purpose, as in choice B.

D: The new information does not link ABE and ESL students as in choice D.

19. All of the following are defined as factors in systematic literacy development EXCEPT:

    A) covering a variety of topics including understanding texts.

    B) varying the strategies by which information is delivered.

    C) **differentiating the format in respect to different learning styles.**

    D) creating lessons plans that students can easily understand.

Learning styles are not discussed in the passage, making choice C the credited answer.

A, B, D: the passage lists "a comprehensive instructional scope that …reading comprehension," "easy-to-follow lesson plans," and "strategies for differentiated instruction."

20. Suppose that the researchers found that more reading instruction was observed in *Sam and Pat* classes, while more English language instruction was observed in control classes. Based on the passage, the researchers would expect that the students in the *Sam and Pat* class to have:

    A) higher levels of success due to a more systematic integration of literacy and reading.

    B) **higher levels of success due to the focus on reading development.**

    C) lower levels of success because of a lack of integration of oral and written learning tasks.

    D) lower levels of success because of a dearth of opportunities for cooperative learning experiences.

The passage focuses on a study using *Sam and Pat* because it offers integrated instruction with a focus on reading comprehension, supporting choice B.

A: the example does not show systematic integration, instead focusing on reading, eliminating choice A.

C, D: the study is built around using *Sam and Pat* for integrated instruction with a "specific focus on reading," so the author would expect higher levels of success, not lower ones.

22. Based upon the passage, the author most likely agrees with which of the following statements?

   A) **The most just person is constantly working at acting justly.**
   B) People that were habituated to be cowards can become courageous if they work hard enough at it.
   C) The lawmaker is the most virtuous person in a society.
   D) Virtues of character are more important than virtues of thinking.

At the top of the third paragraph, the author writes, "Likewise, we become just by doing things that are just, temperate by doing things that are temperate, and courageous by doing things that are courageous." The active state of justice is brought about by being at work at it, or in other words, by doing just things.

B: The author never writes that someone can be reverse habituated, especially given the emphasis he puts on the last sentence, claiming how important it is how one is habituated from childhood.
C, D: Both of these claims are never made.

23. The author makes several references to the harpist and the house builder in order to:

   A) demonstrate how much practice goes into developing virtue of thought.
   B) **demonstrate how virtue of character depends upon being at work in a certain way.**
   C) give examples of virtuous professions that only the most virtuous people can excel at.
   D) prove that the pursuit of virtue is a more important endeavor than the pursuit of the arts.

As the author writes at the end of the second chapter, "...we do acquire virtues by first being at work with them, just as is the case of the arts: home builders learn to build houses by building houses and harpists learn to play the harp by playing the harp." Moreover, in the fourth paragraph, the author describes how a good harpist is one who plays well and a good house builder is one who builds well.

A: As the author says virtue of thinking is the result of teaching, he concludes that it has need of experience and time. He has no need to prove this with an analogy.
C: The author never says these professions are the most virtuous, or that only the most virtuous of people can practice them.
D: The author uses the pursuit of the arts as an analogy for the pursuit of virtue, but never says the one is inferior to the other.

24. Based upon the passage, it can be inferred that the author believes the best way for lawmakers to habituate citizens towards virtue is to:

   A) make laws that require a certain amount of practice at useful arts like house making and pleasurable arts like harp playing.
   B) make laws that allot resources to the education of those with a natural capacity for virtue.
   C) makes laws that require intensive education for all citizens from a very early age.
   D) **make laws that encourage citizens to act justly and temperately.**

The lawmaker's job is to make citizens "good and virtuous by habituating them." Since virtue of character comes from habit, the lawmaker must establish laws that encourage habits in line with virtue in order to make citizens virtuous. Virtues like justice and temperance are not so much learned in school as they are in doing, in being just and temperate.

A: This is never said: the arts are used as analogies.
B: The author never says that those with the natural capacities should receive more or better education.
C: This is never said, and also, we are talking about virtue of character, which is a matter of habit, not of education.

25. Suppose the parents of a newborn boy want him to become a great trumpet player. According to the rationale of the passage, what two things are necessary for this to happen?

    A) He has to have the best teacher and a desire to play well.

    B) He has to practice well and be habituated to behaving like a trumpet player.

    C) **He has to have been born with natural talent and practice well.**

    D) He has to have been born with natural talent and a desire to play well.

At the end of the first paragraph, the author writes, "Therefore, virtues of character come into being neither by nature nor contrary to nature, but rather, they come into being in us who are of a nature to take them on, and they are brought to completion by means of habit." As the arts are used as an analogy for virtue, we can assume that the excellent trumpet player, like the virtuous person, must have the natural capacity and must bring the skill to completion by means of habit, which in this situation would be practicing, playing the instrument.

A: Desire to play well, or be virtuous is not mentioned, and teachers are mentioned in passing.

B: Being habituated to behave like a trumpet player is never mentioned. A more accurate phrase would be must be habituated to practicing and playing like a trumpet player, which is a repeat of the first part of the answer choice.

D: Desire to play well means nothing if the person does not practice and play well.

26. According to the passage, all of the following statements are true EXCEPT:

    A) people become just or unjust by behaving justly or unjustly.

    B) **for the most excellent and inherently virtuous people, there is no need of teachers.**

    C) the senses of sight and sound were not developed by seeing and hearing.

    D) a good government is the one run by lawmakers that properly habituate the people.

All of these things are said explicitly in the passage except for choice B. Moreover, as the author writes in the fourth paragraph, "People become good and bad harpists by playing the harp and house builders become either good or bad at their art by building well or poorly. If it were otherwise, there would be no need for teachers and all people would have been born either good or bad at particular arts." We are born with capacities, but not skills. Those sentences imply that teachers are necessary for all.

27. According to the passage, which of the following will make a person just?

  I. **Acting justly in day to day encounters**

  II. Studying the nature of justice

  III. **Being born with the capacity for justice**

    A) I only

    B) III only

    C) **I and III**

    D) I, II, and III

Items I and III represent the crux of the argument being made in the passage, that virtues of character arise in a person who has "potencies" for them, and that they are brought to completion through habit. Item I is the habit part and Item III is the "potencies" part. The author never says that studying a virtue will allow that person to take on that virtue.

Passage V Explanation

During the early days of **World War II, two groups** of high-level officers began meeting regularly in Washington, D.C. One group was lead by **General Brehon Somervell**, a politically well-connected officer who provided the major motive power behind the construction of the **Pentagon**. Those officers who met with Somervell were primarily interested in creating a **streamlined military structure** that would reduce chains of command between the lowest soldier and the President, but would still have enough **flexibility** to allow **small, quasi-independent groups** the freedom necessary to engage in the kind of **risk-taking** necessary for innovation in any organization. One of the major goals of Somervell's group was to create working papers that could be presented to the President and Congress to convince them to do the necessary reorganization.

Key terms: World War II, Somervell

Opinion: Somervell and his group wanted to streamline the chain of command, create small quasi-independent groups that could undertake risky missions.

Somervell's group began meeting at the very end of 1939, and shortly thereafter another group of retired, semi-retired and reserve officers, centered on **Major General William Donovan**, began to have meetings. Donovan, the only veteran to have received the four highest awards in the United States (the Medal of Honor, the Distinguished Service Cross, the Distinguished Service Medal, and the National Security Medal), was primarily concerned with **shortcomings in America's foreign intelligence** apparatus. He sought to **revive programs** that had been effective during his active service during World War I.

Key terms: Donovan

Opinion: Donovan wanted to build up the foreign intelligence service

Both of these groups of men consisted largely of **anti-establishment thinkers**. While they were strongly **patriotic**, they felt that the **bureaucratic** structures that had built up around the Presidency to manage the United States' national security had **fossilized** into an architecture of positions that **prevented the country from responding swiftly** to new threats, especially that posed by Nazi Germany.

Opinion: Both Donovan's and Somervell's groups weren't part of the establishment and wanted to see swifter response.

Clearly the **urgency created by Hitler's** meteoric rise to prominence and his aggression towards his continental neighbors was a **more potent force** than the **conservatism** of those who were then holding the reins of military power. The **nation as a whole** did not share the level of ambivalence about Nazi Germany that many high level government officials did, as **Audrey O'Connell** convincingly demonstrated in her recent study of the daily tabloid papers that made up most of the media diet of everyday citizens. She soundly refutes the notion that fascist nationalism was a serious thread in the American cultural tapestry of the 1930's and demonstrates that **average American citizens overwhelmingly feared Hitler and favored opposition**.

Key terms: Audrey O'Connell

Contrast: Those at the top of the government had ambivalent feelings about Hitler but the nation as a whole feared him and wanted to intervene in World War II.

FDR, as a man of wide-ranging intellectual engagement, **took at least a passing interest** in the organizational reforms put forth by groups like Somervell's and Donovan's. But he **cannot** have been **strongly supportive** of the work of men who largely hailed from the **Republican party**, or other anti-Democrat foundations. **Among those officers** who were the key architects of Department of Defense reform, and the formation of what would become the Office of Special Services (later the CIA), the majority were either **active members of the Republican party**, or had strong affiliations with those who were.

Contrast: FDR was a Democrat but those encouraging reforms were Republicans

Cause-and-effect: The political alignment of Donovan and Somervell's groups led to FDR not embracing their ideas enthusiastically.

Nonetheless, **FDR** ultimately provided the seal of presidential **approval** to the efforts of **Donovan's group**; **Somervell** would have to **wait** until the end of World War II and the **Eisenhower administration** to see **his plans come to fruition**. FDR's **statements** of approval for reorganizing the military **were strong**, but **saw no action** under his watch. And despite the many successes of the OSS in obtaining key intelligence behind enemy lines in Nazi occupied France and Poland and in neutral Turkey, we must not forget that, at first, **FDR's support was merely nominal**: he allowed the OSS to form, but required that both its **manpower and its budget** be drawn from **existing military structures**.

[Adapted from *Inside Outsiders* by Richard Choate, 2011.]

Opinion: FDR eventually gave support to Donovan's group by nominally approving their efforts.

Contrast: Despite stating his support FDR didn't directly support them but made them draw their budget from other parts of the military budget

Main Idea: At the start of World War II, two groups pushed for changes in the military but their efforts were hampered by the fact that the president was from the opposite political party. Ultimately Donovan's group had their plans go forward but Somervell's group had to wait for a Republican president.

28. The passage suggests that the author believes Somervell's relationship with the larger military hierarchy was one of:
    A) direct antagonistic confrontation.
    B) mutual support in reaching larger goals.
    C) indifference and neglect.
    D) **mixed feelings including points of both support and dissent.**

As a decorated veteran and a very high ranking officer, Somervell was obviously rewarded by the military hierarchy. But the passage tells us that he was also an anti-establishment thinker. Thus he must have had both elements of support and dissent in his relationship with them, making choice D correct.

29. Which of the following, if true, would most *weaken* the author's characterization of Somervell's and Donovan's groups?
    A) **The established military hierarchy in the Joint Chiefs of Staff supported the notion of a simplified command structure and increased financial commitment to foreign intelligence gathering.**
    B) Working papers produced by both groups indicated a need to curb Hitler's aggression nearly a year before the U.S. entered World War II.
    C) Somervell and Donovan themselves made no effort to undermine the authority of FDR's chief military advisors.
    D) Donovan received the nation's four highest awards for work done in conjunction with established military hierarchies.

The author characterizes the groups as anti-establishment and pushing for change to the system. The author's position would be weakened if, in fact, the military establishment did support their proposals. That's what choice A says.

30. The author's description of FDR's attitude towards Somervell's and Donovan's reforms is supported by which of the following passage assertions?
    A) Somervell's and Donovan's groups consisted largely of men from an opposing political party.
    B) FDR's wide-ranging intellect took interest in the proposed reforms.
    C) Eisenhower supported the streamlining of military hierarchy along the lines proposed by Somervell.
    D) **The president provided no new budgeting for the work of the OSS.**

The author suggests that FDR's support was merely nominal since he didn't want to embrace the reforms being suggested by members of an opposing political party. The specific support the author gives for that contention is that FDR wouldn't provide funding for them – he required them to draw manpower and funding from existing military programs. Thus choice D is correct.

31. According to the author, the attitude of FDR towards Somervell's and Donovan's groups was most analogous to which of the following?
   A) **<u>A manager of a football team who reluctantly adopts some of the strategies developed by a rival team.</u>**
   B) A business executive who emulates the marketing strategy of a company that has been successfully selling an unrelated product.
   C) A military commander who insists on giving orders that he knows will lead to the deaths of many troops in order to achieve a larger objective.
   D) A teacher who tolerates a certain amount of misbehaving on the part of students in the interest of classroom tranquility.

We know that FDR was willing to at least begrudgingly allow some of Donovan's plans to move forward, but that he wasn't happy about working with someone from a rival faction. Choice A is a good match here – the manager is willing to adopt strategies from a rival even though he's not happy about it.

32. Based on passage information, a working paper discussing the importance of strengthening the military hierarchy by introducing additional layers in the chain of command would have been adopted by which group?
   A) **<u>Neither</u>**
   B) Donovan's group only
   C) Somervell's group only
   D) Both

Donovan's concern was beefing up foreign intelligence gathering so he would have no interest in or concern with strengthening the military hierarchy. Somervell wanted the exact opposite: streamline it. Thus neither group would favor adding additional layers to the chain of command and the right answer is choice A.

Passage VI Explanation

Fantine, the first of five novels under the general title of ***Les Misérables*** has produced an impression all over Europe, and we already hear of nine translations. It has evidently been "engineered" with immense energy by the French publisher. Translations have appeared in numerous languages almost simultaneously with its publication in Paris. Every resource of bookselling ingenuity has been exhausted in order to make every human being who can read think that the **salvation of his body and soul** depends on his reading *Les Misérables*. **The glory and the obloquy** of the author have both been **forced into aids to a system of puffing** at which **Barnum** himself would stare amazed, and confess that he had never conceived of "a dodge" in which **literary genius and philanthropy** could be allied with the **grossest bookselling humbug**. But we trust, that, after our American showman has recovered from his first shock of surprise, he will vindicate the claim of **America** to be considered the "first nation on the face of the earth," by immediately offering **Dickens** a hundred thousand dollars to superintend his exhibition of dogs, and **Florence Nightingale** a half a million to appear at his exhibition of babies.

Key terms: Fantine, Les Misérables

Cause-and-effect: heavy marketing seems geared towards a goal of extreme sales

Opinion: publicity and marketing on this book is over-the-top and distasteful

The **French bookseller** also piqued the curiosity of the universal public by a story that **Victor Hugo** wrote *Les Misérables* twenty-five years ago, but, being bound to give a certain French publisher all his works after his first celebrated novel, he would not delight the world with this product of his genius until he had forced the said publisher into a compliance with his terms. The publisher shrank aghast from the sum which the author demanded, and **this sum was yearly increased in amount**, as years rolled away and as Victor Hugo's **reputation grew more splendid**. At last the publisher died, **probably from vexation**, and Victor Hugo was free. Then he **condescended** to allow the present publisher to issue *Les Misérables* on the payment of **eighty thousand dollars**. It is not surprising, that, to get his money back, this publisher has been **compelled to resort to tricks which exceed everything** known in the whole history of literature.

[Adapted from "*Fantine*, by Victor Hugo: A Review", *The Atlantic*, by Edwin Percy Whipple, July, 1862.]

Key terms: Victor Hugo

Contrast: Hugo as a new author, Hugo as a phenomenon able to set his own terms; the marketing campaign for Fantine vs. typical book sales

Cause-and-effect: as time went on, Hugo's reputation grew steeply and his price likewise increased; the high cost of purchasing the novel has resulted in extreme efforts by the publisher to maximize sales

Opinion: the anticipation of this novel is purposely inflated and perhaps unwarranted; Hugo has a very high opinion of himself; the publisher's marketing efforts are unheard of.

Main Idea: The behavior in marketing Les Misérables is over-the-top and distasteful and is likely motivated, at least in part, by the outrageous amount of money the publisher had to pay to Victor Hugo.

33. The author would likely agree that:
    A) every human being on the face of the Earth should read *Les Misérables*.
    B) the furor surrounding Victor Hugo's publications is typically over-the-top.
    C) Victor Hugo is more of a celebrity than a legitimate artist.
    D) **the promotional efforts of Hugo's publisher are unseemly.**

The passage is steeped in sarcasm and hyperbole, and the target is the extreme (in the author's opinion) bookselling efforts of the publisher. It's clear the author does not appreciate it.

A: This is stated, but only in the context of the author characterizing the goals of the publisher.
B: The passage suggests several times that this furor is not typical at all, but a first in the history of literature.
C: The passage never directly comments on the quality of Hugo's work, and most of the criticism on the publicity is geared towards the publisher. What has been said or implied about Hugo isn't enough to support this statement.

34. Which of the following, if true, would weaken the author's main argument?
    A) Sales of *Fantine* and successive volumes exceeded all expectations.
    B) *Les Misérables* was, during Hugo's lifetime, a commercial failure.
    C) **Very little of the fanfare over Hugo's novel was a result of marketing by the publisher.**
    D) *Les Misérables* earned high critical praise all over the world.

Since the passage argues that the marketing campaign by the publisher is inappropriate, any indication that the campaign was not as extreme or atypical as it sounds, or any suggestion that the publisher was not responsible for it (e.g., if the popularity of the book arose spontaneously out of the book-buying public or legitimate critics), would weaken this argument. C is a match.

A: The author likely expects high sales, but this is irrelevant to whether the marketing campaign was unreasonable.
B: This would be surprising, but again, sales are irrelevant to whether the campaign was inappropriate, at least from the perspective of ethics or good taste (apparently the passage author's position).
D: The passage never comments on the quality of the work itself. One might be tempted to argue that critical praise could vindicate the marketing efforts and thus weaken the argument, but this is a stretch. The author doesn't base the argument on the publicity being overwrought relative to the value of the work, but overdone, period.

35. What was the author's purpose in recounting the anecdote of the deceased publisher in the final paragraph?
    A) To illustrate the maxim, "he who hesitates is lost".
    B) **To imply that the perceived quality of the novel had become overblown.**
    C) To support the belief that *Les Misérables* was destined to be a masterpiece.
    D) To draw attention to the fact that *Les Misérables* is an early effort from a beginning author.

The author recounts this story somewhat satirically, explaining an unreasonable degree of publisher hype via an equally unreasonable authorial fee. Ultimately this story is in service of the main argument of the passage, as stated in answer choice B.

A: The author doesn't seem to believe that the earlier publisher missed a chance. Rather, that Hugo's asking price was always unreasonable, and no one should have ever paid it.
C: This is not at all supported by the passage.
D: The author does not make note of this point at all.

36. The passage author implies that Victor Hugo:
    A) is a less than skilled writer.
    B) **has a high opinion of himself.**
    C) cares little for public recognition.
    D) is polarizing and almost universally known.

The author states that Hugo "condescended" to sell his novel for $80,000, obviously considered by the author to be an exorbitant price. Answer choice B definitely fits with the tone of the author's description of this circumstance.

A: The passage does not comment on the quality of Hugo's writing directly.

C: This is not supported by the passage.

D: In fact, this statement is supported by the passage, when the "glory and obloquy" of Hugo is brought up in paragraph one, along with all the statements about every man, woman, and child reading his books. However, the statement is not *implied* by the author. It is *explicated*. The statement in B, never made explicit, is still the one that matches for this question.

Passage VII Explanation

It is **not wonderful** that the variety and inconstancy of tastes respecting the attributes and the characters of beauty, should have **led many philosophers to deny** that there exist any certain combinations of forms and of effects to which the term **beauty ought to be invariably attached**.

Cause-and-effect: varied aesthetic tastes led philosophers to deny objective beauty (in context wonderful means "to be a wonder", not "to be very good or desirable")

In his "**Philosophical Dictionary**," **Voltaire**, after quoting some **nonsense** from the **crazy dreamer** who did so much **injury to Greek philosophy**, says: "I am willing to believe that nothing can be more beautiful than this discourse of **Plato**; but it does not give us very clear ideas of the nature of the beautiful. **Ask of a toad what is beauty, pure beauty, the το καλον; he will answer you that it is his female**, with two large round eyes projecting from her little head, a large and flat throat, a yellow belly, and a brown back. Ask the devil, and he will tell you that the beautiful is a pair of horns, four claws, and a tail. Consult, lastly, the philosophers, and they will answer you by rigmarole: they **want something conformable to the archetype of the beautiful in essence**, to the το καλον." **This is wit, not reason: let us look for that to a deeper thinker.**

Key terms: Philosophical Dictionary, Voltaire, Plato, καλον

Contrast: frog's idea of beauty vs. devil vs. philosophers

Cause-and-effect: individual examples of beauty vary wildly, "essence" of beauty very difficult to define; philosophers seek an archetype or essence in defining or understanding something

Opinion: author does not care for Plato; author also considers Voltaire shallow

David Hume says: "It appears that, amid all the variety and caprice of taste, there are certain **general principles of approbation or blame**, whose influence a careful eye may trace in all operations of the mind. Some particular forms or qualities from the original structure of the internal fabric, are calculated to please, and others to displease.... If they fail of their effect in any particular instance, it is from **some apparent defect or imperfection** in the organ.

Key terms: David Hume

Contrast: Voltaire throws up his hands but Hume feels there are general principles related to beauty

Cause-and-effect: beauty or lack of beauty comes from a defect or imperfection in the original structure/fabric

Opinion: from final line of previous paragraph, author considers Hume a deeper thinker/greater philosopher than Voltaire

"In each creature there is a **sound and a defective state**; and the former alone can be supposed to afford us a true standard of taste and sentiment. If, in the sound state of the organ, there be **an entire or a considerable uniformity of sentiment among men, we may thence derive an idea of the perfect beauty**; in like manner as the appearance of objects in daylight, to the eye of a man in health, is denominated their true and real color."

Contrast: sound state vs. defective state; sound state vs. true color

Cause-and-effect: sound state can be determined by unanimity or near-unanimity of human judgment; if an object is of or similar to the sound state, then it will be universally and instinctively perceived as beautiful

To the same purpose writes **<u>Burke</u>**:

"As there will be little doubt that bodies present similar images to the whole species, it must necessarily be allowed, that the **<u>pleasures and the pains which every object excites in one man, it must raise in all mankind</u>**, while it operates naturally, simply, and by its proper powers only. There is hardly any doubt that any man would prefer butter or honey to some nauseous morsel, or to any other bitter drug to which he had not been accustomed; which **<u>proves that his palate is naturally like that of other men in all things</u>**, that it is still like the palate of other men in many things, and only vitiated in some particular points."

Key terms: Burke

Contrast: Hume's idea of a universal ability to identify the "sound state" vs. Burke's universal palate

Cause-and-effect: Burke has same conclusion as Hume, but does not equate beauty with a sound state; Burke explains small differences in aesthetic appeal experienced by different people as minor differences, mentions possibility of becoming accustomed to undesirable things

Main Idea: to argue that the apparent subjectivity of beauty hides some general principles, possibly expounded by Hume and Burke

37. Which of the following can reasonably be inferred from David Hume's argument as quoted in the passage?
  A) **<u>Unlimited cosmetic surgery for all members of the population should lead to increased physical similarity.</u>**
  B) Straight lines and soft color hues are consistent markers of beauty.
  C) Two individuals with the exact same life experiences will lack the usual aesthetic vitiations.
  D) Improvement is unlimited, thus there is no ceiling on beauty.

Hume argues that there is an objective standard of beauty, based on similarity to a sound state. If this is taken to mean there is a single sound state for human beings, or perhaps somewhat dissimilar sound states for men and another for women, this would imply that cosmetic surgery (assuming it is for the purpose of making individuals more beautiful) should also, as a consequence, make people more similar-looking (the ideal nose, cheek bones, et cetera). So A is a definite match. B and D are nowhere in the passage, while C is a reasonable inference, but from Burke's argument, not Hume's.

38. One modern study of the psychology of beauty discovered that perceptions of facial beauty were based on previous experience. Faces that were closer to an average of what the viewer had been used to seeing were considered more beautiful than those faces which deviated from the norm of their experiences. The conclusion was that perception of beauty was heavily influenced by experience rather than being entirely inborn. Based on the passage, whose argument is most weakened by this study?
  A) Plato
  B) Voltaire
  C) Hume
  D) **<u>Burke</u>**

Hume and Burke share the same conclusion, that objective beauty exists, and the above study weakens both of them, by suggesting that experience is far more important than either of them have admitted. Plato is referred to in the passage but his argument is actually not given, so we can discount him, while Voltaire declines to define beauty, arguing, if anything, that beauty is indeed a fairly individual thing, or at least that it appears that way, a conclusion the above study would support. So, which argument is weakened the most? This is a particularly difficult question and will require a closer look at each argument.

Hume hedges somewhat, saying that where there is widespread agreement as to what constitutes beauty of an object (like a human face), then we can inductively reason out the existence of a sound state for that object. He leaves open the possibility, if only barely, that there may not be universal agreement or perhaps not agreement at all. Burke does not speak of an ideal form, simply stating that universal inborn aesthetic preferences exist. He explicitly notes that those individuals whose tastes vary somewhat based on experience have had their senses vitiated (damaged), and that these are perceptual imperfections rather than inborn individual taste. The idea that perception of beauty depends on experience, as in the above study, does not reconcile with Burke's view of experience as marring one's natural ability to identify true beauty, in the same way as a person with damaged hearing cannot sense softer sounds. Burke's argument is more weakened than Hume's by the above study.

39. Which of the following quotations about beauty best exemplifies what Voltaire writes in paragraph two?
    A) Love is blind.
    B) Familiarity breeds contempt.
    C) **Beauty is in the eye of the beholder.**
    D) True beauty transcends personal taste.

Voltaire declines to make much of an argument for what beauty is, other than to say it seems to differ for everyone and finding a common underlying cause has been difficult. His failure to make a strong argument otherwise could be leading to the implicit conclusion that there is no objective universal basis for beauty, which is well-stated in the statement of answer choice C. A and B are somewhat irrelevant, while D is a better fit for Hume or Burke.

40. Plato spoke of ideal forms as existing in another, higher realm, separate from the physical universe. For example, he had argued that any circle drawn by a human hand would be merely an approximation, with small imperfections in the curve, et cetera, compared to the true idea of a circle as mathematically defined. The passage author would likely agree that:
    A) Hume's work on beauty merely retreads Plato's thinking, his idea of a sound state adding nothing new.
    B) Voltaire misunderstood Plato, missing the most relevant contributions of the great philosopher.
    C) Burke's work is inconsistent with Plato, but the former should be favored.
    D) **Hume's similar work on the question of beauty was nevertheless superior to Plato's glancing contribution.**

Ah, so Plato did have something to say about beauty, or at least, the ideas presented in the question stem could certainly be applied to beauty. But what did the author think of Plato? The passage dismisses him as a nonsense-spewing dreamer whom, according to the author, not only did not contribute much to Ancient Greek philosophy but in fact actively damaged it. Voltaire is also given short shrift, but the author compliments Hume as a deep thinker, and likewise seems to at least implicitly acknowledge Burke's ideas as having value. The reader might agree with the answer choice in A, but the pro-Plato and anti-Hume tone do not fit the passage author. Answer choice B is also too positive about Plato. C is a better fit, in terms of tone. Now is it true that Burke's ideas are inconsistent with Plato (as presented in the question stem)? Not really. Plato's ideas about ideal forms are a good match for Hume's idea of the sound state, which themselves complement Burke. Looking at answer choice D, it acknowledges the similarity of Plato's and Hume's work, but still favors Hume. This grudging acknowledgement of the two thinkers' similarity of reasoning is not out of the question for the author, but the conclusion that Hume's work is still superior in fitting with the author's views on the two philosophers, as revealed in the passage. D is the best match.

Passage VIII Explanation

The rack, the thumbscrew, and the knout are still with us; so are the convict's garb and the social wrath, all conspiring against the spirit that is serenely marching on. **Anarchism** could not hope to escape the fate of all other ideas of innovation. Indeed, as the **most revolutionary and uncompromising innovator**, Anarchism must needs **meet with the combined ignorance and venom of the world it aims to reconstruct**.

Key terms: Anarchism

Cause-and-effect: anarchism wants to change the world, but the world will respond with resistance

Opinion: author is pro-anarchism

The strange phenomenon of the opposition to Anarchism is that it brings to light the relation between so-called intelligence and ignorance. And yet this is not so very strange when we consider the relativity of all things. **The ignorant mass has in its favor that it makes no pretense of knowledge or tolerance.** Acting, as it always does, by mere impulse, its reasons are like those of a child. "Why?" "Because." **Yet the opposition of the uneducated to Anarchism deserves the same consideration as that of the intelligent man.**

Contrast: impulsive resistance to philosophy vs. reasoned opposition

Opinion: author considers instinctive, ignorant opposition to anarchism as valid as educated ones

What, then, are the objections? First, **Anarchism is impractical,** though a beautiful ideal. Second, **Anarchism stands for violence and destruction**, hence it must be repudiated as vile and dangerous. **Both the intelligent man and the ignorant mass judge not from a thorough knowledge** of the subject, but either from hearsay or false interpretation.

Contrast: ignorant and educated men both have false impressions of anarchism

Cause-and-effect: objections to anarchism are practicality and violence

Opinion: author does not believe anyone's concerns about anarchism are true/valid

A practical scheme, says **Oscar Wilde**, is either one already in existence, or a scheme that could be carried out under the existing conditions; but it is exactly the existing conditions that one objects to, and any scheme that could accept these conditions is wrong and foolish. **The true criterion of the practical, therefore, is not whether the latter can keep intact the wrong or foolish; rather is it whether the scheme has vitality enough to leave the stagnant waters of the old, and build, as well as sustain, new life**. In the light of this conception, Anarchism is indeed practical. More than any other idea, it is helping to do away with the wrong and foolish; more than any other idea, it is building and sustaining new life.

Key terms: Oscar Wilde

Contrast: idea of practical as fitting existing conditions vs. one that can lead to new and better conditions

Cause-and-effect: revolution is not easy, but a practical scheme can succeed anyway, given enough vitality

Opinion: practicality is useless if it does not make things better

Destruction and violence! How is the ordinary man to know that **the most violent element in society is ignorance**; that its power of destruction is the very thing Anarchism is combating? Nor is he aware that **Anarchism, whose roots, as it were, are part of nature's forces, destroys, not healthful tissue, but parasitic**

growths that feed on the life's essence of society. It is merely clearing the soil from weeds and sagebrush, that it may eventually bear healthy fruit.

Contrast: view of anarchism as violent vs. ignorance as violent

Cause-and-effect: anarchism arises from nature's forces; anarchism destroys the worst elements of society, is not wantonly violent

Opinion: author dismissive of claims of anarchism's violence (literal, metaphorical?), does not come out against use of violence entirely

Someone has said that it requires **less mental effort to condemn than to think**. The widespread mental indolence, so prevalent in society, proves this to be only too true. Rather than to go to the bottom of any given idea, to examine into its origin and meaning, most people will either condemn it altogether, or rely on some superficial or prejudicial definition of non-essentials. **Anarchism urges man to think, to investigate**, to analyze every proposition.

Contrast: unthinking condemnation vs. analytical nature of anarchism

Cause-and-effect: practicing anarchism requires honest, thoughtful analysis of all propositions

Opinion: author considers most members of society intellectually lazy/ignorant

Anarchism is the great liberator of man from the phantoms that have held him captive; it is the arbiter and pacifier of the **two forces for individual and social harmony**. To accomplish that unity, Anarchism has declared war on the pernicious influences which have so far prevented the **harmonious blending of individual and social instincts, the individual and society.**

Contrast: individual good vs. social good; individual and society at odds vs. anarchism's "harmonious blending"

Cause-and-effect: anarchism will improve society but actively attacking societal forces causing individual and society to be at odds

Main Idea: to give a brief overview of core ideas of anarchism and refute common arguments against it

41. Which of the following definitions of the word "practical" best fits the view of the passage author?
    A) A scheme is practical if it assumes the current conditions as less than ideal.
    B) A scheme is proved practical once it's successfully been executed.
    C) **A practical scheme makes things better, rather than wasting energy on the status quo.**
    D) A practical scheme is one whose aims are easily achievable.

B and D are good fits for Oscar Wilde's view of practicality. The author, however, describes practicality as neither easy nor an easy fit for society as it currently stands, but instead as revolutionary, yet with the vigor to see such revolutionary changes through. The reader can infer that Oscar Wilde's conflation of practical with either ease of implementation or preexistence is considered a waste of time by the author, since it does not make society a better place. Having said that, what makes the scheme practical is that it has the vitality to succeed, in the passage author's words. A is tempting, as there would be little point in employing a scheme were there nothing to fix, but C is better, which already assumes a problem to be fixed but explicitly describes success in doing so.

42. It can be inferred from the passage that the passage author considers the apparently violent nature of anarchism:
    A) a pervasive myth.
    B) a necessary evil in combating the forces that corrupt society.
    C) **no more violent in reality than a doctor's removal of a cancerous tumor.**
    D) a necessary response to the equally violent nature of society's ignorant quarters.

The author responds to the accusation of violence not by denying it, but by pointing to more violent elements in society, and the necessity of destroying the targets of anarchism's attacks. This violence, whether metaphorical or physical, is justified, not denied, which eliminates A. That leaves three likely answer choices. D can be eliminated as the argument does not hinge on violence being necessary to combat violence. B and C are both very close, but the tone of the passage, fairly unapologetic, does not fit with the veiled apology suggested by the phrase, "necessary evil". C is a very good fit, however, as the analogy of a violent tumor fits the comparison of parasitic elements versus healthy tissue.

43. Based on the passage description, the philosophy of anarchism can best be described as:
    A) one of incremental, palatable changes summing to wholesale social restructuring.
    B) resting on a few uncompromising, unquestioned propositions that can only lead to complete revolution.
    C) essentially non-violent, intellectually honest and destructive of ignorance and intellectual indolence.
    D) **a predominantly rational philosophy with the aim of improving society by considering nothing immune to scrutiny.**

Answer choice A can be easily dismissed, as palatable is not compatible with uncompromising. However, B, C, and D are all tempting on first glance. B describes the basic propositions as "unquestioned", however, which is contrary to the "question everything" philosophy described in the passage. C describes anarchism as essentially non-violent, but the author's refutation of the complaint of violence was not based on arguing that violence does not occur, but comparing it to other aspects of society that are more violent and damaging, and showing the target of anarchism's destruction as parasitic growths on society rather than healthy tissue. The non-violent description doesn't really fit either, then. That leaves D as the only description that can be applied to anarchism without contradicting the passage.

44. Which of the following, if true, would most *weaken* the passage's argument in favor of anarchism?
    A) **Personality tests suggests anarchists are the group least willing to change their views in light of evidence.**
    B) Anarchists are found to be statistically more likely to deface public property or become violent at protests.
    C) Anarchists tend to be amongst the least happy in societies with incompatible political and cultural mores.
    D) A comprehensive review of the anarchist literature suggests that anarchists are the least likely to be bullied into recanting.

Since anarchism's value depends on its willingness to challenge every assumption, evidence that anarchists themselves held dogmatic beliefs which would not be critically evaluated would hurt the argument in favor of anarchism as a political philosophy. B, on the other hand is irrelevant, as peacefulness or being law-abiding are neither stated nor assumed as evidence in the argument in favor of anarchism. C, too, is irrelevant, as being unhappy with society is not only not an argument against anarchism, but one of the defining characteristics. Since anarchists are supposed to remake society into something better, it would make no sense for them to be satisfied with things as they are. D, if anything, strengthens the argument for anarchism, by supporting the idea that they value truth.

45. Based on the sixth paragraph, the passage author takes for granted that:
    A) it's in human nature to cling to one's prejudices.
    B) **most people will tend to take the path of least resistance.**
    C) introspection comes naturally, but so does rationalization.
    D) anarchism forces people to confront some difficult truths.

Each of these seems reasonable, but only one of the statements in these answer choices is actually assumed by the author. An assumption is unstated but necessary to the validity of the argument. An assumption, if shown to be untrue, makes the argument likewise false. The argument in this case is "ignorantly condemning an idea is easier than carefully analyzing it" (evidence), "people tend to do what is easiest" (assumption), "as a result, ignorance resulting from this type of lazy thinking is widespread" (conclusion). Now if this assumption were incorrect, if, indeed, most individuals tended towards challenging themselves without any external prodding, the conclusion would no longer follow. B, which matches the assumption just identified, is therefore the correct answer choice, but to confirm, check the other options. They might well be true, but what if they weren't? How would that affect the argument? What if individuals were not particularly attached to their prejudices, for example? The argument would still stand, as the argument is not based on attachment but laziness.

46. The title that best represents the views of this passage is:
    A) **The Argument for Anarchism.**
    B) A History of Anarchism.
    C) Anarchism: A Call to Action.
    D) Anarchism: Strengths and Weaknesses.

The author is making a strong, clear argument for anarchism, tackling concerns about the philosophy and refuting them, suggesting no negatives or alternatives to the philosophy. The goal is to explain and defend anarchism, so the balanced, objective approaches the titles of answer choices B and D suggest do not fit. Deciding between A and C is more difficult, but it comes down to whether the goal is to defend anarchism as one's own philosophy or actively convince someone else to subscribe to it. With the acknowledgement and refutation of common concerns, the former is a better fit than the latter, which means answer choice A is the better title than answer choice C.

47. Based on the passage, what does the passage author believe to be at the root of most societal problems?
    A) Rumor and hearsay
    B) **Intellectual laziness**
    C) Selfishness
    D) Pernicious dogma

The author makes note of hearsay and unquestioned beliefs, but relatively in passing compared to the amount of time spent discussing the mental indolence, the difficulty of thinking and the importance in anarchism of questioning and critically examining all one's assumptions, something that is implied not to come naturally. B is the best match.

Passage IX Explanation

Psychology as the **behaviorist** views it is a purely objective **experimental branch of natural science**. Its theoretical goal is the prediction and control of behavior. **Introspection forms no essential part of its methods**, nor is the scientific value of its data dependent upon the readiness with which they lend themselves to **interpretation in terms of consciousness**. The behaviorist, in his efforts to get a unitary scheme of animal response, **recognizes no dividing line between man and brute**. The behavior of man, with all of its refinement and complexity, forms only a part of the behaviorist's total scheme of investigation.

Key terms: Psychology, behaviorist, experimental, natural science

Contrast: pure description and prediction of behavior vs. understanding consciousness; understanding all living things in terms of behavior vs. considering human consciousness different or special

Cause-and-effect: objective, experimentalist approach does not lend itself to theorizing on role or nature of consciousness

It has been maintained by its followers generally that **psychology is a study of the science of the phenomena of consciousness**. It has taken as its problem, on the one hand, **the analysis of complex mental states (or processes) into simple elementary constituents**, and on the other the **construction of complex states when the elementary constituents are given**. The world of physical objects (stimuli, including here anything which may excite activity in a receptor), which forms the total phenomena of the natural scientist, is looked upon merely as means to an end. That end is the production of mental states that may be 'inspected' or 'observed'. The psychological object of observation in the case of an emotion, for example, is the mental state itself. The problem in emotion is the determination of the number and kind of elementary constituents present, their loci, intensity, order of appearance, etc. It is agreed that introspection is the method par excellence by means of which mental states may be manipulated for purposes of psychology. On this assumption, behavior data (including under this term everything which goes under the name of **comparative psychology**) have no value per se. **They possess significance only in so far as they may throw light upon conscious states**. Such data must have at least an analogical or indirect reference to belong to the realm of psychology.

Key terms: comparative psychology

Contrast: behaviorism only cares about rules of behavior while psychology cares only about mental states

Cause-and-effect: psychology's exclusive interest in mental states means behavior data has no intrinsic value, only as evidence of mental states

Indeed, at times, **one finds psychologists who are skeptical of even this analogical reference**. Such skepticism is often shown by the question which is put to the student of behavior, 'what is the bearing of animal work upon human psychology?' I used to have to study over this question. Indeed **it always embarrassed me somewhat**. I was interested in my own work and felt that it was important, and yet I could not trace any close connection between it and **psychology as my questioner understood psychology**. I hope that such a confession will clear the atmosphere to such an extent that we will no longer have **to work under false pretenses**. We must frankly admit that the facts so important to us which we have been able to glean from **extended work upon the senses of animals by the behavior method have contributed only in a fragmentary way to the general theory of human sense organ processes**, nor have they suggested new points of experimental attack. The enormous number of experiments which we have carried out upon learning have likewise contributed little to human psychology. It seems reasonably clear that some kind of compromise must be affected: **either psychology must change its viewpoint so as to take in facts of behavior**, whether or not they have bearings upon the problems of 'consciousness'; **or else behavior must stand alone as a wholly separate and independent science**. Should human psychologists fail to look with favor upon our overtures and refuse to modify their position, the behaviorists will be driven to using human beings as subjects and to employ methods of investigation which are exactly comparable to those now employed in the animal work.

Contrast: goals and methods of behaviorism vs. traditional psychology

Cause-and-effect: some psychologists question whether behavior data has bearing on their conception of psychology (study of consciousness); behavioral studies have contributed to some extent to understanding of human consciousness, but not much, and their value lies elsewhere; the different aims and interest of behaviorism will require either an expansion of the goals of psychology, or a redefinition of behaviorism as outside psychology

Opinion: author is behaviorist, has felt defensive over psychologists questioning value of behavior data; author does not concede there is a single agreed-upon definition of the realm of true psychology; psychologists seen as the old guard, behaviorists are second-tier or subordinate

Main Idea: behaviorism and traditional psychology have separate goals as well as separate methodologies, requiring a reconsideration as to what psychology is about

48. What is the significance of the quotation in the third paragraph, "what is the bearing of animal work upon human psychology"?
   A) The passage author is asking a rhetorical question as a lead in to the many and broad applications of animal behavior studies.
   B) The passage's detailed description of the roundabout connections between these studies and theories of human psychology is given as evidence of the many-faceted and interconnected nature of the discipline.
   C) **The passage author is providing evidence of psychologists' exclusive interest in mental states and dismissal of behavior data as being valuable in itself.**
   D) The passage author is making an argument against further animal research as irrelevant to important psychological questions.

The author, a behaviorist, paraphrases this frequent question as an interrogatory of traditional psychologists, describing the embarrassment and difficulty in answering the question. Read in context, it makes the point that although behavioral data is, to behaviorists, insightful and valuable on its own terms, anything that doesn't shed light on human consciousness is without value to non-behavioral psychologists. Answer choice C correctly describes the author's reason for including the quotation.

49. At the end of the passage, what does the author imply will be the result if psychologists will not reconsider their stance on what constitutes psychology?
   A) **Behaviorists and psychologists will work in isolation, limiting insights into human nature on the whole.**
   B) Human testing will be the only recourse for behavioral science to move forward.
   C) Behaviorism will be forced to adapt by developing theoretical mental models of their own.
   D) Behaviorists will redefine psychology themselves, contesting the psychological view.

The author states that if psychologists are unwilling to alter their views on what psychology can be about, the complete divorce of the two camps into separate disciplines will result in behaviorists studying human psychology from a purely behavioral standpoint, in the same way as animal work. This implies that, at present, there is a degree of give-and-take, psychological theories of mind influencing behavioral research, and perhaps vice-versa. It's further implied that this would be detrimental, perhaps to both groups, and therefore studies of human nature on the whole. Answer choice A matches.

50. Which of the following statements best corresponds to the author's views on behaviorism and psychology?
    A) Behaviorism can offer great insights into human consciousness but the work is less well-regarded than it should be.
    B) **Traditional psychologists unfairly dominate the professional conversation, dismissing the value of behavioral research.**
    C) Behaviorism and traditional psychology should stand as separate sciences since their goals do not overlap.
    D) Traditional psychology is at a dead-end and will be completely superseded by behaviorism.

At no point does the author disparage psychology; however, the passage does not make clear that non-behaviorists do not value behavioral insights that do not impinge on theories of mental states and consciousness. Since the goal of the passage is to explain and defend behaviorism on its own terms, followed with a plea for psychologists to value behavioral studies that don't impinge directly on understanding of human consciousness, it's fair to assume that the author would characterize psychology as displaying minimal appreciation of the behavioral sciences. A sounds somewhat tempting, but it includes a claim about the insights behaviorism makes on human consciousness, while the passage has suggested that knowledge of consciousness gleaned from behavioral data has been fractured and incidental. B is a better match. Checking the other answers to make sure, C is also briefly tempting, as it closely matches language in the passage, but the author does not actually view this outcome as desirable, so it is not a match. D is clearly not a match either.

51. What does the author mean in the third paragraph when mentioning working under false pretenses?
    A) **The author is implying that psychologists are unaware that behaviorists are no longer working towards the same goals as those in traditional psychology.**
    B) The author is alluding to misreported or "fudged" data.
    C) The author is implying that behaviorists are being misleading when they don't explicitly note their research focus in the results of their work.
    D) The author is providing evidence of the exploitative use of behavioral scientists by the field of psychology.

Read in context, the author admits that behavioral data is not primarily useful because it leads to a better understanding of the human mind; however, it is useful in predicting behavior, a worthy goal in its own right. Since the author even uses the word confession, and this is a follow-up to the paraphrased question psychologists apparently always ask, about the implications of experimental behavioral data for human psychology, the implication is that psychologists are unaware that behaviorists have found their own interests and questions to pursue, and are no longer simply trying to provide psychologists with insights into their studied brain states. A is a match.

52. Which of the following differences between behaviorism and traditional psychology is NOT mentioned?
    A) Behaviorism is purely interested in predicting behavior, not understanding consciousness.
    B) Psychology is focused on predicting mental states from elementary constituents or determining constituents from states.
    C) Psychology considers human consciousness qualitatively different from the working of animal minds.
    D) **Behaviorism is quantitative while psychology is more often qualitative.**

The statement in answer choice D is the only one that does not occur anywhere in the passage.

53. It can be assumed from the passage that traditional psychology, in the author's view, is:
    A) complementary in its theoretical trappings to the experimental data of behaviorism.
    B) perhaps overvalued, but absolutely necessary to providing a unifying model for behavioral processing.
    C) no more objective than behaviorism, though admittedly less speculative.
    D) **more subjective than behaviorism, owing to its focus on interpretation of data.**

Traditional psychology is interpretive, while behaviorism is not. Behaviorism is non-subjective for this reason, according to the passage, so it's safe to assume psychology is therefore more subjective for the same reason. None of the other statements listed here can be taken for granted based on the passage.

APPENDIX A: NEXT STEP MCAT - CARS PERFORMANCE TRACKING

DATE	TITLE	STRATEGY	% CORRECT	CONFIDENCE
12/25/2015	Full Section 1	Slow read, took notes	75%	Medium

APPENDIX B: SCORE CONVERSION CHART

Table 1 Raw Score to Scaled Score Conversion for CARS Sections

These scores are rough estimates based on the scaled-to-percentile conversions published by the AAMC for the new format exam. The raw-to-scaled conversions are based on scales from released AAMC exams.

Raw Score (Number of Questions Correct)	Scaled Score	Percentile*
52-53	132	100
50-51	131	99
48-49	130	97
45-47	129	93
42-44	128	87
39-41	127	81
36-38	126	70
33-35	125	58
30-32	124	44
27-29	123	33
24-26	122	23
21-23	121	14
18-20	120	8
14-17	119	3
0 - 13	118	1

* Percentile rank is given in this table as an example of how percentile correlates with scaled score, taken from recent actual MCAT exams. This is for illustration purposes only and does not represent performance of test-takers from the material in this exam.

APPENDIX C: ADDITIONAL VERBAL PRACTICE APPROACHES

In the rest of the book we focused on the three main techniques for reading: the balanced highlighter approach, the slow-read note taking approach, and the fast-read skimming approach.

In this final section of the book, we want to discuss some other more unorthodox approaches.

Author's Opinion Technique

One school of thought says that the only thing that matters is this: "Who is the author? What does she believe?"

Everything else is secondary.

To take this approach to the passage, you don't use the scratch notes or the highlighter. You read briskly, finishing the passage in about 3 minutes. You then stop and **write down the author's main idea**, being sure to capture not just *what* the author says, but *who* she is and *why* she believes what she does.

Under the Author's Opinion approach, the main idea that you jot down will be fairly lengthy. But by skipping other highlighting and note-taking you should have time to write all that down.

The other major aspect of the Author Opinion technique is that when answering the questions, you should answer every single question – even questions that ask you to extrapolate from the passage – on the basis of that overall Author Opinion.

This is the approach advocated by at least a couple of different popular MCAT courses, and many students have success with it. It does require a keen eye for distinguishing between details you can gloss over, and key facts that serve as evidence in the author's argument. But with practice, you can spot the difference.

Skim the Questions First Approach

I recommend against this approach, but some students do find success with it. As with everything, all I can say is: try it and see if you like it.

The reason this idea is out there is that the SAT and ACT reward you for reading the questions first. Many popular prep companies take this approach on those exams. Since anyone taking the MCAT most likely took the SAT or ACT, people will remember this technique from high school and want to try it again.

Here's why it's generally a bad idea for the MCAT: the MCAT is not a "look it up" kind of test. It's a reasoning, analyzing, and synthesizing kind of test. Skimming through the questions just gives you more stuff to think about while you're reading. You don't want your head cluttered while you read – you want to *focus on the passage* and then worry about the questions when they come up.

But okay.

Let's say you're committed to doing this approach.

What should you do?

Two major things: first when you skim through the questions, it really does need to be a *skim*. Don't spend more than 30 – 45 seconds at the most skimming through them; and second, don't even begin to analyze or think about answering them.

The whole point of skimming the questions is just to see certain "buzzwords" that will help guide your reading. If you see the word "epiphenomenalism" show up in three of six questions, you know you'll need to pay attention when that shows up in the passage.

A quick glance at the questions to know what's coming can help you feel more focused while reading.

Attempt the Questions First Approach

If skimming the questions first is, at best, a questionable approach then trying to just jump right to the questions first is a terrible idea. I present it here just for the sake of thoroughness. I have never had a student successfully use this approach, but you can feel free to try it out.

On the questions-first approach, you do the following:

1. Skim all of the questions.
2. Find the questions that make reference to a specific part of the passage.
3. Read the relevant parts of the passage and answer those questions.
4. Answer remaining more general questions by researching each answer choice as needed.

Needless to say, the MCAT style of questioning isn't really conducive to this.

Rephrase the Questions in Your Own Words

This is less a method for reading the passage and more just one popular way for tackling the questions and I recommend it strongly.

As you come to each question, do the following:

1. Read the question once, focusing on, "what are they asking me?"

2. Read the question a second time, and rephrase it in your own words, "what are they telling me in this question, and what are they asking me?"

3. Either do research in the passage, your notes, or move right to process of elimination.

4. Re-read the question immediately followed by your selected answer choice to make sure they fit.

As we mentioned at the start of the book, we haven't included a breakdown of various question types, answer types, etc. You get no points on the MCAT for reading a question and saying, "Ah-HAH! That's an 'apply-the-passage-with-an-author-opinion-inverted-weaken-roman-numeral-except' question! Ha!" Memorizing lots of jargon doesn't actually answer the question itself.

Instead, keep it simple – rephrase the question in your own words and *stick close to the passage*.

Combinations and Variations

Highlight exactly three words in each paragraph

Some folks find they just can't avoid the "paint roller syndrome" when doing highlighting. They end up highlighting huge chunks of text. If you're over-highlighting, then the highlighting becomes pointless.

One variation that some of my students have liked is imposing a super-strict limit: once you've read the paragraph, go back and select exactly three words to highlight. The interface will let you double-click to highlight a word so you can quickly double-click three words. That hyper-strict rule of exactly three words stops you from falling into the trap of highlighting way too much.

Super-extensive notes – never look anything up

Typically even when folks do the note-taking strategy, they can't help but look up some stuff in the passage. Those who find the process of writing is a great way to help them organize and remember things may want to take the note-taking strategy and go really far with it. Write extensive notes and then only ever look to your notes, rather than looking things up in the passage.

Not many students will find this helpful, but if you think you would, give it a try.

Highlighting and Note-taking

The key way to combine these strategies is to limit the highlighting to proper nouns, numbers, technical terms, and any extreme language you see (words like "only", "must", "necessary" and so on) and then use note-taking for the larger synthesis of author's arguments and opinions.

By splitting up the job between note-taking and highlighting many students find it easier to manage. You're highlighting much less – only very specific names and such that you would want to look up later. And you're not using the scratch notes to keep track of where stuff is, but rather what the big ideas are.

Most students who initially opt for the note-taking approach end up settling on some hybrid between note-taking and highlighting. The on-screen highlighting function simply proves too valuable a tool to ignore it altogether.

As always, if you're going to try this sort of hybrid technique, keep good records about how well it works for you and how confident you feel while doing it.

Other variations

You can certainly do any mix-and-match you like: combine highlighting and author opinion, note-taking and author opinion, skimming and highlighting, and so on. Having worked with thousands of students over the years I've seen dozens (or even hundreds!) of slightly different variations on reading techniques. It is the experience of seeing so many different paths to success that has lead to this book's whole philosophy: ***there is no right way to do reading passages; there is only YOUR right way***.

Skipping Around

Some courses will advocate that you should skip around between passages. They suggest that you take time before reading to skim the passage and assign it some sort of difficulty level: "rank it", "triage it", "rate it", etc.

That is fundamentally a bad idea.

Here's why:

What makes the CARS section *hard* is not the content or difficulty of the passage itself.

It's not how difficult and unusual the questions are.

No – what makes the section difficult is only this: how close is the trap answer to the right answer?

You can have an easy passage and straightforward questions, but still absolutely bomb it. If the trap wrong answer is really, really similar to the right answer then you're going to get it wrong, no matter how easy the passage was.

Similarly, you can have a dense, difficult, confusing passage. But if the wrong answers are ridiculously, obviously wrong, then the questions are easy.

So the notion that you can somehow assess difficulty and skip around is absurd. Every passage comes with hard, medium, and easy questions. Your goal is to get to every single passage (even if you have to use the "Panic Mode Method" on that last passage) and to at least get the easy/medium questions right.

Any time you spend skipping around or engaging in a futile effort to "rank" or "triage" the passage is wasted time.

When the CARS section begins, simply take a gulp and take a breath and go ahead and dive right into passage #1. Plow straight on through and come back up for air 90 minutes later at the last passage.

Now, having said that:

If you absolutely hate, Hate, HATE a particular kind of passage, you may feel compelled to skip it. I had one very high-achieving student who had some sort of mental block when it came to art. If the passage started talking about "Caravaggio's loose, expressive brushwork" his brain would just shut down. So in that case, yeah, it made sense for him to just skip any art passages and only do them at the very end.

That should be a rare circumstance, but if it applies to you, then skipping a passage might be necessary.

Skipping Entire Passages

Even the student I mentioned above who would skip art passages would still come back to them at the end and do them with his last 5-10 minutes.

Under no circumstances whatsoever should you plan, from the beginning, to just flat-out guess on an entire passage.

Giving up like that right from the beginning is a very bad idea. No matter how hard it is, every passage comes with at least a few easy questions and giving up right at the beginning is leaving free points on the table.

If you find that you're running out of time, then the issue is to diagnose where that time is going. The average college student reads around 200-300 words per minute. Even on the very bottom of that range, a student could get through a reading passage in under 3 minutes. So if you're running out of time it almost certainly isn't just the reading. Something else is going on.

So, keep moving, don't get bogged down, and plan to do every single passage.

Alternative Study Techniques

Just as every student can find their own way to be successful on the reading passages, so to can every student find a study technique that works best for them. Earlier we discussed the most important study approaches: form a study group, set a study schedule, do CARS practice every day, read philosophy daily, and build your Lessons Learned Journal. Here are some other avenues some of my students have found helpful.

Speed Reading Techniques and Courses

Speed reading courses can teach you a number of techniques to help improve your CARS performance. Before you spend any money, though, research the program carefully. There's lots of really good free websites and programs out there.

If a program is claiming that it can boost your reading speed to something outlandish – 1000 words per minute or more, it may be a scam (that would mean reading an entire CARS passage in 30 seconds!!). To perform well on the MCAT, you really don't need a reading speed much more than the average college student – about 250 words per minute.

However, there are certain habits taught in speed reading courses that can be helpful for the MCAT.

First, many speed-reading courses will teach you to stop back-tracking. For some people, the reason they read slowly is a bad habit of backing up and re-reading words, phrases, or even whole sentences. In particularly bad cases, a person may make a habit of re-reading every single line three or four times, with no increase in comprehension.

Second, speed-reading courses can help you with the mechanics of how you move your eye across the words. They can give you exercises to help build up your eye muscles, and teach you to look at larger chunks of words at once. So instead of moving your eye from word to word like this:

In | this | article | we | will | discuss | the | importance | of | aerobic | exercise | on | mental | performance.

The courses teach you how to move your eye across chunks of words – that is you would only look directly at each of the bold face words below and see the other words in your peripheral vision:

In **this** article | we **will** discuss | the **importance** of | aerobic **exercise** on | mental **performance**.

Finally, speed reading courses can help teach you to stop or reduce sub-vocalizing. We are taught to read phonetically – by linking the printed words to the sounds of speaking the words out loud. This means most people spend their whole lives reading by "hearing" the words inside their head – sub-vocalizing.

As a result, most people never learn to read faster than they could speak out loud – typically a little less than 200 words per minute.

By learning to read while minimizing sub-vocalizing you can often increase your reading speed by a wide margin – up to 300 to 350 word per minute. In an MCAT context, that means comfortably reading the entire passage in under two minutes, without skimming.

Reading whole books

Every MCAT course or expert out there will tell you to do outside reading to help improve your MCAT reading performance. Simply put, you get better at reading by reading!

At the beginning of this book I suggested that you should read philosophy articles from **Reason & Responsibility**. An alternative approach would be to read two or three books in the course of your MCAT prep. Specifically, you should be reading classics of literature – the sort of stuff an AP English class would make you read.

This can be valuable for the student who really struggles with literature-based passages, or for the student who finds that they just can't stay motivated to do technical reading. If you've given it your best shot and you just can't help it – you zone out in like 5 minutes every time you pick up the philosophy textbook, then it's time to try something different. Go pick up a copy of Pride & Prejudice (or even better, read a free copy online at Project Gutenberg).

The advice to do outside reading is no good if you find that you can't follow it. So pick some sort of reading that you **can** stick to and stick to it!

Whatever you choose, the most important thing is to always stop reading at the bottom of each page and summarize the author's overall main idea or opinion and **write it down**.

Reading magazines

I typically recommend against reading magazines since they're not hard enough to simulate MCAT reading.

But, as mentioned above about full books, the only worthwhile outside reading regimen is one that you can actually stick to. So if you need some variety in your reading diet, then magazines can serve well. Moving between a mixture of The Economist, the New York Times Magazine, and Atlantic Monthly can get some variety into your outside reading.

As always, stop at the end of every column of text and jot down the author's main idea.

Doing logic puzzles or logic workbooks

Part of success with the reading passages is being able to see the logical connections the author draws between different concepts. Some students have a really tough time with this because they don't naturally think in a strict, formal-logic kind of way.

If you find that you're repeatedly getting questions wrong because you misunderstood the logic of the author's argument, it may be worth picking up a logic workbook for some practice. Look for something meant for a college "Introduction to Logic" type of class.

Expert Help – Reading Issues

Finally, if you're hitting a big wall with your verbal – consistently getting less than half right, or leaving multiple passages blank – you may need to get some expert help. Rates of reading issues tend to be much higher than most people realize. For example, many estimate that as much as 5 to 10% of the US population may have at least a mild form of dyslexia, yet less than 1 in 5 receive any assistance for it.

If you feel like you've hit a wall in your performance and you see a huge disparity between your ability to succeed in the science sections (and more specifically the discrete questions) and the reading section, you may want to seek out help from an educational psychologist or reading specialist.

Stress Management

The most perfectly-tuned reading technique in the world can't help if you freak out on Test Day. Managing the psychology of the test is every bit as important as mastering the academics. To that end, there are a few things every student should do to help manage stress.

Diet, Exercise, Sleep

Your brain is just another organ in your body. It can't function well if you're neglecting your physiology. This isn't some new-age hocus pocus – you will score higher if you're eating a good diet, getting some aerobic exercise every day, and sticking strictly to a sleep regimen.

Starting approximately three months before Test Day, you should do the following:

1. You must go to bed and wake up at the same time every day.

The MCAT starts at 8am. Depending on how far you have to travel to your test center, and what traffic or public transit systems are like, this can mean having to wake up anywhere from 5am to 7am on Test Day. Whatever time that is, start waking up at that exact time every single day. Yes, it's going to put a cramp on your social life for awhile. But in the grand scheme of things, it's a minor sacrifice to achieve life goals.

2. Do some aerobic exercise first thing in the morning.

When you wake up on Test Day, one of the first things you should do is get your body moving, your heart pumping, and your energy levels high. To that end, go for a quick jog, a swim, or even just a brisk walk. It'll ensure that you're awake, alert and focused to start your day. Plus, a staggering number of studies show a link between exercise and mental functioning. Want to score higher on the MCAT? Exercise!

3. Get yourself on a regular, healthy diet.

I'm not a nutritionist – I'm not qualified to tell you what your best diet choices are. What I can say is that you should decide what works for you, and then stick with it for the three months leading up to Test Day. Don't do anything weird or different as the MCAT approaches, or on Test Day itself.

If your normal morning breakfast is a cup of black coffee, two cigarettes, and a Flintstones chewable, then just keep sticking with that and don't change anything on Test Day. That may not be the best choice for long-term health, but the key for MCAT prep is stability and regularity. Don't make any changes leading up to or on Test Day.

4. Don't change your habits.

I'm a die-hard caffeine addict. When I'm lying on my death bed and dementia has robbed me of the names of my grand-children, I'll still insist that the nurse push some rich, Columbian shade-grown, French-roast coffee into my IV drip.

I've read MCAT advice books where they tell you to kick the coffee. Yeah right. Over my dead body.

We all have some mix of chemicals that we use on some sort of regular basis, whether it's caffeine, nicotine, something we've been prescribed, or even just a jolt of sugary food. As with diet, the absolute essential key here is simply this: homeostasis.

Don't make any changes.

Your MCAT studying is not the time to suddenly start or stop anything unusual. Unfortunately, I've heard all too often stories of students who thought it would be a great idea to get their hands on some ADD meds and take them on Test Day. Needless to say, that always turns into a disaster – unless you've actually been prescribed ADD meds and you take them on a regular basis.

Keep yourself on an even keel for the MCAT. Any attempt at getting some sort of pharmaceutical "edge" will only end in disaster, so don't try.

Visualization

Having a clear image in your head of your goals can go a long way towards helping you achieve them.

To help you visualize your goal, do the following:

1. Take a full practice test – ideally the official AAMC practice test

2. Print out a screen shot of your score report

3. White out the score and write in the score you want

   • This should be something really ambitious, but also something you believe is achievable

4. Tape copies of this ideal score up around your house in places where you will see it regularly

   • The door of the fridge, your bathroom mirror, on the wall over your computer desk, etc.

Having this constant peripheral-vision reminder of success can go a long way towards boosting your confidence and helping you see your success – both literally and metaphorically. This positive reinforcement can keep your enthusiasm up, keep you focused, and keep you working towards that goal.

Focus on the Lessons Learned: Process, not Product

Easily the most common mistake MCAT students make is failing to properly review their practice.

The usual M.O. is to do some timed practice, and then quickly and casually flip through, just checking your wrong answers.

Huge mistake.

When reviewing your work, you need to review every single passage, every single question, every single answer choice. You need to really learn what you're doing. We've discussed the importance of the Lessons Learned Journal earlier in the book. Building the LLJ helps not just with learning how to master the CARS section, it also helps with stress management. By seeing the process of learning, and focusing on your takeaway points, you can help get yourself off the day-to-day emotional rollercoaster of performance.

Your score went up from a 121 to a 123? Great! But so what? What did you learn from it? You're never going to see those passages again. They don't matter – what matters is the lessons you learn.

Had a bad day? Your score dropped from a 129 to a 125? I'm sorry and I hope it goes better next time. But so what? What did you learn from it? You're never going to see those passages again. They don't matter – what matters is the lessons you learn.

Positive Review

Once every three weeks you should do a positive review.

This means after you take a full timed section, go through and **_only_** review the questions you got right. Skip over anything you got wrong.

So you'll be going back through the section and it'll be like this: "Okay #1 got that right, great I found that in the passage, okay got #2 right. Yeah I knew what the author was assuming there, #3 wrong whatever skip it, okay #4 phew! I got it down to two and I guessed right. Oh man I'm so lucky!!"

By reviewing only your right answers, you can emphasize your strengths – see where you're able to succeed. You can get good lessons learned by emphasizing to yourself that you're able to get lots of stuff right and that you'll continue to do so in the future. And it can help dispel the negativity that tends to follow when you just skim through and only review your wrong answers.